תשפ"ב

סֵדֶר הַתְּפִלּוֹת, סֵדֶר קְרִיאַת הַתּוֹרָה,
הֲלָכוֹת וּמִנְהָגִים לְבֵית הַכְּנֶסֶת וְלַבַּיִת

Luaḥ Hashanah
5782

A guide to prayers, readings,
laws, and customs
for the synagogue and for the home

Rabbi Miles B. Cohen
and Leslie Rubin

Resources for Synagogue and Home

This book contains no instance of the Divine name that requires burial (גְנִיזָה *genizah*). Everywhere that such a name appears, the first letter is separated from the remainder of the letters so that the name never appears as an intact unit (for example, אֵ·ל).

To promote ease of use, we do not list the myriad and legitimate variations in liturgical practices. The congregational rabbi, as the *mara de'atra* (the local authority on Jewish practice), has the ultimate responsibility for such decisions in each community.

NOTE: *Luaḥ Hashanah* does not include liturgical or lectionary requirements traditionally associated *only* with Erets Yisra'el.

Published by Miles B. Cohen and Leslie Rubin

ISBN (standard edition) 978-1-950520-05-3
ISBN (large-print/pulpit-size edition) 978-1-950520-06-0
ISBN (electronic edition) 978-1-950520-07-7

DESIGN AND COMPOSITION BY MILES B. COHEN

PRINTED IN THE UNITED STATES OF AMERICA
BY G&H SOHO, INC.
www.ghsoho.com

CONTENTS

ABOUT THE AUTHORS

Rabbi Miles B. Cohen was ordained by the Jewish Theological Seminary of America in 1974. For over twenty years, he worked in curriculum development at the Melton Research Center at JTS, and for many years he taught students preparing to be rabbis, cantors, educators, and lay leaders. He has lectured and conducted workshops all over North America on topics related to synagogue practice. Rabbi Cohen has created guides and interactive software for learning to read Torah, *haftarah,* and *m^e^gillot,* as well as guides for *nusaḥ* skills and Hebrew grammar.

Leslie Rubin is a professional editor, specializing in Jewish studies, who has edited and indexed numerous books on technical and academic subjects. In addition, she developed educational and training materials, with an emphasis on usability and concision.

We again express special thanks to Rabbi Joel Roth of the Jewish Theological Seminary. As always, Rabbi Roth makes himself available throughout the year to clarify and resolve challenging questions of *halakhah* and practice, as well as offering innovative suggestions.

GUIDE TO TRANSLITERATIONS

Careful attention to the transliteration system enables accurate pronunciation of the associated Hebrew words.
When reading transliterations, use the following guidelines:

Consonants

ḥ pronounced in many modern dialects like ***ch*** in *J. S. **Bach**;* in other dialects, pronounced like a harsh or raspy ***h***

kh pronounced like ***ch*** in *J. S. **Bach***

ʼ represents *alef* or *ayin* within a word

Vowels

a pronounced like ***a*** in *father*

ay pronounced like ***ay*** in *kayak*

e pronounced like ***e*** in *bet*

ey pronounced like ***é*** in *café*

i pronounced like ***ie*** in *field*

o pronounced like ***o*** in *nor*

oy pronounced like ***oy*** in *boy*

u pronounced like ***u*** in *flute*

uy pronounced like ***uey*** in *chop suey*

The small, raised vowels represent the *ḥataf* vowels: ^{a}אֲ ^{e}אֱ ^{o}אֳ

These are hurried counterparts of the full vowels: *a*אַ *e*אֶ *o*אֹ

Pronounced *sh^{e}va* (שְׁוָא נָע *sh^{e}va na*), a reduced vowel, is also indicated by ^{e}.

In general, a doubled consonant reflects a *dagesh ḥazak* (for example, *kippur* not *kipur*) because this aids pronunciation of the preceding short vowel. However, doubling usually is not shown after prefixes (for example, *hagadol* not *haggadol*).

Exceptions to the above conventions are made to improve readability (for example, *elul* not *^{e}lul; nitsavim* not *nitstsavim; aliyah* not *^{a}liyyah*).

GUIDE TO SYMBOLS AND CONVENTIONS

Symbols

Symbol	Meaning	Explanation
+	**Add**	Alerts you to *add* a phrase or prayer that usually we do not recite at the particular service or point in the service
✕	**Omit**	Alerts you to *omit* a phrase or prayer that usually we recite at the particular service or point in the service
☞	**Take note**	Calls attention to a required action

Page Numbers in Various Siddurim

The following notations precede page citations for *siddurim* published by the United Synagogue of Conservative Judaism and The Rabbinical Assembly.

L	*Lev Shalem* for Shabbat and Festivals
S	Shabbat and Festival *Sim Shalom*
W	Weekday *Sim Shalom*
F	Full *Sim Shalom* (regular and personal editions)
P	Personal edition of full *Sim Shalom*

Torah Readings

The verse numbers for each aliyah appear both for the reading of the full parashah and for the triennial-cycle reading. The following notations appear in conjunction with instructions for Torah readings:

1 2 3 4 5 6 7	Aliyah numbers
M	Maftir aliyah
°	Aliyah or reading with a special feature that requires attention
☞ °	Explanation of the special feature marked with °

Color-Coded Boxes

Yellow boxes provide instructions for the stated time period, thus replacing multiple occurrences of identical instructions.

Green boxes provide historical or other explanatory background material about holidays, fast days, and special occasions.

Blue boxes provide procedures for *halakhot*, rituals, and customs associated with holidays, fast days, and other occasions.

ABOUT THE YEAR תשפ״ב 5782

Characteristics of the Year

- Year 6 of the 19-year lunar cycle.
  שָׁנָה מְעֻבֶּרֶת, a *leap* year: a 13-month year, adding 1st Adar with 30 days.
  Years 3, 6, 8, 11, 14, 17, and 19 of the lunar cycle are leap years. Each has an extra month.
- A year of type גכ״ז:
  ג Rosh Hashanah falls on יום ג׳, the 3rd day of the week (Tuesday).
  כ שָׁנָה כְּסִדְרָהּ, a *regular* year: the usual 12 months alternate between 30 and 29 days (thus, with the added month, a 384-day year).
  ז Pesaḥ begins on יום ז׳, the 7th day of the week (Shabbat).
- Year 14 (beginning 7 Nisan at midnight) of the 28-year solar cycle.
- שְׁמִטָּה *shemittah* (Sabbatical Year): final year (beginning on Rosh Hashanah) of the 7-year שְׁמִטָּה *shemittah* (Sabbatical Year) cycle.
- Year 3 (beginning on Shabbat Bereshit) of the 3-year Torah-reading cycle followed by some congregations.

Dates to Note

Major holidays

- **Rosh Hashanah** begins Monday night, September 6, 2021.
- **Yom Kippur** begins Wednesday night, September 15, 2021.
- **Sukkot** begins Monday night, September 20, 2021.
- **Shemini Atseret** begins Monday night, September 27, 2021.
- **Simḥat Torah** begins Tuesday night, September 28, 2021.
- **Pesaḥ** begins Friday night, April 15, 2022.
- **Shavu'ot** begins Saturday night, June 4, 2022.

Minor holidays and observances

- **Hosha'na Rabbah** begins Sunday night, September 26, 2021.
- **Ḥanukkah** begins Sunday night, November 28, 2021.
- **Tu Bishvat** begins Sunday night, January 16, 2022.
- **Purim** begins Wednesday night, March 16, 2022.
- **Yom Hasho'ah** (Holocaust Remembrance Day) begins Wednesday night, April 27, 2022.
- **Yom Hazikkaron** (Israel Memorial Day) begins Tuesday night, May 3, 2022 (always observed on the day preceding Yom Ha'atsma'ut).
- **Yom Ha'atsma'ut** (Israel Independence Day) begins Wednesday night, May 4, 2022 (moved to 4 Iyyar).
- **Lag Ba'omer** begins Wednesday night, May 18, 2022.
- **Yom Yerushalayim** (Jerusalem Day) begins Saturday night, May 28, 2022.

Communal fasts

- **Tsom Gedalyah** begins Thursday morning, September 9, 2021.
- **Yom Kippur** begins Wednesday night, September 15, 2021.
- **Asarah Betevet** begins Tuesday morning, December 14, 2021.
- **Ta'anit Ester** begins Wednesday morning, March 16, 2022.
- **Shiv'ah Asar Betammuz** begins Sunday morning, July 17, 2022 .
- **Tish'ah Be'av** begins Saturday night, August 6, 2022.

JEWISH COMMEMORATIONS 5783–5784

5783 • 2022–2023

2022

Rosh Hashanah Day 1 Mon., Sept. 26
Rosh Hashanah Day 2 Tue., Sept. 27
Tsom Gedalyah (fast) Wed., Sept. 28
Yom Kippur Wed., Oct. 5
Sukkot Day 1 Mon., Oct. 10
Sukkot Day 2 Tue., Oct. 11
Hosha'na Rabbah Sun., Oct. 16
Shemini Atseret Mon., Oct. 17
Simḥat Torah Tue., Oct. 18
Ḥanukkah Mon., Dec. 19–Mon., Dec. 26

2023

Asarah Betevet (fast) Tue., Jan. 3
Tu Bishvat Mon., Feb. 6
Ta'anit Ester (fast) Mon., Mar. 6
Purim Tue., Mar. 7
Pesaḥ Day 1 Thu., Apr. 6
Pesaḥ Day 2 Fri., Apr. 7
Pesaḥ Day 7 Wed., Apr. 12
Pesaḥ Day 8 Thu., Apr. 13
Yom Hasho'ah Tue., Apr. 18
Yom Hazikkaron Tue., Apr. 25
Yom Ha'atsma'ut Wed., Apr. 26
Lag Ba'omer Tue., May 9
Yom Yerushalayim Fri., May 19
Shavu'ot Day 1 Fri., May 26
Shavu'ot Day 2 Sat., May 27
Shiv'ah Asar Betammuz (fast) Thu., July 6
Tish'ah Be'av (fast) Thu., July 27

5784 • 2023–2024

2023

Rosh Hashanah Day 1 Sat., Sept. 16
Rosh Hashanah Day 2 Sun., Sept. 17
Tsom Gedalyah (fast) Mon., Sept. 18
Yom Kippur Mon., Sept. 25
Sukkot Day 1 Sat., Sept. 30
Sukkot Day 2 Sun., Oct. 1
Hosha'na Rabbah Fri., Oct. 6
Shemini Atseret Sat., Oct. 7
Simḥat Torah Sun., Oct. 8
Ḥanukkah Fri., Dec. 8–Fri., Dec. 15
Asarah Betevet (fast) Fri., Dec. 22

2024

Tu Bishvat Thu., Jan. 25
Ta'anit Ester (fast) Thu., Mar. 21
Purim Sun., Mar. 24
Pesaḥ Day 1 Tue., Apr. 23
Pesaḥ Day 2 Wed., Apr. 24
Pesaḥ Day 7 Mon., Apr. 29
Pesaḥ Day 8 Tues., Apr. 30
Yom Hasho'ah Mon., May 6
Yom Hazikkaron Mon., May 13
Yom Ha'atsma'ut Tue., May 14
Lag Ba'omer Sun., May 26
Yom Yerushalayim Wed., June 5
Shavu'ot Day 1 Wed., June 12
Shavu'ot Day 2 Thu., June 13
Shiv'ah Asar Betammuz (fast) Tue., July 23
Tish'ah Be'av (fast) Tue., Aug. 13

DURING Elul

MORNINGS

If psalm(s) for the day recited early in the service:

Every day Recite psalm(s) for the day, followed by:
קַדִּישׁ יָתוֹם Mourner's Kaddish (some omit) L121 S82 W100 F52
+ Psalm 27 for the Season of Repentance L113 S80 W92 F40
קַדִּישׁ יָתוֹם Mourner's Kaddish L121 S82 W100 F52

Weekdays + At end of service, sound the shofar* (except on 29 Elul).

If psalm(s) for the day recited at the end of the service:

Every day Recite psalm(s) for the day, followed by:
קַדִּישׁ יָתוֹם Mourner's Kaddish (some omit) L121 S82 W100 F52

Weekdays + Sound the shofar* (except on 29 Elul).
(Some sound the shofar instead after the last
קַדִּישׁ יָתוֹם Mourner's Kaddish.)

Every day + Psalm 27 for the Season of Repentance L113 S80 W92 F40
קַדִּישׁ יָתוֹם Mourner's Kaddish L121 S82 W100 F52

EVENINGS

After עָלֵינוּ Aleynu:
קַדִּישׁ יָתוֹם Mourner's Kaddish (some omit) L58 S82 W100 F52
+ Psalm 27 for the Season of Repentance L59 S80 W92 F40
קַדִּישׁ יָתוֹם Mourner's Kaddish L58 S82 W100 F52

---

*Without anyone reciting a בְּרָכָה *berakhah* or calling out *teki'ah, shevarim,* etc., sound the shofar:
תְּקִיעָה ← שְׁבָרִים ← תְּרוּעָה ← תְּקִיעָה Teki'ah → Shevarim → Teru'ah → Teki'ah

---

Elul 1 אֱלוּל ראשׁ חֹדֶשׁ אֱלוּל Rosh Ḥodesh Elul — Day 2

Sun **8** Aug (evening)

DURING Rosh Ḥodesh **Birkat Hamazon:**
+ יַעֲלֶה וְיָבוֹא Ya'aleh veyavo for Rosh Ḥodesh
L90|95 S340|347 W233|239 F762|780

+ הָרַחֲמָן Haraḥaman for Rosh Ḥodesh
L92|96 S343|348 W235|240 F768

Elul 5781						
	1	2	3	4	5	6
7	8	9	10	11	12	13
14	15	16	17	18	19	20
21	22	23	24	25	26	27
28	29					

Aug | Sep 2021						
	9	10	11	12	13	14
15	16	17	18	19	20	21
22	23	24	25	26	27	28
29	30	31 |	1	2	3	4
5	6					

+ Add ✕ Omit ☞ Take note!

Siddurim

L Lev Shalem for Shabbat and Festivals
S Shabbat and Festival Sim Shalom
W Weekday Sim Shalom
F Full Sim Shalom (both editions)
P Personal Edition of Full Sim Shalom

עַרְבִית

Weekday Amidah:

+ יַעֲלֶה וְיָבוֹא Ya’aleh veyavo for Rosh Ḥodesh W145 F216

קַדִּישׁ שָׁלֵם Full Kaddish W149 F222
עָלֵינוּ Aleynu W150 F224
קַדִּישׁ יָתוֹם Mourner’s Kaddish (some omit) W151 F226
+ Psalm 27 for the Season of Repentance W92 F40
קַדִּישׁ יָתוֹם Mourner’s Kaddish W100 F52

Mon 9 Aug שַׁחֲרִית

Before מִזְמוֹר שִׁיר Mizmor shir (Psalm 30) W14 F50 or at end of service, recite:
Psalm for Monday (Psalm 48) W86 F24
קַדִּישׁ יָתוֹם Mourner’s Kaddish (some omit) W100 F52
+ Psalm 104 for Rosh Ḥodesh W90 F34
קַדִּישׁ יָתוֹם Mourner’s Kaddish (some omit) W100 F52
+ Psalm 27 for the Season of Repentance W92 F40
קַדִּישׁ יָתוֹם Mourner’s Kaddish W100 F52

Weekday Amidah:
+ יַעֲלֶה וְיָבוֹא Ya’aleh veyavo for Rosh Ḥodesh W41 F114

✕ ~~תַּחֲנוּן Taḥanun~~

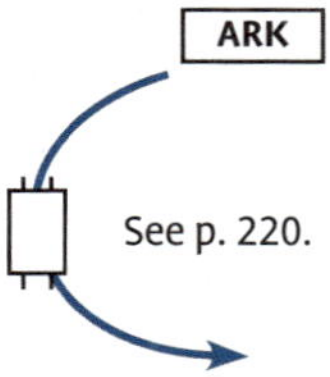

See p. 220.

+ חֲצִי הַלֵּל Short Hallel W50 F380
קַדִּישׁ שָׁלֵם Full Kaddish W56 F392

TORAH SERVICE W65 F138
Remove **1** scroll from ark.

Torah 4 aliyot: פִּינְחָס Pineḥas
בְּמִדְבַּר Bemidbar (Numbers) 28:1–15
[1] 28:1–3 [2] 3–5 [3] 6–10 [4] 11–15 W320 P943

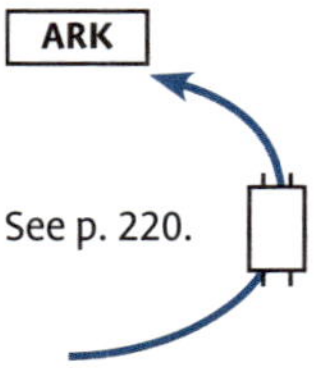

See p. 220.

חֲצִי קַדִּישׁ Short Kaddish W71 F146
Open, raise, display, and wrap scroll.
Return scroll to ark. W76 F150

אַשְׁרֵי Ashrey W78 F152
✕ ~~לַמְנַצֵּחַ Lamenatse·aḥ (Psalm 20)~~
וּבָא לְצִיּוֹן Uva letsiyyon W80 F156

Remove and pack tefillin. (Some remove after Kaddish.)
+ חֲצִי קַדִּישׁ Short Kaddish W103 F428
(If you remove tefillin here, do *not* pack but cover them, so as to begin Musaf together quickly after Kaddish.)

מוּסָף

+ **Rosh Ḥodesh Amidah for weekdays:** W104 F486
Weekday קְדֻשָּׁה Kedushah W105 F488

+ קַדִּישׁ שָׁלֵם Full Kaddish W82 F158
עָלֵינוּ Aleynu W83 F160

If psalms for the day were recited at Shaḥarit:
קַדִּישׁ יָתוֹם Mourner's Kaddish W84 F162
+ Sound the shofar (see procedure on p. 1).

If psalms for the day were not recited at Shaḥarit, add here:
קַדִּישׁ יָתוֹם Mourner's Kaddish (some omit) W84|100 F162|52
Psalm for Monday (Psalm 48) W86 F24
קַדִּישׁ יָתוֹם Mourner's Kaddish (some omit) W100 F52
+ Psalm 104 for Rosh Ḥodesh W90 F34
קַדִּישׁ יָתוֹם Mourner's Kaddish (some omit) W100 F52
+ Sound the shofar (see procedure on p. 1).
+ Psalm 27 for the Season of Repentance W92 F40
קַדִּישׁ יָתוֹם Mourner's Kaddish W84|100 F52

מִנְחָה

Weekday Amidah:
+ יַעֲלֶה וְיָבוֹא Ya'aleh veyavo for Rosh Ḥodesh W127 F178

✕ ~~תַּחֲנוּן Taḥanun~~

Elul 6 אֱלוּל
Sat 14 Aug

שַׁבָּת Shabbat פָּרָשַׁת שֹׁפְטִים Parashat Shofetim

Torah 7 aliyot (minimum): שֹׁפְטִים Shofetim
דְּבָרִים Devarim (Deuteronomy) 16:18–21:9

Annual:	1 16:18–17:13	2 17:14–20	3 18:1–5	4 18:6–13
	5 18:14–19:13	6 19:14–20:9	7 20:10–21:9	M 21:7–9
Triennial:	1 18:6–8	2 18:9–13	3 18:14–17	4 18:18–22
	5 19:1–7	6 19:8–10	7 19:11–13	M 19:11–13

Haftarah יְשַׁעְיָהוּ Yesha'yahu (Isaiah) 51:12–52:12
(4th of 7 haftarot of consolation following Tish'ah Be'av)

מִנְחָה

Torah 3 aliyot from כִּי־תֵצֵא Ki tetse
דְּבָרִים Devarim (Deuteronomy) 21:10–21
1 21:10–14 2 15–17 3 18–21 W313 P934

Chanted also next Monday and Thursday.

Elul 5781						
	1	2	3	4	5	6
7	8	9	10	11	12	13
14	15	16	17	18	19	20
21	22	23	24	25	26	27
28	29					

Aug | Sep 2021						
	9	10	11	12	13	14
15	16	17	18	19	20	21
22	23	24	25	26	27	28
29	30	31 | 1	2	3	4	
5	6					

+ Add ✕ Omit ☞ Take note!

Siddurim
- **L** Lev Shalem for Shabbat and Festivals
- **S** Shabbat and Festival Sim Shalom
- **W** Weekday Sim Shalom
- **F** Full Sim Shalom (both editions)
- **P** Personal Edition of Full Sim Shalom

Elul 7 אֱלוּל
Sat 14 Aug (night)

After Arvit if the moon is visible:
קִדּוּשׁ לְבָנָה Kiddush Levanah L286 W167 F704
For procedures and instructions, see p. 223.

Elul 13 אֱלוּל
Sat 21 Aug

שַׁבָּת Shabbat פָּרָשַׁת כִּי־תֵצֵא Parashat Ki tetse

Torah 7 aliyot (minimum): כִּי־תֵצֵא Ki tetse
דְּבָרִים Devarim (Deuteronomy) 21:10–25:19

Annual:	1 21:10–21	2 21:22–22:7	3 22:8–23:7	4 23:8–24
	5 23:25–24:4	6 24:5–13	7 24:14–25:19°	M 25:17–19°
Triennial:	1 23:8–12	2 23:13–15	3 23:16–19	4 23:20–24
	5 23:25–24:4	6 24:5–9	7 24:10–13	M 24:10–13

☞ °25:19 The proper reading of the 6th-to-last word is זֵכֶר, as it appears in the most reliable manuscripts and in almost all printed editions. No words should be repeated. For more information, see www.milesbcohen.com/LuahResources.

Haftarah יְשַׁעְיָהוּ Yesha'yahu (Isaiah) 54:1–10
(5th of 7 haftarot of consolation following Tish'ah Be'av)

מִנְחָה

Torah 3 aliyot from כִּי־תָבוֹא Ki tavo
דְּבָרִים Devarim (Deuteronomy) 26:1–15°
1 26:1–3 2 4–11 3 12–15 W314 P935

Chanted also next Monday and Thursday.

☞ °26:1–15 The reading extends through verse 15, which enables the correct configuration of the 3 aliyot.

Elul 20 אֱלוּל
Sat 28 Aug

שַׁבָּת Shabbat פָּרָשַׁת כִּי־תָבוֹא Parashat Ki tavo

Torah 7 aliyot (minimum): כִּי־תָבוֹא Ki tavo
דְּבָרִים Devarim (Deuteronomy) 26:1–29:8

Annual:	¹26:1–11	²26:12–15	³26:16–19	⁴27:1–10
	⁵27:11–28:6	⁶28:7–69°	⁷29:1–8	ᴹ29:6–8
Triennial:	¹26:12–15	²26:16–19	³27:1–3	⁴27:4–8
	⁵27:6–10°	⁶27:11–28:3	⁷28:4–6	ᴹ28:4–6

☞ °27:6–8 In the triennial reading, these verses, which are part of the 4th aliyah, are read again in the 5th aliyah.

☞ °28:15–69 This is the תּוֹכֵחָה tokheḥah, verses of rebuke and warning. Because of the ominous nature of these verses, do not divide this lengthy passage into shorter aliyot. However, the chanting may be divided among multiple readers. All the readers must be present at the Torah when the oleh/olah recites the first berakhah. This serves as an implicit appointment of all the readers as sheliḥim (agents) of the oleh/olah.
Chant this section in a somewhat **subdued** voice to symbolically minimize the trepidation that the congregation experiences upon hearing the message of these verses. Be sure that all words and te'amim (tropes, cantillations) remain **clearly** audible to the congregation.
However, for verses 7–14, voicing the promise of God's protection and reward, and for the conclusion, verse 69, chant as usual.

Haftarah יְשַׁעְיָהוּ Yesha'yahu (Isaiah) 60:1–22
(6th of 7 haftarot of consolation following Tish'ah Be'av)

מִנְחָה

Torah 3 aliyot from נִצָּבִים Nitsavim
דְּבָרִים Devarim (Deuteronomy) 29:9–28°
¹29:9–11 ²12–14 ³15–28 W315 P936

Chanted also next Monday and Thursday.

☞ °29:9–28 The reading extends through verse 28, which enables the correct configuration of the 3 aliyot.

Elul 21 אֱלוּל
Sat 28 Aug

מוֹצָאֵי שַׁבָּת Motsa'ey Shabbat Conclusion of Shabbat

עַרְבִית

Saturday night Arvit as usual L264 S281 W137 F200

+ Psalm 27 for the Season of Repentance L59 S80 W92 F40
קַדִּישׁ יָתוֹם Mourner's Kaddish L58 S82 W100 F52

Elul 21 אֱלוּל
Sat 28 Aug (night)

לֵיל סְלִיחוֹת Leyl Seliḥot
Seliḥot at Night

Seliḥot — Penitential Prayers

We recite סְלִיחוֹת *seliḥot* beginning the Saturday night before Rosh Hashanah to prepare ourselves for the upcoming Days of Repentance.

In a year when Rosh Hashanah begins on a Sunday night or Monday night, as in the coming year, we begin סְלִיחוֹת a week earlier so that we have enough time to prepare in advance of Rosh Hashanah.

- Recite the first סְלִיחוֹת at midnight, an expression of our eagerness to begin the process of repentance.
- On subsequent days, recite סְלִיחוֹת before Shaḥarit every morning until Yom Kippur, except Shabbat and Rosh Hashanah.

The standard סְלִיחוֹת liturgy includes:
- אַשְׁרֵי *ashrey* and חֲצִי קַדִּישׁ Short Kaddish
- Various פִּיּוּטִים *piyyutim,* distinct liturgical poems for each day
- The Thirteen Attributes of God, . . . יי יי אֵ·ל רַחוּם וְחַנּוּן *adonay adonay el raḥum veḥannun* (based on Shemot 34:6–7)
- שְׁמַע קוֹלֵנוּ *shema kolenu,* אָשַׁמְנוּ *ashamnu,* and other סְלִיחוֹת prayers that appear in the Yom Kippur liturgy
- Short תַּחֲנוּן *taḥanun*
- קַדִּישׁ שָׁלֵם Full Kaddish

Rosh Hashanah

Looking Ahead to Rosh Hashanah

Teki'at Shofar — Hearing the Sounds of the Shofar

The *mitsvah* of hearing the sounds of the shofar on Rosh Hashanah is not restricted to the synagogue. For a person unable to attend a synagogue service, arrange a shofar blowing where the person lives, so the person fulfills the *mitsvah.*

Preparing to Celebrate with a New Fruit or with New Clothes

The 2nd day of Rosh Hashanah is celebrated Tuesday evening with a "new" fruit (that is, a seasonal fruit that you have not yet tasted this season) or with new clothes, worn for the first time that evening. In preparation, obtain the new fruit or new clothes before Rosh Hashanah begins.

Elul 27 אֱלוּל
Sat 4 Sep

שַׁבָּת Shabbat נִצָּבִים Parashat Nitsavim

Torah 7 aliyot (minimum): נִצָּבִים Nitsavim
דְּבָרִים Devarim (Deuteronomy) 29:9–30:20

Annual: ¹29:9–11 ²29:12–14 ³29:15–28 ⁴30:1–6
⁵30:7–10 ⁶30:11–14 ⁷30:15–20 ᴹ30:15–20 (or 18–20)

Triennial: Chant the full parashah, divided as above.

Haftarah יְשַׁעְיָהוּ Yesha'yahu (Isaiah) 61:10–63:9
(last of 7 haftarot of consolation following Tish'ah Be'av)

× ~~Birkat Haḥodesh~~

מִנְחָה

Torah 3 aliyot from וַיֵּלֶךְ Vayelekh
דְּבָרִים Devarim (Deuteronomy) 31:1–13°
¹31:1–3 ²4–6 ³7–13 W317 P938

Chanted also next Monday.

☞ °31:1–13 The reading extends through verse 13, which enables the correct configuration of the 3 aliyot.

Elul 28 אֱלוּל
Sat 4 Sep

מוֹצָאֵי שַׁבָּת Motsa'ey Shabbat Conclusion of Shabbat

עַרְבִית

Arvit for weekdays L264 S281 W137 F200

Weekday Amidah:

+ אַתָּה חוֹנַנְתָּנוּ Attah ḥonantanu L272 S287 W143 F212

× ~~חֲצִי קַדִּישׁ Short Kaddish~~

× ~~וִיהִי נֹעַם Vihi no'am~~
× ~~יֹשֵׁב בְּסֵתֶר עֶלְיוֹן Yoshev beseter elyon~~
× ~~וְאַתָּה קָדוֹשׁ Ve'attah kadosh~~

קַדִּישׁ שָׁלֵם Full Kaddish L280 S294 W160 F688

Some recite הַבְדָּלָה Havdalah here. L283 S299 W165 F700

עָלֵינוּ Aleynu L281 S297 W163 F696
קַדִּישׁ יָתוֹם Mourner's Kaddish (some omit) L282 S298 W164 F698
+ Psalm 27 for the Season of Repentance L59 S80 W92 F40
קַדִּישׁ יָתוֹם Mourner's Kaddish L58 S82 W100 F52

הַבְדָּלָה Havdalah L283 S299 W165 F700

Elul 5781							Aug | Sep 2021						
	1	2	3	4	5	6		9	10	11	12	13	14
7	8	9	10	11	12	13	15	16	17	18	19	20	21
14	15	16	17	18	19	20	22	23	24	25	26	27	28
21	22	23	24	25	26	27	29	30	31 | 1	2	3	4	
28	29						5	6					

+ Add ✕ Omit ☞ Take note!

Siddurim
- **L** Lev Shalem for Shabbat and Festivals
- **S** Shabbat and Festival Sim Shalom
- **W** Weekday Sim Shalom
- **F** Full Sim Shalom (both editions)
- **P** Personal Edition of Full Sim Shalom

Elul 29 אֱלוּל
Mon 6 Sep (daytime)

עֶרֶב רֹאשׁ הַשָּׁנָה Erev Rosh Hashanah
Day before Rosh Hashanah

+ סְלִיחוֹת Seliḥot (penitential prayers) (including תַּחֲנוּן Taḥanun)

שַׁחֲרִית
✕ ~~תַּחֲנוּן Taḥanun~~
☞ לַמְנַצֵּחַ Lamenatse·aḥ (Psalm 20) W79 F154
✕ ~~תְּקִיעַת שׁוֹפָר Sounding the shofar~~
+ Psalm 27 for the Season of Repentance W92 F40
קַדִּישׁ יָתוֹם Mourner's Kaddish W100 F52

מִנְחָה
✕ ~~תַּחֲנוּן Taḥanun~~

At home
Prepare a flame for Yom Tov. See blue box, below. Light candles. See "Candle Lighting for Rosh Hashanah — Day 1," below.

Before Rosh Hashanah

Preparing a Flame for Yom Tov

On Yom Tov, kindling a *new* fire is not permitted; however, the use of an *existing* fire for cooking or other purposes is permitted.

To light candles for Day 2 of Rosh Hashanah (Tuesday night), ensure that you have a fire burning before candle-lighting time for Day 1 (Monday evening) that will continue to burn until after dark on Tuesday. For example:

- A burning candle that lasts for more than 25 hours
- A pilot light on a gas range (*not* a gas range with an electronic starter)

Rosh Hashanah at Home — Day 1 and Day 2

Candle Lighting for Rosh Hashanah — Day 1

For Day 2, see blue box, p. 11.

1. Before lighting candles, prepare a flame. See above.
2. Light the candles at least 18 minutes before sunset.
3. Recite 2 בְּרָכוֹת *berakhot*: L79 S303 F718

בָּרוּךְ אַתָּה יי, אֱ-לֹהֵינוּ מֶלֶךְ הָעוֹלָם, אֲשֶׁר קִדְּשָׁנוּ בְּמִצְוֹתָיו
וְצִוָּנוּ לְהַדְלִיק נֵר שֶׁל יוֹם טוֹב.

Barukh attah adonay, eloheynu melekh ha'olam,
asher kiddeshanu bemitsvotav, vetsivvanu lehadlik ner shel yom tov.

בָּרוּךְ אַתָּה יי, אֱ-לֹהֵינוּ מֶלֶךְ הָעוֹלָם, שֶׁהֶחֱיָנוּ וְקִיְּמָנוּ וְהִגִּיעָנוּ לַזְּמַן הַזֶּה.

Barukh attah adonay, eloheynu melekh ha'olam,
sheheḥeyanu vekiyyemanu vehiggi'anu lazeman hazeh.

Rosh Hashanah Meals — Day 1 and Day 2

Enjoy festive meals evening and daytime, in the manner of Shabbat meals.

EVENING KIDDUSH L432 S336 F748

Day 1 Recite: 1. Rosh Hashanah קִדּוּשׁ *kiddush*
2. שֶׁהֶחֱיָנוּ *sheheḥeyanu*

Day 2 Wear the new clothes or set the new fruit on the table (see p. 6).
Recite: 1. Rosh Hashanah קִדּוּשׁ *kiddush.* L432 S336 F748
2. שֶׁהֶחֱיָנוּ, with the new clothes or fruit in mind

DAYTIME KIDDUSH L81 S335 F752

Recite: 1. תִּקְעוּ בַחֹדֶשׁ שׁוֹפָר *tik'u vaḥodesh shofar* (Psalm 81:4–5)
2. בּוֹרֵא פְּרִי הַגָּפֶן *bo·re peri hagafen*

HAMOTSI, APPLE AND HONEY, FESTIVE MEAL WITH SINGING, AND BIRKAT HAMAZON

1. Recite הַמּוֹצִיא *hamotsi* over 2 whole חַלָּה *ḥallah* loaves or rolls L81 S313–14 F744|746
   Round חַלָּה loaves are traditional for Rosh Hashanah.

   After reciting הַמּוֹצִיא, it is customary to dip pieces of חַלָּה in honey (instead of the usual salt) and distribute them to those at the table.
2. Dip a piece of apple in honey (evening only, or evening and daytime).
   a. Recite the בְּרָכָה *berakhah* over tree fruit: S336 F715

   בָּרוּךְ אַתָּה יי, אֱ·לֹהֵינוּ מֶלֶךְ הָעוֹלָם, בּוֹרֵא פְּרִי הָעֵץ.

   Barukh attah adonay, eloheynu melekh ha'olam, borey peri ha'ets.

   b. Eat the honey-dipped piece of apple.
   c. Recite the prayer for a sweet year: S336 F750

   יְהִי רָצוֹן מִלְּפָנֶיךָ, יי אֱ·לֹהֵינוּ וֵאלֹהֵי אֲבוֹתֵינוּ,
   שֶׁתְּחַדֵּשׁ עָלֵינוּ שָׁנָה טוֹבָה וּמְתוּקָה.

   Yehi ratson milefanekha, adonay eloheynu veylohey avoteynu,
   sheteḥaddesh aleynu shanah tovah umtukah.
3. Include festive singing, and recite בִּרְכַּת הַמָּזוֹן *birkat hamazon* with Rosh Hashanah additions (see yellow box, p. 10).

THROUGH Hosha'na Rabbah (some continue through Shemini Atseret)

Mornings — **After Psalm for the Day:**
קַדִּישׁ יָתוֹם Mourner's Kaddish (some omit) L58 S82 W100 F52
+ Psalm 27 for the Season of Repentance L59 S80 W92 F40
קַדִּישׁ יָתוֹם Mourner's Kaddish L58 S82 W100 F52

Evenings — **After עָלֵינוּ Aleynu:**
קַדִּישׁ יָתוֹם Mourner's Kaddish (some omit) L58 S82 W100 F52
+ Psalm 27 for the Season of Repentance L59 S80 W92 F40
קַדִּישׁ יָתוֹם Mourner's Kaddish L58 S82 W100 F52

Tishrey 5782						
		1	2	3	4	5
6	7	8	9	10	11	12
13	14	15	16	17	18	19
20	21	22	23	24	25	26
27	28	29	30			

Sep | Oct 2021						
		7	8	9	10	11
12	13	14	15	16	17	18
19	20	21	22	23	24	25
26	27	28	29	30 |	1	2
3	4	5	6			

+ Add ✕ Omit ☞ Take note!

Siddurim
- **L** Lev Shalem for Shabbat and Festivals
- **S** Shabbat and Festival Sim Shalom
- **W** Weekday Sim Shalom
- **F** Full Sim Shalom (both editions)
- **P** Personal Edition of Full Sim Shalom

Tishrey 1 תִּשְׁרֵי — רֹאשׁ הַשָּׁנָה Rosh Hashanah — Day 1

Mon 6 Sep (evening)

DURING Rosh Hashanah

Birkat Hamazon:

\+ יַעֲלֶה וְיָבוֹא Ya'aleh veyavo for Rosh Hashanah
L90|95 S340|347 W233|239 F762|780

\+ הָרַחֲמָן Harahaman for Rosh Hashanah
L92|96 S343 W236|240 F768

עַרְבִית Follow the service in the mahzor, including Kiddush.

קִדּוּשׁ Kiddush for Rosh Hashanah
\+ שֶׁהֶחֱיָנוּ Sheheheyanu

At home See "Rosh Hashanah Meals — Day 1 and Day 2," and "Evening Kiddush," p. 9.

Tue 7 Sep **שַׁחֲרִית** Follow the service in the mahzor.

1st scroll 5 aliyot from וַיֵּרָא Vayera
בְּרֵאשִׁית Bereshit (Genesis) 21:1–34
1 21:1–4 2 21:5–12 3 21:13–21 4 21:22–27 5 21:28–34

Use Yamim Nora'im cantillation.

2nd scroll Maftir aliyah from פִּינְחָס Pinehas
M בְּמִדְבַּר Bemidbar (Numbers) 29:1–6

Use Yamim Nora'im cantillation.

Haftarah for Rosh Hashanah — Day 1
שְׁמוּאֵל א׳ 1 Shemu'el (1 Samuel) 1:1–2:10

מוּסָף Follow the service in the mahzor.

Repetition of the Amidah:
Some congregations include בִּרְכַּת כֹּהֲנִים Birkat kohanim, the Priestly Blessing by the Kohanim (*dukhenen*).
For procedures, see p. 222.

קִדּוּשָׁא רַבָּא Kiddush for Rosh Hashanah L81 S335 F752
See "Daytime Kiddush," p. 9.

At home See "Rosh Hashanah Meals — Day 1 and Day 2," and "Daytime Kiddush," p. 9.

Tashlikh

In the afternoon of Day 1 of Rosh Hashanah (if Shabbat, then Day 2), walk to a natural body of water for the תַּשְׁלִיךְ *tashlikh* ceremony, which is based on the final three verses in the book of the prophet מִיכָה Mikhah (Micah). Symbolically, we cast away our sins—as if into the depths of the sea—and seek God's forgiveness. Many editions of the maḥzor include the text of the ceremony. If you are unable to accomplish this ritual on Rosh Hashanah, you can perform it until Hosha'na Rabbah, although before Yom Kippur is preferable.

מִנְחָה Follow the service in the maḥzor.

In the afternoon Walk to a natural body of water, and recite תַּשְׁלִיךְ Tashlikh. For information, see above.

Candle Lighting for Rosh Hashanah — Day 2

Day 1 ends after dark: when 3 stars appear, or at least 25 minutes after sunset (at least 43 minutes after the time set for lighting candles for Day 1). Some wait longer. For the appropriate time in your community, consult your rabbi.

1. Wait until Day 1 ends.
2. Wear the new clothes or set the new fruit on the table (see p. 6).
3. Do not *strike* a match. Instead, transfer fire to the candles from an *existing* flame (see p. 8) by inserting a match or other stick into the flame.
4. Do not *extinguish* the match or stick. Instead, place it on a non-flammable tray or dish, and let it self-extinguish. Alternately, a wood *safety* match held vertically (flame up) usually self-extinguishes quickly.
5. Recite the בְּרָכָה *berakhah* for Yom Tov candles: L79 S303 F718

   בָּרוּךְ אַתָּה יי, אֱ־לֹהֵינוּ מֶלֶךְ הָעוֹלָם, אֲשֶׁר קִדְּשָׁנוּ בְּמִצְוֹתָיו
   וְצִוָּנוּ לְהַדְלִיק נֵר שֶׁל יוֹם טוֹב.

   Barukh attah adonay, eloheynu melekh ha'olam,
   asher kiddeshanu bemitsvotav vetsivvanu lehadlik ner shel yom tov.
6. Recite שֶׁהֶחֱיָנוּ *sheheḥeyanu*, having in mind the new clothes or new fruit.

   בָּרוּךְ אַתָּה יי, אֱ־לֹהֵינוּ מֶלֶךְ הָעוֹלָם, שֶׁהֶחֱיָנוּ וְקִיְּמָנוּ וְהִגִּיעָנוּ לַזְּמַן הַזֶּה.

   Barukh attah adonay, eloheynu melekh ha'olam,
   sheheḥeyanu vekiyyemanu vehiggi'anu lazeman hazeh.

Tishrey 5782							Sep | Oct 2021						
		1	2	3	4	5			7	8	9	10	11
6	7	8	9	10	11	12	12	13	14	15	16	17	18
13	14	15	16	17	18	19	19	20	21	22	23	24	25
20	21	22	23	24	25	26	26	27	28	29	30	1	2
27	28	29	30				3	4	5	6			

+ Add ✕ Omit ☞ Take note!

Siddurim
- **L** Lev Shalem for Shabbat and Festivals
- **S** Shabbat and Festival Sim Shalom
- **W** Weekday Sim Shalom
- **F** Full Sim Shalom (both editions)
- **P** Personal Edition of Full Sim Shalom

Tishrey 2 תִּשְׁרֵי — Tue 7 Sep
רֹאשׁ הַשָּׁנָה Rosh Hashanah — Day 2

עַרְבִית Follow the service in the maḥzor, including Kiddush.

קִדּוּשׁ Kiddush for Rosh Hashanah
+ שֶׁהֶחֱיָנוּ Sheheḥeyanu

At home Light candles from an existing flame. See "Candle Lighting for Rosh Hashanah — Day 2," p. 11.

See "Rosh Hashanah Meals — Day 1 and Day 2," and "Evening Kiddush," p. 9.

Wed 8 Sep **שַׁחֲרִית** Follow the service in the maḥzor.

1st scroll 5 aliyot from וַיֵּרָא Vayera
בְּרֵאשִׁית Bereshit (Genesis) 22:1–24
[1]22:1–3 [2]22:4–8 [3]22:9–14 [4]22:15–19 [5]22:20–24

Use Yamim Nora'im cantillation.

2nd scroll Maftir aliyah from פִּינְחָס Pineḥas
בְּמִדְבַּר[M] Bemidbar (Numbers) 29:1–6

Use Yamim Nora'im cantillation.

Haftarah for Rosh Hashanah — Day 2
יִרְמְיָהוּ Yirmeyahu (Jeremiah) 31:1–19 (labeled 31:2–20 in some books)

מוּסָף Follow the service in the maḥzor.

Repetition of the Amidah:
Some congregations include בִּרְכַּת כֹּהֲנִים Birkat kohanim, the Priestly Blessing by the Kohanim (*dukhenen*). For procedures, see p. 222.

קִדּוּשָׁא רַבָּא Kiddush for Rosh Hashanah L81 S335 F752
See "Daytime Kiddush," p. 9.

At home See "Rosh Hashanah Meals — Day 1 and Day 2," and "Daytime Kiddush," p. 9.

מִנְחָה Follow the service in the maḥzor.

DURING Aseret Yemey Teshuvah (10 Days of Repentance: Rosh Hashanah – Yom Kippur)

Modifications for Aseret Yemey Teshuvah

Shabbat and weekdays

Every Kaddish (2nd paragraph):

✕ ~~לְעֵלָּא le'eyla~~

\+ לְעֵלָּא לְעֵלָּא le'eyla le'eyla (not לְעֵלָּא וּלְעֵלָּא le'eyla ul'eyla)

Every Amidah:

\+ In the 1st בְּרָכָה berakhah, add זָכְרֵנוּ Zokhrenu.

\+ In the 2nd בְּרָכָה, add מִי כָמוֹךָ Mi khamokha.

Conclusion of the 3rd בְּרָכָה:

✕ ~~הָאֵ-ל הַקָּדוֹשׁ Ha'el hakadosh~~

\+ הַמֶּלֶךְ הַקָּדוֹשׁ Hamelekh hakadosh.

\+ In the next-to-last בְּרָכָה, add וּכְתֹב Ukhtov.

\+ In the last בְּרָכָה, add בְּסֵפֶר חַיִּים Besefer ḥayyim.

Conclusion of the last בְּרָכָה:

✕ ~~הַמְבָרֵךְ . . . בַּשָּׁלוֹם Hamevarekh . . . bashalom~~

\+ עוֹשֵׂה הַשָּׁלוֹם Oseh hashalom.

\+ **Every Shaḥarit after יִשְׁתַּבַּח Yishtabbaḥ (some omit):**

Open ark.

Repeat each verse after the sheliaḥ/sheliḥat tsibbur:

שִׁיר הַמַּעֲלוֹת, מִמַּעֲמַקִּים Shir hama'alot, mima'amakkim (Psalm 130) L450 S254 W62 F134

Close ark.

\+ **Every morning and evening**

Psalm 27 for the Season of Repentance L59 S80 W92 F40

For details, see yellow box, p. 9

Weekdays only

\+ סְלִיחוֹת Seliḥot (penitential prayers) before Shaḥarit

Every weekday Amidah:

Conclusion of הָשִׁיבָה שׁוֹפְטֵינוּ Hashiva shofeteynu:

✕ ~~מֶלֶךְ אוֹהֵב צְדָקָה וּמִשְׁפָּט Melekh ohev tsedakah umishpat~~

\+ הַמֶּלֶךְ הַמִּשְׁפָּט Hamelekh hamishpat.

\+ אָבִינוּ מַלְכֵּנוּ Avinu malkenu W57 F124|188

☞ תַּחֲנוּן Taḥanun

Tishrey 5782						
		1	2	3	4	5
6	7	8	9	10	11	12
13	14	15	16	17	18	19
20	21	22	23	24	25	26
27	28	29	30			

Sep | Oct 2021						
		7	8	9	10	11
12	13	14	15	16	17	18
19	20	21	22	23	24	25
26	27	28	29	30	1	2
3	4	5	6			

+ Add ✕ Omit ☞ Take note!

Siddurim
- **L** Lev Shalem for Shabbat and Festivals
- **S** Shabbat and Festival Sim Shalom
- **W** Weekday Sim Shalom
- **F** Full Sim Shalom (both editions)
- **P** Personal Edition of Full Sim Shalom

Tishrey 3 תִּשְׁרֵי
Wed 8 Sep (evening)

צוֹם גְּדַלְיָה Tsom Gedalyah

Fast of Gedalyah (communal fast, begins Thursday at dawn)
מוֹצָאֵי רֹאשׁ הַשָּׁנָה Motsa'ey Rosh Hashanah
Conclusion of Rosh Hashanah

עַרְבִית

+ Modifications for Aseret Yemey Teshuvah (see p. 13)

Arvit for weekdays L264 S281 W137 F200

Weekday Amidah:
+ אַתָּה חוֹנַנְתָּנוּ Attah ḥonantanu L272 S287 W143 F212

קַדִּישׁ שָׁלֵם Full Kaddish L280 S294 W160 F222

Some recite הַבְדָּלָה Havdalah here. L283 S299 W165 F700
For instructions, see below.

עָלֵינוּ Aleynu L281 S297 W163 F696
קַדִּישׁ יָתוֹם Mourner's Kaddish (some omit) L282 S298 W164 F698
+ Psalm 27 for the Season of Repentance L59 S80 W92 F40
קַדִּישׁ יָתוֹם Mourner's Kaddish L58 S82 W100 F52

+ **Havdalah:** L283 S299 W165 F700
✕ ~~הִנֵּה אֵ-ל יְשׁוּעָתִי Hinneh el yeshu'ati~~
בּוֹרֵא פְּרִי הַגָּפֶן Bo·re peri hagafen
✕ ~~בּוֹרֵא מִינֵי בְשָׂמִים Bo·re miney vesamim~~
✕ ~~בּוֹרֵא מְאוֹרֵי הָאֵשׁ Bo·re me'orey ha'esh~~
הַמַּבְדִּיל בֵּין קֹדֶשׁ לְחֹל Hamavdil beyn kodesh leḥol

Tsom Gedalyah

After Nebuchadnezzar razed Jerusalem in 586 B.C.E., he installed Gedalyah ben Aḥikam as governor of Judah, which was by then a Babylonian province. Later, a Jew was recruited to kill Gedalyah. After the assassination of the governor, the few Jews remaining in Jerusalem dispersed; the last vestiges of Jewish control over Jerusalem ended. Tsom Gedalyah commemorates these events.

- This is a minor fast day, so called because the fast does not begin until dawn.
- The fast (from both eating and drinking) lasts until dark (a minimum of 25 minutes after sunset).
- *Sheliḥey tsibbur,* Torah readers, and those called for *aliyot* should be fasting.
- The preferred fast-day procedures apply when at least six of those who are counted for a *minyan* are fasting.
- If it is ascertained (without causing embarrassment) that fewer than six are fasting, follow the procedures printed in gray and marked with ✦.

Thu 9 Sep (morning)

+ Modifications for Aseret Yemey Teshuvah (see p. 13)

+ סְלִיחוֹת Seliḥot (penitential prayers) before Shaḥarit.

שַׁחֲרִית

+ **After יִשְׁתַּבַּח Yishtabbaḥ (some omit):**
Open ark.
Repeat each verse after the sheliaḥ/sheliḥat tsibbur:
שִׁיר הַמַּעֲלוֹת, מִמַּעֲמַקִּים Shir hama'alot, mima'amakkim (Psalm 130) **W**62 **F**134
Close ark.

Silent weekday Amidah:
Do not add עֲנֵנוּ Anenu.

Repetition of the weekday Amidah:

6 or more fasting + עֲנֵנוּ Anenu, before רְפָאֵנוּ Refa'enu **W**38 **F**110

Fewer than 6 fasting ✦ Add עֲנֵנוּ Anenu in שׁוֹמֵעַ תְּפִלָּה Shome·a tefillah. Replace תַּעֲנִיתֵנוּ ta'anitenu (6th word) with הַתַּעֲנִית הַזֶּה hata'anit hazeh. **W**38 **F**110

+ אָבִינוּ מַלְכֵּנוּ Avinu malkenu **W**57 **F**124
with lines for between Rosh Hashanah and Yom Kippur (omit lines for fast days)

☞ תַּחֲנוּן Taḥanun (וְהוּא רַחוּם Vehu raḥum) **W**59 **F**128
חֲצִי קַדִּישׁ Short Kaddish **W**64 **F**136

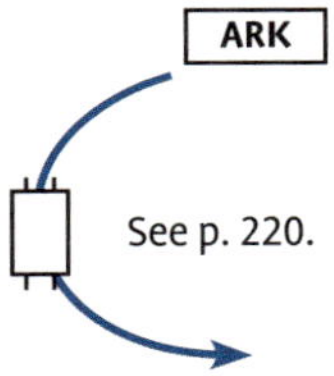

See p. 220.

TORAH SERVICE **W**65 **F**138

Remove **1** scroll from ark.

6 or more fasting

Torah 3 aliyot from כִּי תִשָּׂא Ki tissa
שְׁמוֹת Shemot (Exodus) 32:11–14, 34:1–10
[1]32:11–14° [2]34:1–3 [3]34:4–10° **W**341 **P**979

☞ °At each of the 3 passages indicated below, follow this procedure:
1. The reader pauses before the indicated text.
2. The congregation recites the indicated text.
3. Afterward, the reader chants the indicated text in the manner of the cantillation of High Holiday Torah reading.

32:12 שׁוּב מֵחֲרוֹן אַפֶּךָ וְהִנָּחֵם עַל־הָרָעָה לְעַמֶּךָ׃

34:6–7 יְיָ | יְיָ אֵ֫ל רַחוּם וְחַנּוּן אֶרֶךְ אַפַּיִם וְרַב־חֶסֶד וֶאֱמֶת׃
נֹצֵר חֶסֶד לָאֲלָפִים נֹשֵׂא עָוֺן וָפֶשַׁע וְחַטָּאָה וְנַקֵּה

34:9 וְסָלַחְתָּ לַעֲוֺנֵנוּ וּלְחַטָּאתֵנוּ | וּנְחַלְתָּנוּ׃
To preserve the sense of this passage, maintain the appropriate pause after the טִפְּחָא (וּלְחַטָּאתֵנוּ).

Tishrey 5782						
		1	2	3	4	5
6	7	8	9	10	11	12
13	14	15	16	17	18	19
20	21	22	23	24	25	26
27	28	29	30			

Sep | Oct 2021						
		7	8	9	10	11
12	13	14	15	16	17	18
19	20	21	22	23	24	25
26	27	28	29	30 | 1		2
3	4	5	6			

+ Add ✕ Omit ☞ Take note!

Siddurim
- **L** Lev Shalem for Shabbat and Festivals
- **S** Shabbat and Festival Sim Shalom
- **W** Weekday Sim Shalom
- **F** Full Sim Shalom (both editions)
- **P** Personal Edition of Full Sim Shalom

Fewer than 6 fasting ✦ **Torah** 3 aliyot from וַיֵּלֶךְ Vayelekh
דְּבָרִים Devarim (Deuteronomy) 31:1–13°
^{1}31:1–3 ^{2}4–6 ^{3}7–13 W317 P938

☞°31:1–13 The reading extends through verse 13, which enables the correct configuration of the 3 aliyot.

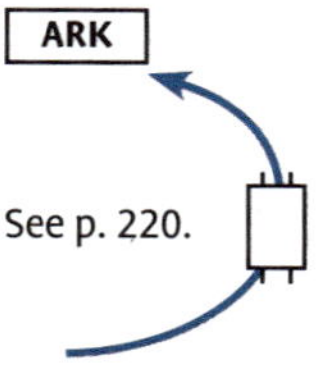

See p. 220.

חֲצִי קַדִּישׁ Short Kaddish W71 F146
Open, raise, display, and wrap scroll.
Return scroll to ark. W76 F150

All minyanim

אַשְׁרֵי Ashrey W78 F152
☞לַמְנַצֵּחַ Lamenatse·aḥ (Psalm 20) W79 F154
Conclude the service as on a usual weekday.

מִנְחָה + Modifications for Aseret Yemey Teshuvah (see p. 13)

אַשְׁרֵי Ashrey W120 F164
חֲצִי קַדִּישׁ Short Kaddish W121 F166

Fewer than 6 fasting ✦ Omit the entire Torah service.
Continue with silent Amidah.

6 or more fasting + **TORAH SERVICE** W65 F138

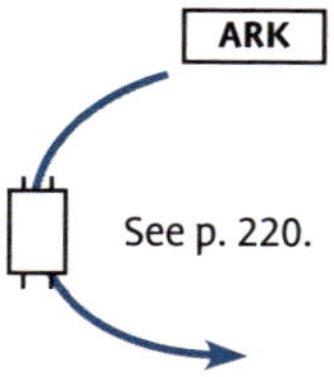

See p. 220.

Remove **1** scroll from ark.

Torah 3 aliyot from כִּי תִשָּׂא Ki tissa
שְׁמוֹת Shemot (Exodus) 32:11–14, 34:1–10
^{1}32:11–14° ^{2}34:1–3 ^{M}34:4–10° W341 P979

☞°Chant as for the morning fast-day reading (p. 15).

☞Do not recite חֲצִי קַדִּישׁ Short Kaddish after maftir aliyah.
Open, raise, display, and wrap scroll.

Recite the בְּרָכָה berakhah before the haftarah. W74 F410 P989

Haftarah יְשַׁעְיָהוּ Yesha'yahu (Isaiah) 55:6–56:8 W342 P980

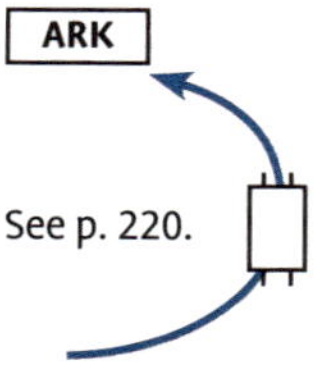

See p. 220.

Recite the 3 concluding haftarah blessings,
through מָגֵן דָּוִד Magen david. W74 F410 P989.

Return scroll to ark. W76 F150
חֲצִי קַדִּישׁ Short Kaddish W121 F166

All minyanim — **Silent weekday Amidah:**

If fasting + עֲנֵנוּ Anenu, in שׁוֹמֵעַ תְּפִלָּה Shome·a tefillah W127 F178

All ✕ ~~שָׁלוֹם רָב Shalom rav~~

+ שִׂים שָׁלוֹם Sim shalom W131 F184

Repetition of the weekday Amidah:

6 or more fasting + עֲנֵנוּ Anenu, before רְפָאֵנוּ Refa'enu W124 F172

Fewer than 6 fasting ✦ Add עֲנֵנוּ Anenu in שׁוֹמֵעַ תְּפִלָּה Shome·a tefillah. Replace תַּעֲנִיתֵנוּ ta'anitenu (6th word) with הַתַּעֲנִית הַזֶּה hata'anit hazeh. W127 F172

All minyanim + בִּרְכַּת כֹּהֲנִים Birkat kohanim W131 F184

✕ ~~שָׁלוֹם רָב Shalom rav~~

+ שִׂים שָׁלוֹם Sim shalom W131 F184

+ אָבִינוּ מַלְכֵּנוּ Avinu malkenu W57 F124
with lines for between Rosh Hashanah and Yom Kippur (omit lines for fast days)

☞ תַּחֲנוּן Tahanun W132 F192

קַדִּישׁ שָׁלֵם Full Kaddish W134 F194
Conclude Minhah as on a usual weekday.

Tishrey 4 תִּשְׁרֵי — עֶרֶב שַׁבָּת Erev Shabbat — Day before Shabbat

Thu 9 Sep — **עַרְבִית** + Modifications for Aseret Yemey Teshuvah (see p. 13)

Fri 10 Sep — **שַׁחֲרִית** + Modifications for Aseret Yemey Teshuvah (see p. 13)

מִנְחָה + Modifications for Aseret Yemey Teshuvah (see p. 13)

✕ ~~אָבִינוּ מַלְכֵּנוּ Avinu malkenu~~ (as on all Friday afternoons)

✕ ~~תַּחֲנוּן Tahanun~~ (as on all Friday afternoons)

Tishrey 5 תִּשְׁרֵי — שַׁבָּת Shabbat — פָּרָשַׁת וַיֵּלֶךְ Parashat Vayelekh

Fri 10 Sep — שַׁבַּת שׁוּבָה Shabbat Shuvah — Shabbat of Repentance

קַבָּלַת שַׁבָּת Kabbalat Shabbat as on a usual Shabbat L7 S13 F252

+ Modifications for Aseret Yemey Teshuvah (see p. 13)

עַרְבִית Shabbat Arvit as usual L39 S28 F279
through וַיְכֻלּוּ Vaykhullu L53 S47 F314

Tishrey 5782						
		1	2	3	4	5
6	7	8	9	10	11	12
13	14	15	16	17	18	19
20	21	22	23	24	25	26
27	28	29	30			

Sep | Oct 2021						
		7	8	9	10	11
12	13	14	15	16	17	18
19	20	21	22	23	24	25
26	27	28	29	30 |	1	2
3	4	5	6			

+ Add ✕ Omit ☞ Take note!

Siddurim
- **L** Lev Shalem for Shabbat and Festivals
- **S** Shabbat and Festival Sim Shalom
- **W** Weekday Sim Shalom
- **F** Full Sim Shalom (both editions)
- **P** Personal Edition of Full Sim Shalom

מָגֵן אָבוֹת Magen avot: L53 S47 F314

✕ ~~הָאֵ·ל הַקָּדוֹשׁ Ha'el Hakadosh~~

+ הַמֶּלֶךְ הַקָּדוֹשׁ Hamelekh Hakadosh

Conclude as on a usual Shabbat.

+ Psalm 27 for the Season of Repentance L59 S80 F40

קַדִּישׁ יָתוֹם Mourner's Kaddish L58 S82 F52

Sat 11 Sep **שַׁחֲרִית** + Modifications for Aseret Yemey Teshuvah (see p. 13)

+ **After יִשְׁתַּבַּח Yishtabbaḥ (some omit):**
Open ark.
Repeat each verse after the sheliaḥ/sheliḥat tsibbur:
שִׁיר הַמַּעֲלוֹת, מִמַּעֲמַקִּים Shir hama'alot, mima'amakkim (Psalm 130) L450 S254 F134
Close ark.

Torah 7 aliyot (minimum): וַיֵּלֶךְ Vayelekh
דְּבָרִים Devarim (Deuteronomy) 31:1–30

Annual:	[1] 31:1–3	[2] 31:4–6	[3] 31:7–9	[4] 31:10–13
	[5] 31:14–19	[6] 31:20–24	[7] 31:25–30	[M] 31:28–30

Triennial: Chant the full parashah, divided as above.

Haftarah for Shabbat Shuvah (when וַיֵּלֶךְ Vayelekh is read)
הוֹשֵׁעַ Hoshe·a (Hosea) 14:2–10 + מִיכָה Mikhah (Micah) 7:18–20°

☞ °There are other selections found in various ḥumashim. This reading is recommended when the parashah is וַיֵּלֶךְ Vayelekh.

מוּסָף + Modifications for Aseret Yemey Teshuvah (see p. 13)

מִנְחָה + Modifications for Aseret Yemey Teshuvah (see p. 13)

Torah 3 aliyot from הַאֲזִינוּ Ha'azinu
דְּבָרִים Devarim (Deuteronomy) 32:1–12°
[1] 32:1–3 [2] 4–6° [3] 7–12 W318 P939

Chanted also next Monday.

☞ °32:1–12 The reading extends through verse 12, which enables the correct configuration of the 3 aliyot.

☞ °32:6 Read הַלְאֲ·דֹנָי hal-adonay. For more information, see p. 25.

☞ צִדְקָתְךָ צֶדֶק Tsidkatekha tsedek L230 S239 W183 F584

Tishrey 5782							Sep | Oct 2021						
		1	2	3	4	5			7	8	9	10	11
6	7	8	9	10	11	12	12	13	14	15	16	17	18
13	14	15	16	17	18	19	19	20	21	22	23	24	25
20	21	22	23	24	25	26	26	27	28	29	30 | 1	2
27	28	29	30				3	4	5	6			

Tishrey 6 תִּשְׁרֵי
Sat 11 Sep

מוֹצָאֵי שַׁבָּת Motsa'ey Shabbat — Conclusion of Shabbat

עַרְבִית

+ Modifications for Aseret Yemey Teshuvah (see p. 13)

Arvit for weekdays L264 S281 W137 F200

Weekday Amidah:

+ אַתָּה חוֹנַנְתָּנוּ Attah ḥonantanu L272 S287 W143 F212

✕ ~~חֲצִי קַדִּישׁ Short Kaddish~~

✕ ~~וִיהִי נֹעַם Vihi no'am~~
✕ ~~יֹשֵׁב בְּסֵתֶר עֶלְיוֹן Yoshev beseter elyon~~
✕ ~~וְאַתָּה קָדוֹשׁ Ve'attah kadosh~~

קַדִּישׁ שָׁלֵם Full Kaddish L280 S294 W160 F688

Some recite הַבְדָּלָה Havdalah here. L283 S299 W165 F700

עָלֵינוּ Aleynu L281 S297 W163 F696
קַדִּישׁ יָתוֹם Mourner's Kaddish (some omit) L282 S298 W164 F698
+ Psalm 27 for the Season of Repentance L59 S80 W92 F40
קַדִּישׁ יָתוֹם Mourner's Kaddish L58 S82 W100 F52

הַבְדָּלָה Havdalah L283 S299 W165 F700

☞ Do not recite Kiddush Levanah until after Yom Kippur.

Sun 12 Sep (daytime) + Modifications for Aseret Yemey Teshuvah (see p. 13)

Tishrey 7 תִּשְׁרֵי
Sun 12 Sep (evening) + Modifications for Aseret Yemey Teshuvah (see p. 13)
Mon 13 Sep (daytime) + Modifications for Aseret Yemey Teshuvah (see p. 13)

Torah 3 aliyot from הַאֲזִינוּ Ha'azinu
דְּבָרִים Devarim (Deuteronomy) 32:1–12°
[1]32:1–3 [2]4–6° [3]7–12 W318 P939

☞ °32:1–12 The reading extends through verse 12, which enables the correct configuration of the 3 aliyot.

☞ °32:6 Read הַלְאֲ·דֹנָי hal-adonay. For more information, see p. 25.

Tishrey 8 תִּשְׁרֵי
Mon 13 Sep (evening) + Modifications for Aseret Yemey Teshuvah (see p. 13)
Tue 14 Sep (daytime) + Modifications for Aseret Yemey Teshuvah (see p. 13)

Tishrey 5782						
		1	2	3	4	5
6	7	8	9	10	11	12
13	14	15	16	17	18	19
20	21	22	23	24	25	26
27	28	29	30			

Sep | Oct 2021						
		7	8	9	10	11
12	13	14	15	16	17	18
19	20	21	22	23	24	25
26	27	28	29	30 |	1	2
3	4	5	6			

+ Add ✕ Omit ☞ Take note!

Siddurim
- **L** Lev Shalem for Shabbat and Festivals
- **S** Shabbat and Festival Sim Shalom
- **W** Weekday Sim Shalom
- **F** Full Sim Shalom (both editions)
- **P** Personal Edition of Full Sim Shalom

Tishrey 9 תִּשְׁרֵי
Tue 14 Sep

עֶרֶב יוֹם כִּפּוּר Erev Yom Kippur
Day before Yom Kippur

עַרְבִית
+ Modifications for Aseret Yemey Teshuvah (see p. 13)

Wed 15 Sep (morning)
+ Modifications for Aseret Yemey Teshuvah (see p. 13)
+ סְלִיחוֹת Seliḥot (penitential prayers)

שַׁחֲרִית
✕ ~~מִזְמוֹר לְתוֹדָה Mizmor letodah (Psalm 100)~~

+ **After יִשְׁתַּבַּח Yishtabbaḥ (some omit):**
Open ark.
Repeat each verse after the sheliaḥ/sheliḥat tsibbur:
שִׁיר הַמַּעֲלוֹת, מִמַּעֲמַקִּים Shir hama'alot, mima'amakkim (Psalm 130) L450 W62 F134
Close ark.

✕ ~~אָבִינוּ מַלְכֵּנוּ Avinu malkenu~~
✕ ~~תַּחֲנוּן Taḥanun~~

אַשְׁרֵי Ashrey L214 W78 F152
✕ ~~לַמְנַצֵּחַ Lamenatse·aḥ (Psalm 20)~~
וּבָא לְצִיּוֹן Uva letsiyyon L216 W80 F156
Conclude Shaḥarit as on a usual weekday.

מִנְחָה
Because of additions to the silent Amidah, use the maḥzor for this Minḥah service.

אַשְׁרֵי Ashrey
חֲצִי קַדִּישׁ Short Kaddish

Silent weekday Amidah:
+ אָשַׁמְנוּ Ashamnu
+ עַל חֵטְא Al ḥet

Repetition of the weekday Amidah:
✕ ~~אָשַׁמְנוּ Ashamnu~~
✕ ~~עַל חֵטְא Al ḥet~~

✕ ~~אָבִינוּ מַלְכֵּנוּ Avinu malkenu~~
✕ ~~תַּחֲנוּן Taḥanun~~
קַדִּישׁ שָׁלֵם Full Kaddish
Conclude Minḥah as usual.

Yom Kippur

Before Yom Kippur

Last Meal before the Fast

The Rabbis considered it a *mitsvah* to eat a festive סְעוּדָה מַפְסֶקֶת *se'udah mafseket* (last meal before a fast) before Yom Kippur begins. If possible, attend Minḥah first and then eat.

Memorial Candle

If a parent or other close relative has died, before lighting the holiday candles, light a memorial candle that will burn throughout Yom Kippur.

Resting Candle

Before Yom Kippur, light a long-burning (about 26 hours) candle. This will serve as נֵר שֶׁשָּׁבַת *ner sheshavat* "a candle that rested," that is, a flame that was burning before Yom Kippur and burned throughout Yom Kippur. At the conclusion of Yom Kippur, use this flame (or a flame lit from it) to light the Havdalah candle.

In the absence of נֵר שֶׁשָּׁבַת, at Havdalah do not light a Havdalah candle and omit the *berakhah* בּוֹרֵא מְאוֹרֵי הָאֵשׁ *bo·re me'orey ha'esh.* (However, after Yom Kippur that falls on Shabbat, in the absence of נֵר שֶׁשָּׁבַת, light a Havdalah candle in the normal manner and recite the *berakhah.*)

A candle lit as a memorial candle also may serve as the resting candle. Ensure it is a candle that will burn long enough (about 26 hours) to be available at the conclusion of Yom Kippur. Many memorial candles do not burn long enough.

Yom Kippur Prohibitions and Practices

The Torah (Vayikra 23:32) refers to Yom Kippur as שַׁבַּת שַׁבָּתוֹן *shabbat shabbaton* (a sabbath of complete rest). Thus, even when Yom Kippur does not fall on Shabbat, it takes on all the restrictions of Shabbat. So, for example, cooking, use of fire, and carrying outside an *eruv* are not permitted.

In addition, the following are not permitted until dark after Yom Kippur:

- Eating and drinking
- Sexual relations
- Bathing (except for minimal washing to remove dirt or after using the toilet)
- Using skin or bath oils
- Wearing leather shoes

Wearing white is customary. During services, some wear a *kittel* (plain white robe).

Before Leaving for the Synagogue

Candle Lighting for Yom Kippur

1. Light the candles at least 18 minutes before sunset.
2. Recite 2 בְּרָכוֹת *berakhot:* S303 F719

בָּרוּךְ אַתָּה יי, אֱ-לֹהֵינוּ מֶלֶךְ הָעוֹלָם, אֲשֶׁר קִדְּשָׁנוּ בְּמִצְוֹתָיו
וְצִוָּנוּ לְהַדְלִיק נֵר שֶׁל יוֹם הַכִּפּוּרִים.

Barukh attah adonay, eloheynu melekh ha'olam, asher kiddeshanu bemitsvotav vetsivvanu lehadlik ner shel yom hakippurim.

בָּרוּךְ אַתָּה יי, אֱ-לֹהֵינוּ מֶלֶךְ הָעוֹלָם, שֶׁהֶחֱיָנוּ וְקִיְּמָנוּ וְהִגִּיעָנוּ לַזְּמַן הַזֶּה.

Barukh attah adonay, eloheynu melekh ha'olam,
sheheḥeyanu vekiyyemanu vehiggi'anu lazeman hazeh.

Blessing the Children

Before leaving for the synagogue, bless the children, L75 S311 F722
even if it is not your custom to do so on Shabbat or Yom Tov.

Before Kol Nidrey

1. Arrive at the synagogue before sunset, while it is still light.
2. Wear a טַלִּית *tallit*. Before putting it on, recite the בְּרָכָה *berakhah*. L102 S62 W2 F4.

Tishrey 10 תִּשְׁרֵי
Wed 15 Sep (evening)

יוֹם כִּפּוּר Yom Kippur

At home

Before leaving for the synagogue:

☞ Wear non-leather shoes.
Light the candles, and bless the children.
See "Candle Lighting for Yom Kippur" and "Blessing the Children," above.

In the synagogue

Before sunset:

☞ Put on a טַלִּית tallit. See "Before Kol Nidrey," above.

כָּל־נִדְרֵי

Remove 2 or more Torah scrolls from ark. (Some congregations conduct a counterclockwise procession around the sanctuary with all the Torah scrolls and then return all but 2 scrolls to ark.)

Hold 2 Torah scrolls, 1 on each side of the sheliaḥ/sheliḥat tsibbur.

Follow the כָּל־נִדְרֵי Kol nidrey liturgy in the maḥzor. Recite the כָּל־נִדְרֵי paragraph 3 times, each recitation louder than the previous one.

Recite שֶׁהֶחֱיָנוּ sheheḥeyanu.

Return scrolls to ark.

עַרְבִית Follow the service in the maḥzor.

☞ After reciting the line **שְׁמַע יִשְׂרָאֵל** Shema Yisra'el, recite . . . **בָּרוּךְ שֵׁם כְּבוֹד** barukh shem kevod . . . *aloud* (rather than in the usual undertone).

Thu 16 Sep **שַׁחֲרִית** Follow the service in the maḥzor.

☞ After reciting the line **שְׁמַע יִשְׂרָאֵל** Shema Yisra'el, recite . . . **בָּרוּךְ שֵׁם כְּבוֹד** barukh shem kevod . . . *aloud* (rather than in the usual undertone).

1st scroll 6 aliyot from **אַחֲרֵי מוֹת** Aḥarey mot
וַיִּקְרָא Vayikra (Leviticus) 16:1–34
[1]16:1–6 [2]16:7–11 [3]16:12–17 [4]16:18–24 [5]16:25–30 [6]16:31–34

Use Yamim Nora'im cantillation.

2nd scroll Maftir aliyah from **פִּינְחָס** Pineḥas
[M]**בְּמִדְבַּר** Bemidbar (Numbers) 29:7–11

Use Yamim Nora'im cantillation.

Haftarah for Yom Kippur morning
יְשַׁעְיָהוּ Yesha'yahu (Isaiah) 57:14–58:14

מוּסָף Follow the service in the maḥzor.

Repetition of the Amidah:
Some congregations include **בִּרְכַּת כֹּהֲנִים** Birkat kohanim, the Priestly Blessing by the Kohanim (*dukhenen*). For procedures, see p. 222.

מִנְחָה Follow the service in the maḥzor.

Torah 3 aliyot from **אַחֲרֵי מוֹת** Aḥarey mot
וַיִּקְרָא Vayikra (Leviticus) 18:1–30
[1]18:1–5 [2]6–21 [M]22–30

Use weekday cantillation, not Yamim Nora'im cantillation.

Haftarah for Yom Kippur afternoon
יוֹנָה Yonah (Jonah) 1:1–4:11 + **מִיכָה** Mikhah (Micah) 7:18–20

נְעִילָה Follow the service in the maḥzor.

Tishrey 5782

	1	2	3	4	5	
6	7	8	9	10	11	12
13	14	15	16	17	18	19
20	21	22	23	24	25	26
27	28	29	30			

Sep | Oct 2021

		7	8	9	10	11
12	13	14	15	16	17	18
19	20	21	22	23	24	25
26	27	28	29	30	1	2
3	4	5	6			

+ Add ✕ Omit ☞ Take note!

Siddurim

L Lev Shalem for Shabbat and Festivals
S Shabbat and Festival Sim Shalom
W Weekday Sim Shalom
F Full Sim Shalom (both editions)
P Personal Edition of Full Sim Shalom

THROUGH HOSHA'NA RABBAH (some congregations, through Shemini Atseret)

+ Psalm 27 for the Season of Repentance L59 S80 W92 F40
For details, see yellow box, p. 9.

THROUGH 24 TISHREY (some congregations, through 1 Ḥeshvan)

✕ ~~תַּחֲנוּן Taḥanun~~

Tishrey 11 תִּשְׁרֵי
Thu 16 Sep

מוֹצָאֵי יוֹם כִּפּוּר Motsa'ey Yom Kippur
Conclusion of Yom Kippur

עַרְבִית

Arvit for weekdays L264 S281 W137 F200

Weekday Amidah:

+ אַתָּה חוֹנַנְתָּנוּ Attah ḥonantanu L272 S287 W143 F212

קַדִּישׁ שָׁלֵם Full Kaddish L280 S294 W160 F222

Some recite הַבְדָּלָה Havdalah here. L283 S299 W165 F700
For instructions, see below.

עָלֵינוּ Aleynu L281 S297 W163 F696
קַדִּישׁ יָתוֹם Mourner's Kaddish (some omit) L282 S298 W164 F698
+ Psalm 27 for the Season of Repentance L59 S80 W92 F40
קַדִּישׁ יָתוֹם Mourner's Kaddish L58 S82 W100 F52

+ **Havdalah:** L283 S299 W165 F700
☞ Light the candle from נֵר שֶׁשָּׁבַת ner sheshavat, a flame lit before Yom Kippur. See "Resting Candle," p. 21.
✕ ~~הִנֵּה אֵ-ל יְשׁוּעָתִי Hinneh el yeshu'ati~~
בּוֹרֵא פְּרִי הַגָּפֶן Bo·re peri hagafen
✕ ~~בּוֹרֵא מִינֵי בְשָׂמִים Bo·re miney vesamim~~
(In the absence of נֵר שֶׁשָּׁבַת ner sheshavat, do not light a Havadalah candle, and omit בּוֹרֵא מְאוֹרֵי הָאֵשׁ.)
בּוֹרֵא מְאוֹרֵי הָאֵשׁ Bo·re me'orey ha'esh

הַמַּבְדִּיל בֵּין קֹדֶשׁ לְחוֹל Hamavdil beyn kodesh leḥol

Tishrey 11 תִּשְׁרֵי
Thu 16 Sep (night)

After Arvit if the moon is visible:
קִדּוּשׁ לְבָנָה Kiddush Levanah L286 W167 F704
For procedures and instructions, see p. 223.

At home

Begin immediately to build your סֻכָּה sukkah, even if you can do only a small first step. See "Looking Ahead to Sukkot," p. 25.

Sukkot

Looking Ahead to Sukkot

Building a Sukkah

- Immediately after Yom Kippur ends (or as soon thereafter as possible), begin to build your סֻכָּה *sukkah*—even if you can do only a small first step.
  This concrete act symbolizes our firm commitment, expressed throughout Yom Kippur, to build *mitsvot* into our everyday lives.
- During the days leading up to Sukkot, complete the *sukkah*.
  It is considered an act of הִדּוּר מִצְוָה *hiddur mitsvah* (beautification of the *mitsvah*) to build and decorate your סֻכָּה in a manner that enhances your enjoyment of the festival.

Acquiring Lulav and Etrog

The *mitsvah* of נְטִילַת לוּלָב *netilat lulav* (taking the *lulav*) requires אַרְבָּעָה מִינִים *arba'ah minim* (4 species): לוּלָב *lulav* (1 palm branch), אֶתְרוֹג *etrog* (1 citron), הֲדַסִּים *hadassim* (3 myrtle branches), and עֲרָבוֹת *aravot* (2 willow branches).

Another act of הִדּוּר מִצְוָה (see above) is to acquire אַרְבָּעָה מִינִים as fresh and unblemished as available and affordable so that their beauty enhances your enjoyment of the festival.

All the branches are placed in a special holder made of woven palm fronds and tied with side fronds from this or another *lulav*. See instructions, p. 27.

Tishrey 12 תִּשְׁרֵי
Sat 18 Sep

שַׁבָּת Shabbat פָּרָשַׁת הַאֲזִינוּ Parashat Ha'azinu

Torah 7 aliyot (minimum): הַאֲזִינוּ Ha'azinu
דְּבָרִים Devarim (Deuteronomy) 32:1–52°

☞°Do not subdivide any of the first 6 aliyot. The divisions below are indicated in the Talmud by the mnemonic הזי"ו ל"ך, which denotes the first letter of each of the 6 aliyot in the poetry section. No other parashah has aliyah divisions mandated by rabbinic tradition.

Annual:	[1]32:1–6° (ה)	[2]32:7–12 (ז)	[3]32:13–18 (י)	[4]32:19–28 (ו)
	[5]32:29–39 (ל)	[6]32:40–43 (ך)	[7]32:44–52	[M]32:48–52
Triennial:	Chant the full parashah, divided as above.			

☞°32:6 Read הַלְאֲ·דֹנָי hal-adonay.
The קְרֵי kerey, the manner in which this word is *read*, is governed by the Masorah, written in the Aleppo Codex (www.aleppocodex.org) and described in Masoretic commentaries such as Minḥat Shay:
(1) Read this as a single word, (2) pronouce the 1st syllable as הַל hal, and (3) then pronounce God's name, *adonay*.
Most books present הַ לְיְ·הֹוָה improperly. As noted in some books,

Notes for Torah reading continue on p. 26.

Tishrey 5782

		1	2	3	4	5
6	7	8	9	10	11	12
13	14	15	16	17	18	19
20	21	22	23	24	25	26
27	28	29	30			

Sep | Oct 2021

		7	8	9	10	11
12	13	14	15	16	17	18
19	20	21	22	23	24	25
26	27	28	29	30	1	2
3	4	5	6			

+ Add ✕ Omit ☞ Take note!

Siddurim
- **L** Lev Shalem for Shabbat and Festivals
- **S** Shabbat and Festival Sim Shalom
- **W** Weekday Sim Shalom
- **F** Full Sim Shalom (both editions)
- **P** Personal Edition of Full Sim Shalom

the ה is to appear as a word standing by itself. This is a feature only of the כְּתִיב k^e^tiv, the manner in which the word is *written* in the Torah scroll; it does not affect the *pronunciation* of the word.

Haftarah שְׁמוּאֵל ב׳ 2 Sh^e^mu'el (2 Samuel) 22:1–51

✕ ~~אַב הָרַחֲמִים Av Haraḥ^a^mim~~

מִנְחָה

Torah 3 aliyot from וְזֹאת הַבְּרָכָה V^e^zot hab^e^rakhah
דְּבָרִים D^e^varim (Deuteronomy) 33:1–17
¹33:1–7 ²8–12 ³13–17 W319 P940

Chanted also next Monday.

✕ ~~צִדְקָתְךָ צֶדֶק Tsidkat^e^kha tsedek~~

Tishrey 13 תִּשְׁרֵי
Sat 18 Sep

מוֹצָאֵי שַׁבָּת Motsa'ey Shabbat Conclusion of Shabbat

עַרְבִית

Arvit for weekdays L264 S281 W137 F200

Weekday Amidah:

+ אַתָּה חוֹנַנְתָּנוּ Attah ḥonantanu L272 S287 W143 F212

✕ ~~חֲצִי קַדִּישׁ Short Kaddish~~

✕ ~~וִיהִי נֹעַם Vihi no'am~~
✕ ~~יֹשֵׁב בְּסֵתֶר עֶלְיוֹן Yoshev b^e^seter elyon~~
✕ ~~וְאַתָּה קָדוֹשׁ Ve'attah kadosh~~

קַדִּישׁ שָׁלֵם Full Kaddish L280 S294 W160 F688

Some recite הַבְדָּלָה Havdalah here. L283 S299 W165 F700

עָלֵינוּ Aleynu L281 S297 W163 F696
קַדִּישׁ יָתוֹם Mourner's Kaddish (some omit) L282 S298 W164 F698
+ Psalm 27 for the Season of Repentance L59 S80 W92 F40
קַדִּישׁ יָתוֹם Mourner's Kaddish L58 S82 W100 F52

הַבְדָּלָה Havdalah L283 S299 W165 F700

Tishrey 14 תִּשְׁרֵי
Mon 20 Sep

עֶרֶב סֻכּוֹת Erev Sukkot Day before Sukkot

שַׁחֲרִית Weekday Shaḥarit as usual W1 F2

✕ ~~תַּחֲנוּן Taḥanun~~

Torah 3 aliyot from וְזֹאת הַבְּרָכָה Vezot haberakhah
דְּבָרִים Devarim (Deuteronomy) 33:1–17
1 33:1–7 2 8–12 3 13–17 W319 P940

☞ לַמְנַצֵּחַ Lamenatse·aḥ (Psalm 20) W79 F154

מִנְחָה ✕ ~~תַּחֲנוּן Taḥanun~~

At home Prepare a flame for Yom Tov. See blue box, below. Light candles. See "Candle Lighting for Sukkot — Day 1," p. 29.

Preparing for Sukkot

The Lulav Assembly

Prepare the 3 kinds of branches of the אַרְבָּעָה מִינִים *arba'ah minim* (4 species) for the performance of the *mitsvah* during Sukkot:

1. Hold the לוּלָב *lulav* (palm branch) with the tip pointing up and the thick spine facing you.
   a. Slide the לוּלָב into the opening in the center of the special holder.
   b. Insert 3 הֲדַסִּים *hadassim* (myrtle branches) into right sleeve of holder.
   c. Insert 2 עֲרָבוֹת *aravot* (willow branches) into left sleeve of holder.
2. Adjust branches so that tips of the עֲרָבוֹת (on the left) do not reach as high as tips of the הֲדַסִּים (on the right). Trim excess at bottom of holder.
3. Using a palm frond from this or another palm branch, tie around the middle of the holder to bind the 3 kinds of branches together.
4. Using additional fronds, tie around the *lulav* in 2 additional places to keep the fronds together. The highest tie must be at least 4 inches from the tip.

For joining the branches with the *etrog* and performing the *mitsvah,* see p. 28.

Preparing a Flame for Yom Tov

On Yom Tov, kindling a *new* fire is not permitted; however, the use of an *existing* fire for cooking or other purposes is permitted.

To light candles for Day 2 of Yom Tov (Tuesday night), ensure that you have a fire burning before candle-lighting time for Day 1 (Monday evening) that will continue to burn until after dark on Tuesday. For example:

- A burning candle that lasts for more than 25 hours
- A pilot light on a gas range (*not* a gas range with an electronic starter)

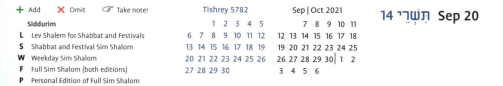

Tishrey 5782							Sep | Oct 2021						
		1	2	3	4	5			7	8	9	10	11
6	7	8	9	10	11	12	12	13	14	15	16	17	18
13	14	15	16	17	18	19	19	20	21	22	23	24	25
20	21	22	23	24	25	26	26	27	28	29	30 | 1		2
27	28	29	30				3	4	5	6			

+ Add ✕ Omit ☞ Take note!

Siddurim
L Lev Shalem for Shabbat and Festivals
S Shabbat and Festival Sim Shalom
W Weekday Sim Shalom
F Full Sim Shalom (both editions)
P Personal Edition of Full Sim Shalom

Mitsvot throughout Sukkot

Eating in the Sukkah

It is a *mitsvah* to eat all meals in the סֻכָּה *sukkah,* except in inclement weather. A beverage or small snack may be consumed while not in the סֻכָּה.

For Kiddush in the sukkah, see blue box, p. 29.

For other occasions, as a symbol of our dwelling in the סֻכָּה, while seated:

1. Recite the בְּרָכָה *berakhah* appropriate for the food you will eat. W228 F714
   - If eating a significant amount of bread or grain products, add:

     בָּרוּךְ אַתָּה יי, אֱ·לֹהֵינוּ מֶלֶךְ הָעוֹלָם, אֲשֶׁר קִדְּשָׁנוּ בְּמִצְוֹתָיו
     וְצִוָּנוּ לֵישֵׁב בַּסֻּכָּה.

     Barukh attah adonay, eloheynu melekh ha'olam,
     asher kiddeshanu bemitsvotav vetsivvanu leshev basukkah.
   - If this is your first time eating in the סֻכָּה this season, add:

     בָּרוּךְ אַתָּה יי, אֱ·לֹהֵינוּ מֶלֶךְ הָעוֹלָם, שֶׁהֶחֱיָנוּ וְקִיְּמָנוּ וְהִגִּיעָנוּ לַזְּמַן הַזֶּה.

     Barukh attah adonay, eloheynu melekh ha'olam,
     sheheḥeyanu vekiyyemanu vehiggi'anu lazeman hazeh.
2. Then eat some of the food.

Upon entering the סֻכָּה for each evening meal, some recite אֻשְׁפִּיזִין *ushpizin,* inviting our revered ancestors to join us in the סֻכָּה as our honored guests. L424 S330

Taking the Lulav and Waving the Lulav (not on Shabbat)

Each day of Sukkot except Shabbat, perform the *mitsvah* of נְטִילַת לוּלָב *netilat lulav* (taking the *lulav*): L315 S131 W49 F379

1. Take the *lulav* assembly in the right hand (if left-handed, in the left hand).
   NOTE: Make sure the thick spine of the *lulav* faces you, with the 3 *hadassim* (myrtles) on the right and the 2 *aravot* (willows) on the left.
2. Hold the *etrog* in your other hand **stem-end up** for reciting the בְּרָכָה *berakhah.*
3. Hold *lulav* and *etrog* together in front of you, and recite the בְּרָכָה:

   בָּרוּךְ אַתָּה יי, אֱ·לֹהֵינוּ מֶלֶךְ הָעוֹלָם, אֲשֶׁר קִדְּשָׁנוּ בְּמִצְוֹתָיו
   וְצִוָּנוּ עַל נְטִילַת לוּלָב.

   Barukh attah adonay, eloheynu melekh ha'olam,
   asher kiddeshanu bemitsvotav vetsivvanu al netilat lulav.

   NOTE: If this is your first time this season, add שֶׁהֶחֱיָנוּ *sheheḥeyanu* (see above).
4. For the נִעֲנוּעִים *ni'nu'im* (waving movements), turn the *etrog* **stem-end down.**
5. Hold *lulav* and *etrog* together. To perform the *mitsvah,* "wave"—that is, extend arms and retract 3 times—in each of 6 directions, as follows:
   a. At home, face east; in the synagogue, face the wall holding the ark.
   b. Wave (1st) to the front, then (2nd) to the right, then (3rd) to the back, and then (4th) to the left, thus proceding in a clockwise direction.
   c. Wave (5th) up (keep *lulav* upright), and then (6th) down (*lulav* still upright).

Sukkot at Home — Day 1 and Day 2

Candle Lighting for Sukkot — Day 1

For Day 2, see blue box, p. 35.

1. Before lighting candles, prepare a flame. See p. 27.
2. Light the candles at least 18 minutes before sunset.
3. Recite 2 בְּרָכוֹת *berakhot:* L79 S303 F718

בָּרוּךְ אַתָּה יי, אֱ·לֹהֵינוּ מֶלֶךְ הָעוֹלָם, אֲשֶׁר קִדְּשָׁנוּ בְּמִצְוֹתָיו
וְצִוָּנוּ לְהַדְלִיק נֵר שֶׁל יוֹם טוֹב.

Barukh attah adonay, eloheynu melekh ha'olam,
asher kiddeshanu bemitsvotav vetsivvanu lehadlik ner shel yom tov.

בָּרוּךְ אַתָּה יי, אֱ·לֹהֵינוּ מֶלֶךְ הָעוֹלָם, שֶׁהֶחֱיָנוּ וְקִיְּמָנוּ וְהִגִּיעָנוּ לַזְּמַן הַזֶּה.

Barukh attah adonay, eloheynu melekh ha'olam,
sheheḥeyanu vekiyyemanu vehiggi'anu lazeman hazeh.

Sukkot Meals — Day 1 and Day 2

When possible, eat in a סֻכָּה *sukkah*. Enjoy festive meals evening and daytime, in the manner of Shabbat meals.
If you usually stand for קִדּוּשׁ *kiddush*, in the סֻכָּה stand for the בְּרָכוֹת *berakhot*, then sit to drink.

EVENING KIDDUSH L79 S334 F742

Recite: Yom Tov קִדּוּשׁ with insertions for Sukkot

At your 1st evening meal in a sukkah this season (Day 1 or Day 2):
לֵישֵׁב בַּסֻּכָּה *leshev basukkah*, then שֶׁהֶחֱיָנוּ *sheheḥeyanu* (see p. 28)
Day 2, not your 1st sukkah meal: שֶׁהֶחֱיָנוּ, then לֵישֵׁב בַּסֻּכָּה (see p. 28)
Not in a sukkah: שֶׁהֶחֱיָנוּ

DAYTIME KIDDUSH L81 S335 F746

Recite: 1. וַיְדַבֵּר מֹשֶׁה *vaydabber mosheh* (Vayikra 23:44)
2. בּוֹרֵא פְּרִי הַגָּפֶן *bo·re peri hagafen*
In a sukkah: לֵישֵׁב בַּסֻּכָּה (see p. 28)
At 1st meal in a sukkah this season: שֶׁהֶחֱיָנוּ (see p. 28) L80 S334 F744

HAMOTSI, FESTIVE MEALS WITH SINGING, AND BIRKAT HAMAZON

Recite הַמּוֹצִיא *hamotsi* over 2 whole חַלָּה *ḥallah* loaves or rolls. L81 S313–14 F744|746
Include festive singing, and recite בִּרְכַּת הַמָּזוֹן *birkat hamazon* with Sukkot additions (see yellow box, p. 30).

Tishrey 5782						
	1	2	3	4	5	
6	7	8	9	10	11	12
13	14	15	16	17	18	19
20	21	22	23	24	25	26
27	28	29	30			

Sep | Oct 2021						
		7	8	9	10	11
12	13	14	15	16	17	18
19	20	21	22	23	24	25
26	27	28	29	30 |	1	2
3	4	5	6			

+ Add ✕ Omit ☞ Take note!

Siddurim
- **L** Lev Shalem for Shabbat and Festivals
- **S** Shabbat and Festival Sim Shalom
- **W** Weekday Sim Shalom
- **F** Full Sim Shalom (both editions)
- **P** Personal Edition of Full Sim Shalom

THROUGOUT SUKKOT

Every Shaḥarit, Minḥah, and Arvit Amidah:

Days 1–7 + יַעֲלֶה וְיָבוֹא Ya'aleh veyavo for Sukkot

Birkat Hamazon:

Days 1–7 + יַעֲלֶה וְיָבוֹא Ya'aleh veyavo for Sukkot L90|95 S340|347 W233|239 F762|780

Days 1 and 2 only + הָרַחֲמָן Haraḥaman for Yom Tov L92|96 S343|348 W236|240 F768

Days 1–7 (some: only Days 3–7) + הָרַחֲמָן Haraḥaman for Sukkot L92|96 S343 W236|240 F768

Every morning and evening

Days 1–7 + Psalm 27 for the Season of Repentance L59 S80 W92 F40
For details, see yellow box, p. 9

Tishrey 15 תִּשְׁרֵי Mon 20 Sep — סֻכּוֹת Sukkot — Day 1

עַרְבִית

Arvit for Yom Tov L39 S28 F279

+ וַיְדַבֵּר מֹשֶׁה Vaydabber mosheh (Vayikra 23:44) L46 S34 F294
חֲצִי קַדִּישׁ Short Kaddish L46 S34 F294

Yom Tov Amidah: L306 S41 F304
+ Insertions for Sukkot

קַדִּישׁ שָׁלֵם Full Kaddish L54 S48 F316

✕ ~~קִדּוּשׁ Kiddush during Arvit~~

עָלֵינוּ Aleynu L56 S51 F320
קַדִּישׁ יָתוֹם Mourner's Kaddish (some omit) L58 S52 F324
+ Psalm 27 for the Season of Repentance L59 S80 F40
קַדִּישׁ יָתוֹם Mourner's Kaddish L58 S82 F52

☞ **At the conclusion of Arvit, in the sukkah,**
קִדּוּשׁ Kiddush for Yom Tov L79 S50 F318
+ Insertions for Sukkot
+ לֵישֵׁב בַּסֻּכָּה Leshev basukkah L80 S50 F320
+ שֶׁהֶחֱיָנוּ Sheheḥeyanu L80 S50 F320

At home See "Sukkot Meals — Day 1 and Day 2" and "Evening Kiddush," p. 29.

Waving the Lulav during Hallel (not on Shabbat)

At 3 points during Hallel, wave the *etrog* and *lulav* assembly (that is, extend and retract arms 3 times) in each of 6 directions. These נִעֲנוּעִים *ni'nu'im* (waving movements) are described more fully in the blue box on p. 28, steps 4–5.

When we chant the name of God, we hold the *lulav* erect, out of respect.

1. At the 4-verse section הוֹדוּ לַיי כִּי טוֹב *hodu ladonay ki tov:* L319 S136 W53 F386

   The *sheliaḥ/sheliḥat tsibbur* chants each verse (waving the *lulav* only during the first 2) and waits for the response from the congregation.

   After the *sheliaḥ/sheliḥat tsibbur* recites each verse, the congregation responds with the following refrain and waving:

	הוֹדוּ	לַיי	כִּי	טוֹב	כִּי	לְעוֹלָם	חַסְדּוֹ.
Refrain	front	hold erect	right	back	left	up	down

	הוֹדוּ	לַיי	כִּי	טוֹב	כִּי	לְעוֹלָם	חַסְדּוֹ.
Verse 1	front	hold erect	right	back	left	up	down

Refrain (הוֹדוּ — see above)

	יֹאמַר	נָא	יִשְׂרָאֵל	כִּי	לְעוֹלָם	חַסְדּוֹ.
Verse 2	front	right	back	left	up	down

Refrain (הוֹדוּ — see above)

Verse 3 יֹאמְרוּ נָא בֵית אַהֲרֹן, כִּי לְעוֹלָם חַסְדּוֹ.

Sheliaḥ/sheliḥat tsibbur does not wave the lulav.

Refrain (הוֹדוּ — see above)

Verse 4 יֹאמְרוּ נָא יִרְאֵי יי, כִּי לְעוֹלָם חַסְדּוֹ.

Sheliaḥ/sheliḥat tsibbur does not wave the lulav.

Refrain (הוֹדוּ — see above)

2. At the verse אָנָּא יי, הוֹשִׁיעָה נָּא *anna adonay, hoshi'ah na:* L320 S137 W55 F388

   The *sheliaḥ/sheliḥat* tsibbur chants the verse, waving the *lulav* as follows:

אָנָּא	יי	הוֹשִׁיעָה	נָּא.
front, then right	hold erect	back, then left	up, then down

   The congregation repeats that verse and the waving.

   The *sheliaḥ/sheliḥat tsibbur* again chants that verse and waves, as does the congregation.

3. Upon reaching the next הוֹדוּ לַיי כִּי טוֹב *hodu ladonay ki tov,* L320 S137 W55 F388 each congregant chants the verse, waving the *lulav* as before:

הוֹדוּ	לַיי	כִּי	טוֹב	כִּי	לְעוֹלָם	חַסְדּוֹ.
front	hold erect	right	back	left	up	down

   Then chant the verse again, waving in the same manner.

Tishrey 5782							Sep | Oct 2021						
		1	2	3	4	5			7	8	9	10	11
6	7	8	9	10	11	12	12	13	14	15	16	17	18
13	14	15	16	17	18	19	19	20	21	22	23	24	25
20	21	22	23	24	25	26	26	27	28	29	30 | 1		2
27	28	29	30				3	4	5	6			

+ Add ✕ Omit ☞ Take note!

Siddurim
L Lev Shalem for Shabbat and Festivals
S Shabbat and Festival Sim Shalom
W Weekday Sim Shalom
F Full Sim Shalom (both editions)
P Personal Edition of Full Sim Shalom

Tue 21 Sep **שַׁחֲרִית**

Here or at Musaf:
+ Psalm 27 for the Season of Repentance W92 F40
קַדִּישׁ יָתוֹם Mourner's Kaddish W100 F52

At the end of the preliminary service,
begin formal chanting at
הָאֵ־ל בְּתַעֲצוּמוֹת עֻזֶּךָ Ha'el beta'atsumot uzzekha. L147 S105 F336

✕ ~~הַכֹּל יוֹדוּךָ Hakol yodukha~~
✕ ~~אֵ־ל אָדוֹן El adon~~
✕ ~~לָאֵ־ל אֲשֶׁר שָׁבַת La'el asher shavat~~
+ הַמֵּאִיר לָאָרֶץ Hame'ir la'arets L152 S109 F342

Yom Tov Amidah: L306 S123 F366
+ Insertions for Sukkot

+ **נְטִילַת לוּלָב Netilat Lulav** L315 S131 F379
Take the luvav and etrog, and recite 2 בְּרָכוֹת berakhot.
See "Taking the Lulav and Waving the Lulav," p. 28.

+ הַלֵּל שָׁלֵם Full Hallel, including waving the lulav L316 S133 F380
See "Waving the Lulav during Hallel," p. 31.

Some congregations recite הוֹשַׁע־נָא Hosha'na and conduct the procession with lulav and etrog here, rather than after the Musaf Amidah. See instructions, p. 34.

קַדִּישׁ שָׁלֵם Full Kaddish L321 S138 F392

YOM TOV TORAH SERVICE L322 S139 F394

+ יי יי אֵ־ל רַחוּם וְחַנּוּן
Adonay adonay el raḥum veḥannun (3 times) L323 S140 F394
+ רִבּוֹנוֹ שֶׁל עוֹלָם Ribbono shel olam L323 S140 F396
+ וַאֲנִי תְפִלָּתִי לְךָ Va'ani tefillati lekha (3 times) L323 S140 F396

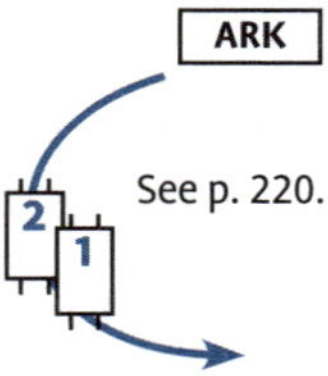

See p. 220.

Remove **2** scrolls from ark in the order they will be read.

1st scroll 5 aliyot from אֱמֹר Emor
וַיִּקְרָא Vayikra (Leviticus) 22:26–23:44
[1]22:26–23:3 [2]23:4–14 [3]23:15–22 [4]23:23–32 [5]23:33–44

Place 2nd scroll on table next to 1st scroll.
חֲצִי קַדִּישׁ Short Kaddish L327 S146 F408
Open, raise, display, and wrap 1st scroll.

2nd scroll Maftir aliyah from פִּינְחָס Pineḥas
בְּמִדְבַּר^M Bemidbar (Numbers) 29:12–16

Open, raise, display, and wrap 2nd scroll.

Haftarah for Sukkot — Day 1
זְכַרְיָה Zekharyah (Zechariah) 14:1–21

Haftarah blessings: L328 S147 F410
☞ Conclude with the Yom Tov בְּרָכָה berakhah L329 S147 F412 with insertions for Sukkot.

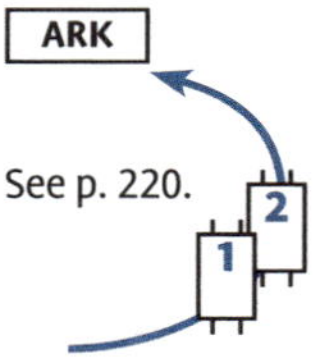

See p. 220.

✕ ~~יְקוּם פֻּרְקָן Yekum purkan~~
✕ ~~אַב הָרַחֲמִים Av Haraḥamim~~

אַשְׁרֵי Ashrey L339 S151 F420
Return scrolls to ark in reverse order. L340 S153 F422
חֲצִי קַדִּישׁ Short Kaddish L342 S155 F428

מוּסָף

Yom Tov Amidah: L343 S166 F456
+ Insertions for Sukkot

Some congregations include in the repetition of the Amidah the Priestly Blessing by the Kohanim (*dukhenen*).
בִּרְכַּת כֹּהֲנִים Birkat kohanim L353 S177 F472
For procedures, see p. 222.

Circling the Sanctuary with Lulav and Etrog

Each day of Sukkot, except Shabbat:

1. Remove a Torah scroll from the ark, and hold it at the reading table. The ark remains open.
2. Form a procession of congregants with *lulav* and *etrog*, reminiscent of the processions of the priests around the altar of the Temple in ancient times.
3. Before beginning the procession, chant the introductory הוֹשַׁע־נָא *hosha'na* lines. L383 S200 W116 F530
4. Make a single counterclockwise circuit around the reading table, Torah scroll, and sanctuary.
5. During the procession, chant the הוֹשַׁע־נָא poem designated for the particular day. Precede and follow each phrase of the poem (or small groups of phrases) with the word הוֹשַׁע־נָא.

+ **Hosha'na**
For procedures for reciting **הוֹשַׁע־נָא** Hosha'na, including procession with lulav and etrog, see the blue box, p. 33.

Open ark, and remove **1** Torah scroll.
Hold scroll at reading table. Ark remains open.

+ **הוֹשַׁע־נָא** Hosha'na for Day 1:
לְמַעַן אֲמִתָּךְ Lema'an amittakh L383 S200 F530+531
+ **כְּהוֹשַׁעְתָּ** Kehosha'ta for weekdays L385 S201 F534
Return scroll to ark.
+ **הוֹשִׁיעָה אֶת־עַמֶּךָ** Hoshi'ah et ammekha L386 S201 F535
Close ark.

קַדִּישׁ שָׁלֵם Full kaddish L203 S181 F506
Continue with **אֵין כֵּא·לֹהֵינוּ** Eyn keloheynu. L204 S182 F508

Here or at Shaharit:
+ Psalm 27 for the Season of Repentance W92 F40
קַדִּישׁ יָתוֹם Mourner's Kaddish W100 F52

קִדּוּשָׁא רַבָּא

Kiddush for Yom Tov, in the sukkah L81 S335 F746
See "Daytime Kiddush," p. 29.

At home

See "Sukkot Meals — Day 1 and Day 2" and "Daytime Kiddush," p. 29.

מִנְחָה

אַשְׁרֵי Ashrey L214 S226 W170 F558
וּבָא לְצִיּוֹן Uva letsiyyon L216 S227 W171 F560
חֲצִי קַדִּישׁ Short Kaddish L217 S229 W173 F564

Yom Tov Amidah: L306 S242 W184 F586
+ Insertions for Sukkot

קַדִּישׁ שָׁלֵם Full Kaddish L230 S247 W189 F596
עָלֵינוּ Aleynu L231 S248 W190 F598
קַדִּישׁ יָתוֹם Mourner's Kaddish L232 S249 W191 F600

Candle Lighting for Sukkot — Day 2

Day 1 ends after dark: when 3 stars appear, or at least 25 minutes after sunset (at least 43 minutes after the time set for lighting candles for Day 1). Some wait longer. For the appropriate time in your community, consult your rabbi.

1. Wait until Day 1 ends.
2. Do not *strike* a match. Instead, transfer fire to the candles from an *existing* flame (see p. 27) by inserting a match or other stick into the flame.
3. Do not *extinguish* the match or stick. Instead, place it on a non-flammable tray or dish, and let it self-extinguish. Alternately, a wood *safety* match held vertically (flame up) usually self-extinguishes quickly.
4. Recite the 2 בְּרָכוֹת *berakhot* (see p. 29). L79 S303 F718

Tishrey 16 תִּשְׁרֵי — Tue 21 Sep

סֻכּוֹת Sukkot — Day 2

עַרְבִית

Arvit for Yom Tov L39 S28 F279
+ וַיְדַבֵּר מֹשֶׁה Vaydabber mosheh (Vayikra 23:44) L46 S34 F294
חֲצִי קַדִּישׁ Short Kaddish L46 S34 F294

Yom Tov Amidah: L306 S41 F304
+ Insertions for Sukkot

קַדִּישׁ שָׁלֵם Full Kaddish L54 S48 F316

✕ ~~קִדּוּשׁ Kiddush during Arvit~~

עָלֵינוּ Aleynu L56 S51 F320
קַדִּישׁ יָתוֹם Mourner's Kaddish (some omit) L58 S52 F324
+ Psalm 27 for the Season of Repentance L59 S80 F40
קַדִּישׁ יָתוֹם Mourner's Kaddish L58 S82 F52

☞ **At the conclusion of Arvit, in the sukkah:**
קִדּוּשׁ Kiddush for Yom Tov L79 S50 F318
+ Insertions for Sukkot
+ שֶׁהֶחֱיָנוּ Sheheḥeyanu L80 S50 F320
+ לֵישֵׁב בַּסֻּכָּה Leshev basukkah L80 S50 F320

At home

Light candles from an existing flame.
See "Candle Lighting for Sukkot — Day 2," above.

See "Sukkot Meals — Day 1 and Day 2" and "Evening Kiddush," p. 29.

Wed 22 Sep שַׁחֲרִית

Here or at Musaf:
+ Psalm 27 for the Season of Repentance W92 F40
קַדִּישׁ יָתוֹם Mourner's Kaddish W100 F52

Tishrey 5782						
		1	2	3	4	5
6	7	8	9	10	11	12
13	14	15	16	17	18	19
20	21	22	23	24	25	26
27	28	29	30			

Sep | Oct 2021						
		7	8	9	10	11
12	13	14	15	16	17	18
19	20	21	22	23	24	25
26	27	28	29	30 |	1	2
3	4	5	6			

+ Add ✕ Omit ☞ Take note!

Siddurim
L Lev Shalem for Shabbat and Festivals
S Shabbat and Festival Sim Shalom
W Weekday Sim Shalom
F Full Sim Shalom (both editions)
P Personal Edition of Full Sim Shalom

At the end of the preliminary service, begin formal chanting at
הָאֵ·ל בְּתַעֲצוּמוֹת עֻזֶּךָ Ha'el beta'atsumot uzzekha. L147 S105 F336

✕ ~~הַכֹּל יוֹדוּךָ Hakol yodukha~~
✕ ~~אֵ·ל אָדוֹן El adon~~
✕ ~~לָאֵ·ל אֲשֶׁר שָׁבַת La'el asher shavat~~
+ הַמֵּאִיר לָאָרֶץ Hame'ir la'arets L152 S109 F342

Yom Tov Amidah: L306 S123 F366
+ Insertions for Sukkot

+ נְטִילַת לוּלָב **Netilat Lulav** L315 S131 F379
Take the luvav and etrog, and recite the בְּרָכָה berakhah. See "Taking the Lulav and Waving the Lulav," p. 28.

+ הַלֵּל שָׁלֵם Full Hallel, including waving the lulav L316 S133 F380
See "Waving the Lulav during Hallel," p. 31.

Some congregations recite הוֹשַׁע־נָא Hosha'na and conduct the procession with lulav and etrog here, rather than after the Musaf Amidah. See instructions, p. 37.

קַדִּישׁ שָׁלֵם Full Kaddish L321 S138 F392

YOM TOV TORAH SERVICE L322 S139 F394

+ יי יי אֵ·ל רַחוּם וְחַנּוּן
Adonay adonay el raḥum veḥannun (3 times) L323 S140 F394
+ רִבּוֹנוֹ שֶׁל עוֹלָם Ribbono shel olam L323 S140 F396
+ וַאֲנִי תְפִלָּתִי לְךָ Va'ani tefillati lekha (3 times) L323 S140 F396

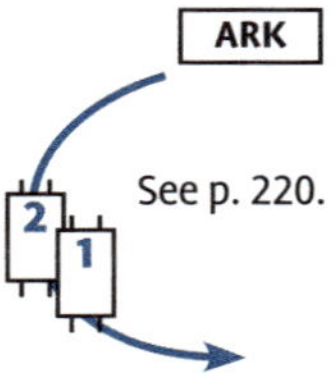

Remove **2** scrolls from ark in the order they will be read.

1st scroll 5 aliyot from אֱמֹר Emor
וַיִּקְרָא Vayikra (Leviticus) 22:26–23:44
[1]22:26–23:3 [2]23:4–14 [3]23:15–22 [4]23:23–32 [5]23:33–44

Place 2nd scroll on table next to 1st scroll.
חֲצִי קַדִּישׁ Short Kaddish L327 S146 F408
Open, raise, display, and wrap 1st scroll.

2nd scroll Maftir aliyah from פִּינְחָס Pineḥas
[M]בְּמִדְבַּר Bemidbar (Numbers) 29:12–16

Open, raise, display, and wrap 2nd scroll.

Haftarah for Sukkot — Day 2
מְלָכִים א' 1 Melakhim (1 Kings) 8:2–21

Haftarah blessings: L328 S147 F410

☞ Conclude with the Yom Tov בְּרָכָה berakhah L329 S147 F412 with insertions for Sukkot.

✕ ~~יְקוּם פֻּרְקָן Yekum purkan~~

✕ ~~אַב הָרַחֲמִים Av Haraḥamim~~

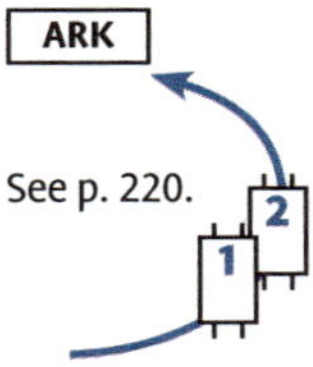

See p. 220.

אַשְׁרֵי Ashrey L339 S151 F420

Return scrolls to ark in reverse order. L340 S153 F422

חֲצִי קַדִּישׁ Short Kaddish L342 S155 F428

מוּסָף

Yom Tov Amidah: L343 S166 F456

+ Insertions for Sukkot

Some congregations include in the repetition of the Amidah the Priestly Blessing by the Kohanim (*dukhenen*).

בִּרְכַּת כֹּהֲנִים Birkat kohanim L353 S177 F472

For procedures, see p. 222.

+ **Hosha'na**

For procedures for reciting הוֹשַׁע־נָא Hosha'na, including procession with lulav and etrog, see p. 33.

Open ark, and remove **1** Torah scroll.
Hold scroll at reading table. Ark remains open.

+ הוֹשַׁע־נָא Hosha'na for Day 2:
אֶבֶן שְׁתִיָּה Even shetiyyah L383+384 S200 F530+531

+ כְּהוֹשַׁעְתָּ Kehosha'ta for weekdays L385 S201 F534

Return scroll to ark.

+ הוֹשִׁיעָה אֶת־עַמֶּךָ Hoshi'ah et ammekha L386 S201 F535

Close ark.

קַדִּישׁ שָׁלֵם Full kaddish L203 S181 F506

Continue with אֵין כֵּא·לֹהֵינוּ Eyn keloheynu. L204 S182 F508

Here or at Shaḥarit:

+ Psalm 27 for the Season of Repentance W92 F40

קַדִּישׁ יָתוֹם Mourner's Kaddish W100 F52

קִדּוּשָׁא רַבָּא

Kiddush for Yom Tov, in the sukkah L81 S335 F746
See "Daytime Kiddush," p. 29.

At home

See "Sukkot Meals — Day 1 and Day 2" and "Daytime Kiddush," p. 29.

מִנְחָה

אַשְׁרֵי Ashrey L214 S226 W170 F558
וּבָא לְצִיּוֹן Uva letsiyyon L216 S227 W171 F560
חֲצִי קַדִּישׁ Short Kaddish L217 S229 W173 F564

Yom Tov Amidah: L306 S242 W184 F586
+ Insertions for Sukkot

קַדִּישׁ שָׁלֵם Full Kaddish L230 S247 W189 F596
עָלֵינוּ Aleynu L231 S248 W190 F598
קַדִּישׁ יָתוֹם Mourner's Kaddish L232 S249 W191 F600

Ḥol Hamo'ed Sukkot

Wearing Tefillin

Whether or not to wear תְּפִלִּין *tefillin* during Ḥol Hamo'ed is a long-standing controversy. Ashkenazic Jews tend to wear תְּפִלִּין; Sephardic and Hasidic Jews tend not to wear תְּפִלִּין. The practice in Israel is not to wear them. Some who wear תְּפִלִּין do not recite the בְּרָכוֹת *berakhot*.

1. Determine your individual practice as follows:
   - If there is an established custom in your family, follow it.
   - If there is no established custom in your family, consult your rabbi.
   - Regardless of your custom, when you are in Israel, do not wear תְּפִלִּין.
2. If you wear תְּפִלִּין, remove them just before the beginning of Hallel.

Tishrey 17 תִּשְׁרֵי
Wed 22 Sep (evening)
through
Tishrey 18 תִּשְׁרֵי
Fri 24 Sep (daytime)

חֹל הַמּוֹעֵד סֻכּוֹת Ḥol Hamo'ed Sukkot Weekdays
חֹל הַמּוֹעֵד Ḥol Hamo'ed (ḤH) — Days 1–2

ḤH Day 1 Wed 22 Sep
ḤH Day 2 Thu 23 Sep (evening)

מוֹצָאֵי יוֹם טוֹב Motsa'ey Yom Tov Conclusion of Yom Tov

עַרְבִית

Arvit for weekdays L264 S281 W137 F200

Weekday Amidah:
ḤH Day 1 Wed 22 Sep + אַתָּה חוֹנַנְתָּנוּ Attah ḥonantanu L272 S287 W143 F212
All evenings + יַעֲלֶה וְיָבוֹא Ya'aleh veyavo for Sukkot L277 S289 W145 F216

All evenings
קַדִּישׁ שָׁלֵם Full Kaddish L280 S294 W160 F222
עָלֵינוּ Aleynu L281 S297 W163 F696
קַדִּישׁ יָתוֹם Mourner's Kaddish (some omit) L282 S298 W164 F698
+ Psalm 27 for the Season of Repentance L59 S80 W92 F40
קַדִּישׁ יָתוֹם Mourner's Kaddish L58 S82 W100 F52

+ Add ✕ Omit ☞ Take note!

Siddurim
- **L** Lev Shalem for Shabbat and Festivals
- **S** Shabbat and Festival Sim Shalom
- **W** Weekday Sim Shalom
- **F** Full Sim Shalom (both editions)
- **P** Personal Edition of Full Sim Shalom

Tishrey 5782							Sep | Oct 2021						
		1	2	3	4	5			7	8	9	10	11
6	7	8	9	10	11	12	12	13	14	15	16	17	18
13	14	15	16	17	18	19	19	20	21	22	23	24	25
20	21	22	23	24	25	26	26	27	28	29	30 | 1	2	
27	28	29	30				3	4	5	6			

17 תִּשְׁרֵי Sep 22
Sep 23
18 תִּשְׁרֵי Sep 24

סֻכּוֹת Sukkot

ḤH Day 1 Wed 22 Sep

+ **Havdalah, in the sukkah:** L283 S299 W165 F700

✕ ~~הִנֵּה אֵ-ל יְשׁוּעָתִי Hinneh el yeshu'ati~~

בּוֹרֵא פְּרִי הַגָּפֶן Bo·re peri hagafen

✕ ~~בּוֹרֵא מִינֵי בְשָׂמִים Bo·re miney vesamim~~

✕ ~~בּוֹרֵא מְאוֹרֵי הָאֵשׁ Bo·re me'orey ha'esh~~

הַמַּבְדִּיל בֵּין קֹדֶשׁ לְחֹל Hamavdil beyn kodesh leḥol

✕ ~~לֵישֵׁב בַּסֻּכָּה Leshev basukkah~~

ḤH Day 1 Thu 23 Sep (morning)
ḤH Day 2 Fri 24 Sep (morning)

שַׁחֲרִית

Shaḥarit for weekdays W1 F2

Here at or Musaf:

+ Psalm 27 for the Season of Repentance W92 F40

קַדִּישׁ יָתוֹם Mourner's Kaddish W100 F52

Weekday Amidah:

+ יַעֲלֶה וְיָבוֹא Ya'aleh veyavo for Sukkot W41 F114

✕ ~~תַּחֲנוּן Taḥanun~~

☞ Those wearing תְּפִלִּין tefillin now remove and pack them.

+ **נְטִילַת לוּלָב Netilat Lulav** W49 F379
Take the luvav and etrog, and recite the בְּרָכָה berakhah.
See "Taking the Lulav and Waving the Lulav," p. 28.

+ הַלֵּל שָׁלֵם Full Hallel, including waving the lulav W50 F380
See "Waving the Lulav during Hallel," p. 31.

Some congregations recite הוֹשַׁע־נָא Hosha'na and conduct the procession with lulav and etrog here, rather than after the Musaf Amidah. See instructions, p. 40.

קַדִּישׁ שָׁלֵם Full Kaddish W56 F392

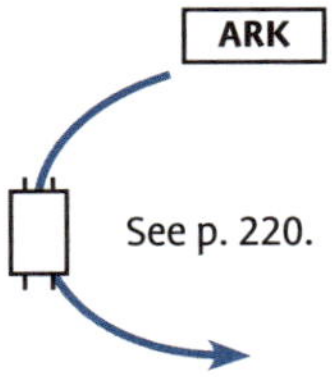

See p. 220.

+ **WEEKDAY TORAH SERVICE** W65 F138
Remove **1** scroll from ark.

Torah 4 aliyot from: פָּרָשַׁת פִּינְחָס Parashat Pineḥas
בְּמִדְבַּר Bemidbar (Numbers) 29

ḤH Day 1 Thu 23 Sep	1 29:17–19	2 20–22	3 23–25	4 17–22	W321 P967
ḤH Day 2 Fri 24 Sep	1 29:20–22	2 23–25	3 26–28	4 20–25	W322 P968

Tishrey 5782						
	1	2	3	4	5	
6	7	8	9	10	11	12
13	14	15	16	17	18	19
20	21	22	23	24	25	26
27	28	29	30			

Sep | Oct 2021						
		7	8	9	10	11
12	13	14	15	16	17	18
19	20	21	22	23	24	25
26	27	28	29	30 |	1	2
3	4	5	6			

+ Add ✕ Omit ☞ Take note!

Siddurim
- **L** Lev Shalem for Shabbat and Festivals
- **S** Shabbat and Festival Sim Shalom
- **W** Weekday Sim Shalom
- **F** Full Sim Shalom (both editions)
- **P** Personal Edition of Full Sim Shalom

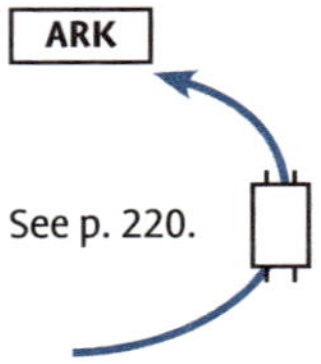

See p. 220.

חֲצִי קַדִּישׁ Short Kaddish W71 F146
Open, raise, display, and wrap scroll.
Return scroll to ark. W76 F150

אַשְׁרֵי Ashrey W78 F152
✕ ~~לַמְנַצֵּחַ Lamenatse·aḥ (Psalm 20)~~
וּבָא לְצִיּוֹן Uva letsiyyon W80 F156

\+ חֲצִי קַדִּישׁ Short Kaddish W103 F428

מוּסָף
\+ **Yom Tov Amidah:** W104+110 F456+462
Weekday קְדֻשָּׁה Kedushah W105 F460
\+ Insertions for Sukkot

ḤH Day 1 Thu 23 Sep + Insertions for Ḥol Hamo'ed Sukkot — Day 1 W111 F466

ḤH Day 2 Fri 24 Sep + Insertions for Ḥol Hamo'ed Sukkot — Day 2 W111 F467

\+ **Hosha'na**
For procedures for reciting הוֹשַׁע־נָא Hosha'na, including procession with lulav and etrog, see p. 33.
Open ark, and remove **1** Torah scroll.
Hold scroll at reading table. Ark remains open.

\+ הוֹשַׁע־נָא Hosha'na W116 F530

ḤH Day 1 Thu 23 Sep + אֶעֱרֹךְ שׁוּעִי E'erokh shu'i W116 F532

ḤH Day 2 Fri 24 Sep + אֵ·ל לְמוֹשָׁעוֹת El lemosha'ot W117 F533

\+ כְּהוֹשַׁעְתָּ Kehosha'ta for weekdays W119 F534
Return scroll to ark.
\+ הוֹשִׁיעָה אֶת־עַמֶּךָ Hoshi'ah et ammekha W119 F535
Close ark.

קַדִּישׁ שָׁלֵם Full Kaddish W82 F158
עָלֵינוּ Aleynu W83 F160
Conclude as on a usual weekday.

Here or at Shaḥarit:
\+ Psalm 27 for the Season of Repentance W92 F40
קַדִּישׁ יָתוֹם Mourner's Kaddish W100 F52

At home See "Eating in the Sukkah," p. 28.

מִנְחָה Minḥah for weekdays L289 S1 W120 F164

Weekday Amidah:

+ יַעֲלֶה וְיָבוֹא Ya'aleh veyavo for Sukkot L298 S7 W127 F178

✕ ~~תַּחֲנוּן Taḥanun~~

ḤH Day 2 Fri 24 Sep (afternoon)

At home Light Shabbat candles as for a usual Shabbat.

Shabbat Ḥol Hamo'ed Sukkot Meals

When possible, eat in a סֻכָּה *sukkah.*

NOTE: Friday evening omit שָׁלוֹם עֲלֵיכֶם *shalom aleykhem* and אֵשֶׁת חַיִל *eshet ḥayil.* Begin with the blessing for the children.

KIDDUSH FOR SHABBAT

If you usually stand, in the סֻכָּה stand for the בְּרָכוֹת *berakhot,* then sit to drink.

Recite: Usual Shabbat קִדּוּשׁ *kiddush*: **Evening** L76 S312 F726 **Daytime** L77 S315 F734

In a sukkah: לֵישֵׁב בַּסֻּכָּה *leshev basukkah* (see p. 28) L80 S312 F744

At 1st meal in a sukkah this season: שֶׁהֶחֱיָנוּ *sheheḥeyanu* (see p. 28) L80 S334 F744

HAMOTSI, FESTIVE MEALS WITH SINGING, BIRKAT HAMAZON, AND HAVDALAH

Proceed as on a usual Shabbat with הַמּוֹצִיא *hamotsi,* festive meals, and singing. Recite בִּרְכַּת הַמָּזוֹן *birkat hamazon* for Shabbat with Sukkot additions (see yellow box, p. 30).

Recite הַבְדָּלָה *havdalah* for after Shabbat—when possible, in a סֻכָּה, L283 S299 W165 F700 and if you will eat a significant amount of bread or grain products, add לֵישֵׁב בַּסֻּכָּה.

Tishrey 19 תִּשְׁרֵי — שַׁבַּת חֹל הַמּוֹעֵד סֻכּוֹת Shabbat Ḥol Hamo'ed Sukkot

Fri 24 Sep (evening)

Ḥol Hamo'ed — Day 3

קַבָּלַת שַׁבָּת ✕ ~~Kabbalat Shabbat~~
through
✕ ~~לְכָה דוֹדִי Lekhah dodi~~

Begin with מִזְמוֹר שִׁיר לְיוֹם הַשַּׁבָּת
Mizmor shir leyom hashabbat (Psalm 92). L27 S23 F266

עַרְבִית Arvit as on a usual Shabbat

✕ ~~וַיְדַבֵּר מֹשֶׁה Vaydabber mosheh~~

Shabbat Amidah:

+ יַעֲלֶה וְיָבוֹא Ya'aleh veyavo for Sukkot L50 S36 F298

וַיְכֻלּוּ Vaykhullu L53 S41 F314

Continue as on a usual Shabbat through
קַדִּישׁ שָׁלֵם Full Kaddish L54 S48 F316

Tishrey 5782

	1	2	3	4	5	
6	7	8	9	10	11	12
13	14	15	16	17	18	19
20	21	22	23	24	25	26
27	28	29	30			

Sep | Oct 2021

		7	8	9	10	11
12	13	14	15	16	17	18
19	20	21	22	23	24	25
26	27	28	29	30	1	2
3	4	5	6			

+ Add ✕ Omit ☞ Take note!

Siddurim
L Lev Shalem for Shabbat and Festivals
S Shabbat and Festival Sim Shalom
W Weekday Sim Shalom
F Full Sim Shalom (both editions)
P Personal Edition of Full Sim Shalom

✕ ~~קִדּוּשׁ Kiddush during Arvit~~

עָלֵינוּ Aleynu L56 S51 F320
קַדִּישׁ יָתוֹם Mourner's Kaddish (some omit) L58 S52 F324
+ Psalm 27 for the Season of Repentance L59 S80 F40
קַדִּישׁ יָתוֹם Mourner's Kaddish L58 S82 F52

☞ **At the conclusion of Arvit, in the sukkah:**
קִדּוּשׁ Kiddush for Shabbat L55 S49 F318
+ לֵישֵׁב בַּסֻּכָּה Leshev basukkah L80 S50 F320

סֻכּוֹת Sukkot

At home See "Shabbat Ḥol Hamo'ed Sukkot Meals" and "Kiddush for Shabbat," p. 41.

Sat 25 Sep **שַׁחֲרִית**

Here or at Musaf:
+ Psalm 27 for the Season of Repentance W92 F40
קַדִּישׁ יָתוֹם Mourner's Kaddish W100 F52

Shaḥarit for Shabbat L99 S61 F2

Shabbat Amidah:
+ יַעֲלֶה וְיָבוֹא Ya'aleh veyavo for Sukkot L163 S118 F360

✕ ~~נְטִילַת לוּלָב Netilat Lulav Taking the lulav and etrog~~

+ הַלֵּל שָׁלֵם Full Hallel L316 S133 F380

Some congregations recite הוֹשַׁע־נָא Hosha'na here, rather than after Musaf. See instructions, p. 43.

קַדִּישׁ שָׁלֵם Full Kaddish L321 S138 F392

+ **Megillah reading:**
Some congregations read
מְגִלַּת קֹהֶלֶת Megillat Kohelet (Scroll of Ecclesiastes), without reciting a בְּרָכָה berakhah.
Some read selections in English. L426 S373 F794
קַדִּישׁ יָתוֹם Mourner's Kaddish L121 S82 F52

SHABBAT TORAH SERVICE L168 S139 F394

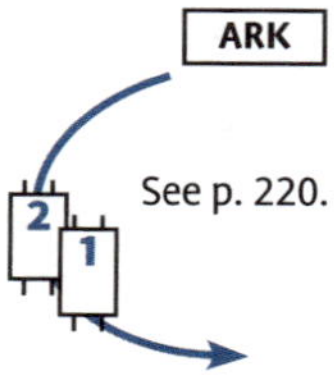

See p. 220.

✕ ~~יי יי אֵ-ל רַחוּם וְחַנּוּן Adonay adonay el raḥum veḥannun~~
✕ ~~רִבּוֹנוֹ שֶׁל עוֹלָם Ribbono shel olam~~
✕ ~~וַאֲנִי תְפִלָּתִי לְךָ Va'ani tefillati lekha~~

Remove **2** scrolls from ark in the order they will be read.

1st scroll 7 aliyot from כִּי תִשָּׂא Ki tissa
שְׁמוֹת Shemot (Exodus) 33:12–34:26
[1]33:12–16 [2]33:17–19 [3]33:20–23 [4]34:1–3
[5]34:4–10° [6]34:11–17 [7]34:18–26

☞ °34:6–7, 9 Chant these verses in the usual manner. Do not chant them in the manner they are chanted on fast days.

Place 2nd scroll on table next to 1st scroll.
חֲצִי קַדִּישׁ Short Kaddish L174 S146 F408
Open, raise, display, and wrap 1st scroll.

+ **2nd scroll** Maftir aliyah from פִּינְחָס Pinehas
M בְּמִדְבַּר Bemidbar (Numbers) 29:23–28

Open, raise, display, and wrap 2nd scroll.

Haftarah for Shabbat Ḥol Hamo'ed Sukkot
יְחֶזְקֵאל Yeḥezkel (Ezekiel) 38:18–39:16

Haftarah blessings: L328 S147 F410
✕ ~~Concluding Shabbat בְּרָכָה berakhah~~
☞ Conclude with the Yom Tov בְּרָכָה berakhah L329 S147 F412 with insertions for Shabbat and Sukkot.

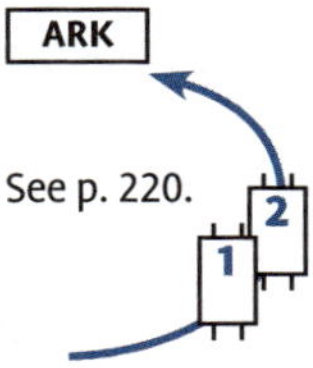

See p. 220.

יְקוּם פֻּרְקָן Yekum purkan L176 S148 F412
✕ ~~אַב הָרַחֲמִים Av Haraḥamim~~

אַשְׁרֵי Ashrey L181 S151 F420
Return scrolls to ark in reverse order. L183 S153 F422

חֲצִי קַדִּישׁ Short Kaddish L184 S155 F428

מוּסָף ☞ **Yom Tov Amidah:** L343 S166 F456
Shabbat קְדֻשָּׁה Kedushah L345 S167 F458
✕ ~~אַדִּיר אַדִּירֵנוּ Addir addirenu~~
+ Insertions for Shabbat
+ Insertions for Sukkot
+ Insertions for Ḥol Hamo'ed Sukkot — Day 3 L350 S172 F467

+ **Hosha'na**
Open ark. Do not remove a Torah scroll.
✕ ~~Lulav and etrog~~
✕ ~~Procession~~

+ הוֹשַׁע־נָא Hosha'na L387 S202 F535
+ אוֹם נְצוּרָה Om netsurah L387–88 S202 F536

סֻכּוֹת Sukkot

Tishrey 5782							Sep | Oct 2021						
		1	2	3	4	5			7	8	9	10	11
6	7	8	9	10	11	12	12	13	14	15	16	17	18
13	14	15	16	17	18	19	19	20	21	22	23	24	25
20	21	22	23	24	25	26	26	27	28	29	30 | 1	2	
27	28	29	30				3	4	5	6			

+ Add ✕ Omit ☞ Take note!

Siddurim
- **L** Lev Shalem for Shabbat and Festivals
- **S** Shabbat and Festival Sim Shalom
- **W** Weekday Sim Shalom
- **F** Full Sim Shalom (both editions)
- **P** Personal Edition of Full Sim Shalom

\+ כְּהוֹשַׁעְתָּ Kehosha'ta for Shabbat L388 S202 F536
\+ הוֹשִׁיעָה אֶת־עַמֶּךָ Hoshi'ah et ammekha L391 S204 F538
Close ark.

קַדִּישׁ שָׁלֵם Full Kaddish L203 S181 F506
Continue with אֵין כֵּא·לֹהֵינוּ Eyn keloheynu. L204 S182 F508

Here or at Shaharit:
\+ Psalm 27 for the Season of Repentance W92 F40
קַדִּישׁ יָתוֹם Mourner's Kaddish W100 F52

סֻכּוֹת Sukkot

קִדּוּשָׁא רַבָּא Daytime Kiddush for Shabbat, in the sukkah L77 S335 F746
See "Kiddush for Shabbat," p. 41.

At home See "Shabbat Ḥol Hamo'ed Sukkot Meals" and "Kiddush for Shabbat," p. 41.

מִנְחָה Minḥah for Shabbat L214 S226 W170 F558

Torah 3 aliyot from וְזֹאת הַבְּרָכָה Vezot haberakhah
דְּבָרִים Devarim (Deuteronomy) 33:1–17
[1]33:1–7 [2]8–12 [3]13–17 W319 P940

Shabbat Amidah: L223 S234 W178 F574
\+ יַעֲלֶה וְיָבוֹא Ya'aleh veyavo for Sukkot L227 S237 W181 F580

✕ ~~צִדְקָתְךָ צֶדֶק Tsidkatekha tsedek~~

Tishrey 20 תִּשְׁרֵי — חֹל הַמּוֹעֵד סֻכּוֹת Ḥol Hamo'ed Sukkot Weekday

Sat 25 Sep (evening)

Ḥol Hamo'ed (ḤH) — Day 4
מוֹצָאֵי שַׁבָּת Motsa'ey Shabbat Conclusion of Shabbat

עַרְבִית Arvit for weekdays L264 S281 W137 F200

Weekday Amidah:
\+ אַתָּה חוֹנַנְתָּנוּ Attah ḥonantanu L272 S287 W143 F212
\+ יַעֲלֶה וְיָבוֹא Ya'aleh veyavo for Sukkot L277 S289 W145 F216

✕ ~~חֲצִי קַדִּישׁ Short Kaddish~~

✕ ~~וִיהִי נֹעַם Vihi no'am~~
✕ ~~יֹשֵׁב בְּסֵתֶר עֶלְיוֹן Yoshev beseter elyon~~
✕ ~~וְאַתָּה קָדוֹשׁ Ve'attah kadosh~~

קַדִּישׁ שָׁלֵם Full Kaddish L280 S294 W160 F222

✕ ~~הַבְדָּלָה Havdalah during Arvit~~

עָלֵינוּ Aleynu L281 S297 W163 F696
קַדִּישׁ יָתוֹם Mourner's Kaddish (some omit) L282 S298 W164 F698
+ Psalm 27 for the Season of Repentance L59 S80 W92 F40
קַדִּישׁ יָתוֹם Mourner's Kaddish L58 S82 W100 F52

הַבְדָּלָה Havdalah for after Shabbat, in the sukkah L283 S299 W165 F700

✕ ~~לֵישֵׁב בַּסֻּכָּה Leshev basukkah~~

Sun 26 Sep **שַׁחֲרִית**

Shaḥarit for weekdays W1 F2

Here or at Musaf:
+ Psalm 27 for the Season of Repentance W92 F40
קַדִּישׁ יָתוֹם Mourner's Kaddish W100 F52

Weekday Amidah:
+ יַעֲלֶה וְיָבוֹא Ya'aleh veyavo for Sukkot W41 F114

✕ ~~תַּחֲנוּן Taḥanun~~

☞ Those wearing תְּפִלִּין tefillin now remove and pack them.

+ **נְטִילַת לוּלָב Netilat Lulav** W49 F379
Take the luvav and etrog, and recite the בְּרָכָה berakhah. See "Taking the Lulav and Waving the Lulav," p. 28.

+ הַלֵּל שָׁלֵם Full Hallel, including waving the lulav W50 F380
See "Waving the Lulav during Hallel," p. 31.

Some congregations recite הוֹשַׁע־נָא Hosha'na and conduct the procession with lulav and etrog here, rather than after the Musaf Amidah. See instructions, p. 46.

קַדִּישׁ שָׁלֵם Full Kaddish W56 F392

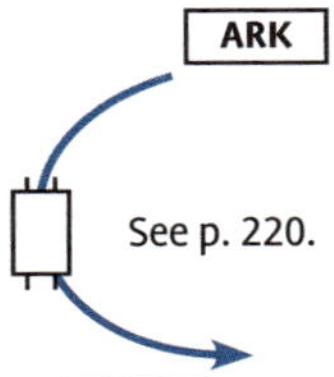

+ **WEEKDAY TORAH SERVICE** W65 F138
Remove **1** scroll from ark.

Torah 4 aliyot from: פָּרָשַׁת פִּינְחָס Parashat Pineḥas
בְּמִדְבַּר Bemidbar (Numbers) 29:26–34
1 29:26–28 2 29–31 3 32–34 4 26–31 W324 P970

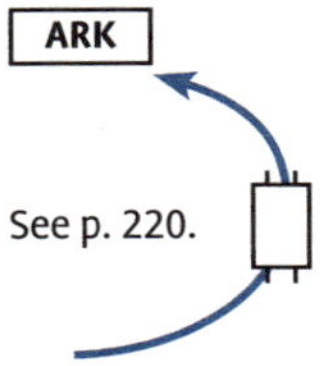

חֲצִי קַדִּישׁ Short Kaddish W71 F146
Open, raise, display, and wrap scroll.
Return scroll to ark. W76 F150

אַשְׁרֵי Ashrey W78 F152
✕ ~~לַמְנַצֵּחַ Lamenatse·aḥ (Psalm 20)~~
וּבָא לְצִיּוֹן Uva letsiyyon W80 F156

\+ חֲצִי קַדִּישׁ Short Kaddish W103 F428

מוּסָף
\+ **Yom Tov Amidah:** W104+110 F456+462
Weekday קְדֻשָּׁה Kedushah W105 F460
\+ Insertions for Sukkot
\+ Insertions for Ḥol Hamo'ed Sukkot — Day 4 W111 F467

\+ **Hosha'na**
For procedures for reciting הוֹשַׁע־נָא Hosha'na, including procession with lulav and etrog, see p. 33.

Open ark and remove **1** Torah scroll.
Hold scroll at reading table. Ark remains open.

\+ הוֹשַׁע־נָא Hosha'na W116 F530
\+ אָדוֹן הַמּוֹשִׁיעַ Adon hamoshia W118 F533
\+ כְּהוֹשַׁעְתָּ Kehosha'ta for weekdays W119 F534
Return scroll to ark.

\+ הוֹשִׁיעָה אֶת־עַמֶּךָ Hoshi'ah et ammekha W119 F535
Close ark.

קַדִּישׁ שָׁלֵם Full Kaddish W82 F158
עָלֵינוּ Aleynu W83 F160
Conclude as on a usual weekday.

Here or at Shaḥarit:
\+ Psalm 27 for the Season of Repentance W92 F40
קַדִּישׁ יָתוֹם Mourner's Kaddish W100 F52

At home See "Eating in the Sukkah," p. 28.

מִנְחָה Minḥah for weekdays L289 S1 W120 F164

Weekday Amidah:
\+ יַעֲלֶה וְיָבוֹא Ya'aleh veyavo for Sukkot L298 S7 W127 F178

✕ ~~תַּחֲנוּן Taḥanun~~

Hosha'na Rabbah

Hosha'na Rabbah, the last day of Sukkot, is the final day of the intense period of reflection and self-evaluation that began on Rosh Hashanah. This day is considered the time of the final sealing of God's judgment. Thus, this day shares with Yom Kippur some themes of repentance and forgiveness. The *sheliaḥ/sheliḥat tsibbur* wears a *kittel* (plain white robe) for the מוּסָף *musaf* service.

The Hosha'na Rabbah service is very complex, combining elements of weekday, festival, and High Holiday services. The נֻסָּח *nusaḥ* (traditional musical chant) for the different sections also reflects the wide range of holiday moods expressed.

A proper נֻסָּח for each section is noted. For some sections, it is understood that there are differing cantorial traditions.

Hosha'na Prayers and Processions

The procedures are the same as those for the previous days (see p. 33).
However, there are 7 Hosha'na prayers and 7 processions around the sanctuary.

1. Remove a Torah scroll from the ark, and hold it at the reading table.
   Many congregations remove all the Torah scrolls from the ark and hold them at the reading table. The ark remains open.
2. Form a procession of congregants with *lulav* and *etrog* reminiscent of the processions of the priests around the altar of the Temple in ancient times.
3. Before beginning the first procession, chant the introductory הוֹשַׁע־נָא *hosha'na* lines. L392 S200 W116 F530
4. For each procession, make a single counterclockwise circuit around the reading table, scroll(s), and sanctuary.
5. During each procession, chant the הוֹשַׁע־נָא poem designated for that procession. Precede and follow each phrase of the poem (or small groups of phrases) with the word הוֹשַׁע־נָא.

Aravot — The 5 Willow Branches

After the processions and liturgical poetry, we take a bundle of 5 עֲרָבוֹת *aravot* (willow branches). Willows require a great deal of water and thus are fitting symbols to accompany liturgy that focuses on our need for rain.

We beat the bundle of עֲרָבוֹת, stripping off a few leaves. This is reminiscent of the Temple ceremony described in the Mishnah (Sukkah 4:6). As we conclude the penitential season, we recognize that separating ourselves from sin is difficult, just as trying to strip leaves from the willow branches is. But just as God's gift of rain enables the willow trees to grow new branches and leaves, our faith enables us to overcome our struggles and feel restored to a fresh life.

Because this unusual ritual can be noisy and disruptive, we return the scroll(s) to the ark and close the ark before beating the עֲרָבוֹת. We are not to beat the עֲרָבוֹת more than 5 times. Beating עֲרָבוֹת is a symbolic ritual act, not a magical one.

Tishrey 5782						
	1	2	3	4	5	
6	7	8	9	10	11	12
13	14	15	16	17	18	19
20	21	22	23	24	25	26
27	28	29	30			

Sep | Oct 2021						
		7	8	9	10	11
12	13	14	15	16	17	18
19	20	21	22	23	24	25
26	27	28	29	30 |	1	2
3	4	5	6			

+ Add ✕ Omit ☞ Take note!

Siddurim
- **L** Lev Shalem for Shabbat and Festivals
- **S** Shabbat and Festival Sim Shalom
- **W** Weekday Sim Shalom
- **F** Full Sim Shalom (both editions)
- **P** Personal Edition of Full Sim Shalom

Tishrey 21 תִּשְׁרֵי Sun 26 Sep

הוֹשַׁעְנָא רַבָּה Hosha'na Rabbah
Last day of Ḥol Hamo'ed

עַרְבִית

Arvit for weekdays L264 W137 F200

Weekday Amidah:

+ יַעֲלֶה וְיָבוֹא Ya'aleh veyavo for Sukkot L277 W145 F216

קַדִּישׁ שָׁלֵם Full Kaddish L280 W160 F688

עָלֵינוּ Aleynu L281 W163 F696

קַדִּישׁ יָתוֹם Mourner's Kaddish (some omit) L282 W164 F698

+ Psalm 27 for the Season of Repentance L59 W92 F40

קַדִּישׁ יָתוֹם Mourner's Kaddish L58 W100 F52

NOTE: To appreciate the Yom Tov enhancements on Hosha'na Rabbah, keep in mind that the service is basically a weekday Ḥol Hamo'ed service. Use a weekday siddur for the weekday sections and a Shabbat/Yom Tov siddur for the Yom Tov sections. The siddur page locators below offer a more coherent prayer experience than a service pieced together from prayers scattered across a Shabbat/Yom Tov siddur.

Mon 27 Sep שַׁחֲרִית

Shaharit for weekdays W1 F2

בִּרְכוֹת הַשַּׁחַר Birkhot hashaḥar W6 F2
Use Yamim Nora'im nusaḥ.

Before מִזְמוֹר שִׁיר Mizmor shir (Psalm 30) or at end of service, recite: W14 F50

Psalm for Monday (Psalm 48) W86 F24
Use weekday minor nusaḥ for the psalms.

קַדִּישׁ יָתוֹם Mourner's Kaddish (some omit) W100 F52

+ Psalm 27 for the Season of Repentance W92 F40

קַדִּישׁ יָתוֹם Mourner's Kaddish W100 F52

מִזְמוֹר שִׁיר (Psalm 30) W14 F50

קַדִּישׁ יָתוֹם Mourner's Kaddish W15 F52

בָּרוּךְ שֶׁאָמַר Barukh she'amar W16 F54
Use Yamim Nora'im nusaḥ.

הוֹדוּ לַיי Hodu ladonay W17 F54
Use weekday minor nusaḥ from here until יִשְׁתַּבַּח.

☞ מִזְמוֹר לְתוֹדָה Mizmor letodah W20 F60

+ Psalms recited on Shabbat and Yom Tov:
☞ Psalms 19, 34, 90, 91, 135, 136, 33, 92, 93 L127–34 S87–95 F60–78

Continue with the usual weekday service from
יְהִי כְבוֹד יי Yehi khevod adonay W20 F80

יִשְׁתַּבַּח Yishtabbaḥ W29 F94
Use weekday Ahavah Rabbah nusaḥ.

Open ark.
Repeat each verse after the sheliaḥ/sheliḥat tsibbur:
+ שִׁיר הַמַּעֲלוֹת, מִמַּעֲמַקִּים Shir hama'alot, mima'amakkim (Psalm 130) W62 F134
Use Seliḥot nusaḥ.
Close ark.

חֲצִי קַדִּישׁ Short Kaddish W29 F94
Use weekday Ahavah Rabbah nusaḥ.

בָּרְכוּ Barekhu and response W30 F96
Use weekday Ahavah Rabbah nusaḥ.

בָּרוּךְ . . . יוֹצֵר אוֹר Barukh . . . yotser or W30 F96
Use Yamim Nora'im nusaḥ through בָּרוּךְ . . . גָּאַל יִשְׂרָאֵל.

Weekday Amidah: W36 F106
Use weekday Amidah (pentatonic) nusaḥ.
+ יַעֲלֶה וְיָבוֹא Ya'aleh veyavo for Sukkot W41 F114

✕ ~~תַּחֲנוּן Taḥanun~~

☞ Those wearing תְּפִלִּין tefillin now remove and pack them.

For instructions on taking the lulav and etrog, see p. 28.
For waving the lulav during Hallel, see p. 31.

+ הַלֵּל שָׁלֵם Full Hallel, including waving the lulav W50 F380
Chant the regular Shalosh Regalim Hallel.

Some congregations recite הוֹשַׁע־נָא Hosha'na and conduct the processions with lulav and etrog here, rather than after the Musaf Amidah. See instructions, p. 51.

קַדִּישׁ שָׁלֵם Full Kaddish L321 S138 W56 F392
Chant quickly in major, as on Shabbat.

☞ **YOM TOV TORAH SERVICE**
Chant as on Yom Tov.

+ אֵין כָּמוֹךָ Eyn Kamokha L322 S139 F394
+ יי יי אֵ-ל רַחוּם וְחַנּוּן
Adonay adonay el raḥum veḥannun (3 times) L323 S140 F394
+ רִבּוֹנוֹ שֶׁל עוֹלָם Ribbono shel olam L323 S140 F396
+ וַאֲנִי תְפִלָּתִי לְךָ Va'ani tefillati lekha (3 times) L323 S140 F396

Tishrey 5782						
		1	2	3	4	5
6	7	8	9	10	11	12
13	14	15	16	17	18	19
20	21	22	23	24	25	26
27	28	29	30			

Sep | Oct 2021						
		7	8	9	10	11
12	13	14	15	16	17	18
19	20	21	22	23	24	25
26	27	28	29	30 |	1	2
3	4	5	6			

+ Add ✕ Omit ☞ Take note!

Siddurim

L Lev Shalem for Shabbat and Festivals
S Shabbat and Festival Sim Shalom
W Weekday Sim Shalom
F Full Sim Shalom (both editions)
P Personal Edition of Full Sim Shalom

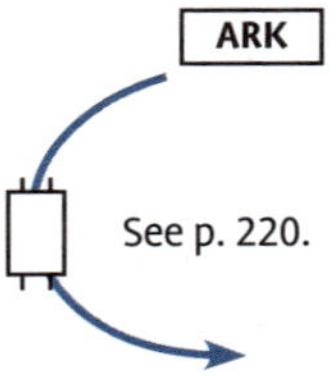

Remove **1** scroll from ark.

שְׁמַע Shema and אֶחָד Eḥad L325 S141 F398
Conclude אֶחָד Eḥad as on High Holidays, with קָדוֹשׁ וְנוֹרָא שְׁמוֹ Kadosh venora shemo.
Chant as on Yamim Nora'im.

גַּדְּלוּ Gaddelu L325 S141 F398
Chant as on Shabbat.

☞ וְיַעֲזֹר Veya'azor L325 S141 F400

Torah 4 aliyot from: פָּרָשַׁת פִּינְחָס Parashat Pineḥas
בְּמִדְבַּר Bemidbar (Numbers) 29:26–34°
[1]29:26–28 [2]29–31 [3]32–34 [4]29–34 W324 P971

☞°Use Yamim Nora'im cantillation for all 4 aliyot.

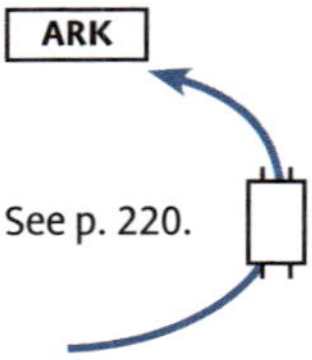

חֲצִי קַדִּישׁ Short Kaddish W71 F146
Use weekday minor nusaḥ.

Open, raise, display, and wrap scroll.

Return scroll to ark. W76 F150

אַשְׁרֵי Ashrey L214 S226 W78 F152
Use weekday minor nusaḥ through וּבָא לְצִיּוֹן.

✕ ~~לַמְנַצֵּחַ Lamenatse·aḥ (Psalm 20)~~
וּבָא לְצִיּוֹן Uva letsiyyon L216 S227 W80 F156

☞ Sheliaḥ/sheliḥat tsibbur customarily wears a *kittel* (plain white robe) for Musaf.

+ חֲצִי קַדִּישׁ Short Kaddish L217 S155 W103 F428
Chant in major as on Shabbat.

מוּסָף

Silent Yom Tov Amidah: L343 S166 F456
+ Insertions for Sukkot
+ Insertions for Hosha'na Rabbah L350 S173 F467

Repetition of the Yom Tov Amidah: L343 S166 F456
Chant as on Shabbat until קְדֻשָּׁה.
Yom Tov קְדֻשָּׁה Kedushah (including אַדִּיר אַדִּירֵנוּ Addir addirenu) L345 S167 F458
Chant as on Yamim Nora'im.

לְדוֹר וָדוֹר Ledor vador, to the end of the Amidah
Use Shalosh Regalim nusaḥ.

+ Insertions for Sukkot
+ Insertions for Hosha'na Rabbah L350 S173 F467

+ **Hosha'na**

For procedures specific to Hosha'na Rabbah for reciting הוֹשַׁע־נָא Hosha'na prayers, including processions with lulav and etrog, see p. 47.

Open ark and remove all Torah scrolls.

+ Recite 7 הוֹשַׁע־נָא Hosha'na prayers during 7 processions. L392–96 S206–8 F538–42
Chant in minor.

+ אֲנִי וָהוֹ הוֹשִׁיעָה־נָּא L385 S209 F542
Chant in major.
כְּהוֹשַׁעְתָּ Kehosha'ta for weekdays L385 S209 F542
Chant in minor.

Put aside the lulav and etrog.
Take a bundle of 5 עֲרָבוֹת aravot (willow branches).

+ תַּעֲנֶה אֱמוּנִים Ta'aneh emunim L397 S210 F544

+ Sheliaḥ/sheliḥat tsibbur, then congregation:
קוֹל מְבַשֵּׂר, מְבַשֵּׂר וְאוֹמֵר
Kol mevasser, mevasser ve'omer L399 S211 F545
Chant in major.
Repeat two more times.

Return all scrolls to ark.

+ הוֹשִׁיעָה אֶת־עַמֶּךָ Hoshi'ah et ammekha L401 S212 F546
Chant in major.
Close ark.

Some beat the עֲרָבוֹת here.
See instructions after Full Kaddish below.

+ יְהִי רָצוֹן Yehi ratson L401 S212 F547

קַדִּישׁ שָׁלֵם Full Kaddish L203 S181 F506
Chant quickly in major, as on Shabbat. Continue as on Shabbat.

+ Beat the עֲרָבוֹת against the floor or other hard surface.
☞ Do *not* beat more than 5 times.

+ אֵין כֵּא·לֹהֵינוּ Eyn keloheynu L204 S182 F508
עָלֵינוּ Aleynu L281 S183 F510

If psalms for the day were not recited at Shaḥarit, add here:
קַדִּישׁ יָתוֹם Mourner's Kaddish (some omit) L282 S184 F512
Psalm for Monday (Psalm 48) L434 S74 F24
Use weekday minor nusaḥ for the psalms.

Tishrey 5782							Sep | Oct 2021						
		1	2	3	4	5			7	8	9	10	11
6	7	8	9	10	11	12	12	13	14	15	16	17	18
13	14	15	16	17	18	19	19	20	21	22	23	24	25
20	21	22	23	24	25	26	26	27	28	29	30 |	1	2
27	28	29	30				3	4	5	6			

+ Add ✕ Omit ☞ Take note!

Siddurim
- **L** Lev Shalem for Shabbat and Festivals
- **S** Shabbat and Festival Sim Shalom
- **W** Weekday Sim Shalom
- **F** Full Sim Shalom (both editions)
- **P** Personal Edition of Full Sim Shalom

קַדִּישׁ יָתוֹם Mourner's Kaddish (some omit) L58 S82 F52

+ Psalm 27 for the Season of Repentance L59 S80 F40

קַדִּישׁ יָתוֹם Mourner's Kaddish L282|58 S184|82 F512|52

At home See "Eating in the Sukkah," p. 28.

מִנְחָה Minḥah for weekdays L289 S1 W120 F164

Weekday Amidah:

+ יַעֲלֶה וְיָבוֹא Ya'aleh veyavo for Sukkot L298 S7 W127 F178

✕ ~~תַּחֲנוּן Taḥanun~~

At home Prepare a flame for Yom Tov. See blue box, below.
Light Yom Tov candles. See blue box, below.

Sheemini Atseret and Simḥat Torah

Preparing for Yom Tov

Preparing a Flame for Yom Tov

Before candle lighting for Sheemini Atseret (Monday evening), prepare a flame. See p. 27.

Sheemini Atseret and Simḥat Torah at Home

Candle Lighting

Sheemini Atseret: See "Candle Lighting for Sukkot — Day 1," p. 29.
Simḥat Torah: See "Candle Lighting for Sukkot — Day 2," p. 35.

Sheemini Atseret and Simḥat Torah Meals

Enjoy festive meals evening and daytime, in the manner of Shabbat meals.

Sheemini Atseret: When possible, eat in a סֻכָּה *sukkah*.
Do *not* recite לֵישֵׁב בַּסֻּכָּה *leshev basukkah*.
If you usually stand for קִדּוּשׁ *kiddush*, in the סֻכָּה stand for the בְּרָכוֹת *berakhot*, then sit to drink.

Simḥat Torah: Do not eat in a *sukkah*.

EVENING KIDDUSH L79 S334 F742

Recite: 1. Yom Tov קִדּוּשׁ with insertions for Sheemini Atseret/Simḥat Torah
2. שֶׁהֶחֱיָנוּ *sheheḥeyanu*

DAYTIME KIDDUSH L81 S335 F746

Recite: 1. וַיְדַבֵּר מֹשֶׁה *vaydabber mosheh* (Vayikra 23:44)
2. בּוֹרֵא פְּרִי הַגָּפֶן *bo·re peri hagafen*

HAMOTSI, FESTIVE MEALS WITH SINGING, AND BIRKAT HAMAZON

Recite הַמּוֹצִיא *hamotsi* over 2 whole חַלָּה *ḥallah* loaves or rolls. L81 S313–14 F744|746
Include festive singing, and recite בִּרְכַּת הַמָּזוֹן *birkat hamazon* with Sheemini Atseret/Simḥat Torah additions (see yellow box, p. 57).

Tishrey 22 תִּשְׁרֵי שְׁמִינִי עֲצֶרֶת Shemini Atseret
Mon 27 Sep

DURING Shemini Atseret and Simḥat Torah

Birkat Hamazon:

+ יַעֲלֶה וְיָבוֹא Ya'aleh veyavo for Shemini Atseret and Simḥat Torah L90|95 S340|347 W233|239 F762|780
+ הָרַחֲמָן Haraḥaman for Yom Tov L92|96 S343|348 W236|240 F768
✕ ~~הָרַחֲמָן Haraḥaman for Sukkot~~

עַרְבִית

Arvit for Yom Tov L39 S28 F279

+ וַיְדַבֵּר מֹשֶׁה Vaydabber mosheh (Vayikra 23:44) L46 S34 F294

חֲצִי קַדִּישׁ Short Kaddish L46 S34 F294

Yom Tov Amidah: L306 S41 F304

+ Insertions for Shemini Atseret

קַדִּישׁ שָׁלֵם Full Kaddish L54 S48 F316

✕ ~~קִדּוּשׁ Kiddush during Arvit~~

עָלֵינוּ Aleynu L56 S51 F320

קַדִּישׁ יָתוֹם Mourner's Kaddish L58 S52 F324

✕ ~~Psalm 27 for the Season of Repentance~~

(Some congregations do recite:
Psalm 27 for the Season of Repentance L59 S80 F40
קַדִּישׁ יָתוֹם Mourner's Kaddish L58 S82 F52)

☞ **At the conclusion of Arvit, in the sukkah:**

קִדּוּשׁ Kiddush for Yom Tov L79 S50 F318
+ Insertions for Shemini Atseret
+ שֶׁהֶחֱיָנוּ Sheheḥeyanu L80 S50 F320
✕ ~~לֵישֵׁב בַּסֻּכָּה Leshev basukkah~~

At home See "Shemini Atseret and Simḥat Torah Meals" and "Evening Kiddush," p. 52.

Tue 28 Sep **שַׁחֲרִית**

✕ ~~Psalm 27 for the Season of Repentance~~

(Some congregations do recite, here or at Musaf:
Psalm 27 for the Season of Repentance L59 S80 F40
קַדִּישׁ יָתוֹם Mourner's Kaddish L58 S82 F52)

Tishrey 5782						
		1	2	3	4	5
6	7	8	9	10	11	12
13	14	15	16	17	18	19
20	21	22	23	24	25	26
27	28	29	30			

Sep | Oct 2021						
		7	8	9	10	11
12	13	14	15	16	17	18
19	20	21	22	23	24	25
26	27	28	29	30 |	1	2
3	4	5	6			

+ Add ✕ Omit ☞ Take note!

Siddurim
- **L** Lev Shalem for Shabbat and Festivals
- **S** Shabbat and Festival Sim Shalom
- **W** Weekday Sim Shalom
- **F** Full Sim Shalom (both editions)
- **P** Personal Edition of Full Sim Shalom

At the end of the preliminary service,
begin formal chanting at
הָאֵ-ל בְּתַעֲצוּמוֹת עֻזֶּךָ Ha'el beta'atsumot uzzekha. L147 S105 F336

✕ ~~הַכֹּל יוֹדוּךָ Hakol yodukha~~
✕ ~~אֵ-ל אָדוֹן El adon~~
✕ ~~לָאֵ-ל אֲשֶׁר שָׁבַת La'el asher shavat~~
+ הַמֵּאִיר לָאָרֶץ Hame'ir la'arets L152 S109 F342

Yom Tov Amidah: L306 S123 F366
+ Insertions for Shemini Atseret

+ הַלֵּל שָׁלֵם Full Hallel L316 S133 F380

קַדִּישׁ שָׁלֵם Full Kaddish L321 S138 F392

YOM TOV TORAH SERVICE L322 S139 F394

+ יי יי אֵ-ל רַחוּם וְחַנּוּן
Adonay adonay el raḥum veḥannun (3 times) L323 S140 F394
+ רִבּוֹנוֹ שֶׁל עוֹלָם Ribbono shel olam L323 S140 F396
+ וַאֲנִי תְפִלָּתִי לְךָ Va'ani tefillati lekha (3 times) L323 S140 F396

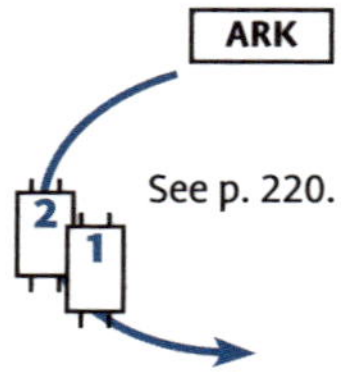

See p. 220.

Remove **2** scrolls from ark in the order they will be read.

1st scroll 5 aliyot from רְאֵה Re'eh
דְּבָרִים Devarim (Deuteronomy) 14:22–16:17
1 14:22–15:23 2 16:1–3 3 16:4–8 4 16:9–12 5 16:13–17
Some divide as follows:
1 14:22–29 2 15:1–18 3 15:19–16:3 4 16:4–8 5 16:9–17

Place 2nd scroll on table next to 1st scroll.
חֲצִי קַדִּישׁ Short Kaddish L327 S146 F408
Open, raise, display, and wrap 1st scroll.

2nd scroll Maftir aliyah from פִּינְחָס Pineḥas
M בְּמִדְבַּר Bemidbar (Numbers) 29:35–30:1

Open, raise, display, and wrap 2nd scroll.

Haftarah for Shemini Atseret
מְלָכִים א׳ 1 Melakhim (1 Kings) 8:54–66

Haftarah blessings:
☞ Conclude with the Yom Tov בְּרָכָה berakhah L329 S147 F412
with insertions for Shemini Atseret.

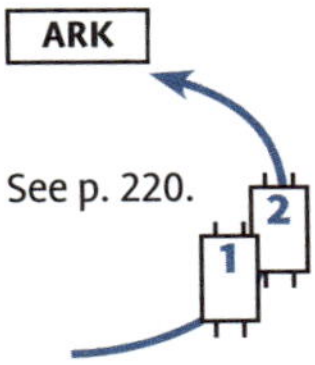

✕ ~~יְקוּם פֻּרְקָן Yekum purkan~~

\+ יִזְכֹּר Yizkor L330 S188 F516

☞ אַב הָרַחֲמִים Av Haraḥamim L446 S151 F420

אַשְׁרֵי Ashrey L339 S151 F420

Return scrolls to ark in reverse order. L340 S153 F422

Mashiv Haruaḥ

Announce before the silent Amidah: "In the silent Amidah, add מַשִּׁיב הָרְוּחַ וּמוֹרִיד הַגָּֽשֶׁם *mashiv haruaḥ umorid hagashem.*"

For congregations that follow the tradition of Erets Yisra'el to add מוֹרִיד הַטָּל *morid hatal* during the summer, instead announce before the silent Amidah: "In the silent Amidah, replace מוֹרִיד הַטָּל *morid hatal* with מַשִּׁיב הָרְוּחַ וּמוֹרִיד הַגָּֽשֶׁם *mashiv haruaḥ umorid hagashem.*"

☞ שְׁלִיחַ/שְׁלִיחַת צִבּוּר sheliaḥ/sheliḥat tsibbur customarily wears a kittel (plain white robe) for Musaf.

חֲצִי קַדִּישׁ Short Kaddish L342 S155 F428

The distinctive traditional melody of this Kaddish anticipates the opening melody of the repetition of the Amidah.

מוּסָף

Silent Yom Tov Amidah: L343 S166 F456

\+ מַשִּׁיב הָרְוּחַ Mashiv haruaḥ L344 S166 F456

\+ Insertions for Shemini Atseret

Open ark.

Repetition of the Yom Tov Amidah: L374 S217 F482

\+ תְּפִלַּת גֶּשֶׁם Tefillat geshem L377 S218 F482

Close ark.

Continue with מְכַלְכֵּל חַיִּים Mekhalkel ḥayyim L344 S166 F456

\+ Insertions for Shemini Atseret

Some congregations include in the repetition of the Amidah the Priestly Blessing by the Kohanim (*dukhenen*).

בִּרְכַּת כֹּהֲנִים Birkat kohanim L353 S177 F472

For procedures, see p. 222.

קַדִּישׁ שָׁלֵם Full Kaddish L203 S181 F506

Continue with אֵין כֵּא·לֹהֵינוּ Eyn keloheynu. L204 S182 F508

Tishrey 5782						
		1	2	3	4	5
6	7	8	9	10	11	12
13	14	15	16	17	18	19
20	21	22	23	24	25	26
27	28	29	30			

Sep | Oct 2021						
		7	8	9	10	11
12	13	14	15	16	17	18
19	20	21	22	23	24	25
26	27	28	29	30	1	2
3	4	5	6			

+ Add ✕ Omit ☞ Take note!

Siddurim
L Lev Shalem for Shabbat and Festivals
S Shabbat and Festival Sim Shalom
W Weekday Sim Shalom
F Full Sim Shalom (both editions)
P Personal Edition of Full Sim Shalom

✕ ~~Psalm 27 for the Season of Repentance~~
(Some congregations do recite, here or at Shaharit:
Psalm 27 for the Season of Repentance L59 S80 F40
קַדִּישׁ יָתוֹם Mourner's Kaddish L58 S82 F52)

קִדּוּשָׁא רַבָּא Kiddush for Yom Tov, in the sukkah L81 S335 F746
See "Daytime Kiddush," p. 52

At home See "Shemini Atseret and Simhat Torah Meals" and "Daytime Kiddush," p. 52.

UNTIL Pesaḥ **Every Amidah:**
+ מַשִּׁיב הָרוּחַ וּמוֹרִיד הַגָּשֶׁם Mashiv haruaḥ umorid hagashem

מִנְחָה
אַשְׁרֵי Ashrey L214 S226 W170 F558
וּבָא לְצִיּוֹן Uva letsiyyon L216 S227 W171 F560
חֲצִי קַדִּישׁ Short Kaddish L217 S229 W173 F564

Yom Tov Amidah: L306 S242 W184 F586
+ מַשִּׁיב הָרוּחַ Mashiv haruaḥ
+ Insertions for Shemini Atseret

קַדִּישׁ שָׁלֵם Full Kaddish L230 S247 W189 F596
עָלֵינוּ Aleynu L231 S248 W190 F598
קַדִּישׁ יָתוֹם Mourner's Kaddish L232 S249 W191 F600

Celebrating with the Torah on Simḥat Torah

Attah Hor'eyta

Whenever we remove the Torah from the ark, we first recite several biblical verses in praise of God. On Simḥat Torah we recite a much larger collection of verses, known as אַתָּה הָרְאֵתָ *attah hor'eyta.* L402 S213 F548

Traditionally, a person recites a verse, and the congregation repeats it. In many congregations, various people take turns leading this recitation.

In congregations where the verses are repeated to accommodate more leaders:
1. Recite the first 10 verses sequentially, through . . . וְיִהְיוּ נָא *veyihyu na. . . .*
2. Repeat this block of 10 verses as necessary.
3. Open the ark, and recite the remaining 9 verses from וַיְהִי בִּנְסֹעַ *vayhi binsoa.*

Hakkafot

Throughout the year, before we read the Torah, we carry the scroll(s) around the sanctuary in procession. On Simḥat Torah, both evening and morning, we carry *all* the Torah scrolls in 7 הַקָּפוֹת *hakkafot* (processions around the sanctuary). These are reminiscent of the processions of the priests around the altar of the Temple in ancient times. The ark remains open during the processions.

For each הַקָּפָה *hakkafah:*

1. Ask a different congregant to lead.
2. Make a counterclockwise circuit around the reading table and sanctuary. During the procession, the leader chants the assigned liturgical verses phrase by phrase. The congregation repeats each phrase. L404 S214 F550
3. Encourage festive singing and dancing.

Tishrey 23 תִּשְׁרֵי שִׂמְחַת תּוֹרָה Simḥat Torah

Tue 28 Sep (evening)

DURING Shemini Atseret and Simḥat Torah

Birkat Hamazon:

+ יַעֲלֶה וְיָבוֹא Ya'aleh veyavo for Shemini Atseret and Simḥat Torah L90|95 S340|347 W233|239 F762|780
+ הָרַחֲמָן Haraḥaman for Yom Tov L92|96 S343|348 W236|240 F768
✕ ~~הָרַחֲמָן Haraḥaman for Sukkot~~

עַרְבִית

Arvit for Yom Tov L39 S28 F279

+ וַיְדַבֵּר מֹשֶׁה Vaydabber mosheh (Vayikra 23:44) L46 S34 F294

חֲצִי קַדִּישׁ Short Kaddish L46 S34 F294

Yom Tov Amidah: L306 S41 F304

+ Insertions for Simḥat Torah

קַדִּישׁ שָׁלֵם Full Kaddish L54 S48 F316

TORAH SERVICE FOR SIMḤAT TORAH L402 S213 F548

אַתָּה הָרְאֵתָ Attah hor'eyta L402 S213 F548
See "Attah Hor'eyta," p. 56.

Remove all Torah scrolls from ark. Ark remains open.

Perform 7 הַקָּפוֹת hakkafot. L404 S214 F550
See "Hakkafot," above.
If congregation leaves sanctuary during הַקָּפוֹת, close ark.

Return all but 1 scroll to ark.

Tishrey 5782

		1	2	3	4	5
6	7	8	9	10	11	12
13	14	15	16	17	18	19
20	21	22	23	24	25	26
27	28	29	30			

Sep | Oct 2021

		7	8	9	10	11
12	13	14	15	16	17	18
19	20	21	22	23	24	25
26	27	28	29	30 |	1	2
3	4	5	6			

+ Add ✕ Omit ☞ Take note!

Siddurim
- **L** Lev Shalem for Shabbat and Festivals
- **S** Shabbat and Festival Sim Shalom
- **W** Weekday Sim Shalom
- **F** Full Sim Shalom (both editions)
- **P** Personal Edition of Full Sim Shalom

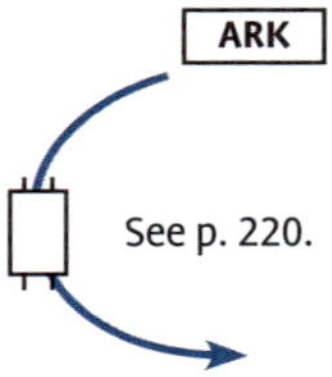

שְׁמַע Shema and אֶחָד Eḥad L325 S141 F398
Conclude אֶחָד Eḥad as on High Holidays, with קָדוֹשׁ וְנוֹרָא שְׁמוֹ Kadosh venora shemo.
Chant as on Yamim Nora'im.

Continue with גַּדְּלוּ Gaddelu, and carry the scroll in a procession, as usual.

☞ וְיַעֲזֹר Veya'azor L325 S141 F400

Torah 3 aliyot from וְזֹאת הַבְּרָכָה Vezot haberakhah
דְּבָרִים Devarim (Deuteronomy) 33:1–17
1 33:1–7 2 8–12 3 13–17 W319 P940

Use Yamim Nora'im cantillation for this reading.

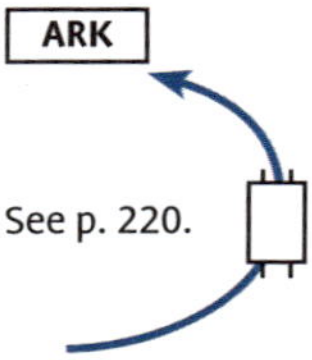

☞ חֲצִי קַדִּישׁ Short Kaddish L327 S146 F408
Open, raise, display, and wrap the scroll.

Return scroll to ark as at Shabbat Minḥah. L221 S232 F570

קִדּוּשׁ Kiddush for Yom Tov L79 S50 F318
+ Insertions for Simḥat Torah
+ שֶׁהֶחֱיָנוּ Sheheḥeyanu L80 S50 F319

עָלֵינוּ Aleynu L56 S51 F320
קַדִּישׁ יָתוֹם Mourner's Kaddish L58 S52 F324

✕ ~~Psalm 27 for the Season of Repentance~~

At home Light Yom Tov candles from an existing flame.
See "Candle Lighting for Sukkot — Day 2," p. 35.

See "Shemini Atseret and Simḥat Torah Meals" and "Evening Kiddush," p. 52.

Wed 29 Sep **שַׁחֲרִית** ✕ ~~Psalm 27 for the Season of Repentance~~

At the end of the preliminary service, begin formal chanting at
הָאֵ·ל בְּתַעֲצוּמוֹת עֻזֶּךָ Ha'el beta'atsumot uzzekha. L147 S105 F336

✕ ~~הַכֹּל יוֹדוּךָ Hakol yodukha~~
✕ ~~אֵ·ל אָדוֹן El adon~~
✕ ~~לָאֵ·ל אֲשֶׁר שָׁבַת La'el asher shavat~~
+ הַמֵּאִיר לָאָרֶץ Hame'ir la'arets L152 S109 F342

Reading the Torah on Simḥat Torah Morning

The 1st Scroll: Completing the Reading of the Torah

After 7 הַקָּפוֹת *hakkafot,* traditionally everyone is called to the Torah. Repeat the first 5 readings until all are called except those to be called for the 2 special *aliyot* (see below) and the מַפְטִיר *maftir aliyah.* If כֹּהֵן *kohen* and לֵוִי *levi* are usually called for the first 2 *aliyot,* call them for the first 2 *aliyot* of each round of 5, until all of them are called. Call the last adult together with all the children (יַעֲמֹד ... עִם כׇּל־הַנְּעָרִים *ya'amod . . . im kol hane'arim*). Spread a large טַלִּית *tallit* above the children. The adult recites the בְּרָכוֹת *berakhot.* Before the second בְּרָכָה, bless the children with הַמַּלְאָךְ הַגֹּאֵל אֹתִי (Bereshit 48:16) S295 F692.

Many congregations hold concurrent Torah readings. After everyone has been called to the Torah, gather again as a single congregation. In some congregations people are called to the Torah as families or other small groups.

Whether one Torah reading or several readings at different stations, at all times at each reading, at least 10 adults must attend to the reading.

Recite מֵרְשׁוּת *mereshut* to call חֲתַן הַתּוֹרָה *ḥatan hatorah* ("groom" of the Torah) or כַּלַּת הַתּוֹרָה *kallat hatorah* ("bride" of the Torah), the person called for the *aliyah* that completes the reading of the Torah. See p. 60.

Chant this parashah using the cantillation of the High Holidays. As we complete the reading of the Torah, we complete the holiday season as well.

The 2nd Scroll: Beginning the Reading of the Torah Anew

We restart the regular Torah reading cycle, symbolizing our continuing dedication to Torah study. Chant using the regular Shabbat cantillation.

Recite מֵרְשׁוּת *mereshut* to call חֲתַן בְּרֵאשִׁית *ḥatan bereshit* ("groom" of Bereshit) or כַּלַּת בְּרֵאשִׁית *kallat bereshit* ("bride" of Bereshit), the person called for the *aliyah* that begins the reading of the Torah anew. See p. 61.

The congregation participates in the festive reading of this section in two ways.

1. Each day of creation ends with the refrain ... וַיְהִי־עֶרֶב וַיְהִי־בֹקֶר יוֹם *vayhi erev vayhi voker yom . . .* ("then was evening, then was morning, the 1st [2nd, 3rd . . .] day"). For each of the 6 occurrences of the refrain (1:5, 8, 13, 19, 23, and 31), follow this procedure:
   a. At the phrase preceding the refrain, the Torah reader uses a prompting melody to alert the congregation.
   b. After the prompt, the reader pauses.
   c. The congregation chants ... וַיְהִי־עֶרֶב וַיְהִי־בֹקֶר יוֹם, the refrain for that day.
   d. When the congregation finishes, the reader chants the refrain from the Torah using the concluding melody phrase of the Shirat Hayam melody.
   e. The reader continues chanting.
2. When the reader reaches וַיְכֻלּוּ *vaykhullu* (2:1), the reader pauses.
   a. The congregation chants the וַיְכֻלּוּ passage (2:1–3).
   b. After the congregation finishes, the reader chants the passage.

Yom Tov Amidah: L306 S123 F366

+ Insertions for Simḥat Torah

Some congregations include in the repetition of the Amidah the Priestly Blessing by the Kohanim (*dukhenen*).

☞ On Simḥat Torah, perform this at Shaḥarit.
בִּרְכַּת כֹּהֲנִים Birkat kohanim L353 S177 F472
For procedures, see p. 222.

+ הַלֵּל שָׁלֵם Full Hallel L316 S133 F380

קַדִּישׁ שָׁלֵם Full Kaddish L321 S138 F392

TORAH SERVICE FOR SIMḤAT TORAH L402 S213 F548

אַתָּה הָרְאֵתָ Attah hor'eyta L402 S213 F548
See "Attah Hor'eyta," p. 56.

Remove all Torah scrolls from ark. Ark remains open.

Perform 7 הַקָּפוֹת hakkafot. L404 S214 F550
See "Hakkafot," p. 57.
If congregation leaves sanctuary during הַקָּפוֹת, close ark.

Return all but 3 scrolls to ark.
(For concurrent readings, retain additional scrolls.)

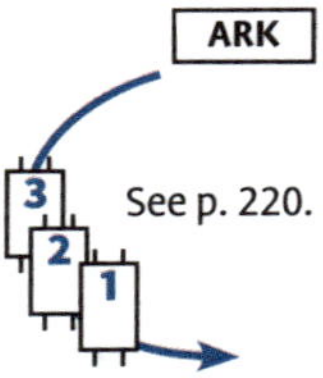

שְׁמַע Shema and אֶחָד Eḥad L325 S141 F398
Conclude אֶחָד Eḥad as on High Holidays, with קָדוֹשׁ וְנוֹרָא שְׁמוֹ Kadosh venora shemo.
Chant as on Yamim Nora'im.

Continue with גַּדְּלוּ Gaddelu, and carry the scrolls in a procession, in the order they will be read, as usual.

1st scroll 5 aliyot from וְזֹאת הַבְּרָכָה Vezot haberakhah
דְּבָרִים Devarim (Deuteronomy) 33:1–26
1 33:1–7 2 33:8–12 3 33:13–17 4 33:18–21 5 33:22–26

Use Yamim Nora'im cantillation for this reading.

Repeat these 5 aliyot until all except those designated for the two ḥatan/kallah aliyot and the person chanting the haftarah have been called to the Torah.
For procedures for this reading, see p. 59.

Ḥatan hatorah / Kallat hatorah
Call חֲתַן הַתּוֹרָה ḥatan hatorah or כַּלַּת הַתּוֹרָה kallat hatorah:
מֵרְשׁוּת Mereshut L406 S215 F552
Use the melody of אַקְדָּמוּת, as chanted on Shavu'ot.

1st scroll Read the concluding section of the Torah.
דְּבָרִים Devarim (Deuteronomy) 33:27–34:12°

Use Yamim Nora'im cantillation for this reading.

☞ °34:12 When the Torah reader concludes a book of the Torah:

1. Close the Torah scroll.
2. **For Oleh:** Congregation chants חֲזַק חֲזַק וְנִתְחַזֵּק ḥazak ḥazak venitḥazzek; oleh remains silent.
   For Olah: Congregation chants חִזְקִי חִזְקִי וְנִתְחַזֵּק ḥizki ḥizki venitḥazzek; olah remains silent.
3. Torah reader repeats congregation's words (oleh/olah remains silent; if Torah reader is the oleh/olah, omit this repetition).
4. Open the Torah scroll.
5. The oleh/olah kisses the Torah scroll, closes it, and continues with the usual concluding berakhah.

Place 2nd scroll on table next to 1st scroll.
☞ Do not recite חֲצִי קַדִּישׁ Short Kaddish here.

Open, raise, display, and wrap 1st scroll.

Ḥatan bereshit / Kallat bereshit

Call חֲתַן בְּרֵאשִׁית ḥatan bereshit or
כַּלַּת בְּרֵאשִׁית kallat bereshit:
מֵרְשׁוּת Mereshut L407 S216 F554

Use the melody of אַקְדָּמוּת, as chanted on Shavu'ot.

2nd scroll Read the opening section of the Torah.
בְּרֵאשִׁית Bereshit (Genesis) °1:1–2:3

Use regular Shabbat cantillation for this reading.

☞ °1:1–2:3 Use special procedures for this reading. See p. 59.

Place 3rd scroll on table next to 2nd scroll.
Place or hold 1st scroll near other scrolls at table.
(Some do not return 1st scroll to table.)

חֲצִי קַדִּישׁ Short Kaddish L327 S146 F408
Open, raise, display, and wrap 2nd scroll.

+ **3rd scroll** Maftir aliyah from פִּינְחָס Pineḥas
M בְּמִדְבַּר Bemidbar (Numbers) 29:35–30:1

Open, raise, display, and wrap 3rd scroll.

Haftarah for Simḥat Torah
יְהוֹשֻׁעַ Yehoshua (Joshua) 1:1–18

Tishrey 5782

		1	2	3	4	5
6	7	8	9	10	11	12
13	14	15	16	17	18	19
20	21	22	23	24	25	26
27	28	29	30			

Sep | Oct 2021

		7	8	9	10	11
12	13	14	15	16	17	18
19	20	21	22	23	24	25
26	27	28	29	30	1	2
3	4	5	6			

+ Add ✕ Omit ☞ Take note!

Siddurim
- **L** Lev Shalem for Shabbat and Festivals
- **S** Shabbat and Festival Sim Shalom
- **W** Weekday Sim Shalom
- **F** Full Sim Shalom (both editions)
- **P** Personal Edition of Full Sim Shalom

Haftarah blessings: L328 S147 F410

☞ Conclude with the Yom Tov בְּרָכָה berakhah L329 S147 F412 with insertions for Simḥat Torah.

✕ ~~יְקוּם פֻּרְקָן Yekum purkan~~
✕ ~~אַב הָרַחֲמִים Av Haraḥamim~~

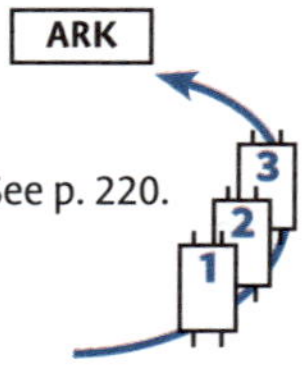

See p. 220.

אַשְׁרֵי Ashrey L339 S151 F420
Return scrolls to ark in reverse order. L340 S153 F422
חֲצִי קַדִּישׁ Short Kaddish L342 S155 F428

מוּסָף

Yom Tov Amidah: L343 S166 F456
+ Insertions for Simḥat Torah

☞ On Simḥat Torah, the Kohanim recite the Priestly Blessing (*dukhenen*) at Shaḥarit, not at Musaf.

קַדִּישׁ שָׁלֵם Full Kaddish L203 S181 F506
Continue with אֵין כֵּא·לֹהֵינוּ Eyn keloheynu. L204 S182 F508

✕ ~~Psalm 27 for the Season of Repentance~~

קִדּוּשָׁא רַבָּא

Kiddush for Yom Tov L81 S335 F746
See "Daytime Kiddush," p. 52

At home

See "Shemini Atseret and Simḥat Torah Meals" and "Daytime Kiddush," p. 52.

מִנְחָה

אַשְׁרֵי Ashrey L214 S226 W170 F558
וּבָא לְצִיּוֹן Uva letsiyyon L216 S227 W171 F560
חֲצִי קַדִּישׁ Short Kaddish L217 S229 W173 F564

Yom Tov Amidah: L306 S242 W184 F586
+ Insertions for Simḥat Torah

קַדִּישׁ שָׁלֵם Full Kaddish L230 S247 W189 F596
עָלֵינוּ Aleynu L231 S248 W190 F598
קַדִּישׁ יָתוֹם Mourner's Kaddish L232 S249 W191 F600

Tishrey 24 תִּשְׁרֵי
Wed 29 Sep

מוֹצָאֵי יוֹם טוֹב Motsa'ey Yom Tov
Conclusion of Yom Tov
אִסְרוּ חַג Isru Ḥag Day after Yom Tov

עַרְבִית

Arvit for weekdays L264 S281 W137 F200

Weekday Amidah:
+ אַתָּה חוֹנַנְתָּנוּ Attah ḥonantanu L272 S287 W143 F212

קַדִּישׁ שָׁלֵם Full Kaddish L280 S294 W160 F222

Some recite הַבְדָּלָה Havdalah here. L283 S299 W165 F700
For instructions, see below.

עָלֵינוּ Aleynu L281 S297 W163 F696
קַדִּישׁ יָתוֹם Mourner's Kaddish L282 S298 W164 F698

+ **Havdalah:** L283 S299 W165 F700
✕ ~~הִנֵּה אֵ-ל יְשׁוּעָתִי Hinneh el yeshu'ati~~
בּוֹרֵא פְּרִי הַגָּפֶן Bo·re peri hagafen
✕ ~~בּוֹרֵא מִינֵי בְשָׂמִים Bo·re miney vesamim~~
✕ ~~בּוֹרֵא מְאוֹרֵי הָאֵשׁ Bo·re me'orey ha'esh~~
הַמַּבְדִּיל בֵּין קֹדֶשׁ לְחֹל Hamavdil beyn kodesh leḥol

Thu 30 Sep **שַׁחֲרִית**

Shaḥarit for weekdays W1 F2

✕ ~~תַּחֲנוּן Taḥanun~~

Torah 3 aliyot from בְּרֵאשִׁית Bereshit
בְּרֵאשִׁית Bereshit (Genesis) 1:1–13
¹1:1–5 ²6–8 ³9–13 W264 P885

☞ לַמְנַצֵּחַ Lamenatse·aḥ (Psalm 20) W79 F154

מִנְחָה ✕ ~~תַּחֲנוּן Taḥanun~~

Tishrey 25 תִּשְׁרֵי
Fri 1 Oct (daytime)

BEGINNING 25 Tishrey Some congregations resume reciting תַּחֲנוּן Taḥanun. Other congregations do not resume until 2 Ḥeshvan.

מִנְחָה ✕ ~~תַּחֲנוּן Taḥanun~~ (as on all Friday afternoons)

Tishrey 26 תִּשְׁרֵי
Sat 2 Oct

שַׁבָּת Shabbat פָּרָשַׁת בְּרֵאשִׁית Parashat Bereshit
שַׁבַּת מְבָרְכִים הַחֹדֶשׁ Shabbat Mevarekhim Haḥodesh

Torah 7 aliyot (minimum): בְּרֵאשִׁית Bereshit
בְּרֵאשִׁית Bereshit (Genesis) 1:1–6:8

Annual:	1 1:1–2:3°	2 2:4–19	3 2:20–3:21	4 3:22–4:18
	5 4:19–26	6 5:1–24	7 5:25–6:8°	M 6:5–8
Triennial:	1 5:1–5	2 5:6–8	3 5:9–14	4 5:15–20
	5 5:21–24	6 5:25–31°	7 5:32–6:8	M 6:5–8

☞°1:1–2:3 Unlike on Simḥat Torah, the congregation does not recite aloud during this reading.
Use only the usual Torah reading melody.

☞°5:29 Note the rare occurrence of the te'amim (tropes) גֵּרְשַׁ֞יִם (֞) and תְּלִישָׁא־גְדוֹלָה (֠) on the same word זֶ֠֞ה. Chant first the melody of גֵּרְשַׁ֞יִם and then the melody of תְּלִישָׁא־גְדוֹלָה consecutively on the 1 syllable of the word. Do **not** chant the word twice.

Haftarah
Ashkenazic: יְשַׁעְיָהוּ Yesha'yahu (Isaiah) 42:5–43:10
Sephardic: יְשַׁעְיָהוּ Yesha'yahu (Isaiah) 42:5–21

+ **Birkat Haḥodesh:** L180 S150 F418
Announce Rosh Ḥodesh Marḥeshvan:
For this formal announcement, use the formal name of the month. Do not announce the month by its popular name "Ḥeshvan."
רֹאשׁ חֹדֶשׁ מַרְחֶשְׁוָן יִהְיֶה בְּיוֹם רְבִיעִי וּבְיוֹם חֲמִישִׁי . . .
Rosh ḥodesh Marḥeshvan yihyeh beyom revi'i uvyom ḥamishi . . .
(Tuesday night, Wednesday, and Thursday)

✕ ~~אַב הָרַחֲמִים Av Haraḥamim~~

מִנְחָה

Torah 3 aliyot from נֹחַ Noaḥ
בְּרֵאשִׁית Bereshit (Genesis) 6:9–22
1 6:9–16 2 17–19 3 20–22 W265 P886

Chanted also next Monday.

☞ Congregations that have not yet resumed reciting תַּחֲנוּן Taḥanun omit צִדְקָתְךָ צֶדֶק Tsidkatekha tsedek.

+ Add ✕ Omit ☞ Take note!

Siddurim

- **L** Lev Shalem for Shabbat and Festivals
- **S** Shabbat and Festival Sim Shalom
- **W** Weekday Sim Shalom
- **F** Full Sim Shalom (both editions)
- **P** Personal Edition of Full Sim Shalom

Tishrey 5782

		1	2	3	4	5
6	7	8	9	10	11	12
13	14	15	16	17	18	19
20	21	22	23	24	25	26
27	28	29	30			

Sep | Oct 2021

		7	8	9	10	11
12	13	14	15	16	17	18
19	20	21	22	23	24	25
26	27	28	29	30	1	2
3	4	5	6			

Tishrey 29 תִּשְׁרֵי
Tue 5 Oct

עֶרֶב רֹאשׁ חֹדֶשׁ Erev Rosh Ḥodesh
Day before Rosh Ḥodesh

מִנְחָה ✕ ~~תַּחֲנוּן Taḥanun~~

Tishrey 30 תִּשְׁרֵי
Tue 5 Oct (evening)

רֹאשׁ חֹדֶשׁ חֶשְׁוָן Rosh Ḥodesh Ḥeshvan — Day 1

DURING Rosh Ḥodesh

Birkat Hamazon:

\+ יַעֲלֶה וְיָבוֹא Ya'aleh veyavo for Rosh Ḥodesh L90|95 S340|347 W233|239 F762|780

\+ הָרַחֲמָן Haraḥaman for Rosh Ḥodesh L92|96 S343|348 W235|240 F768

עַרְבִית

Weekday Amidah:

\+ יַעֲלֶה וְיָבוֹא Ya'aleh veyavo for Rosh Ḥodesh W145 F216

Wed 6 Oct שַׁחֲרִית

Before מִזְמוֹר שִׁיר Mizmor shir (Psalm 30) W14 F50
or at end of service, recite:

Psalm for Wednesday (Psalms 94:1–95:3) W87 F26
קַדִּישׁ יָתוֹם Mourner's Kaddish (some omit) W100 F52
\+ Psalm 104 for Rosh Ḥodesh W90 F34
קַדִּישׁ יָתוֹם Mourner's Kaddish W100 F52

Weekday Amidah:

\+ יַעֲלֶה וְיָבוֹא Ya'aleh veyavo for Rosh Ḥodesh W41 F114

✕ ~~תַּחֲנוּן Taḥanun~~

\+ חֲצִי הַלֵּל Short Hallel W50 F380
קַדִּישׁ שָׁלֵם Full Kaddish W56 F392

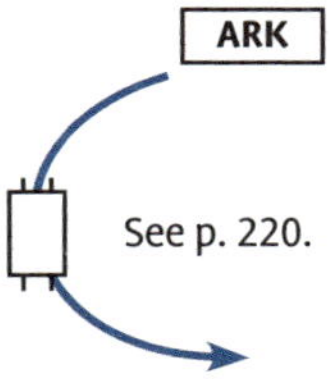

See p. 220.

\+ **TORAH SERVICE** W65 F138
Remove **1** scroll from ark.

Torah 4 aliyot: פִּינְחָס Pineḥas
בְּמִדְבַּר Bemidbar (Numbers) 28:1–15
1 28:1–3 2 3–5 3 6–10 4 11–15 W320 P943

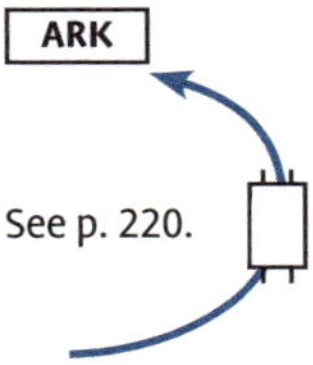

See p. 220.

חֲצִי קַדִּישׁ Short Kaddish W71 F146
Open, raise, display, and wrap scroll.
Return scroll to ark. W76 F150

אַשְׁרֵי Ashrey W78 F152
✕ ~~לַמְנַצֵּחַ Lamenatse·aḥ (Psalm 20)~~
וּבָא לְצִיּוֹן Uva letsiyyon W80 F156

Remove and pack tefillin. (Some remove after Kaddish.)

+ חֲצִי קַדִּישׁ Short Kaddish W103 F428

(If you remove tefillin here, do *not* pack but cover them, so as to begin Musaf together quickly after Kaddish.)

מוּסָף

+ **Rosh Ḥodesh Amidah for weekdays:** W104 F486
Weekday קְדֻשָּׁה Kedushah W105 F488
+ וּלְכַפָּרַת פָּשַׁע Ulkhapparat pasha W107 F494
Add these words only through Rosh Ḥodesh Adar Sheni.

+ קַדִּישׁ שָׁלֵם Full Kaddish W82 F158
עָלֵינוּ Aleynu W83 F160

If psalms for the day were not recited at Shaḥarit, add here:
קַדִּישׁ יָתוֹם Mourner's Kaddish (some omit) W84|100 F162|52
Psalm for Wednesday (Psalms 94:1–95:3) W87 F26
קַדִּישׁ יָתוֹם Mourner's Kaddish (some omit) W100 F52
+ Psalm 104 for Rosh Ḥodesh W90 F34

קַדִּישׁ יָתוֹם Mourner's Kaddish W84|100 F162|52

מִנְחָה

Weekday Amidah:
+ יַעֲלֶה וְיָבוֹא Ya'aleh veyavo for Rosh Ḥodesh W127 F178

✕ ~~תַּחֲנוּן Taḥanun~~

Ḥeshvan 1 חֶשְׁוָן
Wed 6 Oct (evening)

רֹאשׁ חֹדֶשׁ חֶשְׁוָן Rosh Ḥodesh Ḥeshvan — Day 2

DURING Rosh Ḥodesh

Birkat Hamazon:

\+ יַעֲלֶה וְיָבוֹא Ya'aleh veyavo for Rosh Ḥodesh
L90|95 S340|347 W233|239 F762|780

\+ הָרַחֲמָן Harahaman for Rosh Ḥodesh
L92|96 S343|348 W235|240 F768

עַרְבִית

Weekday Amidah:

\+ יַעֲלֶה וְיָבוֹא Ya'aleh veyavo for Rosh Ḥodesh W145 F216

Thu 7 Oct **שַׁחֲרִית**

Before מִזְמוֹר שִׁיר Mizmor shir (Psalm 30) W14 F50
or at end of service, recite:

Psalm for Thursday (Psalm 81) W89 F30
קַדִּישׁ יָתוֹם Mourner's Kaddish (some omit) W100 F52
\+ Psalm 104 for Rosh Ḥodesh W90 F34
קַדִּישׁ יָתוֹם Mourner's Kaddish W100 F52

Weekday Amidah:

\+ יַעֲלֶה וְיָבוֹא Ya'aleh veyavo for Rosh Ḥodesh W41 F114

✕ ~~תַּחֲנוּן Taḥanun~~

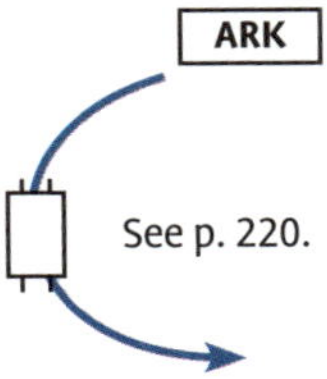

See p. 220.

\+ חֲצִי הַלֵּל Short Hallel W50 F380
קַדִּישׁ שָׁלֵם Full Kaddish W56 F392

TORAH SERVICE W65 F138
Remove **1** scroll from ark.

Torah 4 aliyot: פִּינְחָס Pineḥas
בְּמִדְבַּר Bemidbar (Numbers) 28:1–15
1 28:1–3 2 3–5 3 6–10 4 11–15 W320 P943

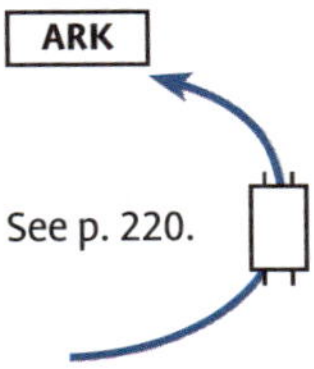

See p. 220.

חֲצִי קַדִּישׁ Short Kaddish W71 F146
Open, raise, display, and wrap scroll.
Return scroll to ark. W76 F150

אַשְׁרֵי Ashrey W78 F152
✕ ~~לַמְנַצֵּחַ Lamenatse·aḥ (Psalm 20)~~
וּבָא לְצִיּוֹן Uva letsiyyon W80 F156

Remove and pack tefillin. (Some remove after Kaddish.)

\+ חֲצִי קַדִּישׁ Short Kaddish W103 F428
(If you remove tefillin here, do *not* pack but cover them, so as to begin Musaf together quickly after Kaddish.)

Ḥeshvan 5782

			1	2	3	
4	5	6	7	8	9	10
11	12	13	14	15	16	17
18	19	20	21	22	23	24
25	26	27	28	29		

Oct | Nov 2021

			7	8	9	
10	11	12	13	14	15	16
17	18	19	20	21	22	23
24	25	26	27	28	29	30
31 |	1	2	3	4		

+ Add ✕ Omit ☞ Take note!

Siddurim
L Lev Shalem for Shabbat and Festivals
S Shabbat and Festival Sim Shalom
W Weekday Sim Shalom
F Full Sim Shalom (both editions)
P Personal Edition of Full Sim Shalom

מוּסָף

+ **Rosh Ḥodesh Amidah for weekdays:** W104 F486
Weekday קְדֻשָּׁה Kedushah W105 F488
+ וּלְכַפָּרַת פָּשַׁע Ulkhapparat pasha W107 F494
Add these words only through Rosh Ḥodesh Adar Sheni.

+ קַדִּישׁ שָׁלֵם Full Kaddish W82 F158
עָלֵינוּ Aleynu W83 F160

If psalms for the day were not recited at Shaḥarit, add here:
קַדִּישׁ יָתוֹם Mourner's Kaddish (some omit) W84|100 F162|52
Psalm for Thursday (Psalm 81) W89 F30
קַדִּישׁ יָתוֹם Mourner's Kaddish (some omit) W100 F52
+ Psalm 104 for Rosh Ḥodesh W90 F34

קַדִּישׁ יָתוֹם Mourner's Kaddish W84|100 F162|52

מִנְחָה

Weekday Amidah:
+ יַעֲלֶה וְיָבוֹא Ya'aleh veyavo for Rosh Ḥodesh W127 F178

✕ ~~תַּחֲנוּן Taḥanun~~

Ḥeshvan 2 חֶשְׁוָן
Fri **8** Oct (daytime)

BEGINNING 2 Ḥeshvan Congregations that have not yet resumed reciting תַּחֲנוּן Taḥanun resume now.

Ḥeshvan 3 חֶשְׁוָן
Sat **9** Oct

שַׁבָּת Shabbat פָּרָשַׁת נֹחַ Parashat Noaḥ

Torah 7 aliyot (minimum): נֹחַ Noaḥ
בְּרֵאשִׁית Bereshit (Genesis) 6:9–11:32

Annual:	1 6:9–22	2 7:1–16	3 7:17–8:14	4 8:15–9:7
	5 9:8–17	6 9:18–10:32	7 11:1–32	M 11:29–32
Triennial:	1 11:1–4	2 11:5–9	3 11:10–13	4 11:14–17
	5 11:18–21	6 11:22–25	7 11:26–32	M 11:29–32

Haftarah
Ashkenazic: יְשַׁעְיָהוּ Yesha'yahu (Isaiah) 54:1–55:5
Sephardic: יְשַׁעְיָהוּ Yesha'yahu (Isaiah) 54:1–10

Siddurim

L Lev Shalem for Shabbat and Festivals
S Shabbat and Festival Sim Shalom
W Weekday Sim Shalom
F Full Sim Shalom (both editions)
P Personal Edition of Full Sim Shalom

		1 2 3		7 8 9		חֶשְׁוָן 3 Oct 9
4 5 6 7 8 9 10			10 11 12 13 14 15 16			חֶשְׁוָן 4 Oct 9
11 12 13 14 15 16 17			17 18 19 20 21 22 23			חֶשְׁוָן 10 Oct 16
18 19 20 21 22 23 24			24 25 26 27 28 29 30			חֶשְׁוָן 17 Oct 23
25 26 27 28 29			31 \| 1 2 3 4

מִנְחָה

Torah 3 aliyot from לֶךְ־לְךָ Lekh lekha
בְּרֵאשִׁית Bereshit (Genesis) 12:1–13
[1]12:1–3 [2]4–9 [3]10–13 W266 P887

Chanted also next Monday and Thursday.

Ḥeshvan 4 חֶשְׁוָן
Sat 9 Oct (night)

After Arvit if the moon is visible:
קִדּוּשׁ לְבָנָה Kiddush Levanah L286 W167 F704
For procedures and instructions, see p. 223.

Ḥeshvan 10 חֶשְׁוָן
Sat 16 Oct

שַׁבָּת Shabbat פָּרָשַׁת לֶךְ־לְךָ Parashat Lekh lekha

Torah 7 aliyot (minimum): לֶךְ־לְךָ Lekh lekha
בְּרֵאשִׁית Bereshit (Genesis) 12:1–17:27

Annual:	[1]12:1–13	[2]12:14–13:4	[3]13:5–18	[4]14:1–20
	[5]14:21–15:6	[6]15:7–17:6	[7]17:7–27	[M]17:24–27
Triennial:	[1]16:1–6	[2]16:7–9	[3]16:10–16	[4]17:1–6
	[5]17:7–17	[6]17:18–23	[7]17:24–27	[M]17:24–27

Haftarah יְשַׁעְיָהוּ Yesha'yahu (Isaiah) 40:27–41:16°

☞°40:31 Read וְקוֹיֵ vekoyey (not vekovey, as printed in many books).

מִנְחָה

Torah 3 aliyot from וַיֵּרָא Vayera
בְּרֵאשִׁית Bereshit (Genesis) 18:1–14
[1]18:1–5 [2]6–8 [3]9–14 W267 P888

Chanted also next Monday and Thursday.

Ḥeshvan 17 חֶשְׁוָן
Sat 23 Oct

שַׁבָּת Shabbat פָּרָשַׁת וַיֵּרָא Parashat Vayera

Torah 7 aliyot (minimum): וַיֵּרָא Vayera
בְּרֵאשִׁית Bereshit (Genesis) 18:1–22:24

Annual:	[1]18:1–14	[2]18:15–33	[3]19:1–20°	[4]19:21–21:4
	[5]21:5–21	[6]21:22–34	[7]22:1–24	[M]22:20–24
Triennial:	[1]21:1–4	[2]21:5–13	[3]21:14–21	[4]21:22–34
	[5]22:1–8	[6]22:9–19	[7]22:20–24	[M]22:20–24

☞°19:16 Note the rare ta'am (trope) | שַׁלְשֶׁלֶת (|): |וַיִּתְמַהְמָהּ

Haftarah
Ashkenazic: מְלָכִים ב׳ 2 Melakhim (2 Kings) 4:1–37
Sephardic: מְלָכִים ב׳ 2 Melakhim (2 Kings) 4:1–23

Ḥeshvan 5782							Oct | Nov 2021						
			1	2	3						7	8	9
4	5	6	7	8	9	10	10	11	12	13	14	15	16
11	12	13	14	15	16	17	17	18	19	20	21	22	23
18	19	20	21	22	23	24	24	25	26	27	28	29	30
25	26	27	28	29			31	1	2	3	4		

+ Add ✕ Omit ☞ Take note!

Siddurim
- **L** Lev Shalem for Shabbat and Festivals
- **S** Shabbat and Festival Sim Shalom
- **W** Weekday Sim Shalom
- **F** Full Sim Shalom (both editions)
- **P** Personal Edition of Full Sim Shalom

מִנְחָה

Torah 3 aliyot from חַיֵּי שָׂרָה Ḥayyey sarah
בְּרֵאשִׁית Bereshit (Genesis) 23:1–16
[1]23:1–7 [2]8–12 [3]13–16 W268 P888

Chanted also next Monday and Thursday.

Ḥeshvan 24 חֶשְׁוָן
Sat 30 Oct

שַׁבָּת Shabbat פָּרָשַׁת חַיֵּי שָׂרָה Parashat Ḥayyey sarah
שַׁבַּת מְבָרְכִים הַחֹדֶשׁ Shabbat Mevarekhim Haḥodesh

Torah 7 aliyot (minimum): חַיֵּי שָׂרָה Ḥayyey sarah
בְּרֵאשִׁית Bereshit (Genesis) 23:1–25:18

Annual:	[1]23:1–16	[2]23:17–24:9	[3]24:10–26°	[4]24:27–52
	[5]24:53–67	[6]25:1–11	[7]25:12–18	[M]25:16–18
Triennial:	[1]24:53–58	[2]24:59–61	[3]24:62–67	[4]25:1–6
	[5]25:7–11	[6]25:12–15	[7]25:16–18	[M]25:16–18

☞° 24:12 Note the rare ta'am (trope) | שַׁלְשֶׁ֓לֶת (׀): וַיֹּאמַ֓ר ׀

Haftarah מְלָכִים א׳ 1 Melakhim (1 Kings) 1:1–31

+ **Birkat Haḥodesh:** L180 S150 F418
Announce Rosh Ḥodesh Kislev:
רֹאשׁ חֹדֶשׁ כִּסְלֵו יִהְיֶה בְּיוֹם שִׁשִּׁי . . .
Rosh ḥodesh Kislev yihyeh beyom shishi . . .
(Thursday night and Friday)

✕ ~~אַב הָרַחֲמִים Av Haraḥamim~~

מִנְחָה

Torah 3 aliyot from תּוֹלְדֹת Toledot
בְּרֵאשִׁית Bereshit (Genesis) 25:19–26:5
[1]25:19–22 [2]23–26 [3]25:27–26:5 W269 P890

Chanted also next Monday and Thursday.

Ḥeshvan 29 חֶשְׁוָן
Thu 4 Nov

עֶרֶב רֹאשׁ חֹדֶשׁ Erev Rosh Ḥodesh
Day before Rosh Ḥodesh

מִנְחָה ✕ ~~תַּחֲנוּן Taḥanun~~

For determining the *yortsayt* of a death on 30 Ḥeshvan, see p. 224.

Kislev 1 כִּסְלֵו — רֹאשׁ חֹדֶשׁ כִּסְלֵו Rosh Ḥodesh Kislev

Thu 4 Nov (evening)

DURING Rosh Ḥodesh

Birkat Hamazon:

\+ יַעֲלֶה וְיָבוֹא Ya’aleh veyavo for Rosh Ḥodesh
L 90|95 S 340|347 W 233|239 F 762|780

\+ הָרַחֲמָן Haraḥaman for Rosh Ḥodesh
L 92|96 S 343|348 W 235|240 F 768

עַרְבִית

Weekday Amidah:

\+ יַעֲלֶה וְיָבוֹא Ya’aleh veyavo for Rosh Ḥodesh W 145 F 216

Fri 5 Nov **שַׁחֲרִית**

Before מִזְמוֹר שִׁיר Mizmor shir (Psalm 30) W 14 F 50
or at end of service, recite:

Psalm for Friday (Psalm 93) W 90 F 32
קַדִּישׁ יָתוֹם Mourner’s Kaddish (some omit) W 100 F 52
\+ Psalm 104 for Rosh Ḥodesh W 90 F 34
קַדִּישׁ יָתוֹם Mourner’s Kaddish W 100 F 52

Weekday Amidah:

\+ יַעֲלֶה וְיָבוֹא Ya’aleh veyavo for Rosh Ḥodesh W 41 F 114

✕ ~~תַּחֲנוּן Taḥanun~~

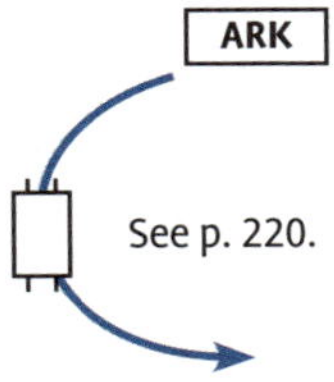

\+ חֲצִי הַלֵּל Short Hallel W 50 F 380
קַדִּישׁ שָׁלֵם Full Kaddish W 56 F 392

\+ **TORAH SERVICE** W 65 F 138
Remove **1** scroll from ark.

Torah 4 aliyot: פִּינְחָס Pineḥas
בְּמִדְבַּר Bemidbar (Numbers) 28:1–15
1 28:1–3 2 3–5 3 6–10 4 11–15 W 320 P 943

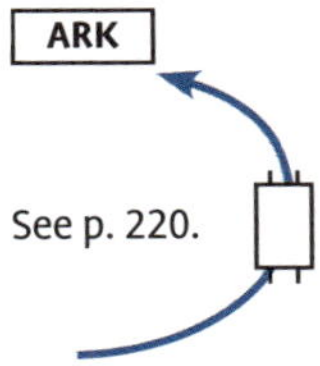

חֲצִי קַדִּישׁ Short Kaddish W 71 F 146
Open, raise, display, and wrap scroll.
Return scroll to ark. W 76 F 150

אַשְׁרֵי Ashrey W 78 F 152
✕ ~~לַמְנַצֵּחַ Lamenatse·aḥ (Psalm 20)~~
וּבָא לְצִיּוֹן Uva letsiyyon W 80 F 156

Remove and pack tefillin. (Some remove after Kaddish.)

\+ חֲצִי קַדִּישׁ Short Kaddish W 103 F 428
(If you remove tefillin here, do *not* pack but cover them, so as to begin Musaf together quickly after Kaddish.)

Kislev 5782						
					1	2
3	4	5	6	7	8	9
10	11	12	13	14	15	16
17	18	19	20	21	22	23
24	25	26	27	28	29	30

Nov | Dec 2021						
					5	6
7	8	9	10	11	12	13
14	15	16	17	18	19	20
21	22	23	24	25	26	27
28	29	30	1	2	3	4

+ Add ✕ Omit ☞ Take note!

Siddurim
L Lev Shalem for Shabbat and Festivals
S Shabbat and Festival Sim Shalom
W Weekday Sim Shalom
F Full Sim Shalom (both editions)
P Personal Edition of Full Sim Shalom

מוּסָף

+ **Rosh Ḥodesh Amidah for weekdays:** W104 F486
Weekday קְדֻשָּׁה Kedushah W105 F488
+ וּלְכַפָּרַת פָּשַׁע Ulkhapparat pasha W107 F494
Add these words only through Rosh Ḥodesh Adar Sheni.

+ קַדִּישׁ שָׁלֵם Full Kaddish W82 F158
עָלֵינוּ Aleynu W83 F160

If psalms for the day were not recited at Shaḥarit, add here:
קַדִּישׁ יָתוֹם Mourner's Kaddish (some omit) W84|100 F162|52
Psalm for Friday (Psalm 93) W90 F32
קַדִּישׁ יָתוֹם Mourner's Kaddish (some omit) W100 F52
+ Psalm 104 for Rosh Ḥodesh W90 F34

קַדִּישׁ יָתוֹם Mourner's Kaddish W84|100 F162|52

מִנְחָה

Weekday Amidah:
+ יַעֲלֶה וְיָבוֹא Ya'aleh veyavo for Rosh Ḥodesh W127 F178

✕ ~~תַּחֲנוּן Taḥanun~~ (as on all Friday afternoons)

Kislev 2 כִּסְלֵו
Sat 6 Nov

שַׁבָּת Shabbat פָּרָשַׁת תּוֹלְדֹת Parashat Toledot

Torah 7 aliyot (minimum): תּוֹלְדֹת Toledot
בְּרֵאשִׁית Bereshit (Genesis) 25:19–28:9

Annual:	1 25:19–26:5	2 26:6–12	3 26:13–22	4 26:23–29
	5 26:30–27:27°	6 27:28–28:4	7 28:5–9°	M 28:7–9°
Triennial:	1 27:28–30	2 27:31–33	3 27:34–37	4 27:38–40
	5 27:41–46	6 28:1–4	7 28:5–9°	M 28:7–9°

☞ °27:25 Note the rare ta'am (trope) מֵירְכָא־כְפוּלָה (֦):
וַיָּבֵא לוֹ יַיִן Connect לוֹ to the preceding and following words without a pause; then pause after the טִפְחָא (יַיִן), as usual.

☞ °28:9 Note the unusual use of the ta'am | מְנַח־לְגַרְמֵיהּ
(= | מְנַח־מַפְסִיק): | אֶת־מָחֲלַת

Haftarah מַלְאָכִי Mal'akhi (Malachi) 1:1–2:7

מִנְחָה

Torah 3 aliyot from וַיֵּצֵא Vayetse
בְּרֵאשִׁית Bereshit (Genesis) 28:10–22
1 28:10–12 2 13–17 3 18–22 W270 P891

Chanted also next Monday and Thursday.

Kislev 9 כִּסְלֵו
Sat 13 Nov

שַׁבָּת Shabbat פָּרָשַׁת וַיֵּצֵא Parashat Vayetse

Torah 7 aliyot (minimum): וַיֵּצֵא Vayetse
בְּרֵאשִׁית Bereshit (Genesis) 28:10–32:3

Annual:	[1] 28:10–22	[2] 29:1–17	[3] 29:18–30:13	[4] 30:14–27
	[5] 30:28–31:16	[6] 31:17–42	[7] 31:43–32:3	[M] 32:1–3
Triennial:	[1] 31:17–21	[2] 31:22–24	[3] 31:25–35	[4] 31:36–42
	[5] 31:43–45	[6] 31:46–50	[7] 31:51–32:3	[M] 32:1–3

Haftarah
Ashkenazic: הוֹשֵׁעַ Hoshe·a (Hosea) 12:13–14:10
Sephardic: הוֹשֵׁעַ Hoshe·a (Hosea) 11:7–12:12

מִנְחָה

Torah 3 aliyot from וַיִּשְׁלַח Vayishlaḥ
בְּרֵאשִׁית Bereshit (Genesis) 32:4–13
[1] 32:4–6 [2] 7–9 [3] 10–13 W271 P892

Chanted also next Monday and Thursday.

Kislev 10 כִּסְלֵו
Sat 13 Nov (night)

After Arvit if the moon is visible:
קִדּוּשׁ לְבָנָה Kiddush Levanah L286 W167 F704
For procedures and instructions, see p. 223.

Kislev 16 כִּסְלֵו
Sat 20 Nov

שַׁבָּת Shabbat פָּרָשַׁת וַיִּשְׁלַח Parashat Vayishlaḥ

Torah 7 aliyot (minimum): וַיִּשְׁלַח Vayishlaḥ
בְּרֵאשִׁית Bereshit (Genesis) 32:4–36:43

Annual:	[1] 32:4–13	[2] 32:14–30	[3] 32:31–33:5	[4] 33:6–20
	[5] 34:1–35:11	[6] 35:12–36:19°	[7] 36:20–43	[M] 36:40–43
Triennial:	[1] 35:16–26°	[2] 35:27–29	[3] 36:1–8	[4] 36:9–19
	[5] 36:20–30	[6] 36:31–39	[7] 36:40–43	[M] 36:40–43

☞ °35:22 Chant as 1 continuous verse. Do not break into 2 verses before וַיִּהְיוּ. Use the te'amim (tropes) indicated below:

וַיְהִי בִּשְׁכֹּן יִשְׂרָאֵל בָּאָרֶץ הַהִוא וַיֵּלֶךְ רְאוּבֵן וַיִּשְׁכַּב אֶת־בִּלְהָה
פִּילֶגֶשׁ אָבִיו וַיִּשְׁמַע יִשְׂרָאֵל וַיִּהְיוּ בְנֵי־יַעֲקֹב שְׁנֵים עָשָׂר׃

Haftarah עֹבַדְיָה Ovadyah (Obadiah) 1:1–21

מִנְחָה

Torah 3 aliyot from וַיֵּשֶׁב Vayeshev
בְּרֵאשִׁית Bereshit (Genesis) 37:1–11
[1] 37:1–3 [2] 4–7 [3] 8–11 W272 P893

Chanted also next Monday and Thursday.

Kislev 5782						
					1	2
3	4	5	6	7	8	9
10	11	12	13	14	15	16
17	18	19	20	21	22	23
24	25	26	27	28	29	30

Nov | Dec 2021						
					5	6
7	8	9	10	11	12	13
14	15	16	17	18	19	20
21	22	23	24	25	26	27
28	29	30 |	1	2	3	4

+ Add ✕ Omit ☞ Take note!

Siddurim
- **L** Lev Shalem for Shabbat and Festivals
- **S** Shabbat and Festival Sim Shalom
- **W** Weekday Sim Shalom
- **F** Full Sim Shalom (both editions)
- **P** Personal Edition of Full Sim Shalom

Kislev 23 כִּסְלֵו
Sat 27 Nov

שַׁבָּת Shabbat פָּרָשַׁת וַיֵּשֶׁב Parashat Vayeshev
שַׁבַּת מְבָרְכִים הַחֹדֶשׁ Shabbat Mevarekhim Haḥodesh

Torah 7 aliyot (minimum): וַיֵּשֶׁב Vayeshev
בְּרֵאשִׁית Bereshit (Genesis) 37:1–40:23

Annual:	^{1}37:1–11	^{2}37:12–22	^{3}37:23–36	^{4}38:1–30
	^{5}39:1–6	^{6}39:7–23°	^{7}40:1–23	^{M}40:20–23
Triennial:	^{1}39:1–6	^{2}39:7–10°	^{3}39:11–18	^{4}39:19–23
	^{5}40:1–8	^{6}40:9–15	^{7}40:16–23	^{M}40:20–23

☞ °39:8 Note the rare ta'am (trope) | שַׁלְשֶׁ֓לֶת (|֓): וַיְמָאֵ֓ן |

Haftarah עָמוֹס Amos (Amos) 2:6–3:8

+ **Birkat Haḥodesh:** L180 S150 F418
Announce Rosh Ḥodesh Tevet:
רֹאשׁ חֹדֶשׁ טֵבֵת יִהְיֶה בְּיוֹם שַׁבַּת קֹדֶשׁ
וּלְמָחֳרָתוֹ בְּיוֹם רִאשׁוֹן . . .
Rosh ḥodesh Tevet yihyeh beyom shabbat kodesh ulmoḥorato beyom rishon . . .
(Friday night, Saturday, and Sunday)

✕ ~~אַב הָרַחֲמִים Av Haraḥamim~~

מִנְחָה

Torah 3 aliyot from מִקֵּץ Mikkets
בְּרֵאשִׁית Bereshit (Genesis) 41:1–14
^{1}41:1–4 ^{2}5–7 ^{3}8–14 W273 P894

☞ Not chanted publicly again until next Shabbat morning.

Kislev 24 כִּסְלֵו
Sat 27 Nov

מוֹצָאֵי שַׁבָּת Motsa'ey Shabbat Conclusion of Shabbat
עֶרֶב חֲנֻכָּה Erev Ḥanukkah Day before Ḥanukkah

עַרְבִית

Arvit for weekdays L264 S281 W137 F200

Weekday Amidah:

+ אַתָּה חוֹנַנְתָּנוּ Attah ḥonantanu L272 S287 W143 F212

☞ חֲצִי קַדִּישׁ Short Kaddish L279 S292 W158 F682

☞ וִיהִי נֹעַם Vihi no'am L279 S292 W158 F684
☞ יוֹשֵׁב בְּסֵתֶר עֶלְיוֹן Yoshev beseter elyon L279 S292 W158 F684
☞ וְאַתָּה קָדוֹשׁ Ve'attah kadosh L216 S293 W159 F684

קַדִּישׁ שָׁלֵם Full Kaddish L280 S294 W160 F688

Conclude as on a usual Saturday night.

Sun 28 Nov **מִנְחָה** ✕ ~~תַּחֲנוּן Taḥanun~~

Ḥanukkah

General Instructions for Candle Lighting at Home

Candle Lighting Times

- Ḥanukkah candles must burn for at least ½ hour; on Shabbat, for 1½ hours.
- Except before and after Shabbat, light Ḥanukkah candles (solid, or oil and wicks) as soon after dark as possible.
- Before Shabbat:
  Allow time for reciting *berakhot,* lighting Ḥanukkah candles, and singing so that Shabbat candles are lit on time.
  1. Light Ḥanukkah candles *before* lighting Shabbat candles.
  2. Light Shabbat candles as usual, at least 18 minutes before sunset.
- After Shabbat:
  In the synagogue, light the Ḥanukkah candles *before* Havdalah.
  At home, light the Ḥanukkah candles *after* Havdalah.

Setup for the Ḥanukkiyyah (Menorah, Candelabra)

1. At home, place the חֲנֻכִּיָּה *ḥanukkiyyah* so that it is visible from outside.
2. Place the candles into the חֲנֻכִּיָּה.
   a. Start at the right end, placing candles from right to left.
   b. Place 1 candle the 1st night, 2 the 2nd night, and so forth.
3. Place the additional שַׁמָּשׁ *shammash* candle into its distinct location.

Lighting and Berakhot

1. Light the שַׁמָּשׁ first.
2. Before lighting the other candles, recite the בְּרָכוֹת *berakhot*: L429 S307 W192 F242

בָּרוּךְ אַתָּה יי, אֱ-לֹהֵינוּ מֶלֶךְ הָעוֹלָם, אֲשֶׁר קִדְּשָׁנוּ בְּמִצְוֹתָיו
וְצִוָּנוּ לְהַדְלִיק נֵר שֶׁל חֲנֻכָּה.

Barukh attah adonay, eloheynu melekh ha'olam,
asher kiddeshanu bemitsvotav vetsivvanu lehadlik ner shel ḥanukkah.

בָּרוּךְ אַתָּה יי, אֱ-לֹהֵינוּ מֶלֶךְ הָעוֹלָם,
שֶׁעָשָׂה נִסִּים לַאֲבוֹתֵינוּ בַּיָּמִים הָהֵם וּבַזְּמַן הַזֶּה.

Barukh attah adonay, eloheynu melekh ha'olam,
she'asah nissim la'avoteinu bayamim hahem uvazeman hazeh.

On the 1st night only, add:

בָּרוּךְ אַתָּה יי, אֱ-לֹהֵינוּ מֶלֶךְ הָעוֹלָם,
שֶׁהֶחֱיָנוּ וְקִיְּמָנוּ וְהִגִּיעָנוּ לַזְּמַן הַזֶּה.

Barukh attah adonay, eloheynu melekh ha'olam,
sheheḥeyanu vekiyyemanu vehiggi'anu lazeman hazeh.

3. Use the שַׁמָּשׁ to light the 1st (left-most) candle.
4. Proceeding left to right, use the שַׁמָּשׁ to light the remaining candles,
   - while reciting הַנֵּרוֹת הַלָּלוּ if reciting from memory.
   - before reciting הַנֵּרוֹת הַלָּלוּ if reading from a text. L429 S308 W193 F242
5. Chant מָעוֹז צוּר. L429 S308 W193 F242

Kislev 5782							Nov | Dec 2021						
					1	2						5	6
3	4	5	6	7	8	9	7	8	9	10	11	12	13
10	11	12	13	14	15	16	14	15	16	17	18	19	20
17	18	19	20	21	22	23	21	22	23	24	25	26	27
24	25	26	27	28	29	30	28	29	30 | 1	2	3	4	

+ Add ✕ Omit ☞ Take note!

Siddurim
L Lev Shalem for Shabbat and Festivals
S Shabbat and Festival Sim Shalom
W Weekday Sim Shalom
F Full Sim Shalom (both editions)
P Personal Edition of Full Sim Shalom

Special Instructions for the Synagogue

Follow the general instructions above, but observe the following modifications:

- Place the חֲנֻכִּיָּה *hanukkiyyah* along the southern wall of the room for prayer.
- Before Arvit, light the Ḥanukkah candles as described in the preceding instructions, *except:*
  1. On Friday afternoon, light the Ḥanukkah candles after Minḥah.
     If Minḥah is delayed, be sure to light the Ḥanukkah candles before Shabbat candle-lighting time (at least 18 minutes before sunset).
  2. After Shabbat, light the Ḥanukkah candles *before* Havdalah.
- Before Shaḥarit (except on Shabbat), light the candles in the manner of the previous evening, but omit the בְּרָכוֹת *berakhot.*

DURING Ḥanukkah

Every Shaḥarit and Minḥah
✕ ~~תַּחֲנוּן Taḥanun~~

Birkat Hamazon:
+ עַל הַנִּסִּים Al Hanissim for Ḥanukkah
L430 S338|345 W231|237 F758

Every Amidah:
+ עַל הַנִּסִּים Al Hanissim for Ḥanukkah

Kislev 25 כִּסְלֵו — חֲנֻכָּה Ḥanukkah — Day 1

Sun 28 Nov

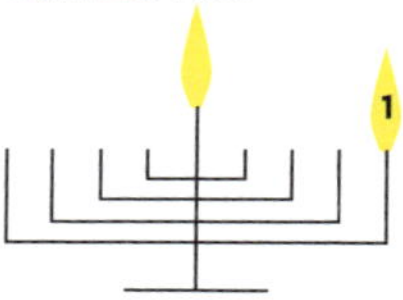

+ In the synagogue, before Arvit, light Ḥanukkah candles (see above). W192 F242

עַרְבִית

Weekday Amidah:
+ עַל הַנִּסִּים Al Hanissim for Ḥanukkah W146 F218

Conclude as on a usual weeknight.

Mon 29 Nov

+ In the synagogue, before Shaḥarit, light Ḥanukkah candles (see above). W192 F242

שַׁחֲרִית

Weekday Amidah:
+ עַל הַנִּסִּים Al Hanissim for Ḥanukkah W42 F116

✕ ~~תַּחֲנוּן Taḥanun~~

+ הַלֵּל שָׁלֵם Full Hallel W50 F380
חֲצִי קַדִּישׁ Short Kaddish W64 F390

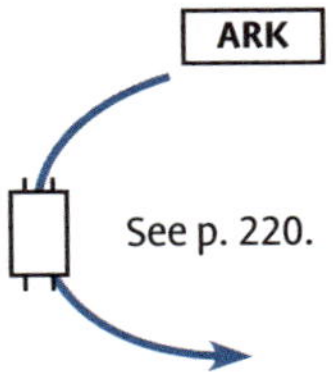

TORAH SERVICE W65 F138
Remove **1** scroll from ark.

Torah 3 aliyot from נָשֹׂא Naso
בְּמִדְבַּר Bemidbar (Numbers) 7:1–17
°1 7:1–11 °2 12–14 °3 15–17 W331 P945

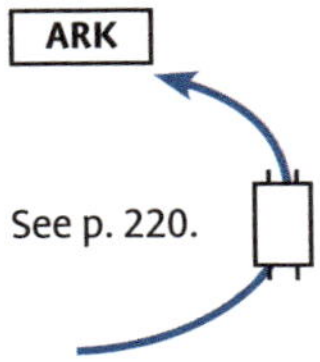

☞°These divisions are preferable to the ones in many siddurim.

חֲצִי קַדִּישׁ Short Kaddish W71 F146
Open, raise, display, and wrap scroll.
Return scroll to ark. W76 F150

אַשְׁרֵי Ashrey W78 F152
× ~~לַמְנַצֵּחַ Lamenatse-aḥ (Psalm 20)~~
וּבָא לְצִיּוֹן Uva letsiyyon W80 F156
קַדִּישׁ שָׁלֵם Full Kaddish W82 F158
עָלֵינוּ Aleynu W83 F160
קַדִּישׁ יָתוֹם Mourner's Kaddish (some omit) W84 F162

If the Psalm for the Day was not recited earlier, add here:
Psalm for Monday (Psalm 48) W86 F24
קַדִּישׁ יָתוֹם Mourner's Kaddish (some omit) W100 F52

\+ Psalm 30 for Ḥanukkah W14 F50
קַדִּישׁ יָתוֹם Mourner's Kaddish W15 F52

מִנְחָה

Weekday Amidah:
\+ עַל הַנִּסִּים Al Hanissim for Ḥanukkah W128 F180

× ~~תַּחֲנוּן Taḥanun~~

Kislev 26 כִּסְלֵו Mon 29 Nov

חֲנֻכָּה Ḥanukkah — Day 2

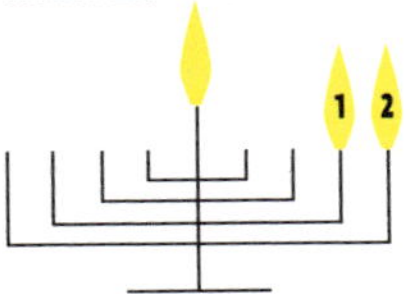

\+ In the synagogue, before Arvit, light Ḥanukkah candles (see p. 76). W192 F242

עַרְבִית

Weekday Amidah:
\+ עַל הַנִּסִּים Al Hanissim for Ḥanukkah W146 F218

Conclude as on a usual weeknight.

Kislev 5782						
					1	2
3	4	5	6	7	8	9
10	11	12	13	14	15	16
17	18	19	20	21	22	23
24	25	26	27	28	29	30

Nov | Dec 2021						
					5	6
7	8	9	10	11	12	13
14	15	16	17	18	19	20
21	22	23	24	25	26	27
28	29	30 | 1	2	3	4	

+ Add ✕ Omit ☞ Take note!

Siddurim

- **L** Lev Shalem for Shabbat and Festivals
- **S** Shabbat and Festival Sim Shalom
- **W** Weekday Sim Shalom
- **F** Full Sim Shalom (both editions)
- **P** Personal Edition of Full Sim Shalom

Tue 30 Nov

+ In the synagogue, before Shaḥarit, light Ḥanukkah candles (see p. 76). W192 F242

שַׁחֲרִית

Weekday Amidah:

+ עַל הַנִּסִּים Al Hanissim for Ḥanukkah W42 F116

✕ ~~תַּחֲנוּן Taḥanun~~

+ הַלֵּל שָׁלֵם Full Hallel W50 F380
חֲצִי קַדִּישׁ Short Kaddish W64 F390

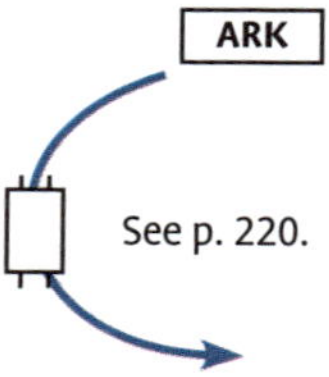

+ **TORAH SERVICE** W65 F138
Remove **1** scroll from ark.

Torah 3 aliyot from נָשֹׂא Naso
בְּמִדְבַּר Bemidbar (Numbers) 7:18–29
[1]7:18–20 [2]21–23 [3]24–29 W332 P946

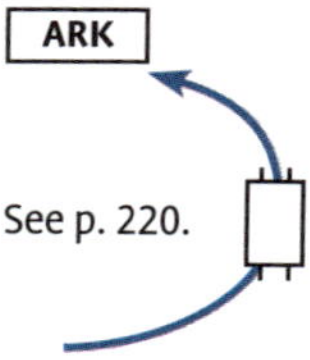

חֲצִי קַדִּישׁ Short Kaddish W71 F146
Open, raise, display, and wrap scroll.
Return scroll to ark. W76 F150

אַשְׁרֵי Ashrey W78 F152
✕ ~~לַמְנַצֵּחַ Lamenatse·aḥ (Psalm 20)~~
וּבָא לְצִיּוֹן Uva letsiyyon W80 F156
קַדִּישׁ שָׁלֵם Full Kaddish W82 F158
עָלֵינוּ Aleynu W83 F160
קַדִּישׁ יָתוֹם Mourner's Kaddish (some omit) W84 F162

If the Psalm for the Day was not recited earlier, add here:
Psalm for Tuesday (Psalm 82) W87 F26
קַדִּישׁ יָתוֹם Mourner's Kaddish (some omit) W100 F52

+ Psalm 30 for Ḥanukkah W14 F50
קַדִּישׁ יָתוֹם Mourner's Kaddish W15 F52

מִנְחָה

Weekday Amidah:

+ עַל הַנִּסִּים Al Hanissim for Ḥanukkah W128 F180

✕ ~~תַּחֲנוּן Taḥanun~~

Kislev 27 כִּסְלֵו
Tue 30 Nov

חֲנֻכָּה Ḥanukkah — Day 3

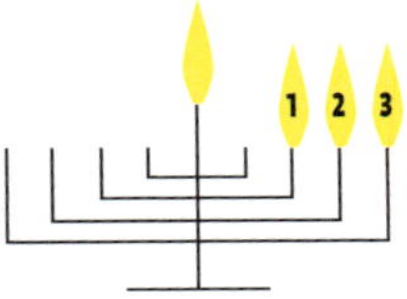

+ In the synagogue, before Arvit, light Ḥanukkah candles (see p. 76). W192 F242

עַרְבִית

Weekday Amidah:

+ עַל הַנִּסִּים Al Hanissim for Ḥanukkah W146 F218

Conclude as on a usual weeknight.

Wed 1 Dec

+ In the synagogue, before Shaḥarit, light Ḥanukkah candles (see p. 76). W192 F242

שַׁחֲרִית

Weekday Amidah:

+ עַל הַנִּסִּים Al Hanissim for Ḥanukkah W42 F116

✕ ~~תַּחֲנוּן Taḥanun~~

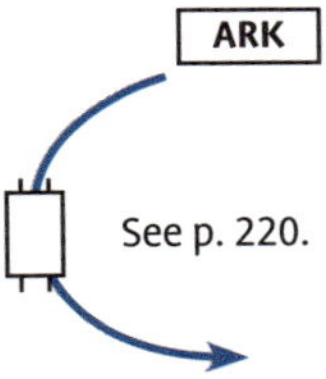

See p. 220.

+ הַלֵּל שָׁלֵם Full Hallel W50 F380
חֲצִי קַדִּישׁ Short Kaddish W64 F390

+ **TORAH SERVICE** W65 F138
Remove **1** scroll from ark.

Torah 3 aliyot from נָשֹׂא Naso
בְּמִדְבַּר Bemidbar (Numbers) 7:24–35
¹7:24–26 ²27–29 ³30–35 W332 P947

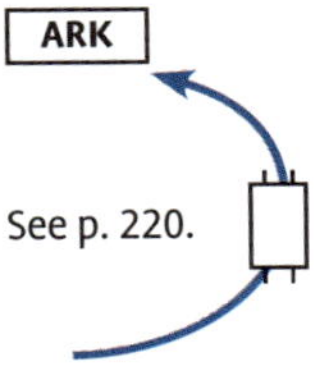

See p. 220.

חֲצִי קַדִּישׁ Short Kaddish W71 F146
Open, raise, display, and wrap scroll.
Return scroll to ark. W76 F150

אַשְׁרֵי Ashrey W78 F152
✕ ~~לַמְנַצֵּחַ Lamenatse·aḥ (Psalm 20)~~
וּבָא לְצִיּוֹן Uva letsiyyon W80 F156
קַדִּישׁ שָׁלֵם Full Kaddish W82 F158
עָלֵינוּ Aleynu W83 F160
קַדִּישׁ יָתוֹם Mourner's Kaddish (some omit) W84 F162

If the Psalm for the Day was not recited earlier, add here:
Psalm for Wednesday (Psalms 94:1–95:3) W87 F26
קַדִּישׁ יָתוֹם Mourner's Kaddish (some omit) W100 F52

+ Psalm 30 for Ḥanukkah W14 F50
קַדִּישׁ יָתוֹם Mourner's Kaddish W15 F52

מִנְחָה

Weekday Amidah:

+ עַל הַנִּסִּים Al Hanissim for Ḥanukkah W128 F180

× ~~תַּחֲנוּן Taḥanun~~

Kislev 28 כִּסְלֵו — חֲנֻכָּה Ḥanukkah — Day 4

Wed 1 Dec

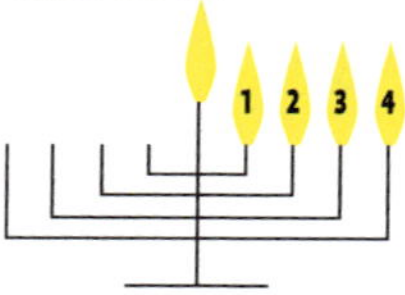

+ In the synagogue, before Arvit, light Ḥanukkah candles (see p. 76). W192 F242

עַרְבִית

Weekday Amidah:

+ עַל הַנִּסִּים Al Hanissim for Ḥanukkah W146 F218

Conclude as on a usual weeknight.

Thu 2 Dec

+ In the synagogue, before Shaḥarit, light Ḥanukkah candles (see p. 76). W192 F242

שַׁחֲרִית

Weekday Amidah:

+ עַל הַנִּסִּים Al Hanissim for Ḥanukkah W42 F116

× ~~תַּחֲנוּן Taḥanun~~

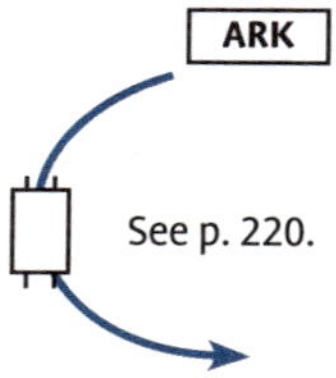

See p. 220.

+ הַלֵּל שָׁלֵם Full Hallel W50 F380
חֲצִי קַדִּישׁ Short Kaddish W64 F390

TORAH SERVICE W65 F138
Remove **1** scroll from ark.

Torah 3 aliyot from נָשֹׂא Naso
בְּמִדְבַּר Bemidbar (Numbers) 7:30–41
[1]7:30–32 [2]33–35 [3]36–41 W333 P948

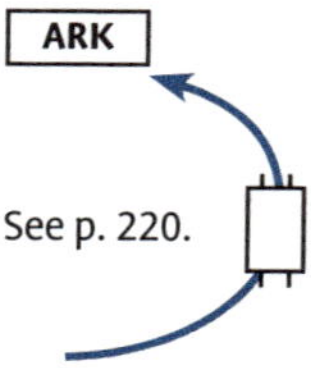

See p. 220.

חֲצִי קַדִּישׁ Short Kaddish W71 F146
Open, raise, display, and wrap scroll.
Return scroll to ark. W76 F150

אַשְׁרֵי Ashrey W78 F152
× ~~לַמְנַצֵּחַ Lamenatse·aḥ (Psalm 20)~~
וּבָא לְצִיּוֹן Uva letsiyyon W80 F156
קַדִּישׁ שָׁלֵם Full Kaddish W82 F158
עָלֵינוּ Aleynu W83 F160
קַדִּישׁ יָתוֹם Mourner's Kaddish (some omit) W84 F162

If the Psalm for the Day was not recited earlier, add here:
Psalm for Thursday (Psalm 81) W89 F30
קַדִּישׁ יָתוֹם Mourner's Kaddish (some omit) W100 F52

+ Psalm 30 for Ḥanukkah W14 F50
קַדִּישׁ יָתוֹם Mourner's Kaddish W15 F52

מִנְחָה

Weekday Amidah:
+ עַל הַנִּסִּים Al Hanissim for Ḥanukkah W128 F180

✕ ~~תַּחֲנוּן Taḥanun~~

Kislev 29 כִּסְלֵו — חֲנֻכָּה Ḥanukkah — Day 5

Thu 2 Dec

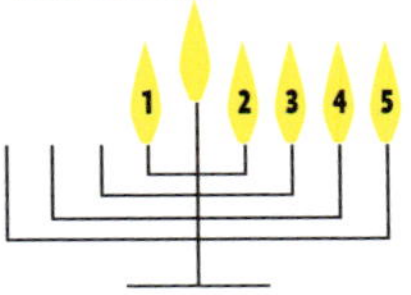

+ In the synagogue, before Arvit, light Ḥanukkah candles (see p. 76). W192 F242

עַרְבִית

Weekday Amidah:
+ עַל הַנִּסִּים Al Hanissim for Ḥanukkah W146 F218

Conclude as on a usual weeknight.

Fri 3 Dec

+ In the synagogue, before Shaḥarit, light Ḥanukkah candles (see p. 76). W192 F242

שַׁחֲרִית

Weekday Amidah:
+ עַל הַנִּסִּים Al Hanissim for Ḥanukkah W42 F116

✕ ~~תַּחֲנוּן Taḥanun~~

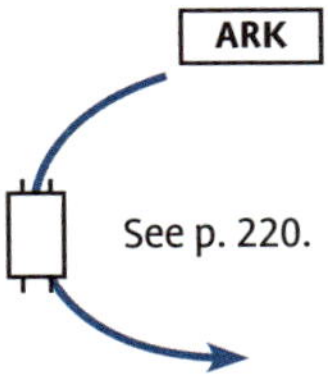

+ הַלֵּל שָׁלֵם Full Hallel W50 F380
חֲצִי קַדִּישׁ Short Kaddish W64 F390

+ **TORAH SERVICE** W65 F138
Remove **1** scroll from ark.

Torah 3 aliyot from נָשֹׂא Naso
בְּמִדְבַּר Bemidbar (Numbers) 7:36–47
[1]7:36–38 [2]39–41 [3]42–47 W333 P949

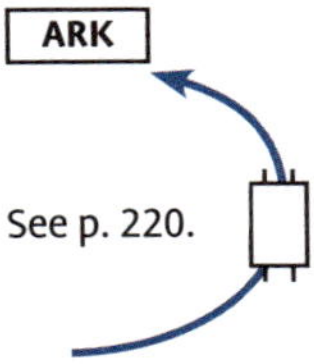

חֲצִי קַדִּישׁ Short Kaddish W71 F146
Open, raise, display, and wrap scroll.
Return scroll to ark. W76 F150

אַשְׁרֵי Ashrey W78 F152
✕ ~~לַמְנַצֵּחַ Lamenatse·aḥ (Psalm 20)~~
וּבָא לְצִיּוֹן Uva letsiyyon W80 F156

חֲנֻכָּה Ḥanukkah

Kislev 5782						
					1	2
3	4	5	6	7	8	9
10	11	12	13	14	15	16
17	18	19	20	21	22	23
24	25	26	27	28	29	30

Nov | Dec 2021						
					5	6
7	8	9	10	11	12	13
14	15	16	17	18	19	20
21	22	23	24	25	26	27
28	29	30 | 1	2	3	4	

+ Add ✕ Omit ☞ Take note!

Siddurim
- **L** Lev Shalem for Shabbat and Festivals
- **S** Shabbat and Festival Sim Shalom
- **W** Weekday Sim Shalom
- **F** Full Sim Shalom (both editions)
- **P** Personal Edition of Full Sim Shalom

קַדִּישׁ שָׁלֵם Full Kaddish W82 F158
עָלֵינוּ Aleynu W83 F160
קַדִּישׁ יָתוֹם Mourner's Kaddish (some omit) W84 F162

If the Psalm for the Day was not recited earlier, add here:
Psalm for Friday (Psalm 93) W90 F32
קַדִּישׁ יָתוֹם Mourner's Kaddish (some omit) W100 F52

+ Psalm 30 for Ḥanukkah W14 F50
קַדִּישׁ יָתוֹם Mourner's Kaddish W15 F52

מִנְחָה

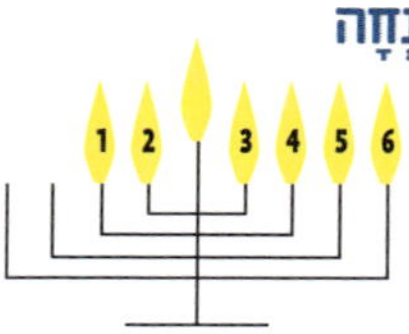

Weekday Amidah:
+ עַל הַנִּסִּים Al Hanissim for Ḥanukkah W128 F180

✕ ~~תַּחֲנוּן Taḥanun~~

At home + Before lighting Shabbat candles, light Ḥanukkah candles (see p. 75). L429 S307 W192 F242

In the synagogue + Before Kabbalat Shabbat, light Ḥanukkah candles (see p. 76). L429 S307 W192 F242

Kislev 30 כִּסְלֵו
Fri 3 Dec (evening)

שַׁבָּת Shabbat פָּרָשַׁת מִקֵּץ Parashat Mikkets
רֹאשׁ חֹדֶשׁ טֵבֵת Rosh Ḥodesh Tevet — Day 1
Ḥanukkah — Day 6

For determining the *yortsayt* of a death on 30 Kislev, see p. 224.

☞ Ensure that Ḥanukkah candles are lit before Shabbat. See blue boxes, pp. 75–76.

DURING Rosh Ḥodesh **Birkat Hamazon:**
+ יַעֲלֶה וְיָבוֹא Ya'aleh veyavo for Rosh Ḥodesh L90|95 S340|347 W233|239 F762|780
+ הָרַחֲמָן Haraḥaman for Rosh Ḥodesh L92|96 S343|348 W235|240 F768

קַבָּלַת שַׁבָּת ☞ Recite Kabbalat Shabbat as on a usual Shabbat. L6 S15 F254

עַרְבִית

Shabbat Amidah:
+ יַעֲלֶה וְיָבוֹא Ya'aleh veyavo for Rosh Ḥodesh L50 S36 F298
+ עַל הַנִּסִּים Al Hanissim for Ḥanukkah L430 S37 F300

Continue Shabbat Arvit service as usual.

Sat 4 Dec שַׁחֲרִית

Before מִזְמוֹר שִׁיר Mizmor shir (Psalm 30) or after Aleynu, recite: L120 S81 F50

Psalm for Shabbat (Psalm 92) L112 S72 F32
קַדִּישׁ יָתוֹם Mourner's Kaddish (some omit) L121 S82 F52
\+ Psalm 104 for Rosh Ḥodesh L114 S78 F34
קַדִּישׁ יָתוֹם Mourner's Kaddish L121 S82 F52

Shabbat Amidah:

\+ יַעֲלֶה וְיָבוֹא Ya'aleh veyavo for Rosh Ḥodesh L163 S118 F360
\+ עַל הַנִּסִּים Al Hanissim for Ḥanukkah L430 S119 F362

\+ הַלֵּל שָׁלֵם Full Hallel L316 S133 F380
קַדִּישׁ שָׁלֵם Full Kaddish L167 S138 F392

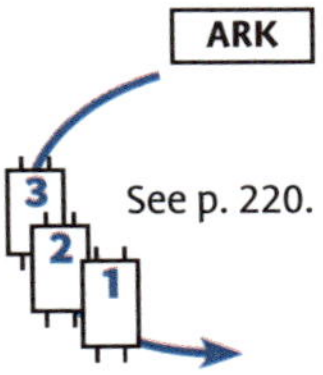

See p. 220.

TORAH SERVICE L168 S139 F394

☞ Remove **3** scrolls from ark in the order they will be read.

1st scroll 6 aliyot (minimum): מִקֵּץ Mikkets
בְּרֵאשִׁית Bereshit (Genesis) 41:1–44:17

Annual:	1 41:1–14	2 41:15–38	3 41:39–52	4 41:53–42:18
	5 42:19–43:15	6 43:16–44:17		
Triennial:	1 43:16–18	2 43:19–25	3 43:26–29	4 43:30–34
	5 44:1–6	6 44:7–17		

Place 2nd scroll on table next to 1st scroll.
☞ Do not recite חֲצִי קַדִּישׁ Short Kaddish here.
Open, raise, display, and wrap 1st scroll.

\+ **2nd scroll** 7th aliyah from פִּינְחָס Pineḥas
7 בְּמִדְבַּר Bemidbar (Numbers) 28:9–15

Place 3rd scroll on table next to 2nd scroll.
Place or hold 1st scroll near other scrolls at table.
(Some do not return 1st scroll to table.)
חֲצִי קַדִּישׁ Short Kaddish L174 S146 F408
Open, raise, display, and wrap 2nd scroll.

3rd scroll Maftir aliyah from נָשֹׂא Naso
M בְּמִדְבַּר Bemidbar (Numbers) 7:42–47°

☞ °Read only these 6 verses, not 12 as on most days of Ḥanukkah.

Open, raise, display, and wrap 3rd scroll.

Kislev 5782

					1	2
3	4	5	6	7	8	9
10	11	12	13	14	15	16
17	18	19	20	21	22	23
24	25	26	27	28	29	30

Nov | Dec 2021

					5	6
7	8	9	10	11	12	13
14	15	16	17	18	19	20
21	22	23	24	25	26	27
28	29	30	1	2	3	4

+ Add ✕ Omit ☞ Take note!

Siddurim

L Lev Shalem for Shabbat and Festivals
S Shabbat and Festival Sim Shalom
W Weekday Sim Shalom
F Full Sim Shalom (both editions)
P Personal Edition of Full Sim Shalom

☞ **Haftarah** for Shabbat Ḥanukkah
זְכַרְיָה Zekharyah (Zechariah) 2:14–4:7

☞ Most Ashkenazic congregations do **not** add verses from other haftarot. Sephardic congregations append the first and last verses of the Shabbat Rosh Ḥodesh and Shabbat Maḥar Ḥodesh haftarot.

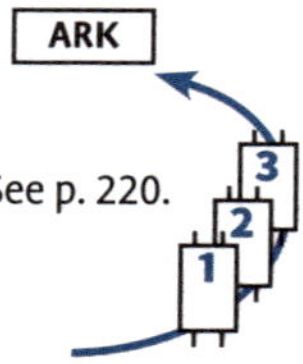

See p. 220.

✕ ~~אַב הָרַחֲמִים Av Haraḥamim~~

אַשְׁרֵי Ashrey L181 S151 F420
Return scrolls to ark in reverse order. L183 S153 F422

חֲצִי קָדִישׁ Short Kaddish L184 S155 F428

מוּסָף

Rosh Hodesh Amidah for Shabbat: L193 S166 F486
Shabbat Kedushah L195 S167 F490
Continuation of Amidah L196 S168 F496
+ וּלְכַפָּרַת פָּשַׁע Ulkhapparat pasha L199 S169 F498
Add these words only through Rosh Ḥodesh Adar Sheni.

+ עַל הַנִּסִּים Al Hanissim for Ḥanukkah L430 S176 F438

קַדִּישׁ שָׁלֵם Full Kaddish L203 S181 F506
אֵין כֵּא·לֹהֵינוּ Eyn keloheynu L204 S182 F508
עָלֵינוּ Aleynu L205 S183 F510
קַדִּישׁ יָתוֹם Mourner's Kaddish (some omit) L207 S184 F512

If the Psalm for the Day was not recited at Shaḥarit, add here:
Psalm for Shabbat (Psalm 92) L112 S72 F32
קַדִּישׁ יָתוֹם Mourner's Kaddish (some omit) L121 S82 F52
+ Psalm 104 for Rosh Hodesh L114 S78 F34
קַדִּישׁ יָתוֹם Mourner's Kaddish (some omit) L121 S82 F52

+ Psalm 30 for Ḥanukkah L120 S81 F50
קַדִּישׁ יָתוֹם Mourner's Kaddish L121 S82 F52

מִנְחָה

Torah 3 aliyot from וַיִּגַּשׁ Vayiggash
בְּרֵאשִׁית Bereshit (Genesis) 44:18–30
1 44:18–20 2 21–24 3 25–30 W274 P895

Chanted also next Thursday.

Shabbat Amidah:
+ יַעֲלֶה וְיָבוֹא Ya'aleh veyavo for Rosh Hodesh L227 S237 F580
+ עַל הַנִּסִּים Al Hanissim for Ḥanukkah L430 S238 F582

✕ ~~צִדְקָתְךָ צֶדֶק Tsidkatekha tsedek~~

חֲנֻכָּה Hanukkah

DURING Ḥanukkah

Continue:

Every Shaḥarit and Minḥah

✕ ~~תַּחֲנוּן Taḥanun~~

Birkat Hamazon:

+ עַל הַנִּסִּים Al Hanissim for Ḥanukkah L430 S338|345 W231|237 F758

Every Amidah:

+ עַל הַנִּסִּים Al Hanissim for Ḥanukkah

Tevet 1 טֵבֵת
Sat 4 Dec (evening)

רֹאשׁ חֹדֶשׁ טֵבֵת Rosh Ḥodesh Tevet — Day 2
חֲנֻכָּה Ḥanukkah — Day 7
מוֹצָאֵי שַׁבָּת Motsa'ey Shabbat Conclusion of Shabbat

DURING Rosh Ḥodesh

Birkat Hamazon:

+ יַעֲלֶה וְיָבוֹא Ya'aleh veyavo for Rosh Ḥodesh L90|95 S340|347 W233|239 F762|780

+ הָרַחֲמָן Haraḥaman for Rosh Ḥodesh L92|96 S343|348 W235|240 F768

עַרְבִית

Arvit for weekdays L264 S281 W137 F200

Weekday Amidah:

+ אַתָּה חוֹנַנְתָּנוּ Attah ḥonantanu L272 S287 W143 F212
+ יַעֲלֶה וְיָבוֹא Ya'aleh veyavo for Rosh Ḥodesh L277 S289 W145 F216
+ עַל הַנִּסִּים Al Hanissim for Ḥanukkah L430 S290 W146 F218

☞ חֲצִי קַדִּישׁ Short Kaddish L269 S292 W158 F682

☞ וִיהִי נֹעַם Vihi no'am L279 S292 W158 F684
☞ יוֹשֵׁב בְּסֵתֶר עֶלְיוֹן Yoshev beseter elyon L279 S292 W158 F684
☞ וְאַתָּה קָדוֹשׁ Ve'attah kadosh L216 S293 W159 F684

קַדִּישׁ שָׁלֵם Full Kaddish L280 S294 W160 F688

Those who recite הַבְדָּלָה Havdalah here:
First light Ḥanukkah candles (see p. 76), L429 S307 W192 F242
then recite הַבְדָּלָה. L283 S299 W165 F700

עָלֵינוּ Aleynu L281 S297 W163 F696
קַדִּישׁ יָתוֹם Mourner's Kaddish L121 S82 W15 F51

Tevet 5782

1	2	3	4	5	6	7
8	9	10	11	12	13	14
15	16	17	18	19	20	21
22	23	24	25	26	27	28
29						

Dec 2021 | Jan 2022

5	6	7	8	9	10	11
12	13	14	15	16	17	18
19	20	21	22	23	24	25
26	27	28	29	30	31	1
2						

+ Add ✕ Omit ☞ Take note!

Siddurim
- **L** Lev Shalem for Shabbat and Festivals
- **S** Shabbat and Festival Sim Shalom
- **W** Weekday Sim Shalom
- **F** Full Sim Shalom (both editions)
- **P** Personal Edition of Full Sim Shalom

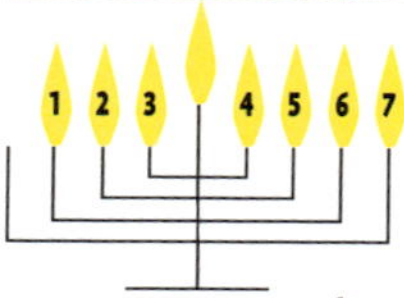

\+ Light Ḥanukkah candles (see p. 76). L429 S307 W192 F242
הַבְדָּלָה Havdalah L283 S299 W165 F700

At home ☞ הַבְדָּלָה Havdalah L283 S299 W165 F700
\+ Light Ḥanukkah candles (see p. 75). L429 S307 W192 F242

Sun 5 Dec

\+ In the synagogue, before Shaḥarit, light Ḥanukkah candles (see p. 76). W192 F242

שַׁחֲרִית

Before מִזְמוֹר שִׁיר Mizmor shir (Psalm 30) W14 F50
or at end of service, recite:
Psalm for Sunday (Psalm 24) W85 F22
קַדִּישׁ יָתוֹם Mourner's Kaddish (some omit) W100 F52
\+ Psalm 104 for Rosh Ḥodesh W90 F34
קַדִּישׁ יָתוֹם Mourner's Kaddish W100 F52

Weekday Amidah:
\+ יַעֲלֶה וְיָבוֹא Ya'aleh veyavo for Rosh Ḥodesh W41 F114
\+ עַל הַנִּסִּים Al Hanissim for Ḥanukkah W42 F116

✕ ~~תַּחֲנוּן Taḥanun~~

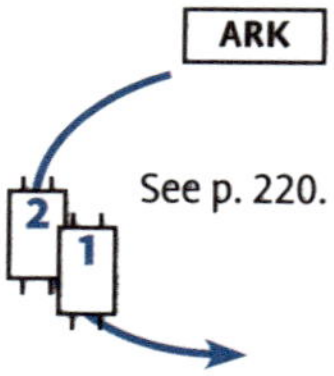

See p. 220.

\+ הַלֵּל שָׁלֵם Full Hallel W50 F380
קַדִּישׁ שָׁלֵם Full Kaddish W56 F392

\+ **TORAH SERVICE** W65 F138
Remove **2** scrolls from ark in the order they will be read.

1st scroll 3 aliyot from פִּינְחָס Pineḥas
בְּמִדְבַּר Bemidbar (Numbers) 28:1–15
1 28:1–5 2 6–10 3 11–15 W336 P943

Place 2nd scroll on table next to 1st scroll.
☞ Do not recite חֲצִי קַדִּישׁ Short Kaddish here.

Open, raise, display, and wrap 1st scroll.

2nd scroll 1 aliyah from נָשֹׂא Naso
4 בְּמִדְבַּר Bemidbar (Numbers) 7:48–53° W333 P951
☞ °Chant only these 6 verses, not 12 as on most days of Ḥanukkah.

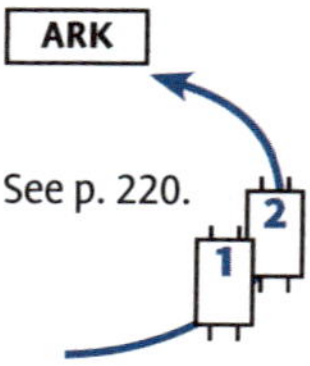

See p. 220.

Place 1st scroll on table next to 2nd scroll.
חֲצִי קַדִּישׁ Short Kaddish W71 F146
Open, raise, display, and wrap 2nd scroll.
Return scrolls to ark in reverse order. W76 F150

אַשְׁרֵי Ashrey W78 F152
✕ ~~לַמְנַצֵּחַ Lamenatse·aḥ (Psalm 20)~~
וּבָא לְצִיּוֹן Uva letsiyyon W80 F156

Remove and pack tefillin. (Some remove after Kaddish.)

\+ חֲצִי קַדִּישׁ Short Kaddish W103 F428

(If you remove tefillin here, do *not* pack but cover them, so as to begin Musaf together quickly after Kaddish.)

מוּסָף

\+ **Rosh Ḥodesh Amidah for weekdays:** W104 F486
Weekday קְדֻשָּׁה Kedushah W105 F488
\+ וּלְכַפָּרַת פָּשַׁע Ulkhapparat pasha W107 F494
Add these words only through Rosh Ḥodesh Adar Sheni.
\+ עַל הַנִּסִּים Al Hanissim for Ḥanukkah W108 F500

\+ קַדִּישׁ שָׁלֵם Full Kaddish W82 F158
עָלֵינוּ Aleynu W83 F160
קַדִּישׁ יָתוֹם Mourner's Kaddish (some omit) W84 F162

If psalms for the day were not recited at Shaḥarit, add here:
Psalm for Sunday (Psalm 24) W85 F22
קַדִּישׁ יָתוֹם Mourner's Kaddish (some omit) W100 F52
\+ Psalm 104 for Rosh Ḥodesh W90 F34
קַדִּישׁ יָתוֹם Mourner's Kaddish (some omit) W100 F52

\+ Psalm 30 for Ḥanukkah W14 F50
קַדִּישׁ יָתוֹם Mourner's Kaddish W15 F52

מִנְחָה

Weekday Amidah:
\+ יַעֲלֶה וְיָבוֹא Ya'aleh veyavo for Rosh Ḥodesh W127 F178
\+ עַל הַנִּסִּים Al Hanissim for Ḥanukkah W128 F180

✕ ~~תַּחֲנוּן Taḥanun~~

Tevet 2 טֵבֵת
Sun 5 Dec

חֲנֻכָּה Ḥanukkah — Day 8

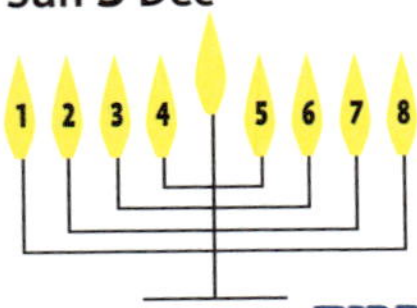

\+ In the synagogue, before Arvit, light Ḥanukkah candles (see p. 76). W192 F242

עַרְבִית

Weekday Amidah:
\+ עַל הַנִּסִּים Al Hanissim for Ḥanukkah W146 F218

Conclude as on a usual weeknight.

חֲנֻכָּה Ḥanukkah

Tevet 5782						
1	2	3	4	5	6	7
8	9	10	11	12	13	14
15	16	17	18	19	20	21
22	23	24	25	26	27	28
29						

Dec 2021 | Jan 2022						
5	6	7	8	9	10	11
12	13	14	15	16	17	18
19	20	21	22	23	24	25
26	27	28	29	30	31	1
2						

+ Add ✕ Omit ☞ Take note!

Siddurim

L Lev Shalem for Shabbat and Festivals
S Shabbat and Festival Sim Shalom
W Weekday Sim Shalom
F Full Sim Shalom (both editions)
P Personal Edition of Full Sim Shalom

Mon 6 Dec

+ In the synagogue, before Shaharit, light Ḥanukkah candles (see p. 76). W192 F242

שַׁחֲרִית

Weekday Amidah:
+ עַל הַנִּסִּים Al Hanissim for Ḥanukkah W42 F116

✕ ~~תַּחֲנוּן Taḥanun~~

+ הַלֵּל שָׁלֵם Full Hallel W50 F380
חֲצִי קַדִּישׁ Short Kaddish W64 F390

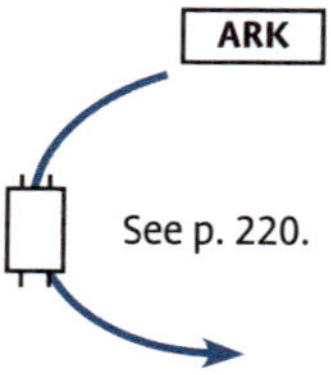

TORAH SERVICE W65 F138
Remove **1** scroll from ark.

☞ **Torah** 3 aliyot from נָשֹׂא Naso + בְּהַעֲלֹתְךָ Beha'alotekha
בְּמִדְבַּר Bemidbar (Numbers) 7:54–8:4
[1]7:54–56 [2]57–59 [3]7:60–8:4 W334–35 P952–54 + 919

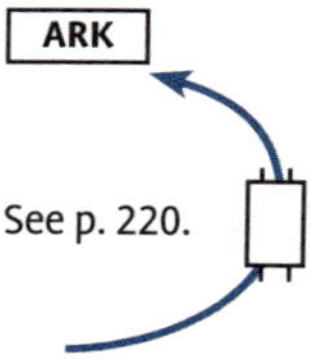

חֲצִי קַדִּישׁ Short Kaddish W71 F146
Open, raise, display, and wrap scroll.
Return scroll to ark. W76 F150

אַשְׁרֵי Ashrey W78 F152
✕ ~~לַמְנַצֵּחַ Lamenatse·aḥ (Psalm 20)~~
וּבָא לְצִיּוֹן Uva letsiyyon W80 F156
קַדִּישׁ שָׁלֵם Full Kaddish W82 F158
עָלֵינוּ Aleynu W83 F160
קַדִּישׁ יָתוֹם Mourner's Kaddish (some omit) W84 F162

If the Psalm for the Day was not recited earlier, add here:
Psalm for Monday (Psalm 48) W86 F24
קַדִּישׁ יָתוֹם Mourner's Kaddish (some omit) W100 F52

+ Psalm 30 for Ḥanukkah W14 F50
קַדִּישׁ יָתוֹם Mourner's Kaddish W15 F52

מִנְחָה

Weekday Amidah:
+ עַל הַנִּסִּים Al Hanissim for Ḥanukkah W128 F180

✕ ~~תַּחֲנוּן Taḥanun~~

Tevet 7 טֵבֵת
Sat 11 Dec

שַׁבָּת Shabbat פָּרָשַׁת וַיִּגַּשׁ Parashat Vayiggash

Torah 7 aliyot (minimum): **וַיִּגַּשׁ** Vayiggash
בְּרֵאשִׁית Bereshit (Genesis) 44:18–47:27

Annual:	[1]44:18–30	[2]44:31–45:7	[3]45:8–18	[4]45:19–27
	[5]45:28–46:27	[6]46:28–47:10	[7]47:11–27	[M]47:25–27
Triennial:	[1]46:28–30	[2]46:31–34	[3]47:1–6	[4]47:7–10
	[5]47:11–19	[6]47:20–22	[7]47:23–27	[M]47:25–27

Haftarah יְחֶזְקֵאל Yeḥezkel (Ezekiel) 37:15–28

מִנְחָה

Torah 3 aliyot from **וַיְחִי** Vayḥi
בְּרֵאשִׁית Bereshit (Genesis) 47:28–48:9
[1]47:28–31 [2]48:1–3 [3]48:4–9 W275 P896

Chanted also next Monday and Thursday.

Tevet 8 טֵבֵת
Sat 11 Dec (night)

After Arvit if the moon is visible:
קִדּוּשׁ לְבָנָה Kiddush Levanah L286 W167 F704
For procedures and instructions, see p. 223.

Tevet 10 טֵבֵת
Mon 13 Dec (evening)

עֲשָׂרָה בְּטֵבֵת Asarah Betevet
10th of Tevet (communal fast, begins Tuesday at dawn)

עַרְבִית Weekday Arvit as usual S281 W137 F200

☞ If you have not yet recited Kiddush Levanah for Tevet, do not recite until Tuesday night after Arvit.

Asarah Betevet

Asarah Betevet marks the beginning of the siege of Jerusalem in 587 B.C.E. by Nebuchadnezzar of Babylonia. The siege ended 18 months later with the destruction of Jerusalem and the 1st Temple.

- This is a minor fast day, so called because the fast does not begin until dawn.
- The fast (from both eating and drinking) lasts until dark (at least 25 minutes after sunset).
- *Sheliḥey tsibbur,* Torah readers, and those called for *aliyot* should be fasting.
- The preferred fast-day procedures apply when at least 6 of those who are counted for a *minyan* are fasting.
- If it is ascertained (without causing embarrassment) that fewer than 6 are fasting, follow the procedures printed in gray and marked with ✦.

Following the suggestion of the Chief Rabbinate in Israel, some observe Asarah Betevet as a Holocaust memorial day by:

- Adding a special memorial prayer at the morning Torah service for those killed in the Holocaust.
  The text of the memorial prayer of the Chief Rabbinate, with translation and explanation, can be found at www.milesbcohen.com/LuahResources.
- Designating a Mourner's Kaddish at the end of the service as a קַדִּישׁ כְּלָלִי *kaddish kelali,* a general Mourner's Kaddish (recited by those having lost one or both parents).

Tue 14 Dec **שַׁחֲרִית**

Silent weekday Amidah:
Do not add עֲנֵנוּ Anenu.

Repetition of the weekday Amidah:

6 or more fasting + עֲנֵנוּ Anenu, before רְפָאֵנוּ Refa'enu W38 F110

Fewer than 6 fasting ✦ Add עֲנֵנוּ Anenu in שׁוֹמֵעַ תְּפִלָּה Shome·a tefillah. Replace תַּעֲנִיתֵנוּ ta'anitenu (6th word) with הַתַּעֲנִית הַזֶּה hata'anit hazeh. W38 F110

6 or more fasting + אָבִינוּ מַלְכֵּנוּ Avinu malkenu W57 F124

Fewer than 6 fasting ✦ Those fasting recite אָבִינוּ מַלְכֵּנוּ individually.

☞ תַּחֲנוּן Taḥanun (וַיֹּאמֶר דָּוִד Vayomer david) W62 F132
חֲצִי קַדִּישׁ Short Kaddish W64 F136

Fewer than 6 fasting ✦ Omit the entire Torah service.
Continue with אַשְׁרֵי Ashrey.

6 or more fasting + **TORAH SERVICE** W65 F138

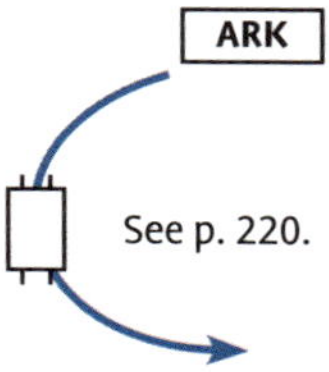

Remove **1** scroll from ark.

Torah 3 aliyot from כִּי תִשָּׂא Ki tissa
שְׁמוֹת Shemot (Exodus) 32:11–14, 34:1–10
¹32:11–14° ²34:1–3 ³34:4–10° W341 P979

☞ °At each of the 3 passages indicated below, follow this procedure:

1. The reader pauses before the indicated text.
2. The congregation recites the indicated text.
3. Afterward, the reader chants the indicated text in the manner of the cantillation of High Holiday Torah reading.

32:12 שׁוּב מֵחֲרוֹן אַפֶּךָ וְהִנָּחֵם עַל־הָרָעָה לְעַמֶּךָ׃

34:6–7 יי | יי אֵ-ל רַחוּם וְחַנּוּן אֶרֶךְ אַפַּיִם וְרַב־חֶסֶד וֶאֱמֶת׃
נֹצֵר חֶסֶד לָאֲלָפִים נֹשֵׂא עָוֺן וָפֶשַׁע וְחַטָּאָה וְנַקֵּה

34:9 וְסָלַחְתָּ לַעֲוֺנֵנוּ וּלְחַטָּאתֵנוּ | וּנְחַלְתָּנוּ׃

To preserve the sense of this passage, maintain the appropriate pause after the טִפְחָא (וּלְחַטָּאתֵנוּ).

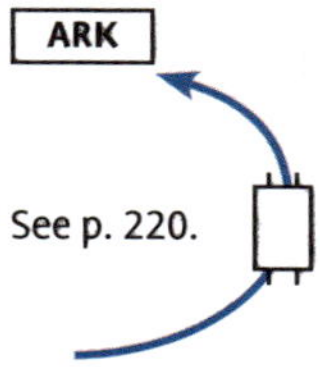

חֲצִי קַדִּישׁ Short Kaddish W71 F146
Open, raise, display, and wrap scroll.
Return scroll to ark. W76 F150

All minyanim **אַשְׁרֵי Ashrey** W78 F152
☞ **לַמְנַצֵּחַ Lamenatse·aḥ (Psalm 20)** W79 F154
Conclude the service in the usual manner.

מִנְחָה **אַשְׁרֵי Ashrey** W120 F164
חֲצִי קַדִּישׁ Short Kaddish W121 F166

Fewer than 6 fasting ✦ Omit the entire Torah service.
Continue with silent Amidah.

6 or more fasting + **TORAH SERVICE** W65 F138

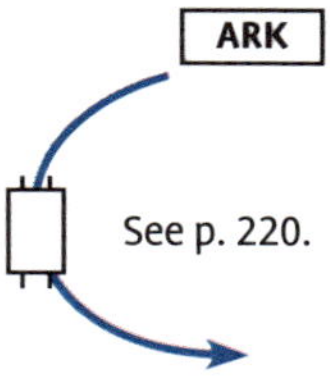

Remove **1** scroll from ark.

Torah 3 aliyot from כִּי תִשָּׂא Ki tissa
שְׁמוֹת Shemot (Exodus) 32:11–14, 34:1–10
¹32:11–14° ²34:1–3 ᴹ34:4–10° W341 P979

☞ °Chant as for the morning fast-day reading (above).

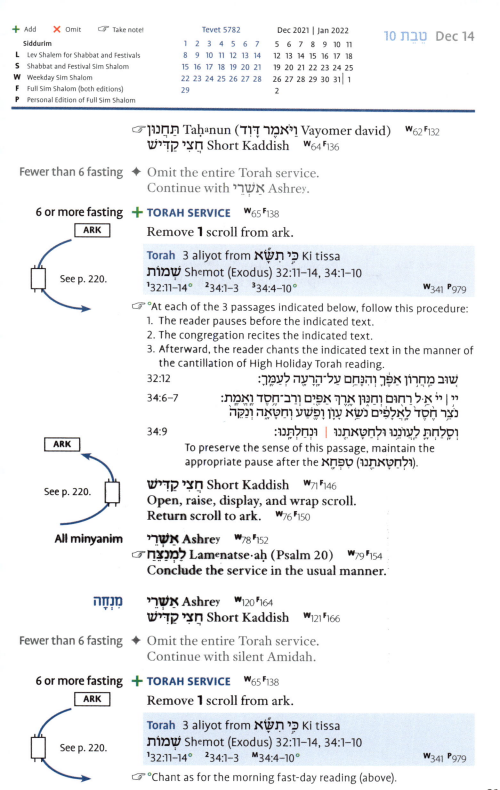

☞ Do not recite חֲצִי קַדִּישׁ Short Kaddish after maftir aliyah.
Open, raise, display, and wrap scroll.

Recite the בְּרָכָה berakhah before the haftarah. W74 F410 P989

Haftarah יְשַׁעְיָהוּ Yesha'yahu (Isaiah) 55:6–56:8 W342 P980

Recite the 3 concluding haftarah blessings, through מָגֵן דָּוִד Magen david. W74 F410 P989.

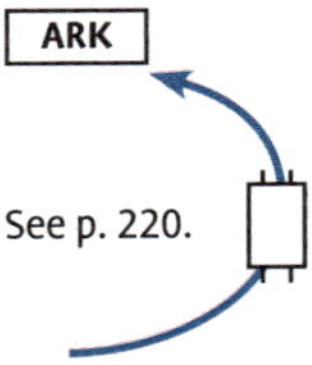

See p. 220.

Return scroll to ark. W76 F150
חֲצִי קַדִּישׁ Short Kaddish W121 F166

All minyanim — **Silent weekday Amidah:**
If fasting + עֲנֵנוּ Anenu, in שׁוֹמֵעַ תְּפִלָּה Shome·a tefillah W127 F178
All ✕ ~~שָׁלוֹם רָב Shalom rav~~
+ שִׂים שָׁלוֹם Sim shalom W131 F184

Repetition of the weekday Amidah:
6 or more fasting + עֲנֵנוּ Anenu, before רְפָאֵנוּ Refa'enu W124 F172
Fewer than 6 fasting ✦ Add עֲנֵנוּ Anenu in שׁוֹמֵעַ תְּפִלָּה Shome·a tefillah. Replace תַּעֲנִיתֵנוּ ta'anitenu (6th word) with הַתַּעֲנִית הַזֶּה hata'anit hazeh. W127 F172
All minyanim + בִּרְכַּת כֹּהֲנִים Birkat kohanim W131 F184
✕ ~~שָׁלוֹם רָב Shalom rav~~
+ שִׂים שָׁלוֹם Sim shalom W131 F184

6 or more fasting + אָבִינוּ מַלְכֵּנוּ Avinu malkenu W57 F188
Fewer than 6 fasting ✦ Those fasting recite אָבִינוּ מַלְכֵּנוּ individually.

☞ תַּחֲנוּן Taḥanun W132 F192

קַדִּישׁ שָׁלֵם Full Kaddish W134 F194
עָלֵינוּ Aleynu W135 F196
קַדִּישׁ יָתוֹם Mourner's Kaddish W136 F198

☞ If you have not yet recited Kiddush Levanah for Tevet, recite it after Arvit at the end of the fast.

Tevet 14 טֵבֵת
Sat 18 Dec

שַׁבָּת Shabbat פָּרָשַׁת וַיְחִי Parashat Vayḥi

Torah 7 aliyot (minimum): וַיְחִי Vayḥi
בְּרֵאשִׁית Bereshit (Genesis) 47:28–50:26

Annual:	1 47:28–48:9	2 48:10–16	3 48:17–22	4 49:1–18
	5 49:19–26	6 49:27–50:20	7 50:21–26 ▮	M 50:23–26
Triennial:	1 49:27–30	2 49:31–33	3 50:1–6	4 50:7–9
	5 50:10–14	6 50:15–20	7 50:21–26 ▮	M 50:23–26

▮ חזק When the Torah reader concludes a book of the Torah:

1. Close the Torah scroll.
2. **For Oleh:** Congregation chants חֲזַק חֲזַק וְנִתְחַזֵּק ḥazak ḥazak venitḥazzek; oleh remains silent.
   For Olah: Congregation chants חִזְקִי חִזְקִי וְנִתְחַזֵּק ḥizki ḥizki venitḥazzek; olah remains silent.
3. Torah reader repeats congregation's words (oleh/olah remains silent; if Torah reader is the oleh/olah, omit this repetition).
4. Open the Torah scroll.
5. The oleh/olah kisses the Torah scroll, closes it, and continues with the usual concluding berakhah.

Haftarah מְלָכִים א׳ 1 Melakhim (1 Kings) 2:1–12

מִנְחָה

Torah 3 aliyot from שְׁמוֹת Shemot
שְׁמוֹת Shemot (Exodus) 1:1–17
1 1:1–7 2 8–12 3 13–17 W276 P897

Chanted also next Monday and Thursday.

Tevet 21 טֵבֵת
Sat 25 Dec

שַׁבָּת Shabbat פָּרָשַׁת שְׁמוֹת Parashat Shemot

Torah 7 aliyot (minimum): שְׁמוֹת Shemot
שְׁמוֹת Shemot (Exodus) 1:1–6:1

Annual:	1 1:1–17	2 1:18–2:10	3 2:11–25	4 3:1–15
	5 3:16–4:17	6 4:18–31	7 5:1–6:1°	M 5:22–6:1
Triennial:	1 4:18–20	2 4:21–26	3 4:27–31	4 5:1–5
	5 5:6–9	6 5:10–14	7 5:15–6:1°	M 5:22–6:1

☞°5:15 Note the rare ta'am (trope) מֵירְכָא־כְפוּלָה (֮): לָמָּה תַעֲשֶׂה כֹה
Connect תַעֲשֶׂה to the preceding and following words, without a pause; then pause, as usual, after the טִפְּחָא (כֹה).

Haftarah
Ashkenazic: יְשַׁעְיָהוּ Yesha'yahu (Isaiah) 27:6–28:13; 29:22–23
Sephardic: יִרְמְיָהוּ Yirmeyahu (Jeremiah) 1:1–2:3

מִנְחָה

Torah 3 aliyot from וָאֵרָא Va'era
שְׁמוֹת Shemot (Exodus) 6:2–13
¹6:2–5 ²6–9 ³10–13 W277 P898

Chanted also next Monday and Thursday.

Tevet 28 טֵבֵת
Sat 1 Jan

שַׁבָּת Shabbat פָּרָשַׁת וָאֵרָא Parashat Va'era
שַׁבַּת מְבָרְכִים הַחֹדֶשׁ Shabbat Mevarekhim Haḥodesh

Torah 7 aliyot (minimum): וָאֵרָא Va'era
שְׁמוֹת Shemot (Exodus) 6:2–9:35

Annual:	¹6:2–13	²6:14–28	³6:29–7:7	⁴7:8–8:6
	⁵8:7–18	⁶8:19–9:16	⁷9:17–35	M9:33–35
Triennial:	¹8:16–23	²8:24–28	³9:1–7	⁴9:8–16
	⁵9:17–21	⁶9:22–26	⁷9:27–35	M9:33–35

Haftarah יְחֶזְקֵאל Yeḥezkel (Ezekiel) 28:25–29:21

+ **Birkat Haḥodesh:** L180 S150 F418
Announce Rosh Ḥodesh Shevat:
רֹאשׁ חֹדֶשׁ שְׁבָט יִהְיֶה בְּיוֹם שֵׁנִי . . .
Rosh ḥodesh Shevat yihyeh beyom sheni . . .
(Sunday night and Monday)

✕ ~~אַב הָרַחֲמִים Av Haraḥamim~~

מִנְחָה

Torah 3 aliyot from בֹּא Bo
שְׁמוֹת Shemot (Exodus) 10:1–11
¹10:1–3 ²4–6 ³7–11 W278 P899

Chanted also next Thursday.

Tevet 29 טֵבֵת
Sun 2 Jan

עֶרֶב רֹאשׁ חֹדֶשׁ Erev Rosh Ḥodesh
Day before Rosh Ḥodesh

מִנְחָה ✕ ~~תַּחֲנוּן Taḥanun~~

Shevat 1 שְׁבָט — ראשׁ חֹדֶשׁ שְׁבָט Rosh Ḥodesh Shevat

Sun 2 Jan (evening)

DURING Rosh Ḥodesh

Birkat Hamazon:

+ יַעֲלֶה וְיָבוֹא Ya'aleh veyavo for Rosh Ḥodesh L90|95 S340|347 W233|239 F762|780

+ הָרַחֲמָן Haraḥaman for Rosh Ḥodesh L92|96 S343|348 W235|240 F768

עַרְבִית

Weekday Amidah:

+ יַעֲלֶה וְיָבוֹא Ya'aleh veyavo for Rosh Ḥodesh W145 F216

Mon 3 Jan **שַׁחֲרִית**

Before מִזְמוֹר שִׁיר Mizmor shir (Psalm 30) W14 F50
or at end of service, recite:

Psalm for Monday (Psalm 48) W86 F24
קַדִּישׁ יָתוֹם Mourner's Kaddish (some omit) W100 F52
+ Psalm 104 for Rosh Ḥodesh W90 F34
קַדִּישׁ יָתוֹם Mourner's Kaddish W100 F52

Weekday Amidah:

+ יַעֲלֶה וְיָבוֹא Ya'aleh veyavo for Rosh Ḥodesh W41 F114

✕ ~~תַּחֲנוּן Taḥanun~~

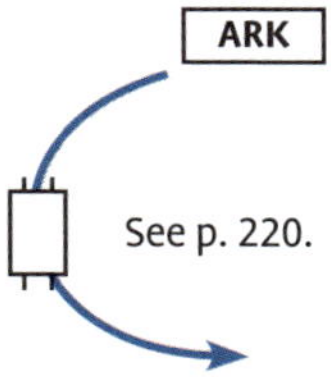

See p. 220.

+ חֲצִי הַלֵּל Short Hallel W50 F380
קַדִּישׁ שָׁלֵם Full Kaddish W56 F392

TORAH SERVICE W65 F138
Remove **1** scroll from ark.

Torah 4 aliyot: פִּינְחָס Pineḥas
בְּמִדְבַּר Bemidbar (Numbers) 28:1–15
1 28:1–3 2 3–5 3 6–10 4 11–15 W320 P943

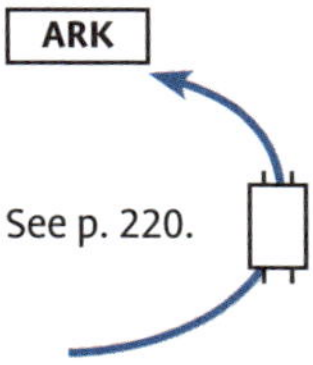

See p. 220.

חֲצִי קַדִּישׁ Short Kaddish W71 F146
Open, raise, display, and wrap scroll.
Return scroll to ark. W76 F150

אַשְׁרֵי Ashrey W78 F152
✕ ~~לַמְנַצֵּחַ Lamenatse·aḥ (Psalm 20)~~
וּבָא לְצִיּוֹן Uva letsiyyon W80 F156

Remove and pack tefillin. (Some remove after Kaddish.)

+ חֲצִי קַדִּישׁ Short Kaddish W103 F428

(If you remove tefillin here, do *not* pack but cover them, so as to begin Musaf together quickly after Kaddish.)

Shevat 5782						
	1	2	3	4	5	6
7	8	9	10	11	12	13
14	15	16	17	18	19	20
21	22	23	24	25	26	27
28	29	30				

Jan | Feb 2022						
	3	4	5	6	7	8
9	10	11	12	13	14	15
16	17	18	19	20	21	22
23	24	25	26	27	28	29
30	31 |	1				

+ Add ✕ Omit ☞ Take note!

Siddurim
L Lev Shalem for Shabbat and Festivals
S Shabbat and Festival Sim Shalom
W Weekday Sim Shalom
F Full Sim Shalom (both editions)
P Personal Edition of Full Sim Shalom

מוּסָף

+ **Rosh Ḥodesh Amidah for weekdays:** W104 F486
Weekday קְדֻשָּׁה Kedushah W105 F488
+ וּלְכַפָּרַת פָּשַׁע Ulkhapparat pasha W107 F494
Add these words only through Rosh Ḥodesh Adar Sheni.

+ קַדִּישׁ שָׁלֵם Full Kaddish W82 F158
עָלֵינוּ Aleynu W83 F160

If psalms for the day were not recited at Shaḥarit, add here:
קַדִּישׁ יָתוֹם Mourner's Kaddish (some omit) W84|100 F162|52
Psalm for Monday (Psalm 48) W86 F24
קַדִּישׁ יָתוֹם Mourner's Kaddish (some omit) W100 F52
+ Psalm 104 for Rosh Ḥodesh W90 F34

קַדִּישׁ יָתוֹם Mourner's Kaddish W84|100 F162|52

מִנְחָה

Weekday Amidah:
+ יַעֲלֶה וְיָבוֹא Ya'aleh veyavo for Rosh Ḥodesh W127 F178

✕ ~~תַּחֲנוּן Taḥanun~~

Shevat 6 שְׁבָט
Sat 8 Jan

שַׁבָּת Shabbat פָּרָשַׁת בֹּא Parashat Bo

Torah 7 aliyot (minimum): בֹּא Bo
שְׁמוֹת Shemot (Exodus) 10:1–13:16

Annual:	1 10:1–11	2 10:12–23	3 10:24–11:3	4 11:4–12:20
	5 12:21–28	6 12:29–51	7 13:1–16	M 13:14–16
Triennial:	1 12:29–32	2 12:33–36	3 12:37–42	4 12:43–51
	5 13:1–4	6 13:5–10	7 13:11–16	M 13:14–16

Haftarah יִרְמְיָהוּ Yirmeyahu (Jeremiah) 46:13–28

מִנְחָה

Torah 3 aliyot from בְּשַׁלַּח Beshallaḥ
שְׁמוֹת Shemot (Exodus) 13:17–14:8
1 13:17–22 2 14:1–4 3 14:5–8 W279 P900

Chanted also next Monday and Thursday.

Shevat 7 שְׁבָט
Sat 8 Jan (night)

After Arvit if the moon is visible:
קִדּוּשׁ לְבָנָה Kiddush Levanah L286 W167 F704
For procedures and instructions, see p. 223.

Siddurim
 1 2 3 4 5 6 3 4 5 6 7 8

L Lev Shalem for Shabbat and Festivals 7 8 9 10 11 12 13 9 10 11 12 13 14 15

S Shabbat and Festival Sim Shalom 14 15 16 17 18 19 20 16 17 18 19 20 21 22

W Weekday Sim Shalom 21 22 23 24 25 26 27 23 24 25 26 27 28 29

F Full Sim Shalom (both editions) 28 29 30 30 31 | 1

P Personal Edition of Full Sim Shalom

Chanting Shirat Hayam

Parashat Beshallaḥ and Pesaḥ — Day 7

The congregation stands during the reading of שִׁירַת הַיָּם *shirat hayam,* as if to reenact the celebration following the crossing of the Sea of Reeds.

According to Ashkenazic practice, we highlight certain verses with the distinctive Shirat Hayam melody. Although traditions differ as to which verses to highlight, a common tradition is: Shemot 15:1b, 2a, 3, 6, 11, 16b, 18, and 21b (a = up to and including the word with ֑; b = after ֑).

In addition, we distinguish parts of three verses (14:22b, 29b, and 31b) that precede the Shirah itself with the same melody. These serve to alert the congregation that something special follows.

Many congregations observe a very old practice. The congregation participates in the chanting of the highlighted verses, as if reenacting the events of Shemot 15:1: "Then Moses and the people Israel sang this song."

There are 2 common patterns of congregational participation. Both rely on the division of the poetic verses into short phrases and the division of the special melody into 2 melody phrases.

Call and Repeat

The Torah reader chants a phrase, and then the congregation repeats that phrase and melody. The reader chants the next phrase, and then the congregation repeats that phrase. For example:

Torah reader chants: אָשִׁ֤ירָה לַיי֙ כִּֽי־גָאֹ֣ה גָּאָ֔ה
Congregation *repeats:* אָשִׁ֤ירָה לַיי֙ כִּֽי־גָאֹ֣ה גָּאָ֔ה

Torah reader chants: ס֥וּס וְרֹכְב֖וֹ רָמָ֥ה בַיָּֽם׃
Congregation *repeats:* ס֥וּס וְרֹכְב֖וֹ רָמָ֥ה בַיָּֽם׃

Call and Respond

The Torah reader chants a phrase; then the congregation chants the following phrase, which (in most cases) completes the verse. The reader then repeats the phrase that the congregation chanted so that the congregation hears every word read directly from the Torah. For example:

Torah reader chants: אָשִׁ֤ירָה לַיי֙ כִּֽי־גָאֹ֣ה גָּאָ֔ה
Congregation *responds:* ס֥וּס וְרֹכְב֖וֹ רָמָ֥ה בַיָּֽם׃
Torah reader *repeats:* ס֥וּס וְרֹכְב֖וֹ רָמָ֥ה בַיָּֽם׃

Whichever procedure your congregation follows, observe carefully the following restrictions so that congregants hear every word read directly from the Torah. Congregants must wait for the Torah reader to stop before they begin to chant. Similarly, the Torah reader must not begin again until congregants have completed their chanting.

Shevat 5782						
	1	2	3	4	5	6
7	8	9	10	11	12	13
14	15	16	17	18	19	20
21	22	23	24	25	26	27
28	29	30				

Jan | Feb 2022						
	3	4	5	6	7	8
9	10	11	12	13	14	15
16	17	18	19	20	21	22
23	24	25	26	27	28	29
30	31 | 1					

+ Add ✕ Omit ☞ Take note!

Siddurim
L Lev Shalem for Shabbat and Festivals
S Shabbat and Festival Sim Shalom
W Weekday Sim Shalom
F Full Sim Shalom (both editions)
P Personal Edition of Full Sim Shalom

Shevat 13 שְׁבָט
Sat 15 Jan (morning)

שַׁבָּת Shabbat פָּרָשַׁת בְּשַׁלַּח Parashat Beshallaḥ
שַׁבַּת שִׁירָה Shabbat Shirah

Shabbat Shirah is the Shabbat of Song. The parashah contains שִׁירַת הַיָּם *shirat hayam,* the song of celebration that Moses, Miriam, and the people Israel sang after the successful crossing of the Sea of Reeds and the defeat of the Egyptian army by the hand of God.
For instructions for the special chanting of this passage, see p. 97.

Torah 7 aliyot (minimum): בְּשַׁלַּח Beshallaḥ
שְׁמוֹת Shemot (Exodus) 13:17–17:16

Annual:	1 13:17–14:8	2 14:9–14	3 14:15–25°	4 14:26–15:26°
	5 15:27–16:10	6 16:11–36	7 17:1–16	M 17:14–16
Triennial:	1 14:26–15:21°	2 15:22–26	3 15:27–16:10	4 16:11–27
	5 16:28–36	6 17:1–7	7 17:8–16	M 17:14–16

☞ °14:22, 29, 31; 15:1–21 For instructions for the special chanting of שִׁירַת הַיָּם Shirat Hayam and of parts of the preceding sections, see p. 97.

☞ °15:11, 16 To preserve the sense of these phrases, maintain the proper pauses after the te'amim (tropes) פַּשְׁטָא (֙) and טִפְחָא (֖):

15:11 מִי־כָמֹכָה בָּאֵלִם֙ | יי מִי כָּמֹכָה | נֶאְדָּר בַּקֹּדֶשׁ . . .

15:16 . . . עַד־יַעֲבֹר עַמְּךָ֙ | יי עַד־יַעֲבֹר | עַם־זוּ קָנִיתָ:

Haftarah
Ashkenazic: שׁוֹפְטִים Shofetim (Judges) 4:4–5:31
Sephardic: שׁוֹפְטִים Shofetim (Judges) 5:1–5:31

מִנְחָה

Torah 3 aliyot from יִתְרוֹ Yitro
שְׁמוֹת Shemot (Exodus) 18:1–12
1 18:1–4 2 5–8 3 9–12 W280 P901

Chanted also next Monday and Thursday.

Shevat 14 שְׁבָט
Sat 15 Jan

מוֹצָאֵי שַׁבָּת Motsa'ey Shabbat Conclusion of Shabbat
עֶרֶב ט"ו בִּשְׁבָט Erev Tu Bishvat Day before Tu Bishvat

עַרְבִית Saturday night Arvit as usual L264 S281 W137 F200

Sun 16 Jan **מִנְחָה** ✕ ~~תַּחֲנוּן Taḥanun~~

Shevat 15 שְׁבָט — ט"ו בִּשְׁבָט Tu Bishvat — 15th of Shevat

Sun 16 Jan (evening)

Tu Bishvat is referred to as the New Year for trees because the fruits of trees that blossom after the 15th of Shevat were counted in ancient times as belonging to the next year for purposes of tithing.

To celebrate, we eat a tree fruit that we have not yet tasted this season, reciting the *berakhot* בּוֹרֵא פְּרִי הָעֵץ *bo·re peri ha'ets* and שֶׁהֶחֱיָנוּ *sheheheyanu.* Other customs include holding a Tu Bishvat seder and eating fruits from Israel.

Mon 17 Jan שַׁחֲרִית ✕ ~~תַּחֲנוּן Tahanun~~
☞ לַמְנַצֵּחַ Lamenatse·ah (Psalm 20) W79 F154

מִנְחָה ✕ ~~תַּחֲנוּן Tahanun~~

Chanting Aseret Hadibberot

Parashat Yitro, and Shavu'ot — Day 1

The congregation stands as they hear this section read, just as the people Israel stood at the foot of Mount Sinai and listened to the voice of God.

The proper chanting of עֲשֶׂרֶת הַדִּבְּרוֹת *aseret hadibberot* requires exceptional attention because this passage is marked with 2 sets of verse divisions and 2 sets of *te'amim* (tropes, cantillation marks). One set, for private study, divides the passage into verses of a usual length, suitable for study. The 2nd set, for public reading, divides the passage into exactly *10* verses. Each verse corresponds to 1 of the 10 pronouncements. The congregation listens to exactly *10* pronouncements, reenacting the events experienced by the people Israel at Mount Sinai.

For the public reading, a long pronouncement, such as that commanding observance of Shabbat, joins several verses into a single long verse. On the other hand, a verse containing 4 very brief pronouncements breaks into 4 separate, very short verses for the public reading.

Over the centuries, the complexity of the task of separating 2 sets of verse divisions and 2 sets of *te'amim* resulted in countless errors in printed *humashim.* The 2 sets of verse divisions led to a confusion in verse *numbering,* which in fact should follow the private reading. There are 22 verses in the chapter, but many editions erroneously count 23. This leads to confusion in labeling the *aliyah* divisions. See Torah reading information on p. 101.

The correct verse divisions and *te'amim* for the public reading appear on p. 100. Only this version, supported by the earliest manuscripts and the most authoritative printed editions, presents *10* pronouncements in *10* verses.

עֲשֶׂרֶת הַדִּבְּרוֹת — פָּרָשַׁת יִתְרוֹ

For Public Reading — טַעֲמָא תְּנִינָא (טַעַם עֶלְיוֹן)

דִּבְּרוֹת

1 אָנֹכִי
יְ־הוָה אֱ־לֹהֶיךָ אֲשֶׁר הוֹצֵאתִיךָ מֵאֶרֶץ מִצְרַיִם מִבֵּית
2 עֲבָדִים: לֹא יִהְיֶה־לְךָ אֱלֹהִים אֲחֵרִים עַל־פָּנַי לֹא
תַעֲשֶׂה־לְךָ פֶסֶל | וְכָל־תְּמוּנָה אֲשֶׁר בַּשָּׁמַיִם | מִמַּעַל
וַאֲשֶׁר בָּאָרֶץ מִתַּחַת וַאֲשֶׁר בַּמַּיִם | מִתַּחַת לָאָרֶץ לֹא־
תִשְׁתַּחֲוֶה לָהֶם וְלֹא תָעָבְדֵם° כִּי אָנֹכִי יְ־הוָה אֱ־לֹהֶיךָ °Read: **to'ovdem**
אֵ־ל קַנָּא פֹּקֵד עֲוֹן אָבֹת עַל־בָּנִים עַל־שִׁלֵּשִׁים
וְעַל־רִבֵּעִים לְשֹׂנְאָי וְעֹשֶׂה חֶסֶד לַאֲלָפִים לְאֹהֲבַי
3 וּלְשֹׁמְרֵי מִצְוֺתָי: לֹא תִשָּׂא אֶת־
שֵׁם־יְ־הוָה אֱ־לֹהֶיךָ לַשָּׁוְא כִּי לֹא יְנַקֶּה יְ־הוָה אֵת
אֲשֶׁר־יִשָּׂא אֶת־שְׁמוֹ לַשָּׁוְא:
4 זָכוֹר אֶת־יוֹם הַשַּׁבָּת לְקַדְּשׁוֹ שֵׁשֶׁת יָמִים תַּעֲבֹד
וְעָשִׂיתָ כָּל־מְלַאכְתֶּךָ וְיוֹם הַשְּׁבִיעִי שַׁבָּת | לַיְ־הוָה
אֱ־לֹהֶיךָ לֹא תַעֲשֶׂה כָל־מְלָאכָה אַתָּה וּבִנְךָ־וּבִתֶּךָ
עַבְדְּךָ וַאֲמָתְךָ וּבְהֶמְתֶּךָ וְגֵרְךָ אֲשֶׁר בִּשְׁעָרֶיךָ
כִּי שֵׁשֶׁת־יָמִים עָשָׂה יְ־הוָה אֶת־הַשָּׁמַיִם וְאֶת־
הָאָרֶץ אֶת־הַיָּם וְאֶת־כָּל־אֲשֶׁר־בָּם וַיָּנַח בַּיּוֹם
הַשְּׁבִיעִי עַל־כֵּן בֵּרַךְ יְ־הוָה אֶת־יוֹם הַשַּׁבָּת
5 וַיְקַדְּשֵׁהוּ: כַּבֵּד אֶת־אָבִיךָ וְאֶת־אִמֶּךָ
לְמַעַן יַאֲרִכוּן יָמֶיךָ עַל הָאֲדָמָה אֲשֶׁר־יְ־הוָה אֱ־לֹהֶיךָ
6 | 7 נֹתֵן לָךְ: לֹא תִרְצָח: לֹא
8 | 9 תִנְאָף: לֹא תִגְנֹב: לֹא־
10 תַעֲנֶה בְרֵעֲךָ עֵד שָׁקֶר: לֹא
תַחְמֹד בֵּית רֵעֶךָ לֹא־
תַחְמֹד אֵשֶׁת רֵעֶךָ וְעַבְדּוֹ וַאֲמָתוֹ וְשׁוֹרוֹ וַחֲמֹרוֹ
וְכֹל אֲשֶׁר לְרֵעֶךָ:

Shevat 20 שְׁבָט
Sat 22 Jan

שַׁבָּת Shabbat פָּרָשַׁת יִתְרוֹ Parashat Yitro

The עֲשֶׂרֶת הַדִּבְּרוֹת ***aseret hadibberot*** section, which appears in Parashat Yitro, is usually called "the 10 commandments." But the Hebrew phrase actually means "the 10 pronouncements."

For the correct text and *te'amim* (tropes, cantillation marks), see p. 100.
For special instructions for the chanting of this passage, see p. 99.

Aseret Hadibberot in the Triennial Cycle

- **Triennial Option A:** The full parashah. The congregation thus experiences עֲשֶׂרֶת הַדִּבְּרוֹת every year.
- **Triennial Option B:** An abbreviated reading. The congregation experiences עֲשֶׂרֶת הַדִּבְּרוֹת only in years 2 and 3 of the cycle.

For details, see below.

Torah 7 aliyot (minimum): יִתְרוֹ Yitro
שְׁמוֹת Shemot (Exodus) 18:1–20:22

Annual:	[1]18:1–12	[2]18:13–23	[3]18:24–27	[4]19:1–6
	[5]19:7–19	°[6]19:20–20:13	°[7]20:14–22	°[M]20:18–22

Triennial:

°Option A	Chant the full parashah, dividing as above.			
°Option B	[1]19:1–6	[2]19:7–9	[3]19:10–13	[4]19:14–19
	°[5]19:20–20:13	°[6]20:14–17	°[7]20:18–22	°[M]20:20–22

☞°**Verse numbers in chapter 20:** In many books, the verses are misnumbered. Use these guidelines to properly divide the reading:

Annual and Triennial Option A
Aliyah **6**: ends לְרֵעֶךָ (20:14 in many books)
Aliyah **7**: וְכָל־הָעָם through עָלָיו (20:15–23 in many books)
Maftir aliyah: וַיֹּאמֶר יי through עָלָיו (20:19–23 in many books)

Triennial Option B
Aliyah **5**: ends לְרֵעֶךָ (20:14 in many books)
Aliyah **6**: וְכָל־הָעָם through הָאֱלֹהִים (20:15–18 in many books)
Aliyah **7**: וַיֹּאמֶר יי through עָלָיו (20:19–23 in many books)
Maftir aliyah: מִזְבַּח אֲדָמָה through עָלָיו (20:21–23 in many books)

☞°20:1–13 Follow the te'amim (tropes) on p. 100 for the public reading of עֲשֶׂרֶת הַדִּבְּרוֹת. For additional instructions for this passage, see p. 99.

☞°Triennial Option B excludes Aseret Hadibberot in year 1 (next year).

Haftarah
Ashkenazic: יְשַׁעְיָהוּ Yesha'yahu (Isaiah) 6:1–7:6; 9:5–6
Sephardic: יְשַׁעְיָהוּ Yesha'yahu (Isaiah) 6:1–13

מִנְחָה

Torah 3 aliyot from מִשְׁפָּטִים Mishpatim
שְׁמוֹת Shemot (Exodus) 21:1–19
[1]21:1–6 [2]7–11 [3]12–19 W281 P901

Chanted also next Monday and Thursday.

Shevat 27 שְׁבָט
Sat 29 Jan

שַׁבָּת Shabbat פָּרָשַׁת מִשְׁפָּטִים Parashat Mishpatim
שַׁבַּת מְבָרְכִים הַחֹדֶשׁ Shabbat Mevarekhim Haḥodesh

Torah 7 aliyot (minimum): מִשְׁפָּטִים Mishpatim
שְׁמוֹת Shemot (Exodus) 21:1–24:18

Annual:	[1]21:1–19	[2]21:20–22:3	[3]22:4–26	[4]22:27–23:5
	[5]23:6–19	[6]23:20–25	[7]23:26–24:18	[M]24:16–18
Triennial:	[1]23:20–25	[2]23:26–30	[3]23:31–33	[4]24:1–6
	[5]24:7–11	[6]24:12–14	[7]24:15–18	[M]24:15–18

Haftarah יִרְמְיָהוּ Yirmeyahu (Jeremiah) 34:8–22, 33:25–26

+ **Birkat Haḥodesh:** L180 S150 F418
Announce Rosh Ḥodesh Adar Rishon:
Do not announce the month as "Adar Alef."
רֹאשׁ חֹדֶשׁ אֲדָר רִאשׁוֹן יִהְיֶה בְּיוֹם שְׁלִישִׁי וּבְיוֹם רְבִיעִי . . .
Rosh ḥodesh Adar Rishon yihyeh beyom shelishi uvyom revi'i . . .
(Monday night, Tuesday, and Wednesday)

✕ ~~אַב הָרַחֲמִים Av Haraḥamim~~

מִנְחָה

Torah 3 aliyot from תְּרוּמָה Terumah
שְׁמוֹת Shemot (Exodus) 25:1–16
[1]25:1–5 [2]6–9 [3]10–16 W282 P902

Chanted also next Monday and Thursday.

Shevat 29 שְׁבָט
Mon 31 Jan

עֶרֶב רֹאשׁ חֹדֶשׁ Erev Rosh Ḥodesh
Day before Rosh Ḥodesh

מִנְחָה ✕ ~~תַּחֲנוּן Taḥanun~~

Shevat 30 שְׁבָט
Mon 31 Jan (evening)

רֹאשׁ חֹדֶשׁ אֲדָר רִאשׁוֹן
Rosh Ḥodesh Adar Rishon — Day 1

DURING Rosh Ḥodesh

Birkat Hamazon:

+ יַעֲלֶה וְיָבוֹא Ya'aleh veyavo for Rosh Ḥodesh L90|95 S340|347 W233|239 F762|780

+ הָרַחֲמָן Haraḥaman for Rosh Ḥodesh L92|96 S343|348 W235|240 F768

עַרְבִית

Weekday Amidah:

+ יַעֲלֶה וְיָבוֹא Ya'aleh veyavo for Rosh Ḥodesh W145 F216

Tue 1 Feb **שַׁחֲרִית**

Before מִזְמוֹר שִׁיר Mizmor shir (Psalm 30) W14 F50
or at end of service, recite:

Psalm for Tuesday (Psalm 82) W87 F26
קַדִּישׁ יָתוֹם Mourner's Kaddish (some omit) W100 F52
+ Psalm 104 for Rosh Ḥodesh W90 F34
קַדִּישׁ יָתוֹם Mourner's Kaddish W100 F52

Weekday Amidah:

+ יַעֲלֶה וְיָבוֹא Ya'aleh veyavo for Rosh Ḥodesh W41 F114

✕ ~~תַּחֲנוּן Taḥanun~~

+ חֲצִי הַלֵּל Short Hallel W50 F380
קַדִּישׁ שָׁלֵם Full Kaddish W56 F392

ARK — See p. 220.

+ **TORAH SERVICE** W65 F138
Remove **1** scroll from ark.

Torah 4 aliyot: פִּינְחָס Pineḥas
בְּמִדְבַּר Bemidbar (Numbers) 28:1–15
1 28:1–3 2 3–5 3 6–10 4 11–15 W320 P943

ARK — See p. 220.

חֲצִי קַדִּישׁ Short Kaddish W71 F146
Open, raise, display, and wrap scroll.
Return scroll to ark. W76 F150

אַשְׁרֵי Ashrey W78 F152
✕ ~~לַמְנַצֵּחַ Lamenatse·aḥ (Psalm 20)~~
וּבָא לְצִיּוֹן Uva letsiyyon W80 F156

Remove and pack tefillin. (Some remove after Kaddish.)

+ חֲצִי קַדִּישׁ Short Kaddish W103 F428

(If you remove tefillin here, do *not* pack but cover them, so as to begin Musaf together quickly after Kaddish.)

Shevat 5782						
	1	2	3	4	5	6
7	8	9	10	11	12	13
14	15	16	17	18	19	20
21	22	23	24	25	26	27
28	29	30				

Jan | Feb 2022						
	3	4	5	6	7	8
9	10	11	12	13	14	15
16	17	18	19	20	21	22
23	24	25	26	27	28	29
30	31 | 1					

+ Add ✕ Omit ☞ Take note!

Siddurim
L Lev Shalem for Shabbat and Festivals
S Shabbat and Festival Sim Shalom
W Weekday Sim Shalom
F Full Sim Shalom (both editions)
P Personal Edition of Full Sim Shalom

מוּסָף

\+ **Rosh Hodesh Amidah for weekdays:** W104 F486
Weekday קְדֻשָּׁה Kedushah W105 F488
\+ וּלְכַפָּרַת פָּשַׁע Ulkhapparat pasha W107 F494
Add these words only through Rosh Hodesh Adar Sheni.

\+ קַדִּישׁ שָׁלֵם Full Kaddish W82 F158
עָלֵינוּ Aleynu W83 F160

If psalms for the day were not recited at Shaharit, add here:
קַדִּישׁ יָתוֹם Mourner's Kaddish (some omit) W84|100 F162|52
Psalm for Tuesday (Psalm 82) W87 F26
קַדִּישׁ יָתוֹם Mourner's Kaddish (some omit) W100 F52
\+ Psalm 104 for Rosh Hodesh W90 F34

קַדִּישׁ יָתוֹם Mourner's Kaddish W84|100 F162|52

מִנְחָה

Weekday Amidah:
\+ יַעֲלֶה וְיָבוֹא Ya'aleh veyavo for Rosh Hodesh W127 F178

✕ ~~תַּחֲנוּן Tahanun~~

1st Adar 1 אֲדָר א׳
Tue 1 Feb (evening)

ראשׁ חֹדֶשׁ אֲדָר רִאשׁוֹן
Rosh Hodesh Adar Rishon — Day 2

For determining the *yortsayt* of a death during Adar, 1st Adar, or 2nd Adar, see p. 224.

DURING Rosh Hodesh

Birkat Hamazon:

+ יַעֲלֶה וְיָבוֹא Ya'aleh veyavo for Rosh Hodesh L90|95 S340|347 W233|239 F762|780

+ הָרַחֲמָן Harahaman for Rosh Hodesh L92|96 S343|348 W235|240 F768

עַרְבִית

Weekday Amidah:

+ יַעֲלֶה וְיָבוֹא Ya'aleh veyavo for Rosh Hodesh W145 F216

Wed 2 Feb **שַׁחֲרִית**

Before מִזְמוֹר שִׁיר Mizmor shir (Psalm 30) W14 F50
or at end of service, recite:

Psalm for Wednesday (Psalms 94:1–95:3) W87 F26
קַדִּישׁ יָתוֹם Mourner's Kaddish (some omit) W100 F52
+ Psalm 104 for Rosh Hodesh W90 F34
קַדִּישׁ יָתוֹם Mourner's Kaddish W100 F52

Weekday Amidah:

+ יַעֲלֶה וְיָבוֹא Ya'aleh veyavo for Rosh Hodesh W41 F114

✕ ~~תַּחֲנוּן Tahanun~~

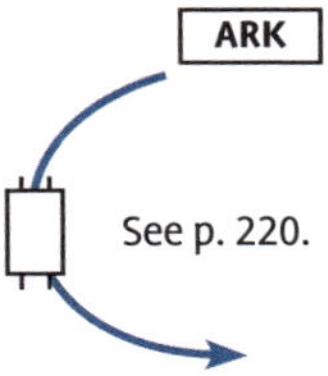

See p. 220.

+ חֲצִי הַלֵּל Short Hallel W50 F380
קַדִּישׁ שָׁלֵם Full Kaddish W56 F392

+ **TORAH SERVICE** W65 F138
Remove **1** scroll from ark.

Torah 4 aliyot: פִּינְחָס Pinehas
בְּמִדְבַּר Bemidbar (Numbers) 28:1–15
[1]28:1–3 [2]3–5 [3]6–10 [4]11–15 W320 P943

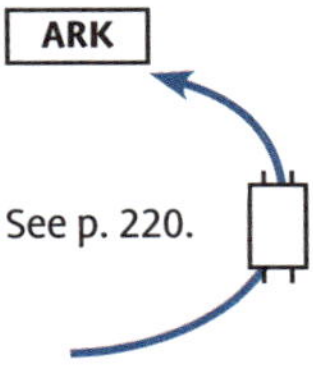

See p. 220.

חֲצִי קַדִּישׁ Short Kaddish W71 F146
Open, raise, display, and wrap scroll.
Return scroll to ark. W76 F150

אַשְׁרֵי Ashrey W78 F152
✕ ~~לַמְנַצֵּחַ Lamenatse·ah (Psalm 20)~~
וּבָא לְצִיּוֹן Uva letsiyyon W80 F156

1st Adar 5782							Feb | Mar 2022						
			1	2	3	4				2	3	4	5
5	6	7	8	9	10	11	6	7	8	9	10	11	12
12	13	14	15	16	17	18	13	14	15	16	17	18	19
19	20	21	22	23	24	25	20	21	22	23	24	25	26
26	27	28	29	30			27	28 |	1	2	3		

+ Add ✕ Omit ☞ Take note!

Siddurim
- **L** Lev Shalem for Shabbat and Festivals
- **S** Shabbat and Festival Sim Shalom
- **W** Weekday Sim Shalom
- **F** Full Sim Shalom (both editions)
- **P** Personal Edition of Full Sim Shalom

Remove and pack tefillin. (Some remove after Kaddish.)

\+ חֲצִי קַדִּישׁ Short Kaddish W103 F428

(If you remove tefillin here, do *not* pack but cover them, so as to begin Musaf together quickly after Kaddish.)

מוּסָף

\+ **Rosh Ḥodesh Amidah for weekdays:** W104 F486

Weekday קְדֻשָּׁה Kedushah W105 F488

\+ וּלְכַפָּרַת פָּשַׁע Ulkhapparat pasha W107 F494

Add these words only through Rosh Ḥodesh Adar Sheni.

\+ קַדִּישׁ שָׁלֵם Full Kaddish W82 F158

עָלֵינוּ Aleynu W83 F160

If psalms for the day were not recited at Shaḥarit, add here:

קַדִּישׁ יָתוֹם Mourner's Kaddish (some omit) W84|100 F162|52

Psalm for Wednesday (Psalms 94:1–95:3) W87 F26

קַדִּישׁ יָתוֹם Mourner's Kaddish (some omit) W100 F52

\+ Psalm 104 for Rosh Ḥodesh W90 F34

קַדִּישׁ יָתוֹם Mourner's Kaddish W84|100 F162|52

מִנְחָה

Weekday Amidah:

\+ יַעֲלֶה וְיָבוֹא Ya'aleh veyavo for Rosh Ḥodesh W127 F178

✕ ~~תַּחֲנוּן Taḥanun~~

1st Adar 4 אֲדָר א׳ — Sat 5 Feb

שַׁבָּת Shabbat פָּרָשַׁת תְּרוּמָה Parashat Terumah

Torah 7 aliyot (minimum): תְּרוּמָה Terumah
שְׁמוֹת Shemot (Exodus) 25:1–27:19

Annual:	[1]25:1–16	[2]25:17–40	[3]26:1–14	[4]26:15–30
	[5]26:31–37	[6]27:1–8	[7]27:9–19	[M]27:17–19
Triennial:	[1]26:31–33	[2]26:34–37	[3]27:1–3	[4]27:4–8
	[5]27:9–12	[6]27:13–16	[7]27:17–19	[M]27:17–19

Haftarah מְלָכִים א׳ 1 Melakhim (1 Kings) 5:26–6:13

מִנְחָה

Torah 3 aliyot from תְּצַוֶּה Tetsavveh
שְׁמוֹת Shemot (Exodus) 27:20–28:12
[1]27:20–28:5 [2]28:6–9 [3]10–12 W283 P903

Chanted also next Monday and Thursday.

1st Adar 5 אֲדָר א׳
Sat 5 Feb (night)

After Arvit if the moon is visible:
קִדּוּשׁ לְבָנָה Kiddush Levanah L286 W167 F704
For procedures and instructions, see p. 223.

1st Adar 11 אֲדָר א׳
Sat 12 Feb

שַׁבָּת Shabbat פָּרָשַׁת תְּצַוֶּה Parashat Tetsavveh

Torah 7 aliyot (minimum): תְּצַוֶּה Tetsavveh
שְׁמוֹת Shemot (Exodus) 27:20–30:10

Annual:	1 27:20–28:12	2 28:13–30	3 28:31–43	4 29:1–18
	5 29:19–37	6 29:38–46	7 30:1–10	M 30:8–10
Triennial:	1 29:19–21	2 29:22–25	3 29:26–30	4 29:31–34
	5 29:35–37	6 29:38–46	7 30:1–10	M 30:8–10

Haftarah יְחֶזְקֵאל Yeḥezkel (Ezekiel) 43:10–27

מִנְחָה

Torah 3 aliyot from כִּי־תִשָּׂא Ki tissa
שְׁמוֹת Shemot (Exodus) 30:11–21°
1 30:11–13 2 14–16 3 17–21 W284 P904

Chanted also next Monday and Thursday.

☞ °30:11–21 Chant only these verses. Do not chant to the end of the 1st Shabbat aliyah.

1st Adar 13 אֲדָר א׳
Mon 14 Feb

עֶרֶב פּוּרִים קָטָן Erev Purim Katan
Day before Purim Katan

מִנְחָה ✕ ~~תַּחֲנוּן Taḥanun~~

1st Adar 14 אֲדָר א׳
Tue 15 Feb

פּוּרִים קָטָן Purim Katan
Fourteenth of 1st Adar

שַׁחֲרִית ✕ ~~תַּחֲנוּן Taḥanun~~

✕ ~~לַמְנַצֵּחַ Lamenatse·aḥ (Psalm 20)~~

מִנְחָה ✕ ~~תַּחֲנוּן Taḥanun~~

1st Adar 5782						
			1	2	3	4
5	6	7	8	9	10	11
12	13	14	15	16	17	18
19	20	21	22	23	24	25
26	27	28	29	30		

Feb | Mar 2022						
			2	3	4	5
6	7	8	9	10	11	12
13	14	15	16	17	18	19
20	21	22	23	24	25	26
27	28 |	1	2	3		

+ Add ✕ Omit ☞ Take note!

Siddurim
L Lev Shalem for Shabbat and Festivals
S Shabbat and Festival Sim Shalom
W Weekday Sim Shalom
F Full Sim Shalom (both editions)
P Personal Edition of Full Sim Shalom

1st Adar 15 אֲדָר א׳ Wed 16 Feb

פּוּרִים שׁוּשַׁן קָטָן Shushan Purim Katan
Fifteenth of 1st Adar

שַׁחֲרִית ✕ ~~תַּחֲנוּן Taḥanun~~

✕ ~~לַמְנַצֵּחַ Lamenatse·aḥ (Psalm 20)~~

מִנְחָה ✕ ~~תַּחֲנוּן Taḥanun~~

1st Adar 18 אֲדָר א׳ Sat 19 Feb

שַׁבָּת Shabbat פָּרָשַׁת כִּי תִשָּׂא Parashat Ki tissa

Torah 7 aliyot (minimum): כִּי תִשָּׂא Ki tissa
שְׁמוֹת Shemot (Exodus) 30:11–34:35

Annual:	1 30:11–31:17	°2 31:18–33:11	3 33:12–16	4 33:17–23
	5 34:1–9°	6 34:10–26	7 34:27–35	M 34:33–35
Triennial:	1 33:12–16	2 33:17–23	3 34:1–9°	4 34:10–17
	5 34:18–21	6 34:22–26	7 34:27–35	M 34:33–35

Annual Reading

☞ °**Aliyah 2** It is traditional to call a **levi** (Levite, descendant of the tribe of Levi) for this aliyah. Only the tribe of Levi remained loyal to Moses and to God (32:26); only a descendant of the tribe of Levi can stand at the Torah with head held high for this aliyah. This practice should be followed even in congregations that do not regularly call a **levi** in the traditional sequence.
Because of the shameful nature of these verses, do not divide this lengthy passage into shorter aliyot. However, the chanting may be divided among multiple readers. All the readers must be present at the Torah when the oleh/olah recites the first berakhah. This serves as an implicit appointment of all the readers as sheliḥim (agents) of the oleh/olah.

☞ °31:18–33:11 Chant most of the story of the golden calf in a somewhat **subdued** voice to symbolically minimize the embarrassment the congregants experience upon hearing the terrible misdeeds of our ancestors. Be sure that all words and te'amim (tropes, cantillations) remain clearly audible to the congregation.
However, chant the following verses as usual:
Shemot 31:18, 32:11–14, 33:1–2, 33:3 only through וּדְבָשׁ, 33:7–11

☞ °32:12, 34:6–7, 9 Chant these verses in the usual manner. Do **not** chant them as chanted on fast days.

Haftarah
Ashkenazic: מְלָכִים א׳ 1 Melakhim (1 Kings) 18:1–39
Sephardic: מְלָכִים א׳ 1 Melakhim (1 Kings) 18:20–39

מִנְחָה

Torah 3 aliyot from וַיַּקְהֵל Vayak·hel
שְׁמוֹת Shemot (Exodus) 35:1–20
[1]35:1–3 [2]4–10 [3]11–20 W285 P905

Chanted also next Monday and Thursday.

1st Adar 25 אֲדָר א׳
Sat **26** Feb (morning)

שַׁבָּת Shabbat פָּרָשַׁת וַיַּקְהֵל Parashat Vayak·hel
שַׁבַּת שְׁקָלִים Shabbat Shekalim
שַׁבַּת מְבָרְכִים הַחֹדֶשׁ Shabbat Mevarekhim Haḥodesh

Shabbat Shekalim is the 1st of 4 special Shabbatot before Pesaḥ. Its name comes from the *maftir aliyah* reading, Shemot 30:11–16, which describes the obligation of every Israelite man to contribute a half shekel.

The contribution served 2 purposes. It provided funds to support the operation of the *mishkan* (portable sanctuary). At the same time, it accomplished a census of Israelite men.

In Temple days, this annual tax was to be paid during Adar. Shabbat Shekalim was scheduled to fall before or on the 1st day of Adar as a reminder of the upcoming obligation. In a leap year Shabbat Shekalim falls before the start of 2nd Adar. Today we observe this obligation by collecting *maḥatsit hashekel* before Purim (see p. 118). The funds support Jewish institutions or other charitable endeavors.

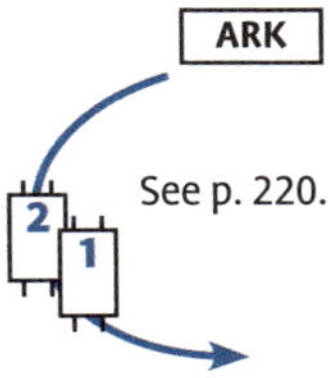

See p. 220.

TORAH SERVICE L168 S139 F394

Remove **2** scrolls from ark in the order they will be read.

1st scroll 7 aliyot (minimum): וַיַּקְהֵל Vayak·hel
שְׁמוֹת Shemot (Exodus) 35:1–38:20

Annual:	[1]35:1–20	[2]35:21–29	[3]35:30–36:7	[4]36:8–19
	[5]36:20–37:16	[6]37:17–29	[7]38:1–20	
Triennial:°	[1]36:20–30	[2]36:31–38	[3]37:1–16	[4]37:17–24
	[5]37:25–29	[6]38:1–8	[7]38:9–20	

☞Triennial: Accords with the CJLS decision of Nov. 16, 2020.

Place 2nd scroll on table next to 1st scroll.
חֲצִי קַדִּישׁ Short Kaddish L174 S146 F408
Open, raise, display, and wrap 1st scroll.

1st Adar 5782						
			1	2	3	4
5	6	7	8	9	10	11
12	13	14	15	16	17	18
19	20	21	22	23	24	25
26	27	28	29	30		

Feb | Mar 2022						
			2	3	4	5
6	7	8	9	10	11	12
13	14	15	16	17	18	19
20	21	22	23	24	25	26
27	28 |	1	2	3		

+ Add ✕ Omit ☞ Take note!

Siddurim
L Lev Shalem for Shabbat and Festivals
S Shabbat and Festival Sim Shalom
W Weekday Sim Shalom
F Full Sim Shalom (both editions)
P Personal Edition of Full Sim Shalom

+ **2nd scroll** Maftir aliyah from כִּי תִשָּׂא Ki tissa
שְׁמוֹת[M] Shemot (Exodus) 30:11–16

Open, raise, display, and wrap 2nd scroll.

☞ **Haftarah** for Shabbat Shekalim
Ashkenazic: מְלָכִים ב׳ 2 Melakhim (2 Kings) 12:1–17
Sephardic: מְלָכִים ב׳ 2 Melakhim (2 Kings) 11:17–12:17

+ **Birkat Haḥodesh:** L180 S150 F418
Announce Rosh Ḥodesh Adar Sheni:
Do not announce the month as “Adar Bet.”
רֹאשׁ חֹדֶשׁ אֲדָר שֵׁנִי יִהְיֶה בְּיוֹם חֲמִישִׁי וּבְיוֹם שִׁשִּׁי . . .
Rosh ḥodesh Adar Sheni yihyeh beyom ḥamishi uvyom shishi . . .
(Wednesday night, Thursday, and Friday)

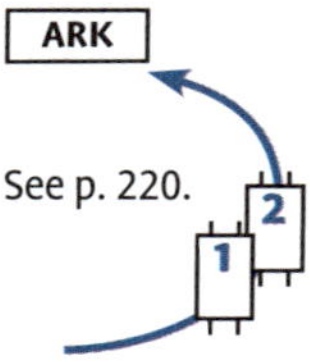

See p. 220.

✕ ~~אַב הָרַחֲמִים Av Haraḥamim~~

אַשְׁרֵי Ashrey L181 S151 F420
Return scrolls to ark in reverse order. L183 S153 F422

חֲצִי קַדִּישׁ Short Kaddish L184 S155 F428

Continue as on a usual Shabbat.

מִנְחָה

Torah 3 aliyot from פְּקוּדֵי Pekudey
שְׁמוֹת Shemot (Exodus) 38:21–39:1
¹38:21–23 ²24–27 ³38:28–39:1 W286 P906

Chanted also next Monday.

☞ צִדְקָתְךָ צֶדֶק Tsidkatekha tsedek L230 S239 W183 F584

1st Adar 29 אֲדָר א׳
Wed 2 Mar

עֶרֶב רֹאשׁ חֹדֶשׁ Erev Rosh Ḥodesh
Day before Rosh Ḥodesh

מִנְחָה ✕ ~~תַּחֲנוּן Taḥanun~~

1st Adar 30 אֲדָר א׳ ראשׁ חֹדֶשׁ אֲדָר שֵׁנִי Rosh Ḥodesh Adar Sheni – Day 1

Wed 2 Mar (evening)

DURING Rosh Ḥodesh

Birkat Hamazon:

+ יַעֲלֶה וְיָבוֹא Ya'aleh veyavo for Rosh Ḥodesh L90|95 S340|347 W233|239 F762|780

+ הָרַחֲמָן Haraḥaman for Rosh Ḥodesh L92|96 S343|348 W235|240 F768

עַרְבִית

Weekday Amidah:

+ יַעֲלֶה וְיָבוֹא Ya'aleh veyavo for Rosh Ḥodesh W145 F216

Thu 3 Mar **שַׁחֲרִית**

Before מִזְמוֹר שִׁיר Mizmor shir (Psalm 30) W14 F50
or at end of service, recite:

Psalm for Thursday (Psalm 81) W89 F30
קַדִּישׁ יָתוֹם Mourner's Kaddish (some omit) W100 F52
+ Psalm 104 for Rosh Ḥodesh W90 F34
קַדִּישׁ יָתוֹם Mourner's Kaddish W100 F52

Weekday Amidah:

+ יַעֲלֶה וְיָבוֹא Ya'aleh veyavo for Rosh Ḥodesh W41 F114

✕ ~~תַּחֲנוּן Taḥanun~~

+ חֲצִי הַלֵּל Short Hallel W50 F380
קַדִּישׁ שָׁלֵם Full Kaddish W56 F392

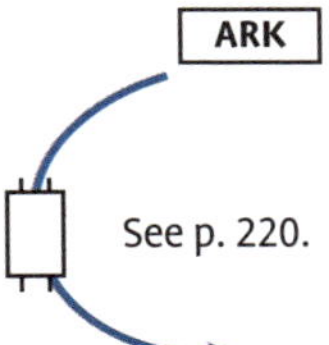

See p. 220.

TORAH SERVICE W65 F138
Remove **1** scroll from ark.

Torah 4 aliyot: פִּינְחָס Pineḥas
בְּמִדְבַּר Bemidbar (Numbers) 28:1–15
[1]28:1–3 [2]3–5 [3]6–10 [4]11–15 W320 P943

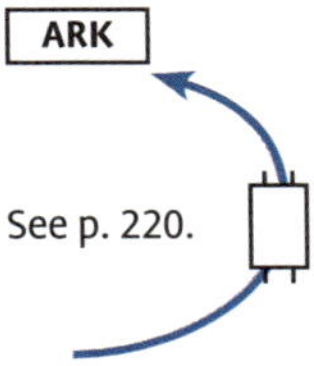

See p. 220.

חֲצִי קַדִּישׁ Short Kaddish W71 F146
Open, raise, display, and wrap scroll.
Return scroll to ark. W76 F150

אַשְׁרֵי Ashrey W78 F152
✕ ~~לַמְנַצֵּחַ Lamenatse·aḥ (Psalm 20)~~
וּבָא לְצִיּוֹן Uva letsiyyon W80 F156

Remove and pack tefillin. (Some remove after Kaddish.)

+ חֲצִי קַדִּישׁ Short Kaddish W103 F428

(If you remove tefillin here, do *not* pack but cover them, so as to begin Musaf together quickly after Kaddish.)

1st Adar 5782						
			1	2	3	4
5	6	7	8	9	10	11
12	13	14	15	16	17	18
19	20	21	22	23	24	25
26	27	28	29	30		

Feb | Mar 2022						
			2	3	4	5
6	7	8	9	10	11	12
13	14	15	16	17	18	19
20	21	22	23	24	25	26
27	28 | 1	2	3			

+ Add ✕ Omit ☞ Take note!

Siddurim

- **L** Lev Shalem for Shabbat and Festivals
- **S** Shabbat and Festival Sim Shalom
- **W** Weekday Sim Shalom
- **F** Full Sim Shalom (both editions)
- **P** Personal Edition of Full Sim Shalom

מוּסָף

\+ **Rosh Ḥodesh Amidah for weekdays:** W104 F486
Weekday קְדֻשָּׁה Kedushah W105 F488
\+ וּלְכַפָּרַת פָּשַׁע Ulkhapparat pasha W107 F494
Add these words only through Rosh Ḥodesh Adar Sheni.

\+ קַדִּישׁ שָׁלֵם Full Kaddish W82 F158
עָלֵינוּ Aleynu W83 F160

If psalms for the day were not recited at Shaḥarit, add here:
קַדִּישׁ יָתוֹם Mourner's Kaddish (some omit) W84|100 F162|52
Psalm for Thursday (Psalm 81) W89 F30
קַדִּישׁ יָתוֹם Mourner's Kaddish (some omit) W100 F52
\+ Psalm 104 for Rosh Ḥodesh W90 F34

קַדִּישׁ יָתוֹם Mourner's Kaddish W84|100 F162|52

מִנְחָה

Weekday Amidah:
\+ יַעֲלֶה וְיָבוֹא Ya'aleh veyavo for Rosh Ḥodesh W127 F178

✕ ~~תַּחֲנוּן Taḥanun~~

2nd Adar 1 אֲדָר ב׳ ראשׁ חֹדֶשׁ אֲדָר שֵׁנִי Rosh Ḥodesh Adar Sheni – Day 2

Thu 3 Mar (evening)

For determining the *yortsayt* of a death during Adar, 1st Adar, or 2nd Adar, see p. 224.

מִשֶּׁנִּכְנַס אֲדָר מַרְבִּין בְּשִׂמְחָה *mishenikhnas adar marbin besimḥah.*
The Rabbis instructed: "From the moment Adar arrives, we are to increase our joy." For a leap year, most authorities apply this dictum only to 2nd Adar, the Adar in which Purim is celebrated. Purim is still 2 weeks away. Yet our mood already begins to change as we anticipate its upcoming celebration.

DURING Rosh Ḥodesh

Birkat Hamazon:
+ יַעֲלֶה וְיָבוֹא Ya'aleh veyavo for Rosh Ḥodesh L90|95 S340|347 W233|239 F762|780
+ הָרַחֲמָן Haraḥaman for Rosh Ḥodesh L92|96 S343|348 W235|240 F768

עַרְבִית

Weekday Amidah:
+ יַעֲלֶה וְיָבוֹא Ya'aleh veyavo for Rosh Ḥodesh W145 F216

Fri 4 Mar **שַׁחֲרִית**

Before מִזְמוֹר שִׁיר Mizmor shir (Psalm 30) W14 F50
or at end of service, recite:
Psalm for Friday (Psalm 93) W90 F32
קַדִּישׁ יָתוֹם Mourner's Kaddish (some omit) W100 F52
+ Psalm 104 for Rosh Ḥodesh W90 F34
קַדִּישׁ יָתוֹם Mourner's Kaddish W100 F52

Weekday Amidah:
+ יַעֲלֶה וְיָבוֹא Ya'aleh veyavo for Rosh Ḥodesh W41 F114

✕ ~~תַּחֲנוּן Taḥanun~~

+ חֲצִי הַלֵּל Short Hallel W50 F380
קַדִּישׁ שָׁלֵם Full Kaddish W56 F392

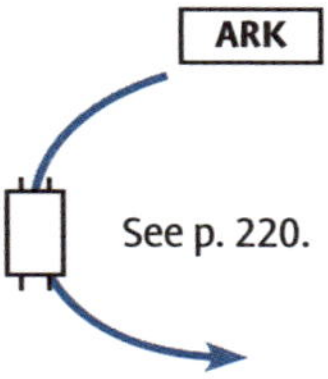

See p. 220.

+ **TORAH SERVICE** W65 F138
Remove **1** scroll from ark.

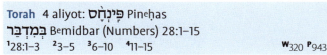

Torah 4 aliyot: פִּינְחָס Pineḥas
בְּמִדְבַּר Bemidbar (Numbers) 28:1–15
¹28:1–3 ²3–5 ³6–10 ⁴11–15 W320 P943

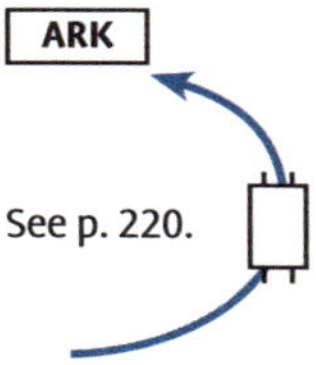

See p. 220.

חֲצִי קַדִּישׁ Short Kaddish W71 F146
Open, raise, display, and wrap scroll.
Return scroll to ark. W76 F150

2nd Adar 5782						
					1	2
3	4	5	6	7	8	9
10	11	12	13	14	15	16
17	18	19	20	21	22	23
24	25	26	27	28	29	

Mar | Apr 2022						
					4	5
6	7	8	9	10	11	12
13	14	15	16	17	18	19
20	21	22	23	24	25	26
27	28	29	30	31 |	1	

+ Add ✕ Omit ☞ Take note!

Siddurim
- **L** Lev Shalem for Shabbat and Festivals
- **S** Shabbat and Festival Sim Shalom
- **W** Weekday Sim Shalom
- **F** Full Sim Shalom (both editions)
- **P** Personal Edition of Full Sim Shalom

אַשְׁרֵי Ashrey W78 F152
✕ ~~לַמְנַצֵּחַ Lamenatse·aḥ (Psalm 20)~~
וּבָא לְצִיּוֹן Uva letsiyyon W80 F156

Remove and pack tefillin. (Some remove after Kaddish.)

+ חֲצִי קַדִּישׁ Short Kaddish W103 F428

(If you remove tefillin here, do *not* pack but cover them, so as to begin Musaf together quickly after Kaddish.)

מוּסָף

+ **Rosh Ḥodesh Amidah for weekdays:** W104 F486
Weekday קְדֻשָּׁה Kedushah W105 F488
+ וּלְכַפָּרַת פָּשַׁע Ulkhapparat pasha W107 F494
Add these words only through Rosh Ḥodesh Adar Sheni.

+ קַדִּישׁ שָׁלֵם Full Kaddish W82 F158
עָלֵינוּ Aleynu W83 F160

If psalms for the day were not recited at Shaḥarit, add here:
קַדִּישׁ יָתוֹם Mourner's Kaddish (some omit) W84|100 F162|52
Psalm for Friday (Psalm 93) W90 F32
קַדִּישׁ יָתוֹם Mourner's Kaddish (some omit) W100 F52
+ Psalm 104 for Rosh Ḥodesh W90 F34

קַדִּישׁ יָתוֹם Mourner's Kaddish W84|100 F162|52

מִנְחָה

Weekday Amidah:
+ יַעֲלֶה וְיָבוֹא Ya'aleh veyavo for Rosh Ḥodesh W127 F178

✕ ~~תַּחֲנוּן Taḥanun~~ (as on all Friday afternoons)

2nd Adar 2 אֲדָר ב׳ Sat 5 Mar

שַׁבָּת Shabbat פָּרָשַׁת פְּקוּדֵי Parashat Pekudey

Torah 7 aliyot (minimum): פְּקוּדֵי Pekudey
שְׁמוֹת Shemot (Exodus) 38:21–40:38

Annual:	1 38:21–39:1	2 39:2–21	3 39:22–32	4 39:33–43
	5 40:1–16	6 40:17–27	7 40:28–38 ▮	M 40:34–38
Triennial:	1 39:22–26	2 39:27–32	3 39:33–43	4 40:1–8
	5 40:9–16	6 40:17–27	7 40:28–38 ▮	M 40:34–38

▮ חזק When the Torah reader concludes a book of the Torah:
1. Close the Torah scroll.
2. **For Oleh:** Congregation chants חֲזַק חֲזַק וְנִתְחַזֵּק ḥazak ḥazak venitḥazzek; oleh remains silent.
For Olah: Congregation chants חִזְקִי חִזְקִי וְנִתְחַזֵּק ḥizki ḥizki venitḥazzek; olah remains silent.

Notes for Torah reading continue on p. 115.

3. Torah reader repeats congregation's words (oleh/olah remains silent; if Torah reader is the oleh/olah, omit this repetition).
4. Open the Torah scroll.
5. The oleh/olah kisses the Torah scroll, closes it, and continues with the usual concluding berakhah.

Haftarah
Ashkenazic: מְלָכִים א׳ 1 Melakhim (1 Kings) 7:51–8:21
Sephardic: מְלָכִים א׳ 1 Melakhim (1 Kings) 7:40–50

מִנְחָה

Torah 3 aliyot from וַיִּקְרָא Vayikra
וַיִּקְרָא Vayikra (Leviticus) 1:1–13
[1]1:1–4 [2]5–9 [3]10–13 W287 P907

Chanted also next Monday and Thursday.

2nd Adar 9 אֲדָר ב׳ Sat 12 Mar (morning)

שַׁבָּת Shabbat פָּרָשַׁת וַיִּקְרָא Parashat Vayikra
שַׁבַּת זָכוֹר Shabbat Zakhor

Shabbat Zakhor, the 2nd of 4 special Shabbatot before Pesaḥ, is named after the first word of the *maftir aliyah* reading, Devarim 25:17–19. It recalls Amalek's cowardly attack upon the weak and weary of the people Israel as they traveled in the wilderness. The people Israel is commanded to remember what Amalek did and to blot out Amalek's name.

The Rabbis prescribed that we fulfill this commandment once a year by reading this passage publicly from a Torah scroll. They chose the Shabbat before Purim for this reading to connect blotting out the name of Amalek to the Purim practice of blotting out the name of Haman, who was a descendant of Amalek.

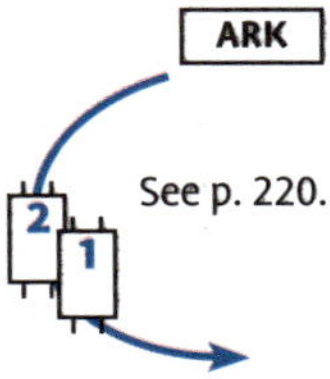

See p. 220.

TORAH SERVICE L168 S139 F394

Remove **2** scrolls from ark in the order they will be read.

1st scroll 7 aliyot (minimum): וַיִּקְרָא Vayikra
וַיִּקְרָא Vayikra (Leviticus) 1:1–5:26

Annual:	[1]1:1–13	[2]1:14–2:6	[3]2:7–16	[4]3:1–17
	[5]4:1–26	[6]4:27–5:10	[7]5:11–26	
Triennial:	[1]4:27–31	[2]4:32–35	[3]5:1–10	[4]5:11–13
	[5]5:14–16	[6]5:17–19	[7]5:20–26	

Place 2nd scroll on table next to 1st scroll.
חֲצִי קַדִּישׁ Short Kaddish L174 S146 F408

Open, raise, display, and wrap 1st scroll.

+ **2nd scroll** Maftir aliyah from כִּי־תֵצֵא Ki tetse
[M]דְּבָרִים Devarim (Deuteronomy) 25:17–19°

☞ °25:19 There should be **no** repetition of this verse or any of its words, despite a widespread practice of reading part or all of this verse twice using variant readings of the 6th-to-last word. The proper reading of this word is זֵכֶר, as it appears in the most reliable manuscripts and in almost all printed editions. For more information, see www.milesbcohen.com/LuahResources.

Open, raise, display, and wrap 2nd scroll.

☞ **Haftarah** for Shabbat Zakhor
Ashkenazic: שְׁמוּאֵל א׳ 1 Shemu'el (1 Samuel) 15:2–34
Sephardic: שְׁמוּאֵל א׳ 1 Shemu'el (1 Samuel) 15:1–34

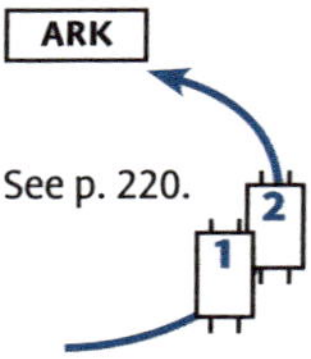

See p. 220.

✕ ~~אַב הָרַחֲמִים Av Harahamim~~

אַשְׁרֵי Ashrey L181 S151 F420
Return scrolls to ark in reverse order. L183 S153 F422

חֲצִי קָדִישׁ Short Kaddish L184 S155 F428

Continue as on a usual Shabbat.

מִנְחָה

Torah 3 aliyot from צַו Tsav
וַיִּקְרָא Vayikra (Leviticus) 6:1–11
[1]6:1–3 [2]4–6 [3]7–11 W288 P908

Chanted also next Monday.

☞ צִדְקָתְךָ צֶדֶק Tsidkatekha tsedek L230 S239 W183 F584

2nd Adar 10 אֲדָר ב׳
Sat 12 Mar (night)

After Arvit if the moon is visible:
קִדּוּשׁ לְבָנָה Kiddush Levanah L286 W167 F704
For procedures and instructions, see p. 223.

✚ Add ✘ Omit ☞ Take note!

Siddurim						
				1 2		4 5
L	Lev Shalem for Shabbat and Festivals	3 4 5 6 7 8 9	6 7 8 9 10 11 12			
S	Shabbat and Festival Sim Shalom	10 11 12 13 14 15 16	13 14 15 16 17 18 19			
W	Weekday Sim Shalom	17 18 19 20 21 22 23	20 21 22 23 24 25 26			
F	Full Sim Shalom (both editions)	24 25 26 27 28 29	27 28 29 30 31 1			
P	Personal Edition of Full Sim Shalom

2nd Adar 13 אֲדָר ב׳ 13 תַּעֲנִית אֶסְתֵּר Ta'anit Ester

Wed 16 Mar (morning) **Fast of Esther (communal fast, begins Wednesday at dawn)**

Ta'anit Ester

Ta'anit Ester commemorates the fasting by the Jews before commencing their defensive battle against Haman's forces. The fast day is named for Esther in remembrance of the 3-day fast she proclaimed for all the Jews in advance of her perilous seeking of an audience with the king to plead for the Jews.

- This is a minor fast day, so called because the fast does not begin until dawn.
- The fast (from both eating and drinking) lasts until dark (a minimum of 25 minutes after sunset).
- *Shelihey tsibbur,* Torah readers, and those called for *aliyot* should be fasting.
- The preferred fast-day procedures apply when at least 6 of those who are counted for a *minyan* are fasting.
- If it is ascertained (without causing embarrassment) that fewer than 6 are fasting, follow the procedures printed in gray and marked with ✦.

שַׁחֲרִית

Silent Weekday Amidah:
Do not add עֲנֵנוּ Anenu.

Repetition of the Weekday Amidah:

6 or more fasting + עֲנֵנוּ Anenu before רְפָאֵנוּ Refa'enu W38 F110

Fewer than 6 fasting ✦ Add עֲנֵנוּ Anenu in שׁוֹמֵעַ תְּפִלָּה Shome·a tefillah. Replace תַּעֲנִיתֵנוּ ta'anitenu (6th word) with הַתַּעֲנִית הַזֶּה hata'anit hazeh. W38 F110

6 or more fasting + אָבִינוּ מַלְכֵּנוּ Avinu malkenu W57 F124

Fewer than 6 fasting ✦ Those fasting recite אָבִינוּ מַלְכֵּנוּ individually.

☞ תַּחֲנוּן Tahanun (וַיֹּאמֶר דָּוִד Vayomer david) W62 F132

חֲצִי קַדִּישׁ Short Kaddish W64 F136

2nd Adar 5782						
					1	2
3	4	5	6	7	8	9
10	11	12	13	14	15	16
17	18	19	20	21	22	23
24	25	26	27	28	29	

Mar | Apr 2022						
					4	5
6	7	8	9	10	11	12
13	14	15	16	17	18	19
20	21	22	23	24	25	26
27	28	29	30	31 |	1	

+ Add ✕ Omit ☞ Take note!

Siddurim
- **L** Lev Shalem for Shabbat and Festivals
- **S** Shabbat and Festival Sim Shalom
- **W** Weekday Sim Shalom
- **F** Full Sim Shalom (both editions)
- **P** Personal Edition of Full Sim Shalom

Fewer than 6 fasting ✦ Omit the entire Torah service. Continue with אַשְׁרֵי Ashrey.

6 or more fasting + **TORAH SERVICE** W65 F138
Remove **1** scroll from ark.

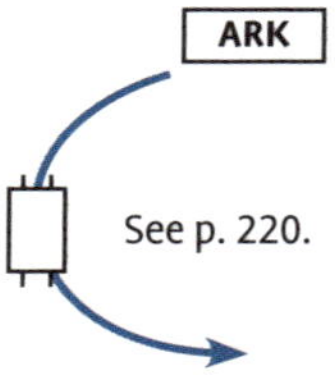

See p. 220.

Torah 3 aliyot from כִּי תִשָּׂא Ki tissa
שְׁמוֹת Shemot (Exodus) 32:11–14, 34:1–10
¹32:11–14° ²34:1–3 ³34:4–10° W341 P979

☞ °At each of the 3 passages indicated below, follow this procedure:
1. The reader pauses before the indicated text.
2. The congregation recites the indicated text.
3. Afterward, the reader chants the indicated text in the manner of the cantillation of High Holiday Torah reading.

32:12 שׁוּב מֵחֲרוֹן אַפֶּךָ וְהִנָּחֵם עַל־הָרָעָה לְעַמֶּךָ׃

34:6–7 יי | יי אֵ‑ל רַחוּם וְחַנּוּן אֶרֶךְ אַפַּיִם וְרַב־חֶסֶד וֶאֱמֶת׃
נֹצֵר חֶסֶד לָאֲלָפִים נֹשֵׂא עָוֺן וָפֶשַׁע וְחַטָּאָה וְנַקֵּה

34:9 וְסָלַחְתָּ לַעֲוֺנֵנוּ וּלְחַטָּאתֵנוּ | וּנְחַלְתָּנוּ׃
To preserve the sense of this passage, maintain the appropriate pause after the טִפְּחָא (וּלְחַטָּאתֵנוּ).

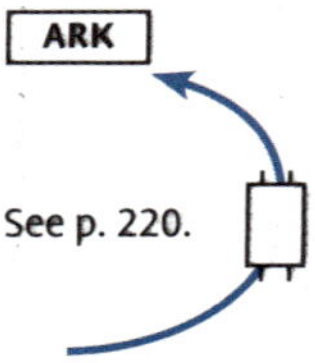

See p. 220.

חֲצִי קַדִּישׁ Short Kaddish W71 F146
Open, raise, display, and wrap scroll.
Return scroll to ark. W76 F150

All minyanim
אַשְׁרֵי Ashrey W78 F152
☞ לַמְנַצֵּחַ Lamenatse·aḥ (Psalm 20) W79 F154
Conclude the service in the usual manner.

מַחֲצִית הַשֶּׁקֶל ***maḥatsit hashekel***, in common practice, is half the basic unit of currency in use in a Jewish community. At Purim time, it is customary to contribute 3 half-shekels (for example, $1.50 in the United States or Canada). This is because in the Torah, the phrase מַחֲצִית הַשֶּׁקֶל appears 3 times in the description of this obligation to contribute (Shemot 30:11–16).

In the Torah, the half-shekel collection was to support operation of the *mishkan*. Later the funds were used for Temple upkeep. This was a tax, instituted as an annual obligation to be paid during the month of Adar.

Currently, the funds support Jewish institutions or other charitable endeavors.

מִנְחָה Before or at Minḥah, we give מַחֲצִית הַשֶּׁקֶל maḥatsit hashekel (see green box, above).

אַשְׁרֵי Ashrey W120 F164
חֲצִי קַדִּישׁ Short Kaddish W121 F166

Fewer than 6 fasting ✦ Omit the entire Torah service. Continue with silent Amidah.

6 or more fasting ➕ **TORAH SERVICE** W65 F138

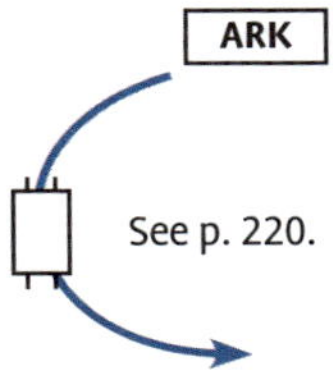

See p. 220.

Remove **1** scroll from ark.

Torah 3 aliyot from כִּי תִשָּׂא Ki tissa
שְׁמוֹת Shemot (Exodus) 32:11–14, 34:1–10
¹32:11–14° ²34:1–3 ᴹ34:4–10° W341 P979

☞ °Chant as for the morning fast-day reading (p. 118).

☞ Do not recite חֲצִי קַדִּישׁ Short Kaddish after maftir aliyah.

Open, raise, display, and wrap scroll.

Recite the בְּרָכָה berakhah before the haftarah. W74 F410 P989

Haftarah יְשַׁעְיָהוּ Yesha'yahu (Isaiah) 55:6–56:8 W342 P980

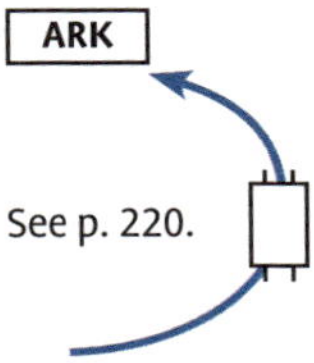

See p. 220.

Recite the 3 concluding haftarah blessings, through מָגֵן דָּוִד Magen david. W74 F410 P989.

Return scroll to ark. W76 F150
חֲצִי קַדִּישׁ Short Kaddish W121 F166

All minyanim **Silent weekday Amidah:**

If fasting ➕ עֲנֵנוּ Anenu, in שׁוֹמֵעַ תְּפִלָּה Shome·a tefillah W127 F178

All ✖ ~~שָׁלוֹם רָב Shalom rav~~
➕ שִׂים שָׁלוֹם Sim shalom W131 F184

Repetition of the weekday Amidah:

6 or more fasting ➕ עֲנֵנוּ Anenu, before רְפָאֵנוּ Refa'enu W124 F172

Fewer than 6 fasting ✦ Add עֲנֵנוּ Anenu in שׁוֹמֵעַ תְּפִלָּה Shome·a tefillah. Replace תַּעֲנִיתֵנוּ ta'anitenu (6th word) with הַתַּעֲנִית הַזֶּה hata'anit hazeh. W127 F172

All minyanim ➕ בִּרְכַּת כֹּהֲנִים Birkat kohanim W131 F184
✖ ~~שָׁלוֹם רָב Shalom rav~~
➕ שִׂים שָׁלוֹם Sim shalom W131 F184

✖ ~~אָבִינוּ מַלְכֵּנוּ Avinu malkenu~~
✖ ~~תַּחֲנוּן Taḥanun~~

קַדִּישׁ שָׁלֵם Full Kaddish W134 F194
עָלֵינוּ Aleynu W135 F196
קַדִּישׁ יָתוֹם Mourner's Kaddish W136 F198

Purim

The 5 Mitsvot of Purim

Five מִצְוֹת *mitsvot* are associated with the celebration of Purim:

1. מִקְרָא מְגִלָּה בְּעַרְבִית *mikra megillah be'arvit.* All Jewish men, women, and children are to listen to the reading of the מְגִלָּה *megillah* at the Arvit service.
2. מִקְרָא מְגִלָּה בְּשַׁחֲרִית *mikra megillah beshaharit.* It is an additional and separate מִצְוָה *mitsvah* for all Jewish men, women, and children to listen to the reading of the מְגִלָּה at the Shaharit service.
3. מַתָּנוֹת לָאֶבְיוֹנִים *mattanot la'evyonim.* To express our joy on Purim, we give gifts of food, drink, money, or clothing to poor people. Fulfill the מִצְוָה by giving at least 1 gift each to 2 poor people during Purim day.
4. מִשְׁלוֹחַ מָנוֹת *mishloah manot.* Another way to express the joy of Purim is to give gifts of food and drink to family and friends. Fulfill the מִצְוָה by giving 2 kinds of food to 1 person during Purim day. More gifts may be given, but it is preferable to maximize gifts to poor people (מַתָּנוֹת לָאֶבְיוֹנִים; see 3 above) rather than to maximize מִשְׁלוֹחַ מָנוֹת.
5. סְעוּדַת פּוּרִים *se'udat purim.* We hold the joyous Purim feast in the afternoon, extending into the evening. (When Purim day is Friday, we hold the feast in the morning.) It features food and drink, as well as "Purim Torah" (parodies of Torah lessons) and a Purim *shpil* (consisting of humorous performances and skits on Purim themes).

Procedure for Chanting Megillat Ester

Before Chanting the Megillah

1. The reader unrolls the מְגִלָּה and folds it like a letter.
2. The congregation stands as the reader recites three בְּרָכוֹת *berakhot* (both evening and morning): S220 W194

בָּרוּךְ אַתָּה יי, אֱ·לֹהֵינוּ מֶלֶךְ הָעוֹלָם, אֲשֶׁר קִדְּשָׁנוּ בְּמִצְוֹתָיו
וְצִוָּנוּ עַל מִקְרָא מְגִלָּה.

בָּרוּךְ אַתָּה יי, אֱ·לֹהֵינוּ מֶלֶךְ הָעוֹלָם,
שֶׁעָשָׂה נִסִּים לַאֲבוֹתֵינוּ בַּיָּמִים הָהֵם וּבַזְּמַן הַזֶּה.

בָּרוּךְ אַתָּה יי, אֱ·לֹהֵינוּ מֶלֶךְ הָעוֹלָם,
שֶׁהֶחֱיָנוּ וְקִיְּמָנוּ וְהִגִּיעָנוּ לַזְּמַן הַזֶּה.

Chanting the Megillah

1. The reader and congregation observe the following customs:
   - When the reader reaches each of אַרְבָּעָה פְּסוּקִים שֶׁל גְּאֻלָּה *arba'ah pesukim shel ge'ullah* ("the 4 redemption verses")—2:5, 8:15, 8:16, and 10:3:
     The reader pauses while the congregation recites the verse.
     When the congregation finishes, the reader chants the verse and continues.

- Whenever the reader chants the name הָמָן *haman,* the congregation makes noise to drown out the name. We do so in response to the commandment תִּמְחֶה אֶת־זֵכֶר עֲמָלֵק *timḥeh et zekher amalek* ("blot out the name of Amalek"; Devarim 25:19). According to tradition, Haman was a descendant of Amalek.

2. To reflect the frequent changes in the mood of the story, the reader adjusts the cantillation by chanting:
   - Traditional enhancements to positive turning points in the story, celebratory moments, and other special verses, including: 1:22, 2:4, 2:17, 5:7, 6:1, 6:10, 7:10, 8:14, 8:15, 8:16, 10:2, and 10:3.
   - Sad and threatening verses using the cantillation system of אֵיכָה *eykhah* (Lamentations): 1:7 (only the 3 words וְכֵלִים מִכֵּלִים שׁוֹנִים), 3:15, 4:1, 4:3 (beginning אֵבֶל גָּדוֹל), and 4:16 (last 3 words only).

   This selection of verses reflects the rabbinic tradition that chapter 6 records God's intervention on behalf of the Jews. After this, no further lamenting is appropriate.
3. The reader chants the names of Haman's 10 sons (9:7–10) in 1 breath.
4. Do *not* follow the mistaken practice of repeating a verse to present supposed variant readings in the מְגִלָּה. The "variants" in 8:11 and 9:2 are old printers' errors. Most recent printed editions have corrected these errors.

   These printers' errors have worked their way into most Ashkenazic scrolls. Even if your scroll contains the errors, read only the correct word, as follows:

   8:11 Read וְלַהֲרֹג even if your scroll has לַהֲרֹג.
   9:2 Read לִפְנֵיהֶם even if your scroll has בִּפְנֵיהֶם.

   Other mistaken practices, growing in popularity, of repeating verses in chapters 2 and 3 have no basis in tradition.

   For more information, see www.milesbcohen.com/LuahResources.

After Chanting the Megillah

- The reader quickly closes the מְגִלָּה.
- The congregation stands for the concluding בְּרָכָה *berakhah*: S220 W194

בָּרוּךְ אַתָּה יי, אֱ־לֹהֵינוּ מֶלֶךְ הָעוֹלָם,
הָרָב אֶת־רִיבֵנוּ, וְהַדָּן אֶת־דִּינֵנוּ, וְהַנּוֹקֵם אֶת־נִקְמָתֵנוּ,
וְהַמְשַׁלֵּם גְּמוּל לְכָל־אוֹיְבֵי נַפְשֵׁנוּ, וְהַנִּפְרָע לָנוּ מִצָּרֵינוּ.
בָּרוּךְ אַתָּה יי, הַנִּפְרָע לְעַמּוֹ יִשְׂרָאֵל מִכָּל־צָרֵיהֶם, הָאֵ־ל הַמּוֹשִׁיעַ.

- In the evening, some add the poem אֲשֶׁר הֵנִיא *asher heni.* W195
- Evening and morning, recite שׁוֹשַׁנַּת יַעֲקֹב *shoshanat ya'akov.* S220 W195

2nd Adar 5782						
					1	2
3	4	5	6	7	8	9
10	11	12	13	14	15	16
17	18	19	20	21	22	23
24	25	26	27	28	29	

Mar | Apr 2022						
					4	5
6	7	8	9	10	11	12
13	14	15	16	17	18	19
20	21	22	23	24	25	26
27	28	29	30	31 |	1	

+ Add ✕ Omit ☞ Take note!

Siddurim
- **L** Lev Shalem for Shabbat and Festivals
- **S** Shabbat and Festival Sim Shalom
- **W** Weekday Sim Shalom
- **F** Full Sim Shalom (both editions)
- **P** Personal Edition of Full Sim Shalom

2nd Adar 14 אֲדָר ב׳ פּוּרִים Purim

Wed **16** Mar (evening)

DURING Purim

Birkat Hamazon:
+ עַל הַנִּסִּים Al Hanissim for Purim L431 W232|238 F760

For information about mitsvot and procedures for Purim, see pp. 120–121.

עַרְבִית

Weekday Arvit as usual until the Amidah L264 S281 W137 F200

Weekday Amidah:
+ עַל הַנִּסִּים Al Hanissim for Purim L431 S290 W146 F218

☞ קַדִּישׁ שָׁלֵם Full Kaddish L280 S294 W149 F222

+ **Megillah reading:**
מְגִלַּת אֶסְתֵּר Megillat Ester (Scroll of Esther)
Follow the procedure described on pp. 120–121.

☞ 8:11 Read וְלַהֲרֹג even if your megillah has לַהֲרֹג.
9:2 Read לִפְנֵיהֶם even if your megillah has בִּפְנֵיהֶם.
Do **not** repeat words, phrases, or verses in an effort to reflect supposed variant readings, which in fact are printer/scribal errors. For more information, see www.milesbcohen.com/LuahResources.

+ וְאַתָּה קָדוֹשׁ Ve'attah kadosh L216 S293 W159 F684

☞ קַדִּישׁ שָׁלֵם Full Kaddish, but omit sentence: L280 S294 W160 F688
✕ ~~תִּתְקַבַּל Titkabal . . .~~

Conclude as on a usual weeknight.

Thu **17** Mar **שַׁחֲרִית**

Weekday Amidah:
+ עַל הַנִּסִּים Al Hanissim for Purim W42 F118

✕ ~~תַּחֲנוּן Taḥanun~~

☞ Do not recite הַלֵּל Hallel.

חֲצִי קַדִּישׁ Short Kaddish W64 F136

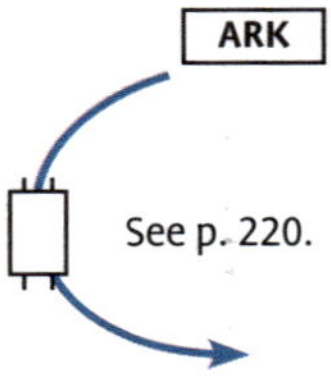

See p. 220.

+ **TORAH SERVICE** W65 F138
Remove **1** scroll from ark.

Torah 3 aliyot from בְּשַׁלַּח Beshallaḥ
שְׁמוֹת Shemot (Exodus) 17:8–16
¹17:8–10 ²11–13 ³14–16 W337 P955

ARK

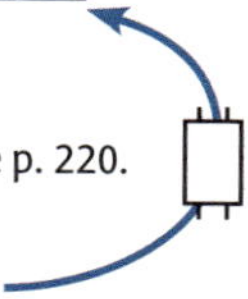

See p. 220.

חֲצִי קַדִּישׁ Short Kaddish W71 F146
Open, raise, display, and wrap scroll.
Return scroll to ark. W76 F150

+ **Megillah reading:**
Follow the procedure described on pp. 120–121.

☞ 8:11 Read וְלַהֲרֹג even if your megillah has לַהֲרֹג.
9:2 Read לִפְנֵיהֶם even if your megillah has בִּפְנֵיהֶם.
Do **not** repeat words, phrases, or verses in an effort to reflect supposed variant readings, which in fact are printer/scribal errors. For more information, see www.milesbcohen.com/LuahResources.

אַשְׁרֵי Ashrey W78 F152
✕ ~~לַמְנַצֵּחַ Lamenatse·aḥ (Psalm 20)~~
וּבָא לְצִיּוֹן Uva letsiyyon W80 F156

קַדִּישׁ שָׁלֵם Full Kaddish W82 F158
עָלֵינוּ Aleynu W83 F160

Conclude as on a usual weekday.

מִנְחָה **Weekday Amidah:**
+ עַל הַנִּסִּים Al Hanissim for Purim W129 F182

✕ ~~תַּחֲנוּן Taḥanun~~

2nd Adar 15 אֲדָר ב׳ פּוּרִים שׁוּשַׁן Shushan Purim
Thu 17 Mar

עַרְבִית Weekday Arvit as usual W137 F200
☞ Do not recite עַל הַנִּסִּים Al Hanissim.

Fri 18 Mar **שַׁחֲרִית** Weekday Shaḥarit as usual W1 F2
☞ Do not recite עַל הַנִּסִּים Al Hanissim.

✕ ~~תַּחֲנוּן Taḥanun~~
✕ ~~לַמְנַצֵּחַ Lamenatse·aḥ (Psalm 20)~~

מִנְחָה Weekday Minḥah as usual L289 S1 W120 F164
☞ Do not recite עַל הַנִּסִּים Al Hanissim.

✕ ~~תַּחֲנוּן Taḥanun~~ (as on all Friday afternoons)

2nd Adar 5782						
					1	2
3	4	5	6	7	8	9
10	11	12	13	14	15	16
17	18	19	20	21	22	23
24	25	26	27	28	29	

Mar | Apr 2022						
					4	5
6	7	8	9	10	11	12
13	14	15	16	17	18	19
20	21	22	23	24	25	26
27	28	29	30	31 |	1	

+ Add ✗ Omit ☞ Take note!

Siddurim
- **L** Lev Shalem for Shabbat and Festivals
- **S** Shabbat and Festival Sim Shalom
- **W** Weekday Sim Shalom
- **F** Full Sim Shalom (both editions)
- **P** Personal Edition of Full Sim Shalom

2nd Adar 16 אֲדָר ב׳ — שַׁבָּת Shabbat פָּרָשַׁת צַו Parashat Tsav
Sat 19 Mar

Torah 7 aliyot (minimum): צַו Tsav
וַיִּקְרָא Vayikra (Leviticus) 6:1–8:36

Annual:	1 6:1–11	2 6:12–7:10	3 7:11–38	4 8:1–13
	5 8:14–21	6 8:22–29°	7 8:30–36	M 8:33–36
Triennial:	1 8:1–5	2 8:6–9	3 8:10–13	4 8:14–17
	5 8:18–21	6 8:22–29°	7 8:30–36	M 8:33–36

☞°8:23 Note the rare ta'am (trope) | שַׁלְשֶׁ֓לֶת (|⸗): וַיִּשְׁחָ֓ט |

Haftarah יִרְמְיָהוּ Yirmeyahu (Jeremiah) 7:21–8:3, 9:22–23

מִנְחָה

Torah 3 aliyot from שְׁמִינִי Shemini
וַיִּקְרָא Vayikra (Leviticus) 9:1–16
1 9:1–6 2 7–10 3 11–16 W289 P909

Chanted also next Monday and Thursday.

2nd Adar 23 אֲדָר ב׳ — שַׁבָּת Shabbat פָּרָשַׁת שְׁמִינִי Parashat Shemini
Sat 26 Mar (morning)

שַׁבַּת פָּרָה Shabbat Parah
שַׁבַּת מְבָרְכִים הַחֹדֶשׁ Shabbat Mevarekhim Haḥodesh

Shabbat Parah is the 3rd of 4 special Shabbatot before Pesaḥ. It falls on the Shabbat before Shabbat Haḥodesh and represents the beginning of preparation for Pesaḥ. The special *maftir aliyah* reading (Bemidbar 19:1–22), in the 2nd Torah scroll, details the matter of the פָּרָה אֲדֻמָּה *parah adummah* (red heifer). In the days of the Temple, the priest would use the ashes of the פָּרָה אֲדֻמָּה to purify people who were in a ritually impure state, which would have prevented them from being eligible to eat of the Pesaḥ sacrifice.

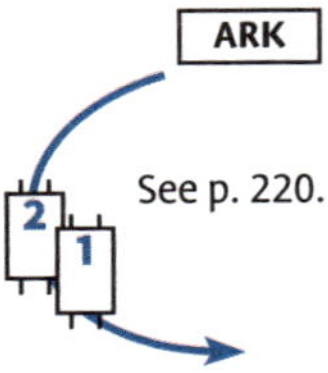

See p. 220.

TORAH SERVICE L168 S139 F394

Remove **2** scrolls from ark in the order they will be read.

1st scroll 7 aliyot (minimum): שְׁמִינִי Shemini
וַיִּקְרָא Vayikra (Leviticus) 9:1–11:47

Annual:	1 9:1–16	2 9:17–23	3 9:24–10:11°	4 10:12–15
	5 10:16–20	6 11:1–32	7 11:33–47	
Triennial:	1 11:1–8	2 11:9–12	3 11:13–19	4 11:20–28
	5 11:29–32	6 11:33–38	7 11:39–47	

☞°10:1 Note the rare ta'am (trope) מֵירְכָא־כְפוּלָה (֦):
אֲשֶׁר לֹ֦א צִוָּה Connect לֹ֦א to the preceding and following words without a pause; then pause after the טִפְּחָא (צִוָּֽה), as usual.

Notes for Torah reading continue on p. 125.

☞°10:4 Note rare occurrence of the te'amim (tropes) גֵּרְשַׁיִם (֞) and תְּלִישָׁא־גְדוֹלָה (֠) on the same word קָרְבּוֹ. Chant first the melody of גֵּרְשַׁיִם and then the melody of תְּלִישָׁא־גְדוֹלָה consecutively on the last syllable of the word (בּוֹ). Do **not** chant the word twice.

☞°10:6 Note the unusual use of the ta'am מֻנַּח־לְגַרְמֵיהּ | (= מֻנַּח־מַפְסִיק |): אַל־תִּפְרָעוּ |

☞°10:8 Note the unusual consecutive occurrences of the ta'am אַל־תֵּשְׁתְּ | אַתָּה | וּבָנֶיךָ אִתָּךְ: (מֻנַּח־מַפְסִיק | =) מֻנַּח־לְגַרְמֵיהּ |

Place 2nd scroll on table next to 1st scroll.
חֲצִי קַדִּישׁ Short Kaddish L174 S146 F408
Open, raise, display, and wrap 1st scroll.

+ **2nd scroll** Maftir aliyah from חֻקַּת Ḥukkat
בְּמִדְבַּר M Bemidbar (Numbers) 19:1–22

Open, raise, display, and wrap 2nd scroll.

☞ **Haftarah** for Shabbat Parah
Ashkenazic: יְחֶזְקֵאל Yeḥezkel (Ezekiel) 36:16–38
Sephardic: יְחֶזְקֵאל Yeḥezkel (Ezekiel) 36:16–36

+ **Birkat Haḥodesh:** L180 S150 F418
Announce Rosh Ḥodesh Nisan:
רֹאשׁ חֹדֶשׁ נִיסָן יִהְיֶה בְּיוֹם שַׁבַּת קֹדֶשׁ . . .
Rosh ḥodesh Nisan yihyeh beyom shabbat kodesh . . .
(Friday night and Saturday)

✕ ~~אַב הָרַחֲמִים Av Haraḥamim~~

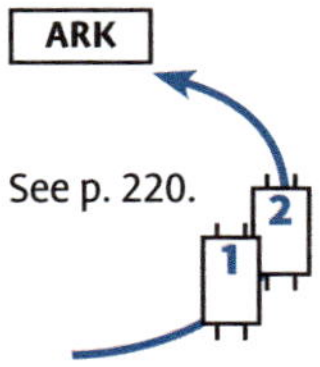

See p. 220.

אַשְׁרֵי Ashrey L181 S151 F420
Return scrolls to ark in reverse order. L183 S153 F422

חֲצִי קַדִּישׁ Short Kaddish L184 S155 F428

Continue as on a usual Shabbat.

מִנְחָה

Torah 3 aliyot from תַּזְרִיעַ Tazria
וַיִּקְרָא Vayikra (Leviticus) 12:1–13:5
1 12:1–4 2 5–8 3 13:1–5 W290 P910

Chanted also next Monday and Thursday.

☞ צִדְקָתְךָ צֶדֶק Tsidkatekha tsedek L230 S239 W183 F584

Nisan 5782							Apr | May 2022						
						1							2
2	3	4	5	6	7	8	3	4	5	6	7	8	9
9	10	11	12	13	14	15	10	11	12	13	14	15	16
16	17	18	19	20	21	22	17	18	19	20	21	22	23
23	24	25	26	27	28	29	24	25	26	27	28	29	30
30							1						

+ Add ✕ Omit ☞ Take note!

Siddurim
- **L** Lev Shalem for Shabbat and Festivals
- **S** Shabbat and Festival Sim Shalom
- **W** Weekday Sim Shalom
- **F** Full Sim Shalom (both editions)
- **P** Personal Edition of Full Sim Shalom

DURING Nisan ✕ ~~תַּחֲנוּן Taḥanun~~

Nisan 1 נִיסָן 1
Fri 1 Apr (evening)

שַׁבָּת Shabbat פָּרָשַׁת תַּזְרִיעַ Parashat Tazria
רֹאשׁ חֹדֶשׁ נִיסָן Rosh Ḥodesh Nisan
שַׁבַּת הַחֹדֶשׁ Shabbat Haḥodesh

Shabbat Haḥodesh is the last of 4 special Shabbatot before Pesaḥ. It falls on the Shabbat before Nisan begins, unless Nisan begins on Shabbat, as it does this year. In that case, Shabbat Haḥodesh coincides with Rosh Ḥodesh.

The special *maftir aliyah* reading for Shabbat Haḥodesh (Shemot 12:1–20) describes the night of the 1st Pesaḥ. Notable features include eating the Pesaḥ lamb sacrifice with unleavened bread and bitter herbs, and painting the blood of the sacrificed lamb on the doorposts of Israelite houses. The passage, containing both the story and various laws of Pesaḥ, connects us to our ancient past and prods us to accelerate preparations for Pesaḥ, which is only a few weeks away.

DURING Rosh Ḥodesh

Birkat Hamazon:

+ יַעֲלֶה וְיָבוֹא Ya'aleh veyavo for Rosh Ḥodesh L90|95 S340|347 W233|239 F762|780

+ הָרַחֲמָן Haraḥaman for Rosh Ḥodesh L92|96 S343|348 W235|240 F768

עַרְבִית

Shabbat Amidah:

+ יַעֲלֶה וְיָבוֹא Ya'aleh veyavo for Rosh Ḥodesh L50 S36 F298

Sat 2 Apr **שַׁחֲרִית**

Before מִזְמוֹר שִׁיר Mizmor shir (Psalm 30) L120 S81 F50
or after Aleynu, recite:

Psalm for Shabbat (Psalm 92) L112 S72 F32
קַדִּישׁ יָתוֹם Mourner's Kaddish (some omit) L121 S82 F52
+ Psalm 104 for Rosh Ḥodesh L114 S78 F34
קַדִּישׁ יָתוֹם Mourner's Kaddish L121 S82 F52

Shabbat Amidah:

+ יַעֲלֶה וְיָבוֹא Ya'aleh veyavo for Rosh Ḥodesh L163 S118 F360

+ חֲצִי הַלֵּל Short Hallel L316 S133 F380
קַדִּישׁ שָׁלֵם Full Kaddish L167 S138 F392

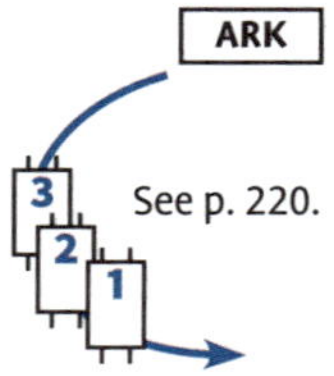

See p. 220.

TORAH SERVICE L168 S139 F394

☞ Remove **3** scrolls from ark in the order they will be read.

Siddurim

- **L** Lev Shalem for Shabbat and Festivals
- **S** Shabbat and Festival Sim Shalom
- **W** Weekday Sim Shalom
- **F** Full Sim Shalom (both editions)
- **P** Personal Edition of Full Sim Shalom

Nisan 5782							Apr | May 2022						
						1							2
2	3	4	5	6	7	8	3	4	5	6	7	8	9
9	10	11	12	13	14	15	10	11	12	13	14	15	16
16	17	18	19	20	21	22	17	18	19	20	21	22	23
23	24	25	26	27	28	29	24	25	26	27	28	29	30
30							1						

1st scroll 6 aliyot (minimum): תַּזְרִ֫יעַ Tazria
וַיִּקְרָא Vayikra (Leviticus) 12:1–13:59

Annual:	[1]12:1–13:5	[2]13:6–17	[3]13:18–23	[4]13:24–28
	[5]13:29–39	[6]13:40–59		
Triennial:°	[1]13:29–34	[2]13:35–39	[3]13:40–42	[4]13:43–46
	[5]13:47–50	[6]13:51–59		

☞ Triennial: Accords with the CJLS decision of Nov. 16, 2020.

Place 2nd scroll on table next to 1st scroll.

☞ Do not recite חֲצִי קַדִּישׁ Short Kaddish here.

Open, raise, display, and wrap 1st scroll.

➕ **2nd scroll** 7th aliyah from פִּינְחָס Pineḥas
בְּמִדְבַּר[7] Bemidbar (Numbers) 28:9–15

Place 3rd scroll on table next to 2nd scroll.
Place or hold 1st scroll near other scrolls at table.
(Some do not return 1st scroll to table.)

חֲצִי קַדִּישׁ Short Kaddish L174 S146 F408
Open, raise, display, and wrap 2nd scroll.

➕ **3rd scroll** Maftir aliyah for Shabbat Haḥodesh
שְׁמוֹת[M] Shemot (Exodus 12:1–20)

Open, raise, display, and wrap 3rd scroll.

☞ **Haftarah** for Shabbat Haḥodesh
Ashkenazic: יְחֶזְקֵאל Yeḥezkel (Ezekiel) 45:16–46:18
Sephardic: יְחֶזְקֵאל Yeḥezkel (Ezekiel) 45:18–46:15

☞ Most Ashkenazic congregations do **not** add verses from the Shabbat Rosh Ḥodesh haftarah. Sephardic congregations append the first and last verses.

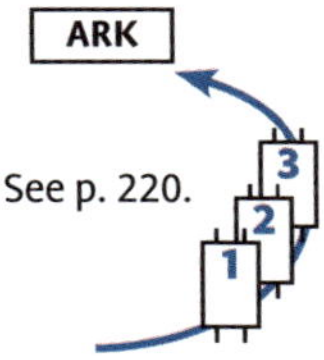

See p. 220.

✕ ~~אַב הָרַחֲמִים Av Haraḥamim~~

אַשְׁרֵי Ashrey L181 S151 F420
Return scrolls to ark in reverse order. L183 S153 F422

חֲצִי קַדִּישׁ Short Kaddish L184 S155 F428

מוּסָף **Rosh Ḥodesh Amidah for Shabbat:** L193 S166 F486
Shabbat קְדֻשָּׁה Kedushah L195 S167 F490
Continuation of Amidah L196 S168 F496

☞ Do *not* continue to add וּלְכַפָּרַת פָּשַׁע Ulkhapparat pasha.

קַדִּישׁ שָׁלֵם Full Kaddish L203 S181 F506
אֵין כֵּא·לֹהֵינוּ Eyn keloheynu L204 S182 F507
עָלֵינוּ Aleynu L205 S183 F508

If psalms for the day were not recited at Shaḥarit, add here:
קַדִּישׁ יָתוֹם Mourner's Kaddish (some omit) L207 S184 F512
Psalm for Shabbat (Psalm 92) L112 S72 F32
קַדִּישׁ יָתוֹם Mourner's Kaddish (some omit) L121 S82 F52
+ Psalm 104 for Rosh Ḥodesh L114 S78 F34

קַדִּישׁ יָתוֹם Mourner's Kaddish L207|121 S184|82 F512|52

מִנְחָה

Torah 3 aliyot from מְצֹרָע Metsora
וַיִּקְרָא Vayikra (Leviticus) 14:1–12
¹14:1–5 ²6–9 ³10–12 W291 P911

Chanted also next Monday and Thursday.

Shabbat Amidah:
+ יַעֲלֶה וְיָבוֹא Ya'aleh veyavo for Rosh Ḥodesh L227 S237 F580

✕ ~~צִדְקָתְךָ צֶדֶק Tsidkatekha tsedek~~

Nisan 8 נִיסָן 8
Sat 9 Apr (morning)

שַׁבָּת Shabbat פָּרָשַׁת מְצֹרָע Parashat Metsora
שַׁבַּת הַגָּדוֹל Shabbat Hagadol

Shabbat Hagadol is the name of the Shabbat preceding Pesaḥ. Some rabbis explain that this Shabbat takes its name from the end of the special haftarah for this day (Mal'akhi 3:23): "I will send the prophet Eliyahu to you before the coming of *the great* [הַגָּדוֹל], fearful day of the Lord." This is a foreshadowing of the role Eliyahu plays at the Pesaḥ seder as a harbinger of the coming of the messianic age. Other rabbis offer alternative explanations for the name.

We do not add a special Torah reading for Shabbat Hagadol.

Torah 7 aliyot (minimum): מְצֹרָע Metsora
וַיִּקְרָא Vayikra (Leviticus) 14:1–15:33

Annual:	¹14:1–12	²14:13–20	³14:21–32	⁴14:33–53
	⁵14:54–15:15	⁶15:16–28	⁷15:29–33	M15:31–33
Triennial:	¹14:33–38	²14:39–47	³14:48–53	⁴14:54–15:7
	⁵15:8–15	⁶15:16–28	⁷15:29–33	M15:31–33

☞ **Haftarah** for Shabbat Hagadol
מַלְאָכִי Mal'akhi (Malachi) 3:4–24°

☞ °After 3:24, repeat 3:23 so that the haftarah ends on a positive note.

✕ ~~אַב הָרַחֲמִים Av Haraḥamim~~

מִנְחָה

Torah 3 aliyot from אַחֲרֵי מוֹת Aḥarey mot
וַיִּקְרָא Vayikra (Leviticus) 16:1–17
1 16:1–6 2 7–11 3 12–17 W292 P912

Chanted also next Monday and Thursday.

✕ ~~צִדְקָתְךָ צֶדֶק Tsidkatekha tsedek~~

Nisan 9 נִיסָן
Sat 9 Apr

מוֹצָאֵי שַׁבָּת Motsa'ey Shabbat Conclusion of Shabbat

עַרְבִית

Arvit for weekdays L264 S281 W137 F200

Weekday Amidah:

+ אַתָּה חוֹנַנְתָּנוּ Attah ḥonantanu L272 S287 W143 F212

☞ חֲצִי קַדִּישׁ Short Kaddish L279 S292 W158 F682

☞ וִיהִי נֹעַם Vihi no'am L279 S292 W158 F684
☞ יוֹשֵׁב בְּסֵתֶר עֶלְיוֹן Yoshev beseter elyon L279 S292 W158 F684
☞ וְאַתָּה קָדוֹשׁ Ve'attah kadosh L216 S293 W159 F684

קַדִּישׁ שָׁלֵם Full Kaddish L280 S294 W160 F688

Conclude as on a usual Saturday night.

Nisan 9 נִיסָן
Sat 9 Apr (night)

After Arvit if the moon is visible:
קִדּוּשׁ לְבָנָה Kiddush Levanah L286 W167 F704
For procedures and instructions, see p. 223.

Pesaḥ

Looking Ahead to Pesaḥ

Cooking for Shabbat and Yom Tov

Cooking is never permitted on Shabbat, and during Shabbat we are not allowed to prepare for Yom Tov. Finish cooking for Shabbat and Yom Tov — Day 1 before Shabbat begins. Finish food preparation for Yom Tov — Day 2 before Shabbat begins or after it ends.

Nisan 5782							Apr | May 2022						
						1							2
2	3	4	5	6	7	8	3	4	5	6	7	8	9
9	10	11	12	13	14	15	10	11	12	13	14	15	16
16	17	18	19	20	21	22	17	18	19	20	21	22	23
23	24	25	26	27	28	29	24	25	26	27	28	29	30
30							1						

+ Add ✗ Omit ☞ Take note!

Siddurim
- **L** Lev Shalem for Shabbat and Festivals
- **S** Shabbat and Festival Sim Shalom
- **W** Weekday Sim Shalom
- **F** Full Sim Shalom (both editions)
- **P** Personal Edition of Full Sim Shalom

Nisan 14 נִיסָן — Thu 14 Apr (evening)

עֶרֶב פֶּסַח Erev Pesaḥ Day before Pesaḥ

בְּדִיקַת חָמֵץ Bedikat Ḥamets The Search for Ḥamets

In Preparation

Searching for Ḥamets

בְּדִיקַת חָמֵץ *bedikat ḥamets* takes place this year on Thursday evening before Pesaḥ. Before the search begins, most people distribute token pieces of bread so that the search is successful. (Some wrap the pieces of bread to prevent inadvertent spilling of crumbs.) Search for *ḥamets* by the light of a candle (traditionally) or a flashlight. Brush חָמֵץ *ḥamets* pieces you find into a wooden spoon using a feather, or collect the wrapped חָמֵץ.

The associated בְּרָכָה *berakhah* and nullification formulas appear near the beginning of the הַגָּדָה *haggadah.*

1. Recite the בְּרָכָה.
2. Search darkened rooms of the home by the light of a candle or flashlight.
3. Collect all token pieces of bread and any חָמֵץ not designated for sale or for consumption in the morning.
4. Recite the first formula for בִּטּוּל חָמֵץ *bittul ḥamets* (nullification of חָמֵץ) in a language you understand.
5. Set aside the חָמֵץ you found until morning.

Fri 15 Apr (morning) בִּעוּר חָמֵץ Bi'ur Ḥamets Destruction of the Ḥamets

Disposing of Ḥamets

We are allowed to possess חָמֵץ *ḥamets* only during the early part of the daylight hours on the morning after the search. Consult your rabbi for the exact time limit in your community. At or before that time, any remaining חָמֵץ in your possession must be destroyed. The associated 2nd formula for בִּטּוּל חָמֵץ *bittul ḥamets* (nullification of חָמֵץ) appears near the beginning of the הַגָּדָה *haggadah.*

1. Do not recite a בְּרָכָה *berakhah.*
2. Destroy the remaining חָמֵץ, including the חָמֵץ found during the search the previous night. Traditionally, this is accomplished by burning. Other methods also are acceptable (for example, flushing it down the toilet, crumbling and scattering it to the wind, disposing of it in a *public* waste receptacle).
3. Immediately afterward, recite the 2nd formula for the nullification of חָמֵץ in a language you understand.

Siddurim																
						1									2

Fri 15 Apr (morning) תַּעֲנִית בְּכוֹרִים Ta’anit Bekhorim

Fast of the Firstborn (individual fast, begins Friday at dawn)

Fast of the Firstborn (Daytime Fast)

In recognition of the rescue of the Israelite firstborn males from the 10th plague while the Egyptian firstborn males died, a firstborn male of a mother or a father observes Fast of the Firstborn on the eve of Pesaḥ.

If the firstborn male is a minor, the father fasts in his place. However, if the father is also a firstborn, the mother fasts in the child’s place.

Fast of the Firstborn is an *individual* fast. Unlike a *communal* fast, it does not introduce public liturgical changes or a special Torah reading. However, if fasting, see instructions at Minḥah below.

Siyyum and Se’udat Mitsvah

If possible, hold a סִיּוּם *siyyum* (completion of study of a tractate of rabbinic literature) to exempt those attending from the obligation to fast.

1. Conduct the סִיּוּם after Shaḥarit.
2. Conclude the סִיּוּם with the special prayers and expanded קַדִּישׁ דְּרַבָּנָן *kaddish derabbanan* for this occasion. Texts can be found at the end of a tractate in many editions of the Talmud and in the *Moreh Derekh* rabbi’s manual.
3. Hold a סְעוּדַת מִצְוָה *se’udat mitsvah* (festive meal celebrating the performance of a *mitsvah*, in this case, the סִיּוּם).

As participants in the סִיּוּם, all firstborns present are permitted to eat at the festive meal and during the rest of the day as well.

שַׁחֲרִית Shaḥarit for weekdays W1 F2

✕ ~~מִזְמוֹר לְתוֹדָה Mizmor letodah (Psalm 100)~~

✕ ~~לַמְנַצֵּחַ Lamenatse·aḥ (Psalm 20)~~

\+ סִיּוּם Siyyum after Shaḥarit (see blue box, above)

\+ סְעוּדַת מִצְוָה Se’udat mitsvah (see blue box, above)

מִנְחָה Minḥah for weekdays W173 F164

Weekday Amidah W122 F168

If fasting + עֲנֵנוּ Anenu, in שׁוֹמֵעַ תְּפִלָּה Shome·a tefillah W127 F178

✕ ~~תַּחֲנוּן Taḥanun~~ (as on all Friday afternoons)

At home Prepare a flame for Yom Tov. See blue box, p. 132. Light candles. See “Candle Lighting for Pesaḥ — Day 1 (Shabbat), p. 132.

פֶּסַח Pesah

Nisan 5782 Apr | May 2022

 1 2

2 3 4 5 6 7 8 3 4 5 6 7 8 9
9 10 11 12 13 14 15 10 11 12 13 14 15 16
16 17 18 19 20 21 22 17 18 19 20 21 22 23
23 24 25 26 27 28 29 24 25 26 27 28 29 30
30 1

✚ Add ✖ Omit ☞ Take note!

Siddurim
L Lev Shalem for Shabbat and Festivals
S Shabbat and Festival Sim Shalom
W Weekday Sim Shalom
F Full Sim Shalom (both editions)
P Personal Edition of Full Sim Shalom

Before Shabbat and Pesaḥ — Day 1

Preparing a Flame for Yom Tov

On Yom Tov, kindling a *new* fire is not permitted; however, the use of an *existing* fire for cooking or other purposes is permitted.

To light candles for Day 2 of Yom Tov (Saturday night), ensure that you have a fire burning before candle-lighting time for Shabbat that will continue to burn until after dark on Saturday. For example:

- A burning candle that lasts for more than 25 hours
- A pilot light on a gas range (*not* a gas range with an electronic starter)

Pesaḥ at Home — Day 1 and Day 2

Candle Lighting for Pesaḥ — Day 1 (Shabbat)

For Day 2, see blue box, p. 137.

1. Before lighting candles, prepare a flame. See above.
2. Light the candles at least 18 minutes before sunset.
3. Recite 2 בְּרָכוֹת *berakhot:* L79 S303 F718

בָּרוּךְ אַתָּה יי, אֱ·לֹהֵינוּ מֶלֶךְ הָעוֹלָם, אֲשֶׁר קִדְּשָׁנוּ בְּמִצְוֹתָיו
וְצִוָּנוּ לְהַדְלִיק נֵר שֶׁל שַׁבָּת וְשֶׁל יוֹם טוֹב.

Barukh attah adonay, eloheynu melekh ha'olam, asher kiddeshanu bemitsvotav vetsivvanu lehadlik ner shel shabbat veshel yom tov.

בָּרוּךְ אַתָּה יי, אֱ·לֹהֵינוּ מֶלֶךְ הָעוֹלָם, שֶׁהֶחֱיָנוּ וְקִיְּמָנוּ וְהִגִּיעָנוּ לַזְּמַן הַזֶּה.

Barukh attah adonay, eloheynu melekh ha'olam,
sheheḥeyanu vekiyyemanu vehiggi'anu lazeman hazeh.

Pesaḥ Meals — Day 1 (Shabbat)

For Day 2, see blue box, p. 137.

NOTE: Omit שָׁלוֹם עֲלֵיכֶם *shalom aleykhem* and אֵשֶׁת חַיִל *eshet ḥayil.* Bless the children before starting the seder.

The Pesaḥ סֵדֶר *seder* tantalizes all 5 of our senses as we celebrate, relive, enjoy, and learn from ceremonies, events, and teachings in the *haggadah.*

In addition to סֵדֶר meals, afternoon meals are also festive occasions, celebrated in the manner of Shabbat meals.

EVENING KIDDUSH L79 S334 F742

Recite:
1. וַיְכֻלּוּ *vaykhullu.*
2. Yom Tov קִדּוּשׁ *kiddush* with insertions for Shabbat and for Pesaḥ
3. שֶׁהֶחֱיָנוּ *sheheḥeyanu*

✚ Add	✗ Omit	☞ Take note!	**Nisan 5782**		**Apr \| May 2022**		נִיסָן **15**	Apr 15

Siddurim																
							1									2

DAYTIME KIDDUSH L81 S335 F746

Recite:
1. וְשָׁמְרוּ *veshameru*
2. זָכוֹר *zakhor* (some omit)
3. עַל־כֵּן בֵּרַךְ *al ken berakh*
4. וַיְדַבֵּר מֹשֶׁה *vaydabber mosheh* (Vayikra 23:44)
5. בּוֹרֵא פְּרִי הַגָּפֶן *bo·re peri hagafen*

HAMOTSI, FESTIVE MEALS WITH SINGING, AND BIRKAT HAMAZON

Recite הַמּוֹצִיא *hamotsi* over 2 whole מַצּוֹת *matsot.* L81 S313–14 F744|746

Include festive singing, and recite בִּרְכַּת הַמָּזוֹן *birkat hamazon* for Shabbat, with Pesaḥ additions (see yellow box, below).

DURING Pesaḥ — **Birkat Hamazon:**

All days + יַעֲלֶה וְיָבוֹא Ya'aleh veyavo for Pesaḥ L90|95 S340|347 W233|239 F762|780

Days 1, 2, 7, and 8 + הָרַחֲמָן Haraḥaman for Yom Tov L92|96 S343|348 W236|240 F768

Every Shaḥarit, Minḥah, and Arvit Amidah:

All days + יַעֲלֶה וְיָבוֹא Ya'aleh veyavo for Pesaḥ

Nisan 15 נִיסָן — שַׁבָּת Shabbat פֶּסַח Pesaḥ — Day 1

Fri 15 Apr

קַבָּלַת שַׁבָּת

✕ ~~Kabbalat Shabbat~~
through
✕ ~~לְכָה דוֹדִי Lekhah dodi~~

Begin with מִזְמוֹר שִׁיר לְיוֹם הַשַּׁבָּת
Mizmor shir leyom hashabbat (Psalm 92). L27 S23 F266

עַרְבִית

Arvit for Yom Tov L39 S28 F279

+ וְשָׁמְרוּ Veshameru L46 S34 F294
+ וַיְדַבֵּר מֹשֶׁה Vaydabber mosheh (Vayikra 23:44) L46 S34 F294

חֲצִי קַדִּישׁ Short Kaddish L46 S34 F294

Yom Tov Amidah: L306 S41 F304

+ מַשִּׁיב הָרוּחַ Mashiv haruaḥ L307 S41 F304
+ Additions for Shabbat
+ Insertions for Pesaḥ

☞ וַיְכֻלּוּ Vaykhullu L53 S47 F314

✕ ~~בָּרוּךְ אַתָּה . . . וָאָרֶץ Barukh attah . . . va'arets~~
✕ ~~מָגֵן אָבוֹת . . . בְּרֵאשִׁית Magen avot . . . bereshit~~
✕ ~~אֱ·לֹהֵינוּ . . . הַשַּׁבָּת Eloheynu . . . hashabbat~~

Nisan 5782							Apr | May 2022						
						1							2
2	3	4	5	6	7	8	3	4	5	6	7	8	9
9	10	11	12	13	14	15	10	11	12	13	14	15	16
16	17	18	19	20	21	22	17	18	19	20	21	22	23
23	24	25	26	27	28	29	24	25	26	27	28	29	30
30							1						

+ Add ✕ Omit ☞ Take note!

Siddurim
- **L** Lev Shalem for Shabbat and Festivals
- **S** Shabbat and Festival Sim Shalom
- **W** Weekday Sim Shalom
- **F** Full Sim Shalom (both editions)
- **P** Personal Edition of Full Sim Shalom

Some congregations add
הַלֵּל שָׁלֵם Full Hallel with בְּרָכוֹת berakhot. L316 S133 F380

Some congregations add selections from
הַלֵּל שָׁלֵם without בְּרָכוֹת. L316 S133 F380

קַדִּישׁ שָׁלֵם Full Kaddish L54 S48 F316

✕ ~~קִדּוּשׁ Kiddush during Arvit~~

עָלֵינוּ Aleynu L56 S51 F320
קַדִּישׁ יָתוֹם Mourner's Kaddish L58 S52 F324

At home + 1st Seder
Follow the procedures in the haggadah.
See also "Pesaḥ Meals — Day 1 (Shabbat)," and "Evening Kiddush" p. 132.

Sat 16 Apr שַׁחֲרִית

At the end of the preliminary service, begin formal chanting at
הָאֵ-ל בְּתַעֲצוּמוֹת עֻזֶּךָ Ha'el beta'atsumot uzzekha. L147 S105 F336

+ הַכֹּל יוֹדוּךָ Hakol yodukha L150 S107 F340
+ אֵ-ל אָדוֹן El adon L151 S108 F342
+ לָאֵ-ל אֲשֶׁר שָׁבַת La'el asher shavat L152 S109 F342
✕ ~~הַמֵּאִיר לָאָרֶץ Hame'ir la'arets~~

Immediately preceding בָּרוּךְ אַתָּה יי גָּאַל יִשְׂרָאֵל L158 S114
some congregations add
בְּרַח דּוֹדִי עַד שֶׁתֶּחְפָּץ Beraḥ dodi ad sheteḥpats. L409 S221

Yom Tov Amidah: L306 S123 F366
+ מַשִּׁיב הָרוּחַ Mashiv haruaḥ L307 S123 F366
+ Additions for Shabbat
+ Insertions for Pesaḥ

+ הַלֵּל שָׁלֵם Full Hallel L316 S133 F380

קַדִּישׁ שָׁלֵם Full Kaddish L321 S138 F392

SHABBAT TORAH SERVICE L322 S139 F394

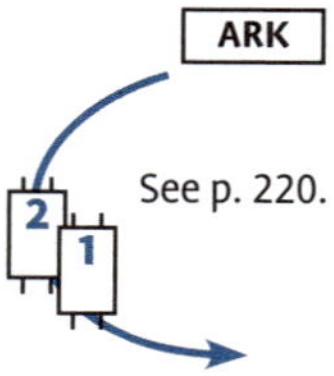

See p. 220.

✕ ~~יי יי אֵ-ל רַחוּם וְחַנּוּן Adonay adonay el raḥum veḥannun~~
✕ ~~רִבּוֹנוֹ שֶׁל עוֹלָם Ribbono shel olam~~
✕ ~~וַאֲנִי תְפִלָּתִי לְךָ Va'ani tefillati lekha~~

Remove **2** scrolls from ark in the order they will be read.

1st scroll 7 aliyot from בֹּא Bo
שְׁמוֹת Shemot (Exodus) 12:21–51
[1] 12:21–24 [2] 12:25–28 [3] 12:29–32 [4] 12:33–36
[5] 12:37–42 [6] 12:43–47 [7] 12:48–51

פֶּסַח Pesah

Place 2nd scroll on table next to 1st scroll.
חֲצִי קַדִּישׁ Short Kaddish L327 S146 F408
Open, raise, display, and wrap 1st scroll.

2nd scroll Maftir aliyah from פִּינְחָס Pinehas
בְּמִדְבַּר M Bemidbar (Numbers) 28:16–25

Open, raise, display, and wrap 2nd scroll.

Haftarah for Pesaḥ — Day 1
Ashkenazic: יְהוֹשֻׁעַ Yehoshua (Joshua) 3:5–7, 5:2–6:1, 6:27
(alternate tradition, 5:2–6:1)
Sephardic: יְהוֹשֻׁעַ Yehoshua (Joshua) 5:2–6:1, 6:27

Haftarah blessings: L328 S147 F410
☞ Conclude with the Yom Tov בְּרָכָה berakhah L329 S147 F412
with insertions for Shabbat and for Pesaḥ.

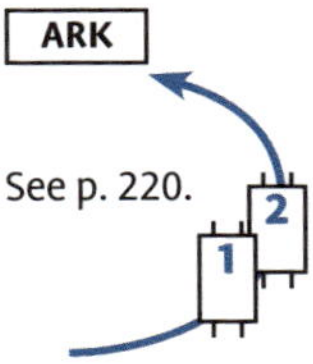

See p. 220.

יְקוּם פֻּרְקָן Yekum purkan L176 S148 F412
✕ ~~אַב הָרַחֲמִים Av Haraḥamim~~

אַשְׁרֵי Ashrey L339 S151 F420
Return scrolls to ark in reverse order. L340 S153 F422

☞ שְׁלִיחַ/שְׁלִיחַת צִבּוּר sheliaḥ/sheliḥat tsibbur customarily wears a *kittel* (plain white robe) for Musaf.

☞ חֲצִי קַדִּישׁ Short Kaddish L342 S155 F428
The distinctive traditional melody of this Kaddish anticipates the opening melody of the repetition of the Amidah.

Morid Hatal
For congregations that follow the tradition of Erets Yisra'el to add מוֹרִיד הַטָּל *morid hatal,* announce before the silent Amidah:
"In the silent Amidah:
Replace מַשִּׁיב הָרוּחַ וּמוֹרִיד הַגָּשֶׁם *mashiv haruaḥ umorid hagashem*
with מוֹרִיד הַטָּל *morid hatal.*"

מוּסָף **Silent Yom Tov Amidah:** L343 S166 F456
☞ מַשִּׁיב הָרוּחַ Mashiv haruaḥ L344 S166 F456
(For congregations that add מוֹרִיד הַטָּל Morid hatal, see the blue box, above.)
+ Additions for Shabbat
+ Insertions for Pesaḥ

פסח Pesaḥ

Nisan 5782						
						1
2	3	4	5	6	7	8
9	10	11	12	13	14	15
16	17	18	19	20	21	22
23	24	25	26	27	28	29
30						

Apr | May 2022						
						2
3	4	5	6	7	8	9
10	11	12	13	14	15	16
17	18	19	20	21	22	23
24	25	26	27	28	29	30
| 1						

\+ Add ✕ Omit ☞ Take note!

Siddurim
- **L** Lev Shalem for Shabbat and Festivals
- **S** Shabbat and Festival Sim Shalom
- **W** Weekday Sim Shalom
- **F** Full Sim Shalom (both editions)
- **P** Personal Edition of Full Sim Shalom

Open ark.

Repetition of the Yom Tov Amidah: L374 S217 F478

\+ תְּפִלַּת טַל Tefillat tal L375 S219 F478

Close ark.

Continue with מְכַלְכֵּל חַיִּים Mekhalkel ḥayyim L344 S166 F456

\+ Additions for Shabbat

\+ Insertions for Pesaḥ

Some congregations include in the repetition of the Amidah the Priestly Blessing by the Kohanim (*dukhenen*).
בִּרְכַּת כֹּהֲנִים Birkat kohanim L353 S177 F472
(Some of these congregations omit it on Shabbat.)
For procedures, see p. 222.

קַדִּישׁ שָׁלֵם Full Kaddish L203 S181 F506
Continue with אֵין כֵּא·לֹהֵינוּ Eyn keloheynu. L204 S182 F508

קִדּוּשָׁא רַבָּא See “Daytime Kiddush,” p. 133.

At home See “Pesaḥ Meals — Day 1 (Shabbat),” and “Daytime Kiddush,” pp. 132–133.

UNTIL Shemini Atseret **Every Amidah:**
✕ ~~מַשִּׁיב הָרוּחַ וּמוֹרִיד הַגָּשֶׁם Mashiv haruaḥ umorid hagashem~~

מִנְחָה

אַשְׁרֵי Ashrey L214 S226 W170 F558
וּבָא לְצִיּוֹן Uva letsiyyon L216 S227 W171 F560
חֲצִי קַדִּישׁ Short Kaddish L217 S229 W173 F564

Torah 3 aliyot from אַחֲרֵי מוֹת Aḥarey mot
וַיִּקְרָא Vayikra (Leviticus) 16:1–17
[1]16:1–6 [2]7–11 [3]12–17 W292 P912

☞ Not chanted publicly again until next Shabbat at Minḥah.

Yom Tov Amidah: L306 S242 W184 F586
✕ ~~מַשִּׁיב הָרוּחַ וּמוֹרִיד הַגָּשֶׁם Mashiv haruaḥ umorid hagashem~~
\+ Additions for Shabbat
\+ Insertions for Pesaḥ

✕ ~~צִדְקָתְךָ צֶדֶק Tsidkatekha tsedek~~

קַדִּישׁ שָׁלֵם Full Kaddish L230 S247 W189 F596
עָלֵינוּ Aleynu L231 S248 W190 F598
קַדִּישׁ יָתוֹם Mourner’s Kaddish L232 S249 W191 F600

Siddurim

- **L** Lev Shalem for Shabbat and Festivals
- **S** Shabbat and Festival Sim Shalom
- **W** Weekday Sim Shalom
- **F** Full Sim Shalom (both editions)
- **P** Personal Edition of Full Sim Shalom

Nisan 5782						
						1
2	3	4	5	6	7	8
9	10	11	12	13	14	15
16	17	18	19	20	21	22
23	24	25	26	27	28	29
30						

Apr | May 2022						
						2
3	4	5	6	7	8	9
10	11	12	13	14	15	16
17	18	19	20	21	22	23
24	25	26	27	28	29	30
1						

Candle Lighting for Pesaḥ — Day 2 (after Shabbat)

Shabbat (Day 1 of Pesaḥ) ends after dark: when 3 stars appear, or at least 25 minutes after sunset (at least 43 minutes after the time set for lighting candles for Day 1). Some wait longer. For the appropriate time in your community, consult your rabbi.

1. Wait until Shabbat ends.
2. Do not *strike* a match. Instead, transfer fire to the candles from an *existing* flame (see p. 132) by inserting a match or other stick into the flame.
3. Do not *extinguish* the match or stick. Instead, place it on a non-flammable tray or dish, and let it self-extinguish. Alternately, a wood *safety* match held vertically (flame up) usually self-extinguishes quickly.
4. Recite 2 בְּרָכוֹת *berakhot*: L79 S303 F718

בָּרוּךְ אַתָּה יי, אֱ·לֹהֵינוּ מֶלֶךְ הָעוֹלָם, אֲשֶׁר קִדְּשָׁנוּ בְּמִצְוֹתָיו
וְצִוָּנוּ לְהַדְלִיק נֵר שֶׁל יוֹם טוֹב.

Barukh attah adonay, eloheynu melekh ha'olam, asher kiddeshanu bemitsvotav vetsivvanu lehadlik ner shel yom tov.

בָּרוּךְ אַתָּה יי, אֱ·לֹהֵינוּ מֶלֶךְ הָעוֹלָם, שֶׁהֶחֱיָנוּ וְקִיְּמָנוּ וְהִגִּיעָנוּ לַזְּמַן הַזֶּה.

Barukh attah adonay, eloheynu melekh ha'olam,
sheheḥeyanu vekiyyemanu vehiggi'anu lazeman hazeh.

Pesaḥ Meals — Day 2 (after Shabbat)

The Pesaḥ סֵדֶר *seder* tantalizes all 5 of our senses as we celebrate, relive, enjoy, and learn from ceremonies, events, and teachings in the *haggadah.*

In addition to סֵדֶר meals, afternoon meals are also festive occasions, celebrated in the manner of Shabbat meals.

EVENING KIDDUSH L79 S334 F742

Do *not* light a Havdalah candle.

Recite:
1. Yom Tov קִדּוּשׁ *kiddush* with insertions for Pesaḥ
2. בּוֹרֵא מְאוֹרֵי הָאֵשׁ *bo·re me'orey ha'esh* (over Yom Tov candles) L80 S335 F744
3. הַמַּבְדִּיל בֵּין קֹדֶשׁ לְקֹדֶשׁ *hamavdil beyn kodesh lekodesh* L80 S335 F744
4. שֶׁהֶחֱיָנוּ *sheheḥeyanu*

DAYTIME KIDDUSH L81 S335 F746

Recite:
1. וַיְדַבֵּר מֹשֶׁה *vaydabber mosheh* (Vayikra 23:44)
2. בּוֹרֵא פְּרִי הַגָּפֶן *bo·re peri hagafen*

HAMOTSI, FESTIVE MEALS WITH SINGING, AND BIRKAT HAMAZON

Recite הַמּוֹצִיא *hamotsi* over 2 whole מַצּוֹת *matsot.* L81 S313–14 F744|746

Include festive singing. Recite בִּרְכַּת הַמָּזוֹן *birkat hamazon* with Pesaḥ additions (see yellow box, p. 133).

FROM the 2nd Night of Pesaḥ UNTIL Shavu'ot

Counting Omer

At night Count Omer each night after dark, preferably at least 23 minutes after sunset. See instructions, p. 221.

If your congregation conducts Arvit before dark, count Omer without reciting a בְּרָכָה berakhah. Encourage congregants to count individually later, after dark, with a בְּרָכָה.

In the morning Count Omer in the synagogue without reciting a בְּרָכָה. This counting fulfills the obligation of those present who neglected to count the previous night.

Nisan 16 נִיסָן
Sat 16 Apr

פֶּסַח Pesaḥ — Day 2

עַרְבִית

Arvit for Yom Tov L39 S28 F279

+ וַיְדַבֵּר מֹשֶׁה Vaydabber mosheh (Vayikra 23:44) L46 S34 F294

חֲצִי קַדִּישׁ Short Kaddish L46 S34 F294

Yom Tov Amidah: L306 S41 F304

+ וַתּוֹדִיעֵנוּ Vatodi'eynu S41 F306

+ Insertions for Pesaḥ

Some congregations add הַלֵּל שָׁלֵם Full Hallel with בְּרָכוֹת berakhot. L316 S133 F380

Some congregations add selections from הַלֵּל שָׁלֵם without בְּרָכוֹת. L316 S133 F380

קַדִּישׁ שָׁלֵם Full Kaddish L54 S48 F316

✕ ~~קִדּוּשׁ Kiddush during Arvit~~

☞ Some count Omer at the seder. Others count here. L63 S55 F237
Day **1** (see instructions, p. 221)

עָלֵינוּ Aleynu L56 S51 F320

קַדִּישׁ יָתוֹם Mourner's Kaddish L58 S52 F324

פֶּסַח Pesah

At home Light candles from an existing flame. See “Candle Lighting for Pesaḥ — Day 2 (after Shabbat),” p. 137.

+ **2nd Seder**
Follow the procedures in the haggadah.

See also “Pesaḥ Meals — Day 2 (after Shabbat),” and “Evening Kiddush,” p. 137.

For those who did not count Omer at Arvit, count here. Day **1** (see instructions, p. 221)

Sun 17 Apr **שַׁחֲרִית** At the end of the preliminary service, begin formal chanting at
הָאֵ·ל בְּתַעֲצוּמוֹת עֻזֶּךָ Ha’el beta’atsumot uzzekha. L147 S105 F336

✕ ~~הַכֹּל יוֹדוּךָ Hakol yodukha~~
✕ ~~אֵ·ל אָדוֹן El adon~~
✕ ~~לָאֵ·ל אֲשֶׁר שָׁבַת La’el asher shavat~~

+ הַמֵּאִיר לָאָרֶץ Hame’ir la’arets L152 S109 F342

Immediately preceding בָּרוּךְ אַתָּה יי גָּאַל יִשְׂרָאֵל L158 S114 some congregations add בְּרַח דּוֹדִי אֶל מָכוֹן לְשִׁבְתָּךְ Beraḥ dodi el makhon leshivtakh. L409 S221

Yom Tov Amidah: L306 S123 F366
+ Insertions for Pesaḥ

+ הַלֵּל שָׁלֵם Full Hallel L316 S133 F380
קַדִּישׁ שָׁלֵם Full Kaddish L321 S138 F392

YOM TOV TORAH SERVICE L322 S139 F394

+ יי יי אֵ·ל רַחוּם וְחַנּוּן
Adonay adonay el raḥum veḥannun (3 times) L323 S140 F394
+ רִבּוֹנוֹ שֶׁל עוֹלָם Ribbono shel olam L323 S140 F396
+ וַאֲנִי תְפִלָּתִי לְךָ Va’ani tefillati lekha (3 times) L323 S140 F396

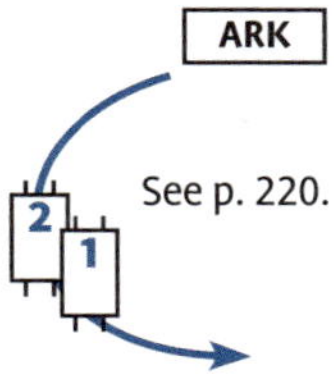

See p. 220.

Remove **2** scrolls from ark in the order they will be read.

1st scroll 5 aliyot from אֱמֹר Emor
וַיִּקְרָא Vayikra (Leviticus) 22:26–23:44
1 22:26–23:3 2 23:4–14 3 23:15–22 4 23:23–32 5 23:33–44

Place 2nd scroll on table next to 1st scroll.
חֲצִי קַדִּישׁ Short Kaddish L327 S146 F408
Open, raise, display, and wrap 1st scroll.

1							2
2	3	4	5	6	7	8	3	4	5	6	7	8	9
9	10	11	12	13	14	15	10	11	12	13	14	15	16
16	17	18	19	20	21	22	17	18	19	20	21	22	23
23	24	25	26	27	28	29	24	25	26	27	28	29	30
30							1						

Siddurim
L Lev Shalem for Shabbat and Festivals
S Shabbat and Festival Sim Shalom
W Weekday Sim Shalom
F Full Sim Shalom (both editions)
P Personal Edition of Full Sim Shalom

2nd scroll Maftir aliyah from פִּינְחָס Pineḥas
בְּמִדְבַּר^M Bemidbar (Numbers) 28:16–25

Open, raise, display, and wrap 2nd scroll.

Haftarah for Pesaḥ — Day 2
מְלָכִים ב׳ 2 Melakhim (2 Kings) 23:1–9, 21–25

Haftarah blessings: L328 S147 F410
☞ Conclude with the Yom Tov בְּרָכָה berakhah with insertions for Pesaḥ. L329 S147 F412

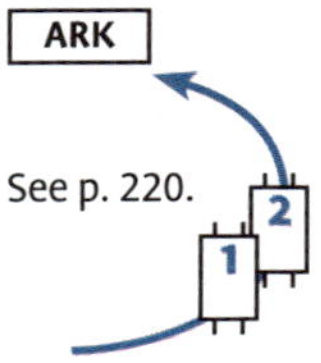

See p. 220.

✕ ~~יְקוּם פֻּרְקָן Yekum purkan~~
✕ ~~אַב הָרַחֲמִים Av Haraḥamim~~

אַשְׁרֵי Ashrey L339 S151 F420
Return scrolls to ark in reverse order. L340 S153 F422
חֲצִי קַדִּישׁ Short Kaddish L342 S155 F428

מוּסָף

Yom Tov Amidah: L343 S166 F456
+ Insertions for Pesaḥ

Some congregations include in the repetition of the Amidah the Priestly Blessing by the Kohanim (*dukhenen*).
בִּרְכַּת כֹּהֲנִים Birkat kohanim L353 S177 F472
For procedures, see p. 222.

קַדִּישׁ שָׁלֵם Full Kaddish L203 S181 F506
Continue with אֵין כֵּא·לֹהֵינוּ Eyn keloheynu. L204 S182 F508

קִדּוּשָׁא רַבָּא See "Daytime Kiddush," p. 137.

At home See "Pesaḥ Meals — Day 2 (after Shabbat)," and "Daytime Kiddush," p. 137.

מִנְחָה

אַשְׁרֵי Ashrey L214 S226 W170 F558
וּבָא לְצִיּוֹן Uva letsiyyon L216 S227 W171 F560
חֲצִי קַדִּישׁ Short Kaddish L217 S229 W173 F564

Yom Tov Amidah: L306 S242 W184 F586
+ Insertions for Pesaḥ

קַדִּישׁ שָׁלֵם Full Kaddish L230 S247 W189 F596
עָלֵינוּ Aleynu L231 S248 W190 F598
קַדִּישׁ יָתוֹם Mourner's Kaddish L232 S249 W191 F600

17 Nisan THROUGH
Dec. 4 at מִנְחָה

Every weekday Amidah:
✕ ~~וְתֵן טַל וּמָטָר לִבְרָכָה Veten tal umatar livrakhah~~
\+ וְתֵן בְּרָכָה Veten berakhah

עַרְבִית L274 W144 F214
שַׁחֲרִית W39 F112
מִנְחָה L295 W125 F174

Nisan 17 נִיסָן חֹל הַמּוֹעֵד פֶּסַח Ḥol Hamo'ed Pesaḥ — Weekdays

Sun 17 Apr (evening)
through
Nisan 20 נִיסָן
Thu 21 Apr (daytime)

Ḥol Hamo'ed (ḤH) — Days 1–4

ḤH Day 1 Sun 17 Apr — מוֹצָאֵי יוֹם טוֹב Motsa'ey Yom Tov Conclusion of Yom Tov
ḤH Day 2 Mon 18 Apr (evening)
ḤH Day 3 Tue 19 Apr (evening)
ḤH Day 4 Wed 20 Apr (evening)

עַרְבִית Arvit for weekdays L264 S281 W137 F200

Weekday Amidah:

ḤH Day 1 Sun 17 Apr + אַתָּה חוֹנַנְתָּנוּ Attah ḥonantanu L272 S287 W143 F212
All evenings + יַעֲלֶה וְיָבוֹא Ya'aleh veyavo for Pesaḥ L277 S289 W145 F216

All evenings קַדִּישׁ שָׁלֵם Full Kaddish L280 S294 W160 F222

\+ Count Omer: L63 S55 W152 F237
ḤH Day 1 Sun 17 Apr Day **2** (see instructions, p. 221)
ḤH Day 2 Mon 18 Apr Day **3** (see instructions, p. 221)
ḤH Day 3 Tue 19 Apr Day **4** (see instructions, p. 221)
ḤH Day 4 Wed 20 Apr Day **5** (see instructions, p. 221)

ḤH Day 1 Sun 17 Apr Some recite הַבְדָּלָה Havdalah here. L283 S299 W165 F700
For instructions, see below.

All evenings עָלֵינוּ Aleynu L281 S297 W163 F696
קַדִּישׁ יָתוֹם Mourner's Kaddish L282 S298 W164 F698

ḤH Day 1 Sun 17 Apr + **Havdalah:** L283 S299 W165 F700
✕ ~~הִנֵּה אֵ-ל יְשׁוּעָתִי Hinneh el yeshu'ati~~
בּוֹרֵא פְּרִי הַגָּפֶן Bo·re peri hagafen
✕ ~~בּוֹרֵא מִינֵי בְשָׂמִים Bo·re miney vesamim~~
✕ ~~בּוֹרֵא מְאוֹרֵי הָאֵשׁ Bo·re me'orey ha'esh~~
הַמַּבְדִּיל בֵּין קֹדֶשׁ לְחֹל Hamavdil beyn kodesh leḥol

Nisan 5782							Apr | May 2022						
						1							2
2	3	4	5	6	7	8	3	4	5	6	7	8	9
9	10	11	12	13	14	15	10	11	12	13	14	15	16
16	17	18	19	20	21	22	17	18	19	20	21	22	23
23	24	25	26	27	28	29	24	25	26	27	28	29	30
30							1						

+ Add ✕ Omit ☞ Take note!

Siddurim
- **L** Lev Shalem for Shabbat and Festivals
- **S** Shabbat and Festival Sim Shalom
- **W** Weekday Sim Shalom
- **F** Full Sim Shalom (both editions)
- **P** Personal Edition of Full Sim Shalom

Ḥol Hamo'ed

Wearing Tefillin

Whether or not to wear תְּפִלִּין *tefillin* during Ḥol Hamo'ed is a long-standing controversy. Ashkenazic Jews tend to wear תְּפִלִּין; Sephardic and Hasidic Jews tend not to wear תְּפִלִּין. The practice in Israel is not to wear them. Some who wear תְּפִלִּין do not recite the בְּרָכוֹת *berakhot*.

1. Determine your individual practice as follows:
   - If there is an established custom in your family, follow it.
   - If there is no established custom in your family, consult your rabbi.
   - Regardless of your custom, when you are in Israel, do not wear תְּפִלִּין.
2. If you wear תְּפִלִּין, remove them just before the beginning of Hallel.

ḤH Day 1 Mon 18 Apr (morning)
ḤH Day 2 Tue 19 Apr (morning)
ḤH Day 3 Wed 20 Apr (morning)
ḤH Day 4 Thu 21 Apr (morning)

שַׁחֲרִית Shaḥarit for weekdays W1 F2

✕ ~~מִזְמוֹר לְתוֹדָה Mizmor letodah (Psalm 100)~~

Weekday Amidah: W36 F106

✕ ~~וְתֵן טַל וּמָטָר לִבְרָכָה Veten tal umatar livrakhah~~

+ וְתֵן בְּרָכָה Veten berakhah W39 F112

+ יַעֲלֶה וְיָבוֹא Ya'aleh veyavo for Pesaḥ W41 F114

✕ ~~תַּחֲנוּן Taḥanun~~

☞ Those wearing תְּפִלִּין tefillin now remove and pack them.

+ חֲצִי הַלֵּל Short Hallel W50 F380

קַדִּישׁ שָׁלֵם Full Kaddish W56 F392

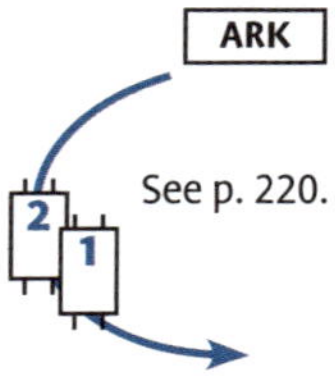

See p. 220.

TORAH SERVICE W65 F138

Remove **2** scrolls from ark in the order they will be read.

ḤH Day 1 Mon 18 Apr

1st scroll 3 aliyot from בֹּא Bo
שְׁמוֹת Shemot (Exodus) 13:1–16
[1]13:1–4 [2]5–10 [3]11–16 W325 P957

ḤH Day 2 Tue 19 Apr

1st scroll 3 aliyot from מִשְׁפָּטִים Mishpatim
שְׁמוֹת Shemot (Exodus) 22:24–23:19
[1]22:24–26 [2]22:27–23:5 [3]23:6–19 W326 P959

ḤH Day 3 Wed 20 Apr

1st scroll 3 aliyot from כִּי תִשָּׂא Ki tissa
שְׁמוֹת Shemot (Exodus) 34:1–26
[1]34:1–3 [2]4–10 [3]11–26 W328 P961

Siddurim 1 2
L Lev Shalem for Shabbat and Festivals 2 3 4 5 6 7 8 3 4 5 6 7 8 9
S Shabbat and Festival Sim Shalom 9 10 11 12 13 14 15 10 11 12 13 14 15 16
W Weekday Sim Shalom 16 17 18 19 20 21 22 17 18 19 20 21 22 23 נִיסָן 20 Apr 21
F Full Sim Shalom (both editions) 23 24 25 26 27 28 29 24 25 26 27 28 29 30
P Personal Edition of Full Sim Shalom 30 | 1

HH Day 4 Thu 21 Apr

> **1st scroll** 3 aliyot from בְּהַעֲלֹתְךָ Beha'alotekha
> בְּמִדְבַּר Bemidbar (Numbers) 9:1–14
> **1** 9:1–5 **2** 6–8 **3** 9–14 **W**329 **P**964

All days Place 2nd scroll on table next to 1st scroll.
 ☞ Do not recite חֲצִי קַדִּישׁ Short Kaddish here.
 Open, raise, display, and wrap 1st scroll.

> **+ 2nd scroll** 1 aliyah from פִּינְחָס Pineḥas
> **4** בְּמִדְבַּר Bemidbar (Numbers) 28:19–25 **W**326 **F**958

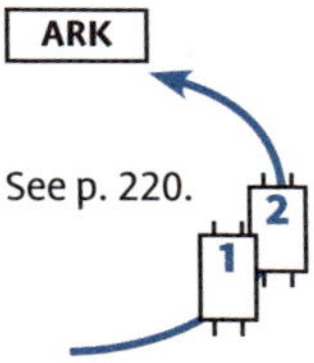

ARK

See p. 220.

Place 1st scroll on table next to 2nd scroll.
חֲצִי קַדִּישׁ Short Kaddish **W**71 **F**146
Open, raise, display, and wrap 2nd scroll.

Return scrolls to ark in reverse order. **W**76 **F**150

אַשְׁרֵי Ashrey **W**78 **F**152
✕ לַמְנַצֵּחַ Lamenatse·aḥ (Psalm 20)
וּבָא לְצִיּוֹן Uva letsiyyon **W**80 **F**156

+ חֲצִי קַדִּישׁ Short Kaddish **W**103 **F**428

מוּסָף **+ Yom Tov Amidah:** **W**104+110 **F**456+462
 Weekday קְדֻשָּׁה Kedushah **W**105 **F**460
 + Insertions for Pesaḥ
 + וְהִקְרַבְתֶּם Vehikravtem for Ḥol Hamo'ed Pesaḥ **W**111 **F**466

 + קַדִּישׁ שָׁלֵם Full Kaddish **W**82 **F**158
 עָלֵינוּ Aleynu **W**83 **F**160
 Conclude as on a usual weekday.

מִנְחָה Minḥah for weekdays **L**289 **S**1 **W**120 **F**164

 Weekday Amidah:
 ✕ וְתֵן טַל וּמָטָר לִבְרָכָה Veten tal umatar livrakhah
 + וְתֵן בְּרָכָה Veten berakhah **L**295 **S**5 **W**144 **F**214
 + יַעֲלֶה וְיָבוֹא Ya'aleh veyavo for Pesaḥ **L**298 **S**7 **W**127 **F**178

 ✕ תַּחֲנוּן Taḥanun

HH Day 4 Thu 21 Apr (afternoon)

At home Prepare an Eruv Tavshilin. See blue box, p. 144.
 Prepare a flame for Yom Tov. See blue box, p. 144.
 Light candles. See "Candle Lighting for Pesaḥ — Day 7,"
 p. 145.

פֶּסַח
Pesaḥ

Before Pesaḥ — Day 7

Preparing an Eruv Tavshilin

When Yom Tov falls on a weekday, cooking is permitted, but only to prepare food for that particular day. On Shabbat all cooking is forbidden. Therefore, preparing food for a Shabbat that follows a Friday Yom Tov presents a difficulty.

To allow cooking for Shabbat on the preceding Friday Yom Tov:
On Thursday before Yom Tov, perform the ritual of עֵרוּב תַּבְשִׁילִין *eruv tavshilin*, the combining (עֵרוּב *eruv*) of the cooking for Yom Tov and Shabbat.

Start the Shabbat cooking Thursday afternoon, following this procedure:

1. Before Yom Tov begins, take two prepared foods, customarily a baked food (for example, מַצָּה *matsah*) and a cooked food (for example, a hard-cooked egg or a piece of cooked chicken or fish).
2. Recite the בְּרָכָה *berakhah*: L78 S306 F716

   בָּרוּךְ אַתָּה יי, אֱ·לֹהֵינוּ מֶלֶךְ הָעוֹלָם, אֲשֶׁר קִדְּשָׁנוּ בְּמִצְוֹתָיו
   וְצִוָּנוּ עַל מִצְוַת עֵרוּב.

   Barukh attah adonay, eloheynu melekh ha'olam,
   asher kiddeshanu bemitsvotav vetsivvanu al mitsvat eruv.
3. In a language you understand, recite a declaration that cooking for Shabbat was begun before—and will be completed on—Yom Tov. L78 S306 F716

   בְּעֵרוּב הַזֶּה יְהִי מֻתָּר לָנוּ לֶאֱפוֹת וּלְבַשֵּׁל וּלְהַטְמִין,
   וּלְהַדְלִיק נֵר, וְלַעֲשׂוֹת כׇּל־צְרָכֵינוּ מִיּוֹם טוֹב לְשַׁבָּת,
   לָנוּ וּלְכׇל־יִשְׂרָאֵל הַדָּרִים בָּעִיר הַזֹּאת.

   By means of this combining (*eruv*), we are permitted to bake, cook, warm, kindle lights, and make all the necessary preparations for Shabbat during the festival (*yom tov*), we and all who live in this city/locale.
4. Set aside the two foods for eating on Shabbat during the day.

The cooking for Shabbat may now be completed on Yom Tov.

Preparing a Flame for Yom Tov

On Yom Tov, kindling a *new* fire is not permitted; however, the use of an *existing* fire for cooking or other purposes is permitted.

To light candles for Day 8 (Shabbat), ensure that you have a fire burning before candle-lighting time for Day 7 (Thursday evening) that will continue to burn until sunset on Friday. For example:

- A burning candle that lasts for more than 25 hours
- A pilot light on a gas range (*not* a gas range with an electronic starter)

Pesaḥ at Home — Day 7

Candle Lighting for Pesaḥ — Day 7

For Day 8 (Shabbat), see blue box, p. 148.

1. Before lighting candles, prepare a flame. See p. 144.
2. Light the candles at least 18 minutes before sunset.
3. Recite only 1 בְּרָכָה *berakhah*: L79 S303 F718

בָּרוּךְ אַתָּה יי, אֱ·לֹהֵינוּ מֶלֶךְ הָעוֹלָם, אֲשֶׁר קִדְּשָׁנוּ בְּמִצְוֹתָיו
וְצִוָּנוּ לְהַדְלִיק נֵר שֶׁל יוֹם טוֹב.

Barukh attah adonay, eloheynu melekh ha'olam,
asher kiddeshanu bemitsvotav vetsivvanu lehadlik ner shel yom tov.

Pesaḥ Meals — Day 7

Enjoy festive meals evening and daytime, in the manner of Shabbat meals.

EVENING KIDDUSH L79 S334 F742

Recite: Yom Tov קִדּוּשׁ *kiddush* with insertions for Pesaḥ
Do *not* add שֶׁהֶחֱיָנוּ *sheheḥeyanu.*

DAYTIME KIDDUSH L81 S335 F746

Recite: 1. וַיְדַבֵּר מֹשֶׁה *vaydabber mosheh* (Vayikra 23:44)
2. בּוֹרֵא פְּרִי הַגָּפֶן *bo·re peri hagafen*

HAMOTSI, FESTIVE MEALS WITH SINGING, AND BIRKAT HAMAZON

Recite הַמּוֹצִיא *hamotsi* over 2 whole מַצּוֹת *matsot.* L81 S313–14 F744|746
Include festive singing, and recite בִּרְכַּת הַמָּזוֹן *birkat hamazon* with Pesaḥ additions (see yellow box, p. 133).

Nisan 21 נִיסָן
Thu 21 Apr

פֶּסַח Pesaḥ — Day 7

עַרְבִית

Arvit for Yom Tov L39 S28 F279

+ וַיְדַבֵּר מֹשֶׁה Vaydabber mosheh (Vayikra 23:44) L46 S34 F294

חֲצִי קַדִּישׁ Short Kaddish L46 S34 F294

Yom Tov Amidah: L306 S41 F304

+ Insertions for Pesaḥ

קַדִּישׁ שָׁלֵם Full Kaddish L54 S48 F316

קִדּוּשׁ Kiddush for Yom Tov
with insertions for Pesaḥ L79 S50 F318

+ Count Omer. L63 S55 W152 F237
Day **6** (see instructions, p. 221)

עָלֵינוּ Aleynu L56 S51 F320
קַדִּישׁ יָתוֹם Mourner's Kaddish L58 S52 F324

Nisan 5782						
						1
2	3	4	5	6	7	8
9	10	11	12	13	14	15
16	17	18	19	20	21	22
23	24	25	26	27	28	29
30						

Apr | May 2022						
						2
3	4	5	6	7	8	9
10	11	12	13	14	15	16
17	18	19	20	21	22	23
24	25	26	27	28	29	30
1						

+ Add ✕ Omit ☞ Take note!

Siddurim
- **L** Lev Shalem for Shabbat and Festivals
- **S** Shabbat and Festival Sim Shalom
- **W** Weekday Sim Shalom
- **F** Full Sim Shalom (both editions)
- **P** Personal Edition of Full Sim Shalom

At home See "Pesaḥ Meals — Day 7" and "Evening Kiddush," p. 145.

Fri 22 Apr **שַׁחֲרִית**

At the end of the preliminary service, begin formal chanting at
הָאֵ-ל בְּתַעֲצוּמוֹת עֻזֶּךָ Ha'el beta'atsumot uzzekha. L147 S105 F336

✕ ~~הַכֹּל יוֹדוּךָ Hakol yodukha~~
✕ ~~אֵ-ל אָדוֹן El adon~~
✕ ~~לָאֵ-ל אֲשֶׁר שָׁבַת La'el asher shavat~~

+ הַמֵּאִיר לָאָרֶץ Hame'ir la'arets L152 S109 F342

Yom Tov Amidah: L306 S123 F366
+ Insertions for Pesaḥ

+ חֲצִי הַלֵּל Short Hallel L316 S133 F380
קַדִּישׁ שָׁלֵם Full Kaddish L321 S138 F392

YOM TOV TORAH SERVICE L322 S139 F394

+ יי יי אֵ-ל רַחוּם וְחַנּוּן
Adonay adonay el raḥum veḥannun (3 times) L323 S140 F394
+ רִבּוֹנוֹ שֶׁל עוֹלָם Ribbono shel olam L323 S140 F396
+ וַאֲנִי תְפִלָּתִי לְךָ Va'ani tefillati lekha (3 times) L323 S140 F396

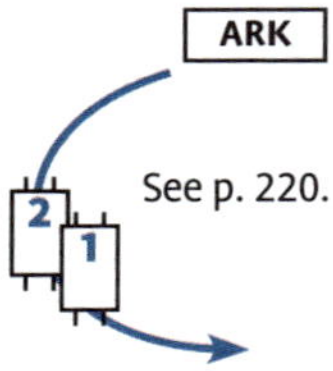

See p. 220.

Remove **2** scrolls from ark in the order they will be read.

1st scroll 5 aliyot from בְּשַׁלַּח Beshallaḥ
שְׁמוֹת Shemot (Exodus) 13:17–15:26
¹13:17–22 ²14:1–8 ³14:9–14 ⁴14:15–25° ⁵14:26–15:26°

☞ °14:22, 29, 31; 15:1–21 For instructions for the special chanting of שִׁירַת הַיָּם Shirat Hayam and of parts of the preceding sections, see p. 97.

☞ °15:11, 16 To preserve the sense of these phrases, maintain the proper pauses after the te'amim (tropes) פַּשְׁטָא ( ) and טִפְּחָא ( ):

15:11 מִי־כָמֹכָה בָּאֵלִם | יי מִי כָּמֹכָה | נֶאְדָּר בַּקֹּדֶשׁ . . .
15:16 . . . עַד־יַעֲבֹר עַמְּךָ | יי עַד־יַעֲבֹר | עַם־זוּ קָנִיתָ:

Place 2nd scroll on table next to 1st scroll.
חֲצִי קַדִּישׁ Short Kaddish L327 S146 F408
Open, raise, display, and wrap 1st scroll.

2nd scroll Maftir aliyah from פִּינְחָס Pineḥas
בְּמִדְבַּר^M Bemidbar (Numbers) 28:19–25

Open, raise, display, and wrap 2nd scroll.

Haftarah for Pesaḥ — Day 7
שְׁמוּאֵל ב׳ 2 Shemu'el (2 Samuel) 22:1–51

Haftarah blessings: L328 S147 F410
☞ Conclude with the Yom Tov בְּרָכָה berakhah L329 S147 F412
with insertions for Pesaḥ.

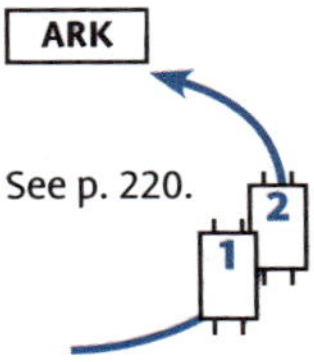

See p. 220.

✕ ~~יְקוּם פֻּרְקָן Yekum purkan~~
✕ ~~אַב הָרַחֲמִים Av Haraḥamim~~

אַשְׁרֵי Ashrey L339 S151 F420
Return scrolls to ark in reverse order. L340 S153 F422
חֲצִי קַדִּישׁ Short Kaddish L342 S155 F428

מוּסָף

Yom Tov Amidah: L343 S166 F456
+ Insertions for Pesaḥ

Some congregations include in the repetition of the Amidah the Priestly Blessing by the Kohanim (*dukhenen*).
בִּרְכַּת כֹּהֲנִים Birkat kohanim L353 S177 F472
For procedures, see p. 222.

קַדִּישׁ שָׁלֵם Full Kaddish L203 S181 F506
Continue with אֵין כֵּא·לֹהֵינוּ Eyn keloheynu. L204 S182 F508

קִדּוּשָׁא רַבָּא

See "Daytime Kiddush," p. 145.

At home

See "Pesaḥ Meals — Day 7" and "Daytime Kiddush," p. 145.

מִנְחָה

אַשְׁרֵי Ashrey L214 S226 W170 F558
וּבָא לְצִיּוֹן Uva letsiyyon L216 S227 W171 F560
חֲצִי קַדִּישׁ Short Kaddish L217 S229 W173 F564

Yom Tov Amidah: L306 S242 W184 F586
+ Insertions for Pesaḥ

קַדִּישׁ שָׁלֵם Full Kaddish L230 S247 W189 F596
עָלֵינוּ Aleynu L231 S248 W190 F598
קַדִּישׁ יָתוֹם Mourner's Kaddish L232 S249 W191 F600

At home

Light candles from an existing flame.
See "Candle Lighting for Pesaḥ — Day 8 (Shabbat)," p. 148.

Nisan 5782							Apr | May 2022						
						1							2
2	3	4	5	6	7	8	3	4	5	6	7	8	9
9	10	11	12	13	14	15	10	11	12	13	14	15	16
16	17	18	19	20	21	22	17	18	19	20	21	22	23
23	24	25	26	27	28	29	24	25	26	27	28	29	30
30							1						

+ Add ✕ Omit ☞ Take note!

Siddurim
- **L** Lev Shalem for Shabbat and Festivals
- **S** Shabbat and Festival Sim Shalom
- **W** Weekday Sim Shalom
- **F** Full Sim Shalom (both editions)
- **P** Personal Edition of Full Sim Shalom

Pesaḥ at Home — Day 8

Candle Lighting for Pesaḥ — Day 8 (Shabbat)

At least 18 minutes before sunset, follow this procedure:

1. Do not *strike* a match. Instead, transfer fire to the candles from an *existing* flame (see p. 144) by inserting a match or other stick into the flame.
2. Do not *extinguish* the match or stick. Instead, place it on a non-flammable tray or dish, and let it self-extinguish. Alternately, a wood *safety* match held vertically (flame up) usually self-extinguishes quickly.
3. Recite only 1 בְּרָכָה *berakhah*: L79 S303 F718

בָּרוּךְ אַתָּה יי, אֱ·לֹהֵינוּ מֶלֶךְ הָעוֹלָם, אֲשֶׁר קִדְּשָׁנוּ בְּמִצְוֹתָיו
וְצִוָּנוּ לְהַדְלִיק נֵר שֶׁל שַׁבָּת וְשֶׁל יוֹם טוֹב.

Barukh attah adonay, eloheynu melekh ha'olam, asher kiddeshanu bemitsvotav vetsivvanu lehadlik ner shel shabbat veshel yom tov.

Pesaḥ Meals — Day 8 (Shabbat)

Enjoy festive meals evening and daytime, in the manner of Shabbat meals.

NOTE: Omit שָׁלוֹם עֲלֵיכֶם *shalom aleykhem* and אֵשֶׁת חַיִל *eshet ḥayil.* Begin with the blessing for the children.

EVENING KIDDUSH L79 S334 F742

Recite: 1. וַיְכֻלּוּ *vaykhullu*
2. Yom Tov קִדּוּשׁ *kiddush* with insertions for Shabbat and for Pesaḥ

Do *not* add שֶׁהֶחֱיָנוּ *sheheḥeyanu.*

DAYTIME KIDDUSH L81 S335 F746

Recite: 1. וְשָׁמְרוּ *veshameru*
2. זָכוֹר *zakhor* (some omit)
3. עַל־כֵּן בֵּרַךְ *al ken berakh*
4. וַיְדַבֵּר מֹשֶׁה *vaydabber mosheh* (Vayikra 23:44)
5. בּוֹרֵא פְּרִי הַגָּפֶן *bo·re peri hagafen*

HAMOTSI, FESTIVE MEALS WITH SINGING, AND BIRKAT HAMAZON

Recite הַמּוֹצִיא *hamotsi* over 2 whole מַצּוֹת *matsot.* L81 S313–14 F744|746

Include festive singing, and recite בִּרְכַּת הַמָּזוֹן *birkat hamazon* for Shabbat, with Pesaḥ additions (see yellow box, p. 133).

Nisan 22 נִיסָן שַׁבָּת Shabbat פֶּסַח Pesaḥ — Day 8

Fri 22 Apr

קַבָּלַת שַׁבָּת ✕ ~~Kabbalat Shabbat~~
through
✕ ~~לְכָה דוֹדִי Lekhah dodi~~

Begin with מִזְמוֹר שִׁיר לְיוֹם הַשַּׁבָּת
Mizmor shir leyom hashabbat (Psalm 92). L27 S23 F266

פֶּסַח Pesaḥ

עַרְבִית Arvit for Yom Tov L39 S28 F279

+ וְשָׁמְרוּ Veshameru L46 S34 F294
+ וַיְדַבֵּר מֹשֶׁה Vaydabber mosheh (Vayikra 23:44) L46 S34 F294

חֲצִי קַדִּישׁ Short Kaddish L46 S34 F294

Yom Tov Amidah: L306 S41 F304
+ Additions for Shabbat
+ Insertions for Pesaḥ

☞ וַיְכֻלּוּ Vaykhullu L53 S47 F314

☞ בָּרוּךְ אַתָּה . . . וָאָרֶץ Barukh attah . . . va'arets L53 S47 F314
☞ מָגֵן אָבוֹת . . . בְרֵאשִׁית Magen avot . . . bereshit L53 S47 F314
☞ אֱ-לֹהֵינוּ . . . הַשַּׁבָּת Eloheynu . . . hashabbat L54 S47 F314

קַדִּישׁ שָׁלֵם Full Kaddish L54 S48 F316

קִדּוּשׁ Kiddush for Yom Tov: L79 S50 F318
✕ ~~וַיְכֻלּוּ Vaykhullu~~
+ Insertions for Shabbat and for Pesaḥ
✕ ~~שֶׁהֶחֱיָנוּ Sheheḥeyanu~~

+ Count Omer. L63 S55 W152 F237
Day **7** (see instructions, p. 221)

עָלֵינוּ Aleynu L56 S51 F320
קַדִּישׁ יָתוֹם Mourner's Kaddish L58 S52 F324

At home See "Pesaḥ Meals — Day 8 (Shabbat)" and "Evening Kiddush," p. 148.

Sat 23 Apr **שַׁחֲרִית** At the end of the preliminary service, begin formal chanting at
הָאֵ-ל בְּתַעֲצוּמוֹת עֻזֶּךָ Ha'el beta'atsumot uzzekha. L147 S105 F336

+ הַכֹּל יוֹדוּךָ Hakol yodukha L150 S107 F340
+ אֵ-ל אָדוֹן El adon L151 S108 F342
+ לָאֵ-ל אֲשֶׁר שָׁבַת La'el asher shavat L152 S109 F342

✕ ~~הַמֵּאִיר לָאָרֶץ Hame'ir la'arets~~

Yom Tov Amidah: L306 S123 F366
+ Additions for Shabbat
+ Insertions for Pesaḥ

Nisan 5782							Apr | May 2022						
						1							2
2	3	4	5	6	7	8	3	4	5	6	7	8	9
9	10	11	12	13	14	15	10	11	12	13	14	15	16
16	17	18	19	20	21	22	17	18	19	20	21	22	23
23	24	25	26	27	28	29	24	25	26	27	28	29	30
30							1						

+ Add ✕ Omit ☞ Take note!

Siddurim
- **L** Lev Shalem for Shabbat and Festivals
- **S** Shabbat and Festival Sim Shalom
- **W** Weekday Sim Shalom
- **F** Full Sim Shalom (both editions)
- **P** Personal Edition of Full Sim Shalom

+ חֲצִי הַלֵּל Short Hallel L316 S133 F380

קַדִּישׁ שָׁלֵם Full Kaddish L321 S138 F392

+ **Megillah reading:**
Some congregations read מְגִלַּת שִׁיר הַשִּׁירִים Megillat Shir Hashirim (Scroll of Song of Songs), without reciting a בְּרָכָה berakhah.
Some read selections in English. L7 S377 F788

קַדִּישׁ יָתוֹם Mourner's Kaddish L121 S82 F52

SHABBAT TORAH SERVICE L322 S139 F394

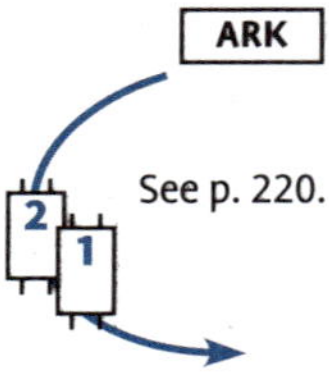

See p. 220.

✕ ~~יי יי אֵ-ל רַחוּם וְחַנּוּן Adonay adonay el raḥum veḥannun~~
✕ ~~רִבּוֹנוֹ שֶׁל עוֹלָם Ribbono shel olam~~
✕ ~~וַאֲנִי תְפִלָּתִי לְךָ Va'ani tefillati lekha~~

Remove **2** scrolls from ark in the order they will be read.

1st scroll 7 aliyot from רְאֵה Re'eh
דְּבָרִים Devarim (Deuteronomy) 14:22–16:17
1 14:22–29 2 15:1–18 3 15:19–23 4 16:1–3
5 16:4–8 6 16:9–12 7 16:13–17

Place 2nd scroll on table next to 1st scroll.
חֲצִי קַדִּישׁ Short Kaddish L327 S146 F408
Open, raise, display, and wrap 1st scroll.

2nd scroll Maftir aliyah from פִּינְחָס Pineḥas
M בְּמִדְבַּר Bemidbar (Numbers) 28:19–25

Open, raise, display, and wrap 2nd scroll.

Haftarah for Pesaḥ — Day 8
יְשַׁעְיָהוּ Yesha'yahu (Isaiah) 10:32–12:6

Haftarah blessings: L328 S147 F410
☞ Conclude with the Yom Tov בְּרָכָה berakhah L329 S147 F412 with insertions for Shabbat and for Pesaḥ.

☞ יְקוּם פֻּרְקָן Yekum purkan L176 S148 F412

+ יִזְכֹּר Yizkor L330 S188 F516

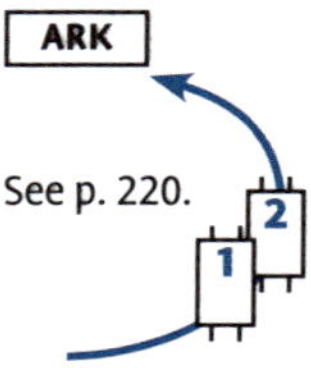

See p. 220.

☞ אַב הָרַחֲמִים Av haraḥamim L446 S151 F420

אַשְׁרֵי Ashrey L339 S151 F420
Return scrolls to ark in reverse order. L340 S153 F422
חֲצִי קַדִּישׁ Short Kaddish L342 S155 F428

פֶּסַח Pesaḥ

מוּסָף

Yom Tov Amidah: L343 S166 F456
+ Additions for Shabbat
+ Insertions for Pesaḥ

Some congregations include in the repetition of the Amidah the Priestly Blessing by the Kohanim (*dukhenen*).
בִּרְכַּת כֹּהֲנִים Birkat kohanim L353 S177 F472
(Some congregations omit on Shabbat.)
For procedures, see p. 222.

קַדִּישׁ שָׁלֵם Full Kaddish L203 S181 F506
Continue with אֵין כֵּא·לֹהֵינוּ Eyn keloheynu. L204 S182 F508

קִדּוּשָׁא רַבָּא

See "Daytime Kiddush — Day 8 (Shabbat)," p. 148.

At home

See "Pesaḥ Meals — Day 8 (Shabbat)" and "Daytime Kiddush," p. 148.

מִנְחָה

אַשְׁרֵי Ashrey L214 S226 W170 F558
וּבָא לְצִיּוֹן Uva letsiyyon L216 S227 W171 F560
חֲצִי קַדִּישׁ Short Kaddish L217 S229 W173 F564

Torah 3 aliyot from אַחֲרֵי מוֹת Aḥarey mot
וַיִּקְרָא Vayikra (Leviticus) 16:1–17
¹16:1–6 ²7–11 ³12–17 W292 P912

Chanted also next Monday and Thursday.

Yom Tov Amidah: L306 S242 W184 F586
+ Additions for Shabbat
+ Insertions for Pesaḥ

✕ ~~צִדְקָתְךָ צֶדֶק Tsidkatekha tsedek~~

קַדִּישׁ שָׁלֵם Full Kaddish L230 S247 W189 F596
עָלֵינוּ Aleynu L231 S248 W190 F598
קַדִּישׁ יָתוֹם Mourner's Kaddish L232 S249 W191 F600

Nisan 23 נִיסָן
Sat 23 Apr

מוֹצָאֵי שַׁבָּת וְיוֹם טוֹב Motsa'ey Shabbat Veyom Tov
Conclusion of Shabbat and Yom Tov
אִסְרוּ חַג Isru Ḥag Day after Yom Tov

עַרְבִית

Arvit for weekdays L264 S281 W137 F200

Weekday Amidah:
+ אַתָּה חוֹנַנְתָּנוּ Atta ḥonantanu L272 S287 W143 F212

Nisan 5782							Apr | May 2022						
						1							2
2	3	4	5	6	7	8	3	4	5	6	7	8	9
9	10	11	12	13	14	15	10	11	12	13	14	15	16
16	17	18	19	20	21	22	17	18	19	20	21	22	23
23	24	25	26	27	28	29	24	25	26	27	28	29	30
30							1						

+ Add ✕ Omit ☞ Take note!

Siddurim
- **L** Lev Shalem for Shabbat and Festivals
- **S** Shabbat and Festival Sim Shalom
- **W** Weekday Sim Shalom
- **F** Full Sim Shalom (both editions)
- **P** Personal Edition of Full Sim Shalom

☞ חֲצִי קַדִּישׁ Short Kaddish L269 S292 W158 F682

☞ וִיהִי נֹעַם Vihi no'am L279 S292 W158 F684
☞ יוֹשֵׁב בְּסֵתֶר עֶלְיוֹן Yoshev beseter elyon L279 S292 W158 F684
☞ וְאַתָּה קָדוֹשׁ Ve'attah kadosh L216 S293 W159 F684

קַדִּישׁ שָׁלֵם Full Kaddish L280 S294 W160 F688
+ Count Omer. L63 S55 W152 F237
Day **8** (see instructions, p. 221)

Some recite הַבְדָּלָה Havdalah here. L283 S299 W165 F700
For instructions, see below.

עָלֵינוּ Aleynu L281 S297 W163 F696
קַדִּישׁ יָתוֹם Mourner's Kaddish L282 S298 W164 F698

הַבְדָּלָה Havdalah as at the end of a usual Shabbat L283 S299 W165 F700

DURING Nisan Continue:
✕ ~~תַּחֲנוּן Taḥanun~~

Sun 24 Apr שַׁחֲרִית Shaḥarit for weekdays W1 F2
☞ מִזְמוֹר לְתוֹדָה Mizmor letodah W20 F60
✕ ~~תַּחֲנוּן Taḥanun~~
☞ לַמְנַצֵּחַ Lamenatse·aḥ (Psalm 20) W79 F154

מִנְחָה ✕ ~~תַּחֲנוּן Taḥanun~~

Nisan 24 נִיסָן
Sun 24 Apr עַרְבִית + Before עָלֵינוּ Aleynu, count Omer. L63 S55 W152 F237
Day **9** (see instructions, p. 221)

Nisan 25 נִיסָן
Mon 25 Apr עַרְבִית + Before עָלֵינוּ Aleynu, count Omer. L63 S55 W152 F237
Day **10** (see instructions, p. 221)

Nisan 26 נִיסָן
Tue 26 Apr עַרְבִית + Before עָלֵינוּ Aleynu, count Omer. L63 S55 W152 F237
Day **11** (see instructions, p. 221)

Nisan 27 נִיסָן
Wed 27 Apr (evening)

יוֹם הַשּׁוֹאָה וְהַגְּבוּרָה Yom Hasho'ah Vehagevurah
Holocaust and Heroism Remembrance Day

Yom Hasho'ah Vehagevurah

The Knesset in Israel has officially designated 27 Nisan as a day to commemorate the Holocaust and to honor the heroes of the resistance movements during the period of the Holocaust.

Although no fixed liturgy for the occasion has yet emerged, many congregations mark the occasion with changes in the service. The following are customs practiced and resources used in various congregations:

- Reading all of (or selections from) *Megillat Hashoah: The Shoah Scroll.* This work, comprising six chapters in memory of the six million, is available from The Rabbinical Assembly at www.rabbinicalassembly.org/resources-ideas/publications.
- Reading additional texts appropriate to Holocaust commemoration and the heroic efforts of resistance fighters. Modern *siddurim* offer a selection of such readings. L450 S387 W198 F828
- Reciting a נַחֵם *naḥem* prayer for Yom Hasho'ah in each Amidah, such as the one in *Siddur Sim Shalom for Weekdays* (pp. 40, 127, 145).
- Lighting a single memorial candle, or lighting six *yortsayt* candles.
  Yellow memorial candles have become a powerful symbol for this purpose through the efforts of the Federation of Jewish Men's Clubs. For more details, visit www.yellowcandles.org.
- Reciting אֵ-ל מָלֵא רַחֲמִים *El ma·le raḥamim.* L336 S196 W200 F522
  For the text of a Holocaust remembrance אֵ-ל מָלֵא רַחֲמִים prayer from the Chief Rabbinate of the State of Israel, with translation and explanation, visit www.milesbcohen.com/LuahResources.
- Adding a קַדִּישׁ כְּלָלִי *kaddish kelali*, a general Mourner's Kaddish (recited by those who have lost one or both parents).

עַרְבִית Arvit for weekdays L264 S281 W137 F200

+ Additions for יוֹם הַשּׁוֹאָה Yom Hasho'ah (see box, above)

+ Before עָלֵינוּ Aleynu, count Omer. L63 S55 W152 F237
Day **12** (see instructions, p. 221)

Thu 28 Apr **שַׁחֲרִית** Shaḥarit for weekdays W1 F2

+ Additions for יוֹם הַשּׁוֹאָה Yom Hasho'ah (see box, above)

Some omit לַמְנַצֵּחַ Lamenatse·aḥ (Psalm 20).

מִנְחָה Minḥah for weekdays W120 F164

+ Additions for יוֹם הַשּׁוֹאָה Yom Hasho'ah (see box, above)

Nisan 5782						
						1
2	3	4	5	6	7	8
9	10	11	12	13	14	15
16	17	18	19	20	21	22
23	24	25	26	27	28	29
30						

Apr | May 2022						
						2
3	4	5	6	7	8	9
10	11	12	13	14	15	16
17	18	19	20	21	22	23
24	25	26	27	28	29	30
1						

+ Add ✕ Omit ☞ Take note!

Siddurim
- **L** Lev Shalem for Shabbat and Festivals
- **S** Shabbat and Festival Sim Shalom
- **W** Weekday Sim Shalom
- **F** Full Sim Shalom (both editions)
- **P** Personal Edition of Full Sim Shalom

Nisan 28 נִיסָן
Thu 28 Apr

עַרְבִית + Before עָלֵינוּ Aleynu, count Omer. L63 S55 W152 F237
Day **13** (see instructions, p. 221)

Nisan 29 נִיסָן
Fri 29 Apr

שַׁבָּת Shabbat פָּרָשַׁת אַחֲרֵי מוֹת Parashat Aḥarey mot
שַׁבָּת מָחָר חֹדֶשׁ Shabbat Maḥar Ḥodesh
שַׁבַּת מְבָרְכִים הַחֹדֶשׁ Shabbat Mevarekhim Haḥodesh

עַרְבִית + Before עָלֵינוּ Aleynu, count Omer. L63 S55 W152 F237
Day **14** (see instructions, p. 221)

Sat 30 Apr

Torah 7 aliyot (minimum): אַחֲרֵי מוֹת Aḥarey mot
וַיִּקְרָא Vayikra (Leviticus) 16:1–18:30

Annual:	1 16:1–17	2 16:18–24	3 16:25–34	4 17:1–7
	5 17:8–18:5	6 18:6–21	7 18:22–30	M 18:28–30
Triennial:°	1 17:1–7	2 17:8–12	3 17:13–16	4 18:1–5
	5 18:6–21	6 18:22–25	7 18:26–30	M 18:26–30

☞Triennial: Accords with the CJLS decision of Nov. 16, 2020.

☞**Haftarah** for Shabbat Maḥar Ḥodesh
שְׁמוּאֵל א׳ 1 Shemu'el (1 Samuel) 20:18–42

+ **Birkat Haḥodesh:** L180 S150 F418
Announce Rosh Ḥodesh Iyyar:
רֹאשׁ חֹדֶשׁ אִיָּר יִהְיֶה בְּיוֹם רִאשׁוֹן וּבְיוֹם שֵׁנִי . . .
Rosh ḥodesh Iyyar yihyeh beyom rishon uvyom sheni . . .
(Saturday night, Sunday, and Monday)

☞Recite אַב הָרַחֲמִים Av haraḥamim L446 S151 F420
during Omer period, even if congregation usually omits.

מִנְחָה

Torah 3 aliyot from קְדֹשִׁים Kedoshim
וַיִּקְרָא Vayikra (Leviticus) 19:1–14
1 19:1–4 2 5–10 3 11–14 W293 P914

☞Not chanted publicly again until next Shabbat morning.

✕ ~~צִדְקָתְךָ צֶדֶק Tsidkatekha tsedek~~

Nisan 30 נִיסָן — Sat 30 Apr (evening)

רֹאשׁ חֹדֶשׁ אִיָּר Rosh Ḥodesh Iyyar — Day 1

מוֹצָאֵי שַׁבָּת Motsa'ey Shabbat Conclusion of Shabbat

DURING Rosh Ḥodesh

Birkat Hamazon:

+ יַעֲלֶה וְיָבוֹא Ya'aleh veyavo for Rosh Ḥodesh L90|95 S340|347 W233|239 F762|780

+ הָרַחֲמָן Haraḥaman for Rosh Ḥodesh L92|96 S343|348 W235|240 F768

עַרְבִית

Arvit for weekdays L264 S281 W137 F200

Weekday Amidah:

+ אַתָּה חוֹנַנְתָּנוּ Attah ḥonantanu L272 S287 W143 F212
+ יַעֲלֶה וְיָבוֹא Ya'aleh veyavo for Rosh Ḥodesh L277 S289 W145 F216

Continue as on a usual Saturday night through
קַדִּישׁ שָׁלֵם Full Kaddish L280 S294 W160 F688

+ Count Omer. L63 S55 W152 F237
Day **15** (see instructions, p. 221)

Some recite הַבְדָּלָה Havdalah here. L283 S299 W165 F700

עָלֵינוּ Aleynu L281 S297 W163 F696
קַדִּישׁ יָתוֹם Mourner's Kaddish L282 S298 W164 F698

הַבְדָּלָה Havdalah L283 S299 W165 F700

Sun 1 May — שַׁחֲרִית

Before מִזְמוֹר שִׁיר Mizmor shir (Psalm 30) W14 F50
or at end of service, recite:

Psalm for Sunday (Psalm 24) W85 F22
קַדִּישׁ יָתוֹם Mourner's Kaddish (some omit) W100 F52
+ Psalm 104 for Rosh Ḥodesh W90 F34
קַדִּישׁ יָתוֹם Mourner's Kaddish W100 F52

Weekday Amidah:

+ יַעֲלֶה וְיָבוֹא Ya'aleh veyavo for Rosh Ḥodesh W41 F114

✕ ~~תַּחֲנוּן Taḥanun~~

+ חֲצִי הַלֵּל Short Hallel W50 F380
קַדִּישׁ שָׁלֵם Full Kaddish W56 F392

Nisan 5782							Apr | May 2022						
						1							2
2	3	4	5	6	7	8	3	4	5	6	7	8	9
9	10	11	12	13	14	15	10	11	12	13	14	15	16
16	17	18	19	20	21	22	17	18	19	20	21	22	23
23	24	25	26	27	28	29	24	25	26	27	28	29	30
30							1						

+ Add ✕ Omit ☞ Take note!

Siddurim
- **L** Lev Shalem for Shabbat and Festivals
- **S** Shabbat and Festival Sim Shalom
- **W** Weekday Sim Shalom
- **F** Full Sim Shalom (both editions)
- **P** Personal Edition of Full Sim Shalom

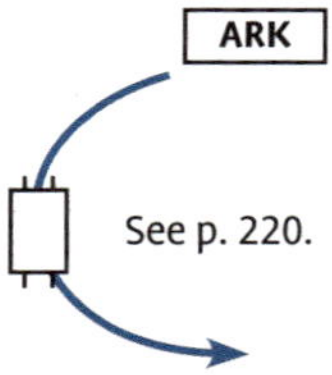

See p. 220.

\+ **TORAH SERVICE** W65 F138
Remove **1** scroll from ark.

Torah 4 aliyot: פִּינְחָס Pineḥas
בְּמִדְבַּר Bemidbar (Numbers) 28:1–15
[1]28:1–3 [2]3–5 [3]6–10 [4]11–15 W320 P943

חֲצִי קַדִּישׁ Short Kaddish W71 F146
Open, raise, display, and wrap scroll.
Return scroll to ark. W76 F150

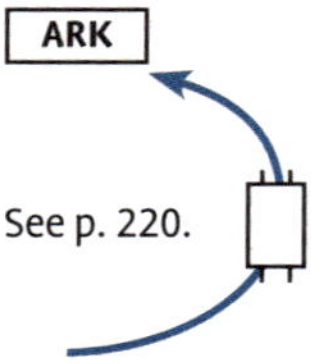

See p. 220.

אַשְׁרֵי Ashrey W78 F152
✕ ~~לַמְנַצֵּחַ Lamenatse·aḥ (Psalm 20)~~
וּבָא לְצִיּוֹן Uva letsiyyon W80 F156

Remove and pack tefillin. (Some remove after Kaddish.)

\+ חֲצִי קַדִּישׁ Short Kaddish W103 F428
(If you remove tefillin here, do *not* pack but cover them, so as to begin Musaf together quickly after Kaddish.)

מוּסָף

\+ **Rosh Ḥodesh Amidah for weekdays:** W104 F486
Weekday קְדֻשָּׁה Kedushah W105 F488
☞ Do *not* continue to add וּלְכַפָּרַת פָּשַׁע Ulkhapparat pasha.

\+ קַדִּישׁ שָׁלֵם Full Kaddish W82 F158
עָלֵינוּ Aleynu W83 F160

If psalms for the day were not recited at Shaḥarit, add here:
קַדִּישׁ יָתוֹם Mourner's Kaddish (some omit) W84|100 F162|52
Psalm for Sunday (Psalm 24) W85 F22
קַדִּישׁ יָתוֹם Mourner's Kaddish (some omit) W100 F52
\+ Psalm 104 for Rosh Ḥodesh W90 F34

קַדִּישׁ יָתוֹם Mourner's Kaddish W84|100 F162|52

מִנְחָה

Weekday Amidah:
\+ יַעֲלֶה וְיָבוֹא Ya'aleh veyavo for Rosh Ḥodesh W127 F178

✕ ~~תַּחֲנוּן Taḥanun~~

Iyyar 1 אִיָּר
Sun 1 May (evening)

רֹאשׁ חֹדֶשׁ אִיָּר Rosh Ḥodesh Iyyar — Day 2

DURING Rosh Ḥodesh

Birkat Hamazon:
+ יַעֲלֶה וְיָבוֹא Ya'aleh veyavo for Rosh Ḥodesh L90|95 S340|347 W233|239 F762|780
+ הָרַחֲמָן Haraḥaman for Rosh Ḥodesh L92|96 S343|348 W235|240 F768

עַרְבִית

Weekday Amidah:
+ יַעֲלֶה וְיָבוֹא Ya'aleh veyavo for Rosh Ḥodesh W145 F216

+ Before עָלֵינוּ Aleynu, count Omer. L63 S55 W152 F237
Day **16** (see instructions, p. 221)

Mon 2 May **שַׁחֲרִית**

Before מִזְמוֹר שִׁיר Mizmor shir (Psalm 30) W14 F50
or at end of service, recite:
Psalm for Monday (Psalm 48) W86 F24
קַדִּישׁ יָתוֹם Mourner's Kaddish (some omit) W100 F52
+ Psalm 104 for Rosh Ḥodesh W90 F34
קַדִּישׁ יָתוֹם Mourner's Kaddish W100 F52

Weekday Amidah:
+ יַעֲלֶה וְיָבוֹא Ya'aleh veyavo for Rosh Ḥodesh W41 F114

✕ ~~תַּחֲנוּן Taḥanun~~

+ חֲצִי הַלֵּל Short Hallel W50 F380
קַדִּישׁ שָׁלֵם Full Kaddish W56 F392

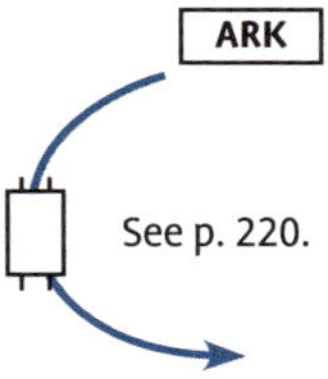

See p. 220.

TORAH SERVICE W65 F138
Remove **1** scroll from ark.

Torah 4 aliyot: פִּינְחָס Pineḥas
בְּמִדְבַּר Bemidbar (Numbers) 28:1–15
[1]28:1–3 [2]3–5 [3]6–10 [4]11–15 W320 P943

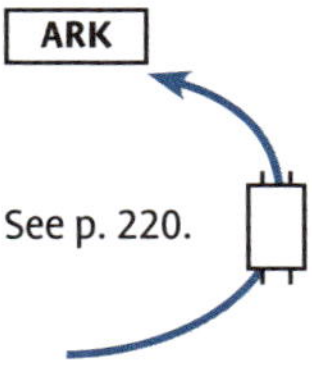

See p. 220.

חֲצִי קַדִּישׁ Short Kaddish W71 F146
Open, raise, display, and wrap scroll.
Return scroll to ark. W76 F150

אַשְׁרֵי Ashrey W78 F152
✕ ~~לַמְנַצֵּחַ Lamenatse·aḥ (Psalm 20)~~
וּבָא לְצִיּוֹן Uva letsiyyon W80 F156

Remove and pack tefillin. (Some remove after Kaddish.)

+ חֲצִי קַדִּישׁ Short Kaddish W103 F428
(If you remove tefillin here, do *not* pack but cover them, so as to begin Musaf together quickly after Kaddish.)

מוּסָף
+ **Rosh Ḥodesh Amidah for weekdays:** W104 F486
Weekday קְדֻשָּׁה Kedushah W105 F488
☞ Do *not* continue to add וּלְכַפָּרַת פָּשַׁע Ulkhapparat pasha.

+ קַדִּישׁ שָׁלֵם Full Kaddish W82 F158
עָלֵינוּ Aleynu W83 F160

If psalms for the day were not recited at Shaḥarit, add here:
קַדִּישׁ יָתוֹם Mourner's Kaddish (some omit) W84|100 F162|52
Psalm for Monday (Psalm 48) W86 F24
קַדִּישׁ יָתוֹם Mourner's Kaddish (some omit) W100 F52
+ Psalm 104 for Rosh Ḥodesh W90 F34
קַדִּישׁ יָתוֹם Mourner's Kaddish W84|100 F162|52

מִנְחָה
Weekday Amidah:
+ יַעֲלֶה וְיָבוֹא Ya'aleh veyavo for Rosh Ḥodesh W127 F178

✕ ~~תַּחֲנוּן Taḥanun~~

Iyyar 2 אִיָּר
Mon 2 May
עַרְבִית
+ Before עָלֵינוּ Aleynu, count Omer. L63 S55 W152 F237
Day **17** (see instructions, p. 221)

BEGINNING 2 Iyyar Resume reciting תַּחֲנוּן Taḥanun.

Iyyar 3 אִיָּר
Tue 3 May (evening)

יוֹם הַזִּכָּרוֹן Yom Hazikkaron
Remembrance Day

Yom Hazikkaron

The Knesset in Israel has officially designated the day before Yom Ha'atsma'ut as יוֹם הַזִּכָּרוֹן, Remembrance Day for Fallen Soldiers and Victims of Terrorism. Appropriate observances include:

- Adding relevant readings to the service
- Lighting a *yortsayt* candle
- Reciting אֵ-ל מָלֵא רַחֲמִים *El ma-le raḥamim* W73 F522
- Reciting a communal קַדִּישׁ יָתוֹם Mourner's Kaddish W84 F524

Siddurim

	1	2	3	4	5	6		2	3	4	5	6	7			May 4	
L Lev Shalem for Shabbat and Festivals	7	8	9	10	11	12	13	8	9	10	11	12	13	14		אִיָּר 4	May 4
S Shabbat and Festival Sim Shalom	14	15	16	17	18	19	20	15	16	17	18	19	20	21			
W Weekday Sim Shalom	21	22	23	24	25	26	27	22	23	24	25	26	27	28			
F Full Sim Shalom (both editions)	28	29						29	30								
P Personal Edition of Full Sim Shalom

עַרְבִית + Additions for יוֹם הַזִּכָּרוֹן Yom Hazikkaron (see box, p. 158)

+ Before עָלֵינוּ Aleynu, count Omer. L63 S55 W152 F237
Day **18** (see instructions, p. 221)

Wed 4 May **שַׁחֲרִית** + Additions for יוֹם הַזִּכָּרוֹן Yom Hazikkaron (see box, p. 158)

מִנְחָה ✕ ~~תַּחֲנוּן Taḥanun~~

Iyyar 4 אִיָּר — יוֹם הָעַצְמָאוּת Yom Ha'atsma'ut

Wed 4 May (evening) — **Independence Day**

Yom Ha'atsma'ut

The Knesset in Israel has officially designated 5 Iyyar as **יוֹם הָעַצְמָאוּת**, Independence Day. When that date falls on Thursday night and Friday, as it does this year, Yom Ha'atsma'ut is moved to 4 Iyyar so that festivities do not interfere with the beginning of Shabbat.

In addition to the ritual observances, the following are customary:
- Eating a festive meal that includes foods from Israel
- Singing songs related to Israel

Also, all mourning practices associated with the Omer period are suspended. For example:
- Weddings and other communal celebrations are permitted.
- Haircuts are permitted.

DURING Yom Ha'atsma'ut

Birkat Hamazon:
+ עַל הַנִּסִּים Al Hanissim for Yom Ha'atsma'ut W232|238 F760

עַרְבִית **Weekday Amidah:**
+ עַל הַנִּסִּים Al Hanissim for Yom Ha'atsma'ut W147 F218

Some recite הַלֵּל שָׁלֵם Full Hallel. W50 F380

קַדִּישׁ שָׁלֵם Full Kaddish W149 F222

+ Prayers, readings, and songs for Yom Ha'atsma'ut W205–8

+ Before עָלֵינוּ Aleynu, count Omer. L63 S55 W152 F237
Day **19** (see instructions, p. 221)

May 5   4 אִיָּר

Iyyar 5782

	1	2	3	4	5	6
7	8	9	10	11	12	13
14	15	16	17	18	19	20
21	22	23	24	25	26	27
28	29					

May 2022

	2	3	4	5	6	7
8	9	10	11	12	13	14
15	16	17	18	19	20	21
22	23	24	25	26	27	28
29	30					

+ Add   ✕ Omit   ☞ Take note!

Siddurim

- **L** Lev Shalem for Shabbat and Festivals
- **S** Shabbat and Festival Sim Shalom
- **W** Weekday Sim Shalom
- **F** Full Sim Shalom (both editions)
- **P** Personal Edition of Full Sim Shalom

Thu 5 May   **שַׁחֲרִית**

Weekday Shaḥarit as usual W1 F2
through מִזְמוֹר לְתוֹדָה Mizmor letodah (Psalm 100) W20 F60

+ Psalms recited on Shabbat and Yom Tov:
☞ Psalms 19, 34, 90, 91, 135, 136, 33, 92, 93 L127–34 S87–95 F60–78
Use weekday minor nusaḥ for the psalms.

Continue with the usual weekday service from
יְהִי כְבוֹד יי Yehi khevod adonay. W20 F80

Weekday Amidah:

+ עַל הַנִּסִּים Al hanissim for Yom Ha'atsma'ut W42 F118

✕ ~~תַּחֲנוּן Taḥanun~~

הַלֵּל שָׁלֵם Full Hallel W50 F380

ARK

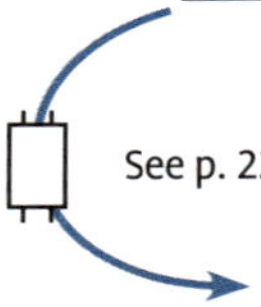

See p. 220.

חֲצִי קַדִּישׁ Short Kaddish W56 F390

TORAH SERVICE W65 F138

Remove **1** scroll from ark.

3 aliyot from עֵקֶב Ekev
°דְּבָרִים Devarim (Deuteronomy) 7:12–8:18
1 7:12–21   2 7:22–8:6   M 8:7–18   W343 P983

☞ °If your congregation does not read the Yom Ha'atsma'ut reading:
1. Read the regular weekday reading (קְדֹשִׁים Kedoshim; see p. 154).
2. Later, read the haftarah below, **omitting** all בְּרָכוֹת berakhot.

חֲצִי קַדִּישׁ Short Kaddish W71 F146
Open, raise, display, and wrap scroll.

+ Recite the בְּרָכָה berakhah before the haftarah. W74 F410 P989

Haftarah יְשַׁעְיָהוּ Yesha'yahu (Isaiah) 10:32–12:6 W345 P987

+ Recite the 3 concluding haftarah blessings,
through מָגֵן דָּוִד. W74 F410 P989.

ARK

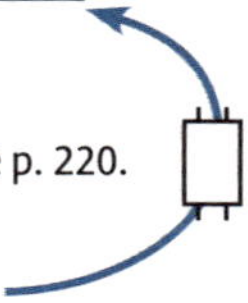

See p. 220.

+ תְּפִלָּה לִשְׁלוֹם הַמְּדִינָה Prayer for the State of Israel W75 F416

Return scroll to ark. W76 F150

אַשְׁרֵי Ashrey W78 F152
✕ ~~לַמְנַצֵּחַ Lamenatseaḥ (Psalm 20)~~
וּבָא לְצִיּוֹן Uva letsiyyon W80 F156

+ קַדִּישׁ שָׁלֵם Full Kaddish W82 F158

+ Prayers, readings, and songs for Yom Ha'atsma'ut W205–8

Conclude weekday Shaḥarit as usual.

מִנְחָה

Weekday Amidah:

+ עַל הַנִּסִּים Al hanissim for Yom Ha'atsma'ut W129 F182

✕ ~~תַּחֲנוּן Taḥanun~~

Iyyar 5 אִיָּר
Thu 5 May

עַרְבִית + Before עָלֵינוּ Aleynu, count Omer. L63 S55 W152 F237
Day **20** (see instructions, p. 221)

Iyyar 6 אִיָּר
Fri 6 May

שַׁבָּת Shabbat פָּרָשַׁת קְדֹשִׁים Parashat Kedoshim

עַרְבִית + Before עָלֵינוּ Aleynu, count Omer. L63 S55 W152 F237
Day **21** (see instructions, p. 221)

Sat 7 May

Torah 7 aliyot (minimum): קְדֹשִׁים Kedoshim
וַיִּקְרָא Vayikra (Leviticus) 19:1–20:27

Annual:	1 19:1–14	2 19:15–22	3 19:23–32	4 19:33–37
	5 20:1–7	6 20:8–22	7 20:23–27	M 20:25–27
Triennial:	1 19:15–18	2 19:19–22	3 19:23–32	4 19:33–37
	5 20:1–7	6 20:8–22	7 20:23–27	M 20:25–27

Haftarah

☞ Ashkenazic: עָמוֹס Amos (Amos) 9:7–15
Sephardic: יְחֶזְקֵאל Yeḥezkel (Ezekiel) 20:2–20

☞ Recite אַב הָרַחֲמִים Av haraḥamim L446 S151 F420
during Omer period, even if congregation usually omits.

מִנְחָה

Torah 3 aliyot: אֱמֹר Emor
וַיִּקְרָא Vayikra (Leviticus) 21:1–15
1 21:1–6 2 7–12° 3 13–15 W294 P914

Chanted also next Monday and Thursday.

☞ °21:10 Note the unusual use of the ta'am (trope) | מֻנַּח־לְגַרְמֵיהּ
(= מֻנַּח־מַפְסִיק |): עַל־רֹאשׁוֹ |

Iyyar 5782						
	1	2	3	4	5	6
7	8	9	10	11	12	13
14	15	16	17	18	19	20
21	22	23	24	25	26	27
28	29					

May 2022						
	2	3	4	5	6	7
8	9	10	11	12	13	14
15	16	17	18	19	20	21
22	23	24	25	26	27	28
29	30					

+ Add ✕ Omit ☞ Take note!

Siddurim
- **L** Lev Shalem for Shabbat and Festivals
- **S** Shabbat and Festival Sim Shalom
- **W** Weekday Sim Shalom
- **F** Full Sim Shalom (both editions)
- **P** Personal Edition of Full Sim Shalom

Iyyar 7 אִיָּר
Sat 7 May

מוֹצָאֵי שַׁבָּת Motsa'ey Shabbat Conclusion of Shabbat

עַרְבִית

Saturday night Arvit as usual L264 S281 W137 F200
through קַדִּישׁ שָׁלֵם Full Kaddish L280 S294 W160 F688

+ Count Omer. L63 S55 W152 F237
Day **22** (see instructions, p. 221)

Some recite הַבְדָּלָה Havdalah here. L283 S299 W165 F700

עָלֵינוּ Aleynu L281 S297 W163 F696
קַדִּישׁ יָתוֹם Mourner's Kaddish L282 S298 W164 F698

הַבְדָּלָה Havdalah L283 S299 W165 F700

Iyyar 7 אִיָּר
Sat 7 May (night)

After Arvit if the moon is visible:
קִדּוּשׁ לְבָנָה Kiddush Levanah L286 W167 F704
For procedures and instructions, see p. 223.

Iyyar 8 אִיָּר
Sun 8 May **עַרְבִית**
+ Before עָלֵינוּ Aleynu, count Omer. L63 S55 W152 F237
Day **23** (see instructions, p. 221)

Iyyar 9 אִיָּר
Mon 9 May **עַרְבִית**
+ Before עָלֵינוּ Aleynu, count Omer. L63 S55 W152 F237
Day **24** (see instructions, p. 221)

Iyyar 10 אִיָּר
Tue 10 May **עַרְבִית**
+ Before עָלֵינוּ Aleynu, count Omer. L63 S55 W152 F237
Day **25** (see instructions, p. 221)

Iyyar 11 אִיָּר
Wed 11 May **עַרְבִית**
+ Before עָלֵינוּ Aleynu, count Omer. L63 S55 W152 F237
Day **26** (see instructions, p. 221)

Iyyar 12 אִיָּר
Thu 12 May **עַרְבִית**
+ Before עָלֵינוּ Aleynu, count Omer. L63 S55 W152 F237
Day **27** (see instructions, p. 221)

Iyyar 13 אִיָּר Fri 13 May — שַׁבָּת Shabbat פָּרָשַׁת אֱמֹר Parashat Emor

עַרְבִית + Before עָלֵינוּ Aleynu, count Omer. L63 S55 W152 F237
Day **28** (see instructions, p. 221)

Sat 14 May

Torah 7 aliyot (minimum): אֱמֹר Emor
וַיִּקְרָא Vayikra (Leviticus) 21:1–24:23

Annual:	1 21:1–15°	2 21:16–22:16	3 22:17–33	4 23:1–22
	5 23:23–32	6 23:33–44	7 24:1–23	M 24:21–23
Triennial:	1 23:23–25	2 23:26–32	3 23:33–44	4 24:1–4
	5 24:5–9	6 24:10–12	7 24:13–23	M 24:21–23

☞ °21:10 Note the unusual use of the ta'am (trope) | מְֻנַּח־לְגַרְמֵיהּ
(= | מְֻנַּח־מַפְסִיק): | עַל־רֹאשׁוֹ

Haftarah יְחֶזְקֵאל Yeḥezkel (Ezekiel) 44:15–31

☞ Recite אַב הָרַחֲמִים Av haraḥamim L446 S151 F420
during Omer period, even if congregation usually omits.

מִנְחָה **Torah** 3 aliyot from בְּהַר Behar
וַיִּקְרָא Vayikra (Leviticus) 25:1–13
1 25:1–3 2 4–7 3 8–13 W295 P915

Chanted also next Monday and Thursday.

☞ צִדְקָתְךָ צֶדֶק Tsidkatekha tsedek L230 S239 W183 F584

Iyyar 14 אִיָּר Sat 14 May (evening) — פֶּסַח שֵׁנִי Pesaḥ Sheni — The 2nd Pesaḥ

מוֹצָאֵי שַׁבָּת Motsa'ey Shabbat Conclusion of Shabbat

Pesaḥ Sheni is described in Bemidbar 9:6–14. People who were unable to partake of the Pesaḥ offering because of a particular ritual impurity or because of distant travel were obligated to perform a "make-up" Pesaḥ offering a month later. Pesaḥ Sheni is, therefore, a somewhat festive occasion.
As a reminder of this 2nd Pesaḥ offering, some eat מַצָּה *matsah* on this day.

עַרְבִית Saturday night Arvit as usual L264 S281 W137 F200
through קַדִּישׁ שָׁלֵם Full Kaddish L280 S294 W160 F688

+ Count Omer. L63 S55 W152 F237
Day **29** (see instructions, p. 221)

Some recite הַבְדָּלָה Havdalah here. L283 S299 W165 F700

עָלֵינוּ Aleynu L281 S297 W163 F696
קַדִּישׁ יָתוֹם Mourner's Kaddish L282 S298 W164 F698

הַבְדָּלָה Havdalah L283 S299 W165 F700

Sun 15 May שַׁחֲרִית ✕ ~~תַּחֲנוּן Taḥanun~~
☞ לַמְנַצֵּחַ Lamenatse·aḥ (Psalm 20) W79 F154

מִנְחָה ✕ ~~תַּחֲנוּן Taḥanun~~

Iyyar 15 אִיָּר
Sun 15 May עַרְבִית + Before עָלֵינוּ Aleynu, count Omer. L63 S55 W152 F237
Day **30** (see instructions, p. 221)

Iyyar 16 אִיָּר
Mon 16 May עַרְבִית + Before עָלֵינוּ Aleynu, count Omer. L63 S55 W152 F237
Day **31** (see instructions, p. 221)

Iyyar 17 אִיָּר
Tue 17 May **עֶרֶב לַ"ג בָּעֹמֶר Erev Lag Ba'omer**
Day before Lag Ba'omer

עַרְבִית + Before עָלֵינוּ Aleynu, count Omer. L63 S55 W152 F237
Day **32** (see instructions, p. 221)

Wed 18 May מִנְחָה ✕ ~~תַּחֲנוּן Taḥanun~~

Iyyar 18 אִיָּר — לַ"ג בָּעֹמֶר Lag Ba'omer — Day 33 of the Omer
Wed 18 May (evening)

Lag Ba'omer

Lag Ba'omer is a festive occasion, celebrating happy events from the rabbinic period. Although Lag Ba'omer has no liturgical additions or specific rituals, we customarily celebrate with outdoor activities or picnics.

Mourning practices associated with the Omer period are suspended.
For example:

- Weddings and other communal celebrations are permitted.
- Haircuts are permitted. (In a year when Lag Ba'omer falls immediately after Shabbat, a haircut is permitted on Friday prior to Shabbat.)

עַרְבִית + Before עָלֵינוּ Aleynu, count Omer. L63 S55 W152 F237
Day **33** (see instructions, p. 221)

+ Add ✕ Omit ☞ Take note!

Siddurim
- **L** Lev Shalem for Shabbat and Festivals
- **S** Shabbat and Festival Sim Shalom
- **W** Weekday Sim Shalom
- **F** Full Sim Shalom (both editions)
- **P** Personal Edition of Full Sim Shalom

Iyyar 5782

	1	2	3	4	5	6
7	8	9	10	11	12	13
14	15	16	17	18	19	20
21	22	23	24	25	26	27
28	29					

May 2022

	2	3	4	5	6	7
8	9	10	11	12	13	14
15	16	17	18	19	20	21
22	23	24	25	26	27	28
29	30					

18 אִיָּר May 19
19 אִיָּר May 19
20 אִיָּר May 20
May 21

Thu 19 May שַׁחֲרִית ✕ ~~תַּחֲנוּן Taḥanun~~
☞ לַמְנַצֵּחַ Lamenatse·aḥ (Psalm 20) W79 F154

מִנְחָה ✕ ~~תַּחֲנוּן Taḥanun~~

Iyyar 19 אִיָּר
Thu 19 May עַרְבִית + Before עָלֵינוּ Aleynu, count Omer. L63 S55 W152 F237
Day **34** (see instructions, p. 221)

Iyyar 20 אִיָּר
Fri 20 May

שַׁבָּת Shabbat פָּרָשַׁת בְּהַר Parashat Behar

עַרְבִית + Before עָלֵינוּ Aleynu, count Omer. L63 S55 W152 F237
Day **35** (see instructions, p. 221)

Sat 21 May

Torah 7 aliyot (minimum): בְּהַר Behar
וַיִּקְרָא Vayikra (Leviticus) 25:1–26:2

Annual:	1 25:1–13	2 25:14–18	3 25:19–24	4 25:25–28
	5 25:29–38	6 25:39–46	7 25:47–26:2	M 25:55–26:2
Triennial:°	1 25:29–34	2 25:35–38	3 25:39–43	4 25:44–46
	5 25:47–50	6 25:51–54	7 25:55–26:2	M 25:55–26:2

☞ Triennial: Accords with the CJLS decision of Nov. 16, 2020.

Haftarah
Ashkenazic: יִרְמְיָהוּ Yirmeyahu (Jeremiah) 32:6–27
Sephardic: יִרְמְיָהוּ Yirmeyahu (Jeremiah) 32:6–22

☞ Recite אַב הָרַחֲמִים Av haraḥamim L446 S151 F420
during Omer period, even if congregation usually omits.

מִנְחָה **Torah** 3 aliyot from בְּחֻקֹּתַי Beḥukkotay
וַיִּקְרָא Vayikra (Leviticus) 26:3–13°
1 26:3–5 2 6–9 3 10–13 W296 P916

Chanted also next Monday and Thursday.

☞ °26:3–13 The reading extends through verse 13, which enables the correct configuration of the 3 aliyot.

Iyyar 5782						
	1	2	3	4	5	6
7	8	9	10	11	12	13
14	15	16	17	18	19	20
21	22	23	24	25	26	27
28	29					

May 2022						
	2	3	4	5	6	7
8	9	10	11	12	13	14
15	16	17	18	19	20	21
22	23	24	25	26	27	28
29	30					

+ Add ✕ Omit ☞ Take note!

Siddurim
- **L** Lev Shalem for Shabbat and Festivals
- **S** Shabbat and Festival Sim Shalom
- **W** Weekday Sim Shalom
- **F** Full Sim Shalom (both editions)
- **P** Personal Edition of Full Sim Shalom

Iyyar 21 אִיָּר
Sat **21** May

מוֹצָאֵי שַׁבָּת Motsa'ey Shabbat Conclusion of Shabbat

עַרְבִית

Saturday night Arvit as usual L264 S281 W137 F200
through קַדִּישׁ שָׁלֵם Full Kaddish L280 S294 W160 F688

+ Count Omer. L63 S55 W152 F237
Day **36** (see instructions, p. 221)

Some recite הַבְדָּלָה Havdalah here. L283 S299 W165 F700

עָלֵינוּ Aleynu L281 S297 W163 F696
קַדִּישׁ יָתוֹם Mourner's Kaddish L282 S298 W164 F698

הַבְדָּלָה Havdalah L283 S299 W165 F700

Iyyar 22 אִיָּר
Sun **22** May **עַרְבִית** + Before עָלֵינוּ Aleynu, count Omer. L63 S55 W152 F237
Day **37** (see instructions, p. 221)

Iyyar 23 אִיָּר
Mon **23** May **עַרְבִית** + Before עָלֵינוּ Aleynu, count Omer. L63 S55 W152 F237
Day **38** (see instructions, p. 221)

Iyyar 24 אִיָּר
Tue **24** May **עַרְבִית** + Before עָלֵינוּ Aleynu, count Omer. L63 S55 W152 F237
Day **39** (see instructions, p. 221)

Iyyar 25 אִיָּר
Wed **25** May **עַרְבִית** + Before עָלֵינוּ Aleynu, count Omer. L63 S55 W152 F237
Day **40** (see instructions, p. 221)

Iyyar 26 אִיָּר
Thu **26** May **עַרְבִית** + Before עָלֵינוּ Aleynu, count Omer. L63 S55 W152 F237
Day **41** (see instructions, p. 221)

Iyyar 27 אִיָּר
Fri 27 May

שַׁבָּת Shabbat פָּרָשַׁת בְּחֻקֹּתַי Parashat Beḥukkotay
שַׁבַּת מְבָרְכִים הַחֹדֶשׁ Shabbat Mevarekhim Haḥodesh

עַרְבִית + Before עָלֵינוּ Aleynu, count Omer. L63 S55 W152 F237
Day **42** (see instructions, p. 221)

Sat 28 May

Torah 7 aliyot (minimum): בְּחֻקֹּתַי Beḥukkotay
וַיִּקְרָא Vayikra (Leviticus) 26:3–27:34

Annual:	[1]26:3–5	[2]26:6–9	[3]26:10–46°	[4]27:1–15
	[5]27:16–21	[6]27:22–28	[7]27:29–34▮	[M]27:32–34
Triennial:	[1]27:1–4	[2]27:5–8	[3]27:9–15	[4]27:16–21
	[5]27:22–25	[6]27:26–28	[7]27:29–34▮	[M]27:32–34

☞ °26:14–44 This is the תּוֹכֵחָה tokheḥah, verses of rebuke and warning. Because of the ominous nature of these verses, do not divide this lengthy passage into shorter aliyot. However, the chanting may be divided among multiple readers. All the readers must be present at the Torah when the oleh/olah recites the first berakhah. This serves as an implicit appointment of all the readers as sheliḥim (agents) of the oleh/olah.
Chant this section in a somewhat **subdued** voice to symbolically minimize the trepidation the congregation experiences upon hearing the message of these verses. Be sure that all words and te'amim (tropes, cantillations) remain clearly audible to the congregation.
For the verses voicing promise of God's protection and reward (10–13, 42, and 45) and for the concluding summary verse (46), chant as usual.

▮ חזק When the Torah reader concludes a book of the Torah:

1. Close the Torah scroll.
2. **For Oleh:** Congregation chants חֲזַק חֲזַק וְנִתְחַזֵּק ḥazak ḥazak venitḥazzek; oleh remains silent.
   For Olah: Congregation chants חִזְקִי חִזְקִי וְנִתְחַזֵּק ḥizki ḥizki venitḥazzek; olah remains silent.
3. Torah reader repeats congregation's words (oleh/olah remains silent; if Torah reader is the oleh/olah, omit this repetition).
4. Open the Torah scroll.
5. The oleh/olah kisses the Torah scroll, closes it, and continues with the usual concluding berakhah.

Haftarah יִרְמְיָהוּ Yirmeyahu (Jeremiah) 16:19–17:14

Iyyar 5782						
	1	2	3	4	5	6
7	8	9	10	11	12	13
14	15	16	17	18	19	20
21	22	23	24	25	26	27
28	29					

May 2022						
	2	3	4	5	6	7
8	9	10	11	12	13	14
15	16	17	18	19	20	21
22	23	24	25	26	27	28
29	30					

+ Add ✕ Omit ☞ Take note!

Siddurim
- **L** Lev Shalem for Shabbat and Festivals
- **S** Shabbat and Festival Sim Shalom
- **W** Weekday Sim Shalom
- **F** Full Sim Shalom (both editions)
- **P** Personal Edition of Full Sim Shalom

\+ **Birkat Haḥodesh:** L180 S150 F418
Announce Rosh Ḥodesh Sivan:
רֹאשׁ חֹדֶשׁ סִיוָן יִהְיֶה בְּיוֹם שְׁלִישִׁי . . .
Rosh ḥodesh Sivan yihyeh beyom shelishi . . .
(Monday night and Tuesday)

☞ Recite אַב הָרַחֲמִים Av haraḥamim L446 S151 F420
during Omer period, even if congregation usually omits.

מִנְחָה

Torah 3 aliyot from בְּמִדְבַּר Bemidbar
בְּמִדְבַּר Bemidbar (Numbers) 1:1–19
1 1:1–4 2 5–16 3 17–19 W297 P917

Chanted also next Monday and Thursday.

✕ ~~צִדְקָתְךָ צֶדֶק Tsidkatekha tsedek~~

Iyyar 28 אִיָּר
Sat 28 May (evening)

יוֹם יְרוּשָׁלַיִם Yom Yerushalayim

Jerusalem Day
מוֹצָאֵי שַׁבָּת Motsa'ey Shabbat Conclusion of Shabbat

Yom Yerushalayim

The Knesset in Israel has officially designated 28 Iyyar as יוֹם יְרוּשָׁלַיִם Jerusalem Day to celebrate the reunification of Jerusalem during the Six-Day War in 1967. Celebratory psalms and readings are added to the service.

Mourning practices associated with the Omer period are suspended. For example:
- Weddings and other communal celebrations are permitted.
- Haircuts are permitted.

עַרְבִית

Saturday night Arvit as usual L264 S281 W137 F200
through קַדִּישׁ שָׁלֵם Full Kaddish L280 S294 W160 F688

\+ Prayers, readings, and songs for Yom Yerushalayim W209–14

\+ Count Omer. L63 S55 W152 F237
Day **43** (see instructions, p. 221)

Some recite הַבְדָּלָה Havdalah here. L283 S299 W165 F700

עָלֵינוּ Aleynu L281 S297 W163 F696
קַדִּישׁ יָתוֹם Mourner's Kaddish L282 S298 W164 F698

הַבְדָּלָה Havdalah L283 S299 W165 F700

Sun 29 May שַׁחֲרִית

Weekday Shaḥarit as usual W1 F2
through מִזְמוֹר לְתוֹדָה Mizmor letodah (Psalm 100) W20 F60

+ Psalms recited on Shabbat and Yom Tov:
☞ Psalms 19, 34, 90, 91, 135, 136, 33, 92, 93 S87–95 F60–78
Use weekday minor nusaḥ for the psalms.

Continue with the usual weekday service from
יְהִי כְבוֹד יי Yehi khevod adonay W20 F80
through the weekday Amidah.

✕ ~~תַּחֲנוּן Taḥanun~~

+ הַלֵּל שָׁלֵם Full Hallel W50 F380

חֲצִי קַדִּישׁ Short Kaddish W56 F390

+ תְּפִלָּה לִשְׁלוֹם הַמְּדִינָה Prayer for the State of Israel W75 F416
+ Other additions for Yom Yerushalayim W209–14

אַשְׁרֵי Ashrey W78 F152
✕ ~~לַמְנַצֵּחַ Lamenatseaḥ (Psalm 20)~~
וּבָא לְצִיּוֹן Uva letsiyyon W80 F156
קַדִּישׁ שָׁלֵם Full Kaddish W82 F158

Conclude as on a usual weekday.

מִנְחָה ✕ ~~תַּחֲנוּן Taḥanun~~

Iyyar 29 אִיָּר
Sun 29 May

עֶרֶב רֹאשׁ חֹדֶשׁ Erev Rosh Ḥodesh
Day before Rosh Ḥodesh

עַרְבִית + Before עָלֵינוּ Aleynu, count Omer. L63 S55 W152 F237
Day **44** (see instructions, p. 221)

Mon 30 May מִנְחָה ✕ ~~תַּחֲנוּן Taḥanun~~

Sivan 5782						
		1	2	3	4	5
6	7	8	9	10	11	12
13	14	15	16	17	18	19
20	21	22	23	24	25	26
27	28	29	30			

May | Jun 2022						
		31	1	2	3	4
5	6	7	8	9	10	11
12	13	14	15	16	17	18
19	20	21	22	23	24	25
26	27	28	29			

+ Add ✕ Omit ☞ Take note!

Siddurim
- **L** Lev Shalem for Shabbat and Festivals
- **S** Shabbat and Festival Sim Shalom
- **W** Weekday Sim Shalom
- **F** Full Sim Shalom (both editions)
- **P** Personal Edition of Full Sim Shalom

Sivan 1 סִיוָן — Mon 30 May (evening)

רֹאשׁ חֹדֶשׁ סִיוָן Rosh Ḥodesh Sivan

DURING Rosh Ḥodesh

Birkat Hamazon:

\+ יַעֲלֶה וְיָבוֹא Ya'aleh veyavo for Rosh Ḥodesh L90|95 S340|347 W233|239 F762|780

\+ הָרַחֲמָן Haraḥaman for Rosh Ḥodesh L92|96 S343|348 W235|240 F768

עַרְבִית

Weekday Amidah:

\+ יַעֲלֶה וְיָבוֹא Ya'aleh veyavo for Rosh Ḥodesh W145 F216

\+ Before עָלֵינוּ Aleynu, count Omer. L63 S55 W152 F237
Day **45** (see instructions, p. 221)

Tue 31 May **שַׁחֲרִית**

Before מִזְמוֹר שִׁיר Mizmor shir (Psalm 30) or at end of service, recite: W14 F50
Psalm for Tuesday (Psalm 82) W87 F26
קַדִּישׁ יָתוֹם Mourner's Kaddish (some omit) W100 F52
\+ Psalm 104 for Rosh Ḥodesh W90 F34
קַדִּישׁ יָתוֹם Mourner's Kaddish W100 F52

Weekday Amidah:

\+ יַעֲלֶה וְיָבוֹא Ya'aleh veyavo for Rosh Ḥodesh W41 F114

✕ ~~תַּחֲנוּן Taḥanun~~

\+ חֲצִי הַלֵּל Short Hallel W50 F380
קַדִּישׁ שָׁלֵם Full Kaddish W56 F392

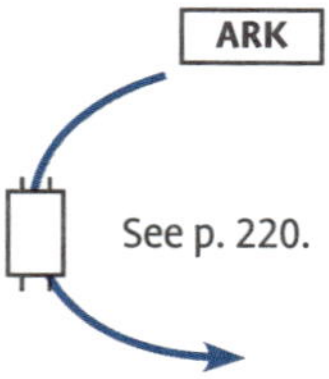

See p. 220.

\+ **TORAH SERVICE** W65 F138
Remove **1** scroll from ark.

Torah 4 aliyot: פִּינְחָס Pineḥas
בְּמִדְבַּר Bemidbar (Numbers) 28:1–15
1 28:1–3 2 3–5 3 6–10 4 11–15 W320 P943

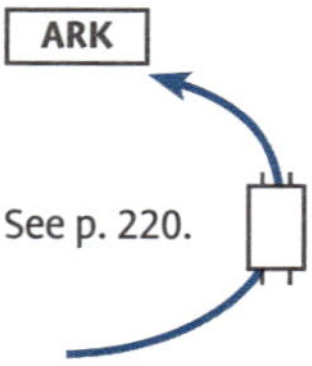

See p. 220.

חֲצִי קַדִּישׁ Short Kaddish W71 F146
Open, raise, display, and wrap scroll.
Return scroll to ark. W76 F150

אַשְׁרֵי Ashrey W78 F152
✕ ~~לַמְנַצֵּחַ Lamenatse·aḥ (Psalm 20)~~
וּבָא לְצִיּוֹן Uva letsiyyon W80 F156

Remove and pack tefillin. (Some remove after Kaddish.)

+ חֲצִי קַדִּישׁ Short Kaddish W103 F428
(If you remove tefillin here, do *not* pack but cover them, so as to begin Musaf together quickly after Kaddish.)

מוּסָף + **Rosh Ḥodesh Amidah for weekdays:** W104 F486
Weekday קְדֻשָּׁה Kedushah W105 F488
☞ Do *not* continue to add וּלְכַפָּרַת פָּשַׁע Ulkhapparat pasha.

+ קַדִּישׁ שָׁלֵם Full Kaddish W82 F158
עָלֵינוּ Aleynu W83 F160

If psalms for the day were not recited at Shaḥarit, add here:
קַדִּישׁ יָתוֹם Mourner's Kaddish (some omit) W84|100 F162|52
Psalm for Tuesday (Psalm 82) W87 F26
קַדִּישׁ יָתוֹם Mourner's Kaddish (some omit) W100 F52
+ Psalm 104 for Rosh Ḥodesh W90 F34

קַדִּישׁ יָתוֹם Mourner's Kaddish W84|100 F162|52

מִנְחָה **Weekday Amidah:**
+ יַעֲלֶה וְיָבוֹא Ya'aleh veyavo for Rosh Ḥodesh W127 F178

✕ ~~תַּחֲנוּן Taḥanun~~

Sivan 2 סִיוָן
Tue 31 May

עַרְבִית + Before עָלֵינוּ Aleynu, count Omer. L63 S55 W152 F237
Day **46** (see instructions, p. 221)

Wed 1 Jun **שַׁחֲרִית** ✕ ~~תַּחֲנוּן Taḥanun~~
☞ לַמְנַצֵּחַ Lamenatse·aḥ (Psalm 20) W79 F154

מִנְחָה ✕ ~~תַּחֲנוּן Taḥanun~~

Sivan 3 סִיוָן
Wed 1 Jun

עַרְבִית + Before עָלֵינוּ Aleynu, count Omer. L63 S55 W152 F237
Day **47** (see instructions, p. 221)

Thu 2 Jun **שַׁחֲרִית** ✕ ~~תַּחֲנוּן Taḥanun~~
☞ לַמְנַצֵּחַ Lamenatse·aḥ (Psalm 20) W79 F154

מִנְחָה ✕ ~~תַּחֲנוּן Taḥanun~~

Sivan 4 סִיוָן
Thu 2 Jun

עַרְבִית + Before עָלֵינוּ Aleynu, count Omer. L63 S55 W152 F237
Day **48** (see instructions, p. 221)

Sivan 5782						
		1	2	3	4	5
6	7	8	9	10	11	12
13	14	15	16	17	18	19
20	21	22	23	24	25	26
27	28	29	30			

May | Jun 2022						
		31	1	2	3	4
5	6	7	8	9	10	11
12	13	14	15	16	17	18
19	20	21	22	23	24	25
26	27	28	29			

+ Add ✕ Omit ☞ Take note!

Siddurim
- **L** Lev Shalem for Shabbat and Festivals
- **S** Shabbat and Festival Sim Shalom
- **W** Weekday Sim Shalom
- **F** Full Sim Shalom (both editions)
- **P** Personal Edition of Full Sim Shalom

Fri 3 Jun

שַׁחֲרִית ✕ ~~תַּחֲנוּן Taḥanun~~
☞ לַמְנַצֵּחַ Lamenatse·aḥ (Psalm 20) W79 F154

מִנְחָה ✕ ~~תַּחֲנוּן Taḥanun~~ (as on all Friday afternoons)

Shavu'ot

Before Shabbat

Cooking for Shabbat and Yom Tov

Cooking is never permitted on Shabbat, and during Shabbat we are not allowed to prepare for Yom Tov. Finish cooking for Shabbat before Shabbat begins. Finish food preparation for Yom Tov — Day 1 before Shabbat begins or after it ends.

Preparing a Flame for Yom Tov

On Yom Tov, kindling a *new* fire is not permitted; however, the use of an *existing* fire for cooking or other purposes is permitted.

To light candles for Yom Tov (Saturday night), ensure you have a fire burning before candle-lighting time for Shabbat that will continue to burn until after dark on Saturday. For example:

- A burning candle that lasts for more than 25 hours
- A pilot light on a gas range (*not* a gas range with an electronic starter)

Similarly, in the synagogue ensure a long-burning candle is lit so that בּוֹרֵא מְאוֹרֵי הָאֵשׁ *bo·re me'orey ha'esh* may be recited there after Shabbat.

Sivan 5 סִיוָן
Fri 3 Jun

שַׁבָּת Shabbat פָּרָשַׁת בְּמִדְבַּר Parashat Bemidbar
עֶרֶב שָׁבוּעוֹת Erev Shavu'ot Day before Shavu'ot

עַרְבִית + Before עָלֵינוּ Aleynu, count Omer. L63 S55 W152 F237
Day **49** (see instructions, p. 221)

Sat 4 Jun

Torah 7 aliyot (minimum): בְּמִדְבַּר Bemidbar
בְּמִדְבַּר Bemidbar (Numbers) 1:1–4:20

Annual:	[1] 1:1–19	[2] 1:20–54	[3] 2:1–34	[4] 3:1–13
	[5] 3:14–39	[6] 3:40–51	[7] 4:1–20	[M] 4:17–20
Triennial:	[1] 3:14–20	[2] 3:21–26	[3] 3:27–39	[4] 3:40–43
	[5] 3:44–51	[6] 4:1–10	[7] 4:11–20	[M] 4:17–20

Haftarah הוֹשֵׁעַ Hoshe·a (Hosea) 2:1–22

☞ Recite אַב הָרַחֲמִים Av haraḥamim L446 S151 F420
during Omer period, even if congregation usually omits.

מִנְחָה

Torah 3 aliyot from נָשֹׂא Naso
בְּמִדְבַּר Bemidbar (Numbers) 4:21–4:33°
[1]4:21–24 [2]25–28 [3]29–33° W298 P918

Chanted also next Thursday.

☞ °4:21–33 Some continue reading through 4:37. This is not necessary.

✕ ~~צִדְקָתְךָ צֶדֶק Tsidkatekha tsedek~~

Shavu'ot — Day 1 and Day 2

Candle Lighting for Shavu'ot — Day 1 (after Shabbat)

For Day 2, see p. 177.

Shabbat ends after dark: when 3 stars appear or at least 25 minutes after sunset (43 minutes after the time set for Shabbat candle lighting). Some wait longer. For the appropriate time in your community, consult your rabbi.

1. Wait until Shabbat ends.
2. Do *not strike* a match. Instead, transfer fire to the candles from an *existing* flame (see p. 172) by inserting a match or other stick into the flame.
3. Do *not extinguish* the match or stick. Instead, place it on a non-flammable tray or dish, and let it self-extinguish. Alternately, a wood *safety* match held vertically (flame up) usually self-extinguishes quickly.
4. Recite 2 בְּרָכוֹת *berakhot* (both nights): L79 S303 F718

בָּרוּךְ אַתָּה יי, אֱ־לֹהֵינוּ מֶלֶךְ הָעוֹלָם, אֲשֶׁר קִדְּשָׁנוּ בְּמִצְוֹתָיו
וְצִוָּנוּ לְהַדְלִיק נֵר שֶׁל יוֹם טוֹב.

Barukh attah adonay, eloheynu melekh ha'olam,
asher kiddeshanu bemitsvotav vetsivvanu lehadlik ner shel yom tov.

בָּרוּךְ אַתָּה יי, אֱ־לֹהֵינוּ מֶלֶךְ הָעוֹלָם, שֶׁהֶחֱיָנוּ וְקִיְּמָנוּ וְהִגִּיעָנוּ לַזְּמַן הַזֶּה.

Barukh attah adonay, eloheynu melekh ha'olam,
sheheḥeyanu vekiyyemanu vehiggi'anu lazeman hazeh.

NOTE: To light candles for Yom Tov — Day 2 (Sunday night), you must have a fire that will continue to burn until after dark on Sunday. If this necessitates lighting another long-burning candle, follow instructions 2 and 3 above for transferring the flame.

שבועות Shavu'ot

Sivan 5782						
		1	2	3	4	5
6	7	8	9	10	11	12
13	14	15	16	17	18	19
20	21	22	23	24	25	26
27	28	29	30			

May | Jun 2022						
		31	1	2	3	4
5	6	7	8	9	10	11
12	13	14	15	16	17	18
19	20	21	22	23	24	25
26	27	28	29			

+ Add ✕ Omit ☞ Take note!

Siddurim
- **L** Lev Shalem for Shabbat and Festivals
- **S** Shabbat and Festival Sim Shalom
- **W** Weekday Sim Shalom
- **F** Full Sim Shalom (both editions)
- **P** Personal Edition of Full Sim Shalom

Shavu'ot Meals — Day 1 (after Shabbat)

For Day 2, see blue box, p. 178.

Enjoy festive meals evening and daytime, in the manner of Shabbat meals. Meals consisting of dairy foods are customary on Shavu'ot. Some follow this practice only for the first day of Shavu'ot.

EVENING KIDDUSH L79 S334 F742

Do *not* light a Havdalah candle.

Recite:
1. Yom Tov קִדּוּשׁ *kiddush* with insertions for Shavu'ot
2. בּוֹרֵא מְאוֹרֵי הָאֵשׁ *bo·re me'orey ha'esh* (over Yom Tov candles) L80 S335 F744
3. הַמַּבְדִּיל בֵּין קֹדֶשׁ לְקֹדֶשׁ *hamavdil beyn kodesh lekodesh* L80 S335 F744
4. שֶׁהֶחֱיָנוּ *sheheḥeyanu*

DAYTIME KIDDUSH L81 S335 F746

Recite:
1. וַיְדַבֵּר מֹשֶׁה *vaydabber mosheh* (Vayikra 23:44)
2. בּוֹרֵא פְּרִי הַגָּפֶן *bo·re peri hagafen*

HAMOTSI, FESTIVE MEALS WITH SINGING, AND BIRKAT HAMAZON

Recite הַמּוֹצִיא *hamotsi* over 2 whole חַלָּה *ḥallah* loaves or rolls. L81 S313–14 F744|746
Include festive singing, and recite בִּרְכַּת הַמָּזוֹן *birkat hamazon* with Shavu'ot additions (see yellow box, below).

Tikkun Leyl Shavu'ot

On the first night, some follow the kabbalistic tradition of participating in a תִּקּוּן לֵיל שָׁבוּעוֹת *tikkun leyl shavu'ot,* a night of Torah study, to thoroughly prepare for reliving God's revelation at Sinai during the morning Torah service.

Sivan 6 סִיוָן — שָׁבוּעוֹת Shavu'ot — Day 1

Sat 4 Jun (evening)

DURING Shavu'ot

Birkat Hamazon:

+ יַעֲלֶה וְיָבוֹא Ya'aleh veyavo for Shavu'ot L90|95 S340|347 W233|239 F762|780

+ הָרַחֲמָן Haraḥaman for Yom Tov L92|96 S343|348 W236|240 F768

עַרְבִית Arvit for Yom Tov L39 S28 F279

+ וַיְדַבֵּר מֹשֶׁה Vaydabber mosheh (Vayikra 23:44) L46 S34 F294

חֲצִי קַדִּישׁ Short Kaddish L46 S34 F294

Yom Tov Amidah: L306 S41 F304

+ וַתּוֹדִיעֵנוּ Vatodi'eynu L309 S41 F306

+ Insertions for Shavu'ot

קַדִּישׁ שָׁלֵם Full Kaddish L54 S48 F316

קִדּוּשׁ Kiddush for Yom Tov after Shabbat: L79 S50 F318

+ Insertions for Shavu'ot
Do *not* light a Havdalah candle.
+ If you have a flame burning from before Shabbat, recite over that flame:
בּוֹרֵא מְאוֹרֵי הָאֵשׁ Bo·re me'orey ha'esh L80 S50 F320
If not, do *not* recite that berakhah.
+ הַמַּבְדִּיל בֵּין קֹדֶשׁ לְקֹדֶשׁ Hamavdil beyn kodesh lekodesh
+ שֶׁהֶחֱיָנוּ Sheheḥeyanu L80 S50 F319

עָלֵינוּ Aleynu L56 S51 F320
קַדִּישׁ יָתוֹם Mourner's Kaddish L58 S52 F324

☞ Do not recite Kiddush Levanah until Monday night after Arvit.

At home

Light candles after dark.
See "Candle Lighting for Shavu'ot — Day 1 (after Shabbat)," p. 173.

Recite קִדּוּשׁ Kiddush after dark. L79 S334 F742
See "Shavu'ot Meals — Day 1 (after Shabbat) " and "Evening Kiddush," p. 174.

Sun 5 Jun **שַׁחֲרִית**

At the end of the preliminary service, begin formal chanting at
הָאֵ·ל בְּתַעֲצוּמוֹת עֻזֶּךָ Ha'el beta'atsumot uzzekha. L147 S105 F336

✕ ~~הַכֹּל יוֹדוּךָ Hakol yodukha~~
✕ ~~אֵ·ל אָדוֹן El adon~~
✕ ~~לָאֵ·ל אֲשֶׁר שָׁבַת La'el asher shavat~~
+ הַמֵּאִיר לָאָרֶץ Hame'ir la'arets L152 S109 F342

Yom Tov Amidah: L306 S123 F366
+ Insertions for Shavu'ot

+ הַלֵּל שָׁלֵם Full Hallel L316 S133 F380

קַדִּישׁ שָׁלֵם Full Kaddish L321 S138 F392

Sivan 5782						
		1	2	3	4	5
6	7	8	9	10	11	12
13	14	15	16	17	18	19
20	21	22	23	24	25	26
27	28	29	30			

May | Jun 2022						
		31	1	2	3	4
5	6	7	8	9	10	11
12	13	14	15	16	17	18
19	20	21	22	23	24	25
26	27	28	29			

+ Add ✕ Omit ☞ Take note!

Siddurim
L Lev Shalem for Shabbat and Festivals
S Shabbat and Festival Sim Shalom
W Weekday Sim Shalom
F Full Sim Shalom (both editions)
P Personal Edition of Full Sim Shalom

YOM TOV TORAH SERVICE L322 S139 F394

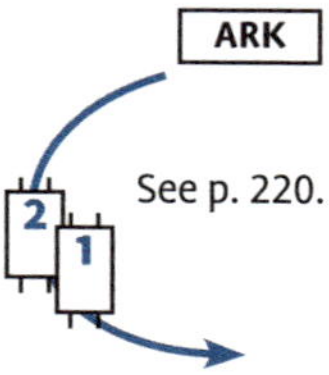

See p. 220.

+ יי יי אֵ-ל רַחוּם וְחַנּוּן
Adonay adonay el raḥum veḥannun (3 times) L323 S140 F394
+ רִבּוֹנוֹ שֶׁל עוֹלָם Ribbono shel olam L323 S140 F396
+ וַאֲנִי תְפִלָּתִי לְךָ Va'ani tefillati lekha (3 times) L323 S140 F396

Remove **2** scrolls from ark in the order they will be read.

+ Just before the person called for the 1st aliyah begins the 1st בְּרָכָה berakhah, recite אַקְדָּמוּת Akdamut. L413 S222 F526
Torah reader and congregation chant alternate couplets.

1st scroll 5 aliyot from יִתְרוֹ Yitro
שְׁמוֹת Shemot (Exodus) 19:1–°20:22
¹19:1–6 ²19:7–13 ³19:14–19 °⁴19:20–20:13 °⁵20:14–22

☞ °**Verse numbers in chapter 20:** In many books, the verses are misnumbered. Use these guidelines to properly divide the reading:
Aliyah **4**: ends לְרֵעֶךָ (20:14 in many books).
Aliyah **5**: וְכָל־הָעָם through עָלָיו (20:15–23 in many books)

☞ °20:1–13 Follow the te'amim (tropes) on p. 100 for the public reading of עֲשֶׂרֶת הַדִּבְּרוֹת. For additional instructions for this passage, see p. 99.

Place 2nd scroll on table next to 1st scroll.

חֲצִי קַדִּישׁ Short Kaddish L327 S146 F408
Open, raise, display, and wrap 1st scroll.

2nd scroll Maftir aliyah from פִּינְחָס Pineḥas
ᴹבְּמִדְבַּר Bemidbar (Numbers) 28:26–31

Open, raise, display, and wrap 2nd scroll.

Haftarah for Shavu'ot — Day 1
יְחֶזְקֵאל Yeḥezkel (Ezekiel) 1:1–28; 3:12

Haftarah blessings: L328 S147 F410
☞ Conclude with the Yom Tov בְּרָכָה berakhah L329 S147 F412 with insertions for Shavu'ot.

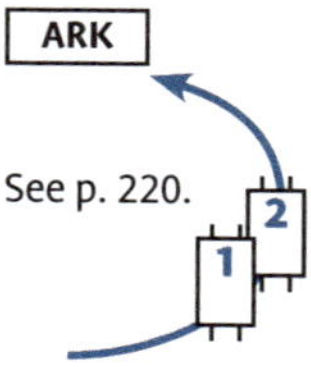

See p. 220.

✕ ~~יְקוּם פֻּרְקָן Yekum purkan~~
✕ ~~אַב הָרַחֲמִים Av Haraḥamim~~

אַשְׁרֵי Ashrey L339 S151 F420
Return scrolls to ark in reverse order. L340 S153 F422
חֲצִי קַדִּישׁ Short Kaddish L342 S155 F428

שבועות Shavu'ot

מוּסָף

Yom Tov Amidah: L343 S166 F456

+ Insertions for Shavu'ot

Some congregations include in the repetition of the Amidah the Priestly Blessing by the Kohanim (*dukhenen*).
בִּרְכַּת כֹּהֲנִים Birkat kohanim L353 S177 F472
For procedures, see p. 222.

קַדִּישׁ שָׁלֵם Full kaddish L203 S181 F506
Continue with אֵין כֵּא·לֹהֵינוּ Eyn keloheynu. L204 S182 F508

קְדוּשָּׁא רַבָּא See "Daytime Kiddush," p. 174.

At home See "Shavu'ot Meals — Day 1 (after Shabbat)" and "Daytime Kiddush," p. 174.

מִנְחָה

אַשְׁרֵי Ashrey L214 S226 W170 F558
וּבָא לְצִיּוֹן Uva letsiyyon L216 S227 W171 F560
חֲצִי קַדִּישׁ Short Kaddish L217 S229 W173 F564

Yom Tov Amidah: L306 S242 W184 F586

+ Insertions for Shavu'ot

קַדִּישׁ שָׁלֵם Full Kaddish L230 S247 W189 F596
עָלֵינוּ Aleynu L231 S248 W190 F598
קַדִּישׁ יָתוֹם Mourner's Kaddish L232 S249 W191 F600

Candle Lighting for Shavu'ot — Day 2

Day 1 ends after dark: when 3 stars appear, or at least 25 minutes after sunset (at least 43 minutes after the time set for lighting candles on Day 1). Some wait longer. For the appropriate time in your community, consult your rabbi.

1. Wait until Day 1 ends.
2. Do not *strike* a match. Instead, transfer fire to the candles from an *existing* flame (see p. 172) by inserting a match or other stick into the flame.
3. Do not *extinguish* the match or stick. Instead, place it on a non-flammable tray or dish, and let it self-extinguish. Alternately, a wood *safety* match held vertically (flame up) usually self-extinguishes quickly.
4. Recite the same 2 בְּרָכוֹת *berakhot* as on Day 1 (see p. 173). L79 S303 F718

Sivan 5782						
		1	2	3	4	5
6	7	8	9	10	11	12
13	14	15	16	17	18	19
20	21	22	23	24	25	26
27	28	29	30			

May | Jun 2022						
		31	1	2	3	4
5	6	7	8	9	10	11
12	13	14	15	16	17	18
19	20	21	22	23	24	25
26	27	28	29			

+ Add ✕ Omit ☞ Take note!

Siddurim
- **L** Lev Shalem for Shabbat and Festivals
- **S** Shabbat and Festival Sim Shalom
- **W** Weekday Sim Shalom
- **F** Full Sim Shalom (both editions)
- **P** Personal Edition of Full Sim Shalom

Shavu'ot Meals — Day 2

Enjoy festive meals evening and daytime, in the manner of Shabbat meals. Meals consisting of dairy foods are customary on Shavu'ot. Some follow this practice only for the first day of Shavu'ot.

EVENING KIDDUSH L79 S334 F742

Recite: 1. Yom Tov קִדּוּשׁ with insertions for Shavu'ot
2. שֶׁהֶחֱיָנוּ *sheheḥeyanu*

DAYTIME KIDDUSH L81 S335 F746

Recite: 1. וַיְדַבֵּר מֹשֶׁה *vaydabber mosheh* (Vayikra 23:44)
2. בּוֹרֵא פְּרִי הַגָּפֶן *bo·re peri hagafen*

HAMOTSI, FESTIVE MEALS WITH SINGING, AND BIRKAT HAMAZON

Recite הַמּוֹצִיא *hamotsi* over 2 whole חַלָּה *ḥallah* loaves or rolls. L81 S313–14 F744|746
Include festive singing. Recite בִּרְכַּת הַמָּזוֹן *birkat hamazon* with Shavu'ot additions (see yellow box, p. 174).

Sivan 7 סִיוָן — שָׁבוּעוֹת Shavu'ot — Day 2

Sun 5 Jun

עַרְבִית

Arvit for Yom Tov L39 S28 F279

+ וַיְדַבֵּר מֹשֶׁה Vaydabber mosheh (Vayikra 23:44) L46 S34 F294

חֲצִי קַדִּישׁ Short Kaddish L46 S34 F294

Yom Tov Amidah: L306 S41 F304

+ Insertions for Shavu'ot

קַדִּישׁ שָׁלֵם Full Kaddish L54 S48 F316

+ קִדּוּשׁ Kiddush for Yom Tov with insertions for Shavu'ot L79 S50 F318

+ שֶׁהֶחֱיָנוּ Sheheḥeyanu L80 S50 F319

עָלֵינוּ Aleynu L56 S51 F320

קַדִּישׁ יָתוֹם Mourner's Kaddish L58 S52 F324

☞ Do not recite Kiddush Levanah until Monday night after Arvit.

At home

Light candles from an existing flame.
See "Candle Lighting for Yom Tov — Day 2," p. 177.

See "Shavu'ot Meals — Day 2" and "Evening Kiddush," above.

Mon 6 Jun שַׁחֲרִית

At the end of the preliminary service, begin formal chanting at
הָאֵ-ל בְּתַעֲצוּמוֹת עֻזֶּךָ Ha'el beta'atsumot uzzekha. L147 S105 F336

✕ ~~הַכֹּל יוֹדוּךָ Hakol yodukha~~
✕ ~~אֵ-ל אָדוֹן El adon~~
✕ ~~לָאֵ-ל אֲשֶׁר שָׁבַת La'el asher shavat~~

+ הַמֵּאִיר לָאָרֶץ Hame'ir la'arets L152 S109 F342

Yom Tov Amidah: L306 S123 F366
+ Insertions for Shavu'ot

+ הַלֵּל שָׁלֵם Full Hallel L316 S133 F380
קַדִּישׁ שָׁלֵם Full Kaddish L321 S138 F392

+ **Megillah reading:**
Some congregations read
מְגִלַּת רוּת Megillat Rut (Scroll of Ruth),
without reciting a בְּרָכָה berakhah.
Some read selections in English. L333 S383 F790
קַדִּישׁ יָתוֹם Mourner's Kaddish L338 S82 F52

YOM TOV TORAH SERVICE L322 S139 F394

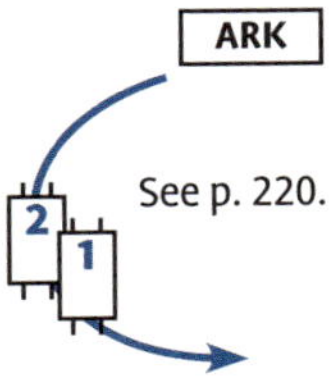

See p. 220.

+ יי יי אֵ-ל רַחוּם וְחַנּוּן
Adonay adonay el raḥum veḥannun (3 times) L323 S140 F394
+ רִבּוֹנוֹ שֶׁל עוֹלָם Ribbono shel olam L323 S140 F396
+ וַאֲנִי תְפִלָּתִי לְךָ Va'ani tefillati lekha (3 times) L323 S140 F396

Remove **2** scrolls from ark in the order they will be read.

1st scroll 5 aliyot from רְאֵה Re'eh
דְּבָרִים Devarim (Deuteronomy) 15:19–16:17
1 15:19–23 2 16:1–3 3 16:4–8 4 16:9–12 5 16:13–17

Place 2nd scroll on table next to 1st scroll.
חֲצִי קַדִּישׁ Short Kaddish L327 S146 F408
Open, raise, display, and wrap 1st scroll.

2nd scroll Maftir aliyah from פִּינְחָס Pineḥas
M בְּמִדְבַּר Bemidbar (Numbers) 28:26–31

Open, raise, display, and wrap 2nd scroll.

Sivan 5782

		1	2	3	4	5
6	7	8	9	10	11	12
13	14	15	16	17	18	19
20	21	22	23	24	25	26
27	28	29	30			

May | Jun 2022

		31	1	2	3	4
5	6	7	8	9	10	11
12	13	14	15	16	17	18
19	20	21	22	23	24	25
26	27	28	29			

+ Add ✕ Omit ☞ Take note!

Siddurim
- **L** Lev Shalem for Shabbat and Festivals
- **S** Shabbat and Festival Sim Shalom
- **W** Weekday Sim Shalom
- **F** Full Sim Shalom (both editions)
- **P** Personal Edition of Full Sim Shalom

Haftarah for Shavu'ot — Day 2
Ashkenazic: חֲבַקּוּק Ḥavakkuk (Habakkuk) 3:1–19°
Sephardic: חֲבַקּוּק Ḥavakkuk (Habakkuk) 2:20–3:19°

☞ °3:19 יֱהֹוִה אֲ·דֹנָי — Read: elohim adonay.

Haftarah blessings: L328 S147 F410
☞ Conclude with the Yom Tov בְּרָכָה berakhah L329 S147 F412
with insertions for Shavu'ot.

✕ ~~יְקוּם פֻּרְקָן Yekum purkan~~

+ יִזְכֹּר Yizkor L330 S188 F516

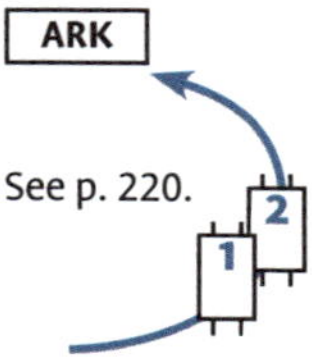

See p. 220.

☞ אַב הָרַחֲמִים Av Haraḥamim L446 S151 F420

אַשְׁרֵי Ashrey L339 S151 F420
Return scrolls to ark in reverse order. L340 S153 F422
חֲצִי קַדִּישׁ Short Kaddish L342 S155 F428

מוּסָף

Yom Tov Amidah: L343 S166 F456
+ Insertions for Shavu'ot

Some congregations include in the repetition of the Amidah the Priestly Blessing by the Kohanim (*dukhenen*).
בִּרְכַּת כֹּהֲנִים Birkat kohanim L353 S177 F472
For procedures, see p. 222.

קַדִּישׁ שָׁלֵם Full kaddish L203 S181 F506
Continue with אֵין כֵּא·לֹהֵינוּ Eyn keloheynu. L204 S182 F508

קִדּוּשָׁא רַבָּא See "Daytime Kiddush," p. 178.

At home See "Shavu'ot Meals — Day 2" and "Daytime Kiddush," p. 178.

מִנְחָה

אַשְׁרֵי Ashrey L214 S226 W170 F558
וּבָא לְצִיּוֹן Uva letsiyyon L216 S227 W171 F560
חֲצִי קַדִּישׁ Short Kaddish L217 S229 W173 F564

Yom Tov Amidah: L306 S242 W184 F586
+ Insertions for Shavu'ot

קַדִּישׁ שָׁלֵם Full Kaddish L230 S247 W189 F596
עָלֵינוּ Aleynu L231 S248 W190 F598
קַדִּישׁ יָתוֹם Mourner's Kaddish L232 S249 W191 F600

+ Add ✕ Omit ☞ Take note!

Siddurim

- **L** Lev Shalem for Shabbat and Festivals
- **S** Shabbat and Festival Sim Shalom
- **W** Weekday Sim Shalom
- **F** Full Sim Shalom (both editions)
- **P** Personal Edition of Full Sim Shalom

Sivan 5782

		1	2	3	4	5
6	7	8	9	10	11	12
13	14	15	16	17	18	19
20	21	22	23	24	25	26
27	28	29	30			

May | Jun 2022

		31	1	2	3	4
5	6	7	8	9	10	11
12	13	14	15	16	17	18
19	20	21	22	23	24	25
26	27	28	29			

8 סִיוָן Jun 6
Jun 7
9 סִיוָן Jun 8

Sivan 8 סִיוָן
Mon 6 Jun

מוֹצָאֵי יוֹם טוֹב Motsa'ey Yom Tov Conclusion of Yom Tov
אִסְרוּ חַג Isru Ḥag Day after Yom Tov

עַרְבִית

Arvit for weekdays L264 S281 W137 F200

Weekday Amidah:

+ אַתָּה חוֹנַנְתָּנוּ Atta ḥonantanu L272 S287 W143 F212

קַדִּישׁ שָׁלֵם Full Kaddish L280 S294 W160 F222

Some recite הַבְדָּלָה Havdalah here. L283 S299 W165 F700
For instructions, see below.

עָלֵינוּ Aleynu L281 S297 W163 F696
קַדִּישׁ יָתוֹם Mourner's Kaddish L282 S298 W164 F698

+ **Havdalah:** L283 S299 W165 F700
✕ ~~הִנֵּה אֵ-ל יְשׁוּעָתִי Hinneh el yeshu'ati~~
בּוֹרֵא פְּרִי הַגָּפֶן Bo·re peri hagafen
✕ ~~בּוֹרֵא מִינֵי בְשָׂמִים Bo·re miney vesamim~~
✕ ~~בּוֹרֵא מְאוֹרֵי הָאֵשׁ Bo·re me'orey ha'esh~~
הַמַּבְדִּיל בֵּין קֹדֶשׁ לְחֹל Hamavdil beyn kodesh leḥol

Mon 6 Jun (night)

After Arvit if the moon is visible:
קִדּוּשׁ לְבָנָה Kiddush Levanah L286 W167 F704
For procedures and instructions, see p. 223.

Tue 7 Jun **שַׁחֲרִית**

Shaḥarit for weekdays W1 F2

✕ ~~תַּחֲנוּן Taḥanun~~
☞ לַמְנַצֵּחַ Lamenatse·aḥ (Psalm 20) W79 F154

מִנְחָה ✕ ~~תַּחֲנוּן Taḥanun~~

Sivan 9 סִיוָן
Wed 8 Jun (daytime)

BEGINNING 9 Sivan Resume reciting תַּחֲנוּן Taḥanun.
(Some congregations do not resume until 13 Sivan.)

Sivan 5782						
	1	2	3	4	5	
6	7	8	9	10	11	12
13	14	15	16	17	18	19
20	21	22	23	24	25	26
27	28	29	30			

May | Jun 2022						
		31	1	2	3	4
5	6	7	8	9	10	11
12	13	14	15	16	17	18
19	20	21	22	23	24	25
26	27	28	29			

+ Add ✕ Omit ☞ Take note!

Siddurim
- **L** Lev Shalem for Shabbat and Festivals
- **S** Shabbat and Festival Sim Shalom
- **W** Weekday Sim Shalom
- **F** Full Sim Shalom (both editions)
- **P** Personal Edition of Full Sim Shalom

Sivan 12 סִיוָן
Sat 11 Jun

שַׁבָּת Shabbat פָּרָשַׁת נָשֹׂא Parashat Naso

Torah 7 aliyot (minimum): נָשֹׂא Naso
בְּמִדְבַּר Bemidbar (Numbers) 4:21–7:89

Annual:	[1] 4:21–37°	[2] 4:38–49	[3] 5:1–10	[4] 5:11–6:27
	[5] 7:1–41	[6] 7:42–71	[7] 7:72–89	[M] 7:87–89
Triennial:	[1] 7:1–11	[2] 7:12–23	[3] 7:24–35	[4] 7:36–47
	[5] 7:48–59	[6] 7:60–71	[7] 7:72–89	[M] 7:87–89

☞ °4:26 Note the unusual consecutive occurrences of the ta'am (trope)
וְאֶת־מָסַךְ | פֶּתַח | שַׁעַר הֶחָצֵר :(מֻנַּח־מַפְסִיק | =) מֻנַּח־לְגַרְמֵיהּ |

Haftarah שׁוֹפְטִים Shofetim (Judges) 13:2–25

מִנְחָה

Torah 3 aliyot from בְּהַעֲלֹתְךָ Beha'alotekha
בְּמִדְבַּר Bemidbar (Numbers) 8:1–14
[1] 8:1–4 [2] 5–9 [3] 10–14 — W299 P919

Chanted also next Monday and Thursday.

☞ צִדְקָתְךָ צֶדֶק Tsidkatekha tsedek L230 S239 W183 F584
Omit if your congregation does not resume reciting תַּחֲנוּן Taḥanun until 13 Sivan.

Sivan 13 סִיוָן
Sun 12 Jun (daytime)

BEGINNING 13 Sivan Congregations that have not yet resumed reciting תַּחֲנוּן Taḥanun resume now.

Sivan 19 סִיוָן
Sat 18 Jun

שַׁבָּת Shabbat פָּרָשַׁת בְּהַעֲלֹתְךָ Parashat Beha'alotekha

Torah 7 aliyot (minimum): בְּהַעֲלֹתְךָ Beha'alotekha
בְּמִדְבַּר Bemidbar (Numbers) 8:1–12:16

Annual:	1 8:1–14	2 8:15–26	3 9:1–14	4 9:15–10:10
	5 10:11–34°	6 10:35–11:29°	7 11:30–12:16	M 12:14–16
Triennial:	1 10:35–11:9°	2 11:10–18	3 11:19–22	4 11:23–29
	5 11:30–35	6 12:1–13	7 12:14–16	M 12:14–16

☞° 10:15–16, 19–20, 23–24, 26–27 Chant these 4 pairs of verses using the "desert traveling melody," based on Shirat Hayam melody.

☞° 10:35–36 This pair of verses is marked before and after with the "twisted nun" symbol. No special treatment is required.

☞° 11:1–6 Chant in a somewhat **subdued** voice to symbolically minimize the embarrassment the congregants experience upon hearing the terrible misdeeds of our ancestors. Be sure that all words and te'amim (tropes, cantillations) remain clearly audible to the congregation.

Haftarah זְכַרְיָה Zekharyah (Zechariah) 2:14–4:7°

☞° 3:2 Note the rare ta'am (trope) מֵירְכָא־כְפוּלָה (֮):
הֲלוֹא זֶה אוּד Connect זֶה to the preceding and following words, without a pause; then pause after the טִפְּחָא (אוּד), as usual.

מִנְחָה

Torah 3 aliyot from שְׁלַח־לְךָ Shelaḥ lekha
בְּמִדְבַּר Bemidbar (Numbers) 13:1–20
1 13:1–3 2 4–16 3 17–20 W300 P920

Chanted also next Monday and Thursday.

Sivan 5782						
		1	2	3	4	5
6	7	8	9	10	11	12
13	14	15	16	17	18	19
20	21	22	23	24	25	26
27	28	29	30			

May | Jun 2022						
		31	1	2	3	4
5	6	7	8	9	10	11
12	13	14	15	16	17	18
19	20	21	22	23	24	25
26	27	28	29			

+ Add ✕ Omit ☞ Take note!

Siddurim
- **L** Lev Shalem for Shabbat and Festivals
- **S** Shabbat and Festival Sim Shalom
- **W** Weekday Sim Shalom
- **F** Full Sim Shalom (both editions)
- **P** Personal Edition of Full Sim Shalom

Sivan 26 סִיוָן
Sat 25 Jun

שַׁבָּת Shabbat פָּרָשַׁת שְׁלַח־לְךָ Parashat Shelaḥ lekha
שַׁבַּת מְבָרְכִים הַחֹדֶשׁ Shabbat Mevarekhim Haḥodesh

Torah 7 aliyot (minimum): שְׁלַח־לְךָ Shelaḥ lekha
בְּמִדְבַּר Bemidbar (Numbers) 13:1–15:41

Annual:	1 13:1–20	2 13:21–14:7°	3 14:8–25	4 14:26–15:7
	5 15:8–16	6 15:17–26	7 15:27–41	M 15:37–41
Triennial:	1 15:8–10	2 15:11–16	3 15:17–21	4 15:22–26
	5 15:27–31	6 15:32–36	7 15:37–41	M 15:37–41

☞°14:3 Note the rare ta'am (trope) מֵירְכָא־כְפוּלָה (״):
הֲלוֹא טוֹב לָנוּ Connect טוֹב to the preceding and following words, without a pause; then pause after the טִפְחָא (לָנוּ), as usual.

Haftarah יְהוֹשֻׁעַ Yehoshua (Joshua) 2:1–24

+ **Birkat Haḥodesh:** L180 S150 F418
Announce Rosh Ḥodesh Tammuz:
רֹאשׁ חֹדֶשׁ תַּמּוּז יִהְיֶה בְּיוֹם רְבִיעִי וּבְיוֹם חֲמִישִׁי . . .
Rosh ḥodesh Tammuz yihyeh beyom revi'i uvyom ḥamishi . . .
(Tuesday night, Wednesday, and Thursday)

✕ ~~אַב הָרַחֲמִים Av Haraḥamim~~

מִנְחָה

Torah 3 aliyot from קֹרַח Koraḥ
בְּמִדְבַּר Bemidbar (Numbers) 16:1–13
1 16:1–3 2 4–7 3 8–13 W301 P921

Chanted also next Monday.

Sivan 29 סִיוָן
Tue 28 Jun

עֶרֶב רֹאשׁ חֹדֶשׁ Erev Rosh Ḥodesh
Day before Rosh Ḥodesh

מִנְחָה ✕ ~~תַּחֲנוּן Taḥanun~~

Sivan 30 סִיוָן — רֹאשׁ חֹדֶשׁ תַּמּוּז Rosh Ḥodesh Tammuz — Day 1

Tue 28 Jun (evening)

DURING Rosh Ḥodesh

Birkat Hamazon:

\+ יַעֲלֶה וְיָבוֹא Ya'aleh veyavo for Rosh Ḥodesh L90|95 S340|347 W233|239 F762|780

\+ הָרַחֲמָן Haraḥaman for Rosh Ḥodesh L92|96 S343|348 W235|240 F768

עַרְבִית

Weekday Amidah:

\+ יַעֲלֶה וְיָבוֹא Ya'aleh veyavo for Rosh Ḥodesh W145 F216

Wed 29 Jun **שַׁחֲרִית**

Before מִזְמוֹר שִׁיר Mizmor shir (Psalm 30) W14 F50
or at end of service, recite:

Psalm for Wednesday (Psalms 94:1–95:3) W87 F26
קַדִּישׁ יָתוֹם Mourner's Kaddish (some omit) W100 F52
\+ Psalm 104 for Rosh Ḥodesh W90 F34
קַדִּישׁ יָתוֹם Mourner's Kaddish W100 F52

Weekday Amidah:

\+ יַעֲלֶה וְיָבוֹא Ya'aleh veyavo for Rosh Ḥodesh W41 F114

✕ ~~תַּחֲנוּן Taḥanun~~

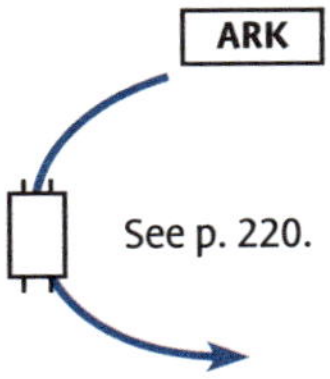

See p. 220.

\+ חֲצִי הַלֵּל Short Hallel W50 F380
קַדִּישׁ שָׁלֵם Full Kaddish W56 F392

\+ **TORAH SERVICE** W65 F138
Remove **1** scroll from ark.

Torah 4 aliyot: פִּינְחָס Pineḥas
בְּמִדְבַּר Bemidbar (Numbers) 28:1–15
1 28:1–3 2 3–5 3 6–10 4 11–15 W320 P943

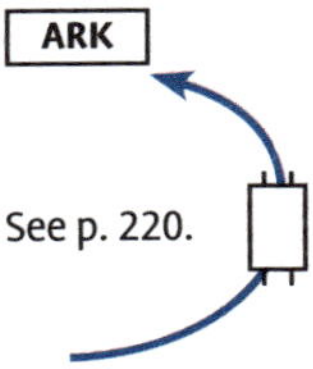

See p. 220.

חֲצִי קַדִּישׁ Short Kaddish W71 F146
Open, raise, display, and wrap scroll.
Return scroll to ark. W76 F150

אַשְׁרֵי Ashrey W78 F152
✕ ~~לַמְנַצֵּחַ Lamenatse·aḥ (Psalm 20)~~
וּבָא לְצִיּוֹן Uva letsiyyon W80 F156

Remove and pack tefillin. (Some remove after Kaddish.)

+ חֲצִי קַדִּישׁ Short Kaddish W103 F428

(If you remove tefillin here, do *not* pack but cover them, so as to begin Musaf together quickly after Kaddish.)

מוּסָף

+ **Rosh Ḥodesh Amidah for weekdays:** W104 F486

Weekday קְדֻשָּׁה Kedushah W105 F488

☞ Do *not* continue to add וּלְכַפָּרַת פָּשַׁע Ulkhapparat pasha.

+ קַדִּישׁ שָׁלֵם Full Kaddish W82 F158

עָלֵינוּ Aleynu W83 F160

If psalms for the day were not recited at Shaḥarit, add here:

קַדִּישׁ יָתוֹם Mourner's Kaddish (some omit) W84|100 F162|52

Psalm for Wednesday (Psalms 94:1–95:3) W87 F26

קַדִּישׁ יָתוֹם Mourner's Kaddish (some omit) W100 F52

+ Psalm 104 for Rosh Ḥodesh W90 F34

קַדִּישׁ יָתוֹם Mourner's Kaddish W84|100 F162|52

מִנְחָה

Weekday Amidah:

+ יַעֲלֶה וְיָבוֹא Ya'aleh veyavo for Rosh Ḥodesh W127 F178

✕ ~~תַּחֲנוּן Taḥanun~~

Tammuz 1 תַּמּוּז — רֹאשׁ חֹדֶשׁ תַּמּוּז Rosh Ḥodesh Tammuz — Day 2

Wed 29 Jun (evening)

DURING Rosh Ḥodesh

Birkat Hamazon:

+ יַעֲלֶה וְיָבוֹא Ya'aleh veyavo for Rosh Ḥodesh L90|95 S340|347 W233|239 F762|780

+ הָרַחֲמָן Haraḥaman for Rosh Ḥodesh L92|96 S343|348 W235|240 F768

עַרְבִית

Weekday Amidah:

+ יַעֲלֶה וְיָבוֹא Ya'aleh veyavo for Rosh Ḥodesh W145 F216

Thu 30 Jun **שַׁחֲרִית**

Before מִזְמוֹר שִׁיר Mizmor shir (Psalm 30) W14 F50 or at end of service, recite:

Psalm for Thursday (Psalm 81) W89 F30

קַדִּישׁ יָתוֹם Mourner's Kaddish (some omit) W100 F52

+ Psalm 104 for Rosh Ḥodesh W90 F34

קַדִּישׁ יָתוֹם Mourner's Kaddish W100 F52

Weekday Amidah:

+ יַעֲלֶה וְיָבוֹא Ya'aleh veyavo for Rosh Ḥodesh W41 F114

✕ ~~תַּחֲנוּן Taḥanun~~

+ חֲצִי הַלֵּל Short Hallel W50 F380

קַדִּישׁ שָׁלֵם Full Kaddish W56 F392

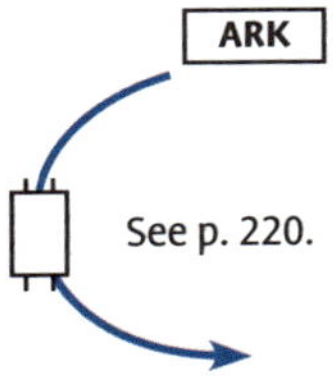

See p. 220.

TORAH SERVICE W65 F138

Remove **1** scroll from ark.

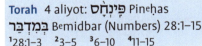

Torah 4 aliyot: פִּינְחָס Pineḥas
בְּמִדְבַּר Bemidbar (Numbers) 28:1–15
[1]28:1–3 [2]3–5 [3]6–10 [4]11–15 W320 P943

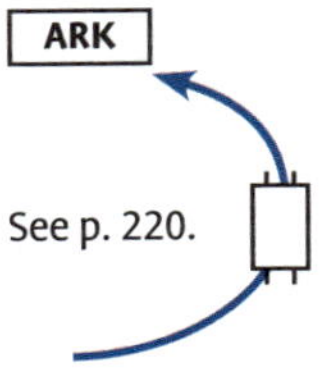

See p. 220.

חֲצִי קַדִּישׁ Short Kaddish W71 F146

Open, raise, display, and wrap scroll.

Return scroll to ark. W76 F150

אַשְׁרֵי Ashrey W78 F152

✕ ~~לַמְנַצֵּחַ Lamenatse·aḥ (Psalm 20)~~

וּבָא לְצִיּוֹן Uva letsiyyon W80 F156

Remove and pack tefillin. (Some remove after Kaddish.)

Tammuz 5782

				1	2	3
4	5	6	7	8	9	10
11	12	13	14	15	16	17
18	19	20	21	22	23	24
25	26	27	28	29		

Jun | Jul 2022

				30	1	2
3	4	5	6	7	8	9
10	11	12	13	14	15	16
17	18	19	20	21	22	23
24	25	26	27	28		

+ Add ✕ Omit ☞ Take note!

Siddurim
L Lev Shalem for Shabbat and Festivals
S Shabbat and Festival Sim Shalom
W Weekday Sim Shalom
F Full Sim Shalom (both editions)
P Personal Edition of Full Sim Shalom

\+ חֲצִי קַדִּישׁ Short Kaddish W103 F428
(If you remove tefillin here, do *not* pack but cover them, so as to begin Musaf together quickly after Kaddish.)

מוּסָף
\+ **Rosh Ḥodesh Amidah for weekdays:** W104 F486
Weekday קְדֻשָּׁה Kedushah W105 F488
☞ Do *not* continue to add וּלְכַפָּרַת פָּשַׁע Ulkhapparat pasha.

\+ קַדִּישׁ שָׁלֵם Full Kaddish W82 F158
עָלֵינוּ Aleynu W83 F160

If psalms for the day were not recited at Shaḥarit, add here:
קַדִּישׁ יָתוֹם Mourner's Kaddish (some omit) W84|100 F162|52
Psalm for Thursday (Psalm 81) W89 F30
קַדִּישׁ יָתוֹם Mourner's Kaddish (some omit) W100 F52
\+ Psalm 104 for Rosh Ḥodesh W90 F34

קַדִּישׁ יָתוֹם Mourner's Kaddish W84|100 F162|52

מִנְחָה
Weekday Amidah:
\+ יַעֲלֶה וְיָבוֹא Ya'aleh veyavo for Rosh Ḥodesh W127 F178

✕ ~~תַּחֲנוּן Taḥanun~~

Tammuz 3 תַּמּוּז
Sat 2 Jul

שַׁבָּת Shabbat פָּרָשַׁת קֹרַח Parashat Koraḥ

Torah 7 aliyot (minimum): קֹרַח Koraḥ
בְּמִדְבַּר Bemidbar (Numbers) 16:1–18:32

Annual:	[1] 16:1–13	[2] 16:14–19	[3] 16:20–17:8	[4] 17:9–15
	[5] 17:16–24	[6] 17:25–18:20	[7] 18:21–32	[M] 18:30–32
Triennial:	[1] 17:25–18:7	[2] 18:8–10	[3] 18:11–13	[4] 18:14–20
	[5] 18:21–24	[6] 18:25–29	[7] 18:30–32	[M] 18:30–32

Haftarah שְׁמוּאֵל א׳ 1 Shemu'el (1 Samuel) 11:14–12:22

מִנְחָה
Torah 3 aliyot from חֻקַּת Ḥukkat
בְּמִדְבַּר Bemidbar (Numbers) 19:1–17
[1] 19:1–6 [2] 7–9 [3] 10–17 W302 P922

Chanted also next Monday and Thursday.

Tammuz 4 תַּמּוּז
Sat 2 Jul (night)

After Arvit if the moon is visible:
קִדּוּשׁ לְבָנָה Kiddush Levanah L286 W167 F704
For procedures and instructions, see p. 223.

Tammuz 10 תַּמּוּז
Sat 9 Jul

שַׁבָּת Shabbat פָּרָשַׁת חֻקַּת Parashat Ḥukkat

Torah 7 aliyot (minimum): חֻקַּת Ḥukkat
בְּמִדְבַּר Bemidbar (Numbers) 19:1–22:1

Annual:	1 19:1–17	2 19:18–20:6	3 20:7–13	4 20:14–21
	5 20:22–21:9	6 21:10–20°	7 21:21–22:1	M 21:34–22:1
Triennial:°	1 20:22–21:3	2 21:4–10	3 21:11–16	4 21:17–20°
	5 21:21–25	6 21:26–33	7 21:34–22:1	M 21:34–22:1

☞ Triennial: Accords with the CJLS decision of Nov. 16, 2020.

☞ °21:19 Chant this verse using the "desert traveling melody," based on the Shirat Hayam melody.

Haftarah שׁוֹפְטִים Shofetim (Judges) 11:1–33

מִנְחָה

Torah 3 aliyot from בָּלָק Balak
בְּמִדְבַּר Bemidbar (Numbers) 22:2–12
1 22:2–4 2 5–7° 3 8–12° W303 P923

Chanted also next Monday and Thursday.

☞ The following notes apply to readers using Israeli pronunciation:
°22:6 אָרָה־לִּי Read: ora-li (vowel of א is kamets katan)
°22:11 קָבָה־לִּי Read: kova-li (vowel of ק is kamets katan)

Because 17 Tammuz falls on Shabbat, we delay the fast-day observance one day. See p. 191.

Tammuz 17 תַּמּוּז
Sat 16 Jul

שַׁבָּת Shabbat פָּרָשַׁת בָּלָק Parashat Balak

Torah 7 aliyot (minimum): בָּלָק Balak
בְּמִדְבַּר Bemidbar (Numbers) 22:2–25:9

Annual:	1 22:2–12°	2 22:13–20°	3 22:21–38	4 22:39–23:12°
	5 23:13–26°	6 23:27–24:13	7 24:14–25:9	M 25:7–9
Triennial:	1 22:39–23:5	2 23:6–12°	3 23:13–26°	4 23:27–30
	5 24:1–13	6 24:14–25	7 25:1–9	M 25:7–9

☞ The following notes apply to readers using Israeli pronunciation:

°22:6	אָרָה־לִּי	Read: ora-li (vowel of א is kamets katan)
°22:11	קָבָה־לִּי	Read: kova-li (vowel of ק is kamets katan)
°22:17	קָבָה־לִּי	Read: kova-li (vowel of ק is kamets katan)
°23:7	אָרָה־לִּי	Read: ora-li (vowel of א is kamets katan)
°23:13	וְקָבְנוֹ־לִי	Read: vekovno-li (vowel of ק is kamets katan)
°23:25	תִקֳּבֶנּוּ	Read: tikkovennu (every ֳ [ḥataf kamets] is pronounced "o")

Haftarah מִיכָה Mikhah (Micah) 5:6–6:8

מִנְחָה

Torah 3 aliyot from פִּינְחָס Pineḥas
בְּמִדְבַּר Bemidbar (Numbers) 25:10–26:4
1 25:10–12 2 13–15 3 25:16–26:4° W304 P924

Chanted also next Monday and Thursday.

☞ °26:1 (in some books incorrectly marked as 25:19)
וַיְהִי אַחֲרֵי הַמַּגֵּפָה וַיֹּאמֶר . . .
Despite the break in the text after הַמַּגֵּפָה, this is a single verse until לֵאמֹר. Chant the אֶתְנַחְתָּא of הַמַּגֵּפָה as usual, and continue with the rest of the verse.

☞ צִדְקָתְךָ צֶדֶק Tsidkatekha tsedek L230 S239 W183 F584

+ Add **✕** Omit ☞ Take note!

Siddurim

- **L** Lev Shalem for Shabbat and Festivals
- **S** Shabbat and Festival Sim Shalom
- **W** Weekday Sim Shalom
- **F** Full Sim Shalom (both editions)
- **P** Personal Edition of Full Sim Shalom

Tammuz 5782

				1	2	3
4	5	6	7	8	9	10
11	12	13	14	15	16	17
18	19	20	21	22	23	24
25	26	27	28	29		

Jun | Jul 2022

				30	1	2
3	4	5	6	7	8	9
10	11	12	13	14	15	16
17	18	19	20	21	22	23
24	25	26	27	28		

The 3 Weeks

Shiv'ah Asar Betammuz inaugurates a 3-week mourning period that concludes on Tish'ah Be'av.

During these weeks, avoid concerts and public celebrations such as weddings. Some refrain from haircuts.

Tammuz 18 תַּמּוּז
Sat 16 Jul

שִׁבְעָה עָשָׂר בְּתַמּוּז Shiv'ah Asar Betammuz

17th of Tammuz (communal fast, begins Sunday at dawn)

מוֹצָאֵי שַׁבָּת Motsa'ey Shabbat Conclusion of Shabbat

עַרְבִית Saturday night Arvit as usual L264 S281 W137 F200

Shiv'ah Asar Betammuz

On this date in 70 C.E., soldiers of the Roman army broke through the walls of Jerusalem. Three weeks later, on the 9th of Av, they destroyed the 2nd Temple.

This year the 17th of Tammuz falls on Shabbat. Therefore, we delay the fast until the 18th of Tammuz.

- This is a minor fast day, so called because the fast does not begin until dawn.
- The fast (from both eating and drinking) lasts until dark (a minimum of 25 minutes after sunset).
- *Sheliḥey tsibbur*, Torah readers, and those called for *aliyot* should be fasting.
- The preferred fast-day procedures apply when at least 6 of those who are counted for a *minyan* are fasting.
- If it is ascertained (without causing embarrassment) that fewer than 6 are fasting, follow the procedures printed in gray and marked with ✦.

Sun 17 Jul **שַׁחֲרִית**

Silent weekday Amidah:
Do not add עֲנֵנוּ Anenu.

Repetition of the weekday Amidah:

6 or more fasting **+** עֲנֵנוּ Anenu, before רְפָאֵנוּ Refa'enu W38 F110

Fewer than 6 fasting ✦ Add עֲנֵנוּ Anenu in שׁוֹמֵעַ תְּפִלָּה Shome·a tefillah. Replace תַּעֲנִיתֵנוּ ta'anitenu (6th word) with הַתַּעֲנִית הַזֶּה hata'anit hazeh. W38 F110

6 or more fasting **+** אָבִינוּ מַלְכֵּנוּ Avinu malkenu W57 F124

Fewer than 6 fasting ✦ Those fasting recite אָבִינוּ מַלְכֵּנוּ individually.

☞ תַּחֲנוּן Taḥanun (וַיֹּאמֶר דָּוִד Vayomer david) W62 F132
חֲצִי קַדִּישׁ Short Kaddish W64 F136

Tammuz 5782						
				1	2	3
4	5	6	7	8	9	10
11	12	13	14	15	16	17
18	19	20	21	22	23	24
25	26	27	28	29		

Jun | Jul 2022						
				30	1	2
3	4	5	6	7	8	9
10	11	12	13	14	15	16
17	18	19	20	21	22	23
24	25	26	27	28		

+ Add ✕ Omit ☞ Take note!

Siddurim
- **L** Lev Shalem for Shabbat and Festivals
- **S** Shabbat and Festival Sim Shalom
- **W** Weekday Sim Shalom
- **F** Full Sim Shalom (both editions)
- **P** Personal Edition of Full Sim Shalom

Fewer than 6 fasting ✦ Omit the entire Torah service.
Continue with אַשְׁרֵי Ashrey.

6 or more fasting + **TORAH SERVICE** W65 F138

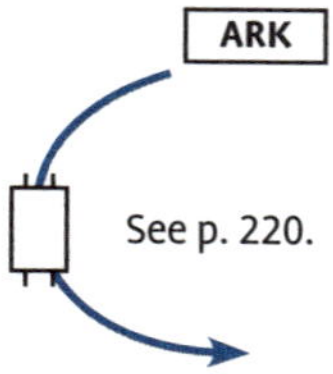

Remove **1** scroll from ark.

Torah 3 aliyot from כִּי תִשָּׂא Ki tissa
שְׁמוֹת Shemot (Exodus) 32:11–14, 34:1–10
1 32:11–14° 2 34:1–3 3 34:4–10° W341 P979

☞ °At each of the 3 passages indicated below, follow this procedure:
1. The reader pauses before the indicated text.
2. The congregation recites the indicated text.
3. Afterward, the reader chants the indicated text in the manner of the cantillation of High Holiday Torah reading.

32:12 שׁוּב מֵחֲרוֹן אַפֶּךָ וְהִנָּחֵם עַל־הָרָעָה לְעַמֶּךָ׃

34:6–7 יי | יי אֵ-ל רַחוּם וְחַנּוּן אֶרֶךְ אַפַּיִם וְרַב־חֶסֶד וֶאֱמֶת׃
נֹצֵר חֶסֶד לָאֲלָפִים נֹשֵׂא עָוֹן וָפֶשַׁע וְחַטָּאָה וְנַקֵּה

34:9 וְסָלַחְתָּ לַעֲוֹנֵנוּ וּלְחַטָּאתֵנוּ | וּנְחַלְתָּנוּ׃

To preserve the sense of this passage, maintain the appropriate pause after the טִפְחָא (וּלְחַטָּאתֵנוּ).

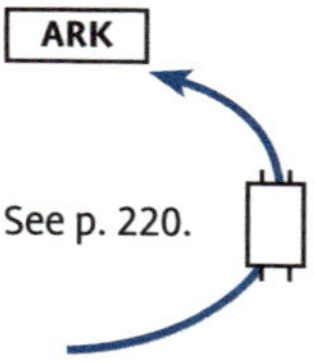

חֲצִי קַדִּישׁ Short Kaddish W71 F146
Open, raise, display, and wrap scroll.
Return scroll to ark. W76 F150

All minyanim אַשְׁרֵי Ashrey W78 F152
☞ לַמְנַצֵּחַ Lamenatse·aḥ (Psalm 20) W79 F154
Conclude the service in the usual manner.

מִנְחָה

אַשְׁרֵי Ashrey W120 F164
חֲצִי קַדִּישׁ Short Kaddish W121 F166

Fewer than 6 fasting ✦ Omit the entire Torah service.
Continue with silent Amidah.

6 or more fasting + **TORAH SERVICE** W65 F138

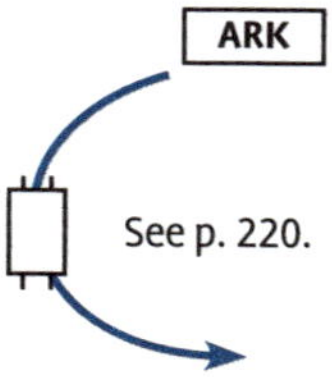

Remove **1** scroll from ark.

Torah 3 aliyot from כִּי תִשָּׂא Ki tissa
שְׁמוֹת Shemot (Exodus) 32:11–14, 34:1–10
1 32:11–14° 2 34:1–3 M 34:4–10° W341 P979

☞ °Chant as for the morning fast-day reading (above).

☞ Do not recite חֲצִי קַדִּישׁ Short Kaddish after maftir aliyah.

Open, raise, display, and wrap scroll.

Recite the בְּרָכָה berakhah before the haftarah. W74 F410 P989

Haftarah יְשַׁעְיָהוּ Yesha'yahu (Isaiah) 55:6–56:8 W342 P980

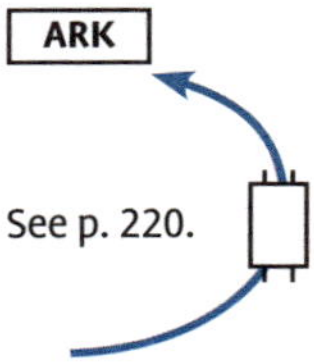

See p. 220.

Recite the 3 concluding haftarah blessings, through מָגֵן דָּוִד Magen david. W74 F410 P989.

Return scroll to ark. W76 F150
חֲצִי קַדִּישׁ Short Kaddish W121 F166

All minyanim — **Silent weekday Amidah:**

If fasting + עֲנֵנוּ Anenu, in שׁוֹמֵעַ תְּפִלָּה Shome·a tefillah W127 F178

All ✕ ~~שָׁלוֹם רָב Shalom rav~~
+ שִׂים שָׁלוֹם Sim shalom W131 F184

Repetition of the weekday Amidah:

6 or more fasting + עֲנֵנוּ Anenu, before רְפָאֵנוּ Refa'enu W124 F172

Fewer than 6 fasting ✦ Add עֲנֵנוּ Anenu in שׁוֹמֵעַ תְּפִלָּה Shome·a tefillah. Replace תַּעֲנִיתֵנוּ ta'anitenu (6th word) with הַתַּעֲנִית הַזֶּה hata'anit hazeh. W127 F172

All minyanim + בִּרְכַּת כֹּהֲנִים Birkat kohanim W131 F184
✕ ~~שָׁלוֹם רָב Shalom rav~~
+ שִׂים שָׁלוֹם Sim shalom W131 F184

6 or more fasting + אָבִינוּ מַלְכֵּנוּ Avinu malkenu W57 F188

Fewer than 6 fasting ✦ Those fasting recite אָבִינוּ מַלְכֵּנוּ individually.

☞ תַּחֲנוּן Taḥanun W132 F192

קַדִּישׁ שָׁלֵם Full Kaddish W134 F194
עָלֵינוּ Aleynu W135 F196
קַדִּישׁ יָתוֹם Mourner's Kaddish W136 F198

Tammuz 5782							Jun | Jul 2022						
				1	2	3					30	1	2
4	5	6	7	8	9	10	3	4	5	6	7	8	9
11	12	13	14	15	16	17	10	11	12	13	14	15	16
18	19	20	21	22	23	24	17	18	19	20	21	22	23
25	26	27	28	29			24	25	26	27	28		

+ Add ✕ Omit ☞ Take note!

Siddurim
L Lev Shalem for Shabbat and Festivals
S Shabbat and Festival Sim Shalom
W Weekday Sim Shalom
F Full Sim Shalom (both editions)
P Personal Edition of Full Sim Shalom

Tammuz 24 תַּמּוּז
Sat 23 Jul

שַׁבָּת Shabbat פָּרָשַׁת פִּינְחָס Parashat Pineḥas
שַׁבַּת מְבָרְכִים הַחֹדֶשׁ Shabbat Mevarekhim Haḥodesh

Torah 7 aliyot (minimum): פִּינְחָס Pineḥas
בְּמִדְבַּר Bemidbar (Numbers) 25:10–30:1

Annual:	[1]25:10–26:4°	[2]26:5–51	[3]26:52–27:5	[4]27:6–23
	[5]28:1–15	[6]28:16–29:11	[7]29:12–30:1	[M]29:35–30:1
Triennial:	[1]28:16–25	[2]28:26–31	[3]29:1–6	[4]29:7–11
	[5]29:12–16	[6]29:17–28	[7]29:29–30:1	[M]29:35–30:1

☞ °26:1 (in some books incorrectly marked as 25:19)
וַיְהִי אַחֲרֵי הַמַּגֵּפָה וַיֹּאמֶר . . .
Despite the break in the text after הַמַּגֵּפָה, this is a single verse until לֵאמֹר. Chant the אֶתְנַחְתָּא of הַמַּגֵּפָה as usual, and continue with the rest of the verse.

☞ **Haftarah** יִרְמְיָהוּ Yirmeyahu (Jeremiah) 1:1–2:3
(1st of 3 haftarot of rebuke preceding Tish'ah Be'av)

+ **Birkat Haḥodesh:** L180 S150 F418
Announce Rosh Ḥodesh Menaḥem Av:
For this formal announcement, use the formal name of the month. Do not announce the month by its popular name "Av."
רֹאשׁ חֹדֶשׁ מְנַחֵם אָב יִהְיֶה בְּיוֹם שִׁשִּׁי . . .
Rosh ḥodesh Menaḥem Av yihyeh beyom shishi . . .
(Thursday night and Friday)

✕ ~~אַב הָרַחֲמִים Av Haraḥamim~~

מִנְחָה

Torah 3 aliyot from מַטּוֹת Mattot
בְּמִדְבַּר Bemidbar (Numbers) 30:2–17
[1]30:2–9 [2]10–13 [3]14–17 W305 P925

Chanted also next Monday and Thursday.

Tammuz 29 תַּמּוּז
Thu 28 Jul

עֶרֶב רֹאשׁ חֹדֶשׁ Erev Rosh Ḥodesh
Day before Rosh Ḥodesh

מִנְחָה ✕ ~~תַּחֲנוּן Taḥanun~~

The 9 Days

Restrictions

The Rabbis instructed: מִשֶּׁנִּכְנַס אָב מְמַעֲטִין בְּשִׂמְחָה *mishenikhnas av mema'atin besimḥah* "From the moment Av arrives, we are to diminish our rejoicing."

As Tish'ah Be'av nears, the mourning that began with Shiv'ah Asar Betammuz (see p. 190) intensifies. From Rosh Ḥodesh Av through Tish'ah Be'av, we observe additional restrictions. For example, we refrain from:

- Eating meat
- Drinking wine
- Purchasing or wearing new clothes
- Getting a haircut

Restrictions on meat and wine are suspended on Shabbat and also for a סְעוּדַת מִצְוָה *se'udat mitsvah* (mandatory festive meal), celebrating events such as:

- בְּרִית מִילָה *berit milah* (ritual circumcision)
- פִּדְיוֹן הַבֵּן *pidyon haben* (redemption of a male firstborn child)
- סִיּוּם *siyyum* (completion of study of a tractate of rabbinic literature)

This year the 9th of Av falls on Shabbat. Therefore, we delay the observance of Tish'ah Be'av until the 10th of Av.

We continue to refrain from eating meat and drinking wine throughout the night following the fast.

Av 1 אָב — רֹאשׁ חֹדֶשׁ אָב Rosh Ḥodesh Av

Thu 28 Jul (evening)

DURING Rosh Ḥodesh

Birkat Hamazon:

+ יַעֲלֶה וְיָבוֹא Ya'aleh veyavo for Rosh Ḥodesh L90|95 S340|347 W233|239 F762|780

+ הָרַחֲמָן Haraḥaman for Rosh Ḥodesh L92|96 S343|348 W235|240 F768

עַרְבִית

Weekday Amidah:

+ יַעֲלֶה וְיָבוֹא Ya'aleh veyavo for Rosh Ḥodesh W145 F216

Fri 29 Jul

שַׁחֲרִית

Before מִזְמוֹר שִׁיר Mizmor shir (Psalm 30) W14 F50
or at end of service, recite:

Psalm for Friday (Psalm 93) W90 F32
קַדִּישׁ יָתוֹם Mourner's Kaddish (some omit) W100 F52
+ Psalm 104 for Rosh Ḥodesh W90 F34
קַדִּישׁ יָתוֹם Mourner's Kaddish W100 F52

Av 5782						
					1	2
3	4	5	6	7	8	9
10	11	12	13	14	15	16
17	18	19	20	21	22	23
24	25	26	27	28	29	30

Jul | Aug 2022						
					29	30
31	1	2	3	4	5	6
7	8	9	10	11	12	13
14	15	16	17	18	19	20
21	22	23	24	25	26	27

+ Add ✕ Omit ☞ Take note!

Siddurim
- **L** Lev Shalem for Shabbat and Festivals
- **S** Shabbat and Festival Sim Shalom
- **W** Weekday Sim Shalom
- **F** Full Sim Shalom (both editions)
- **P** Personal Edition of Full Sim Shalom

Weekday Amidah:

\+ יַעֲלֶה וְיָבוֹא Ya'aleh veyavo for Rosh Ḥodesh W41 F114

✕ ~~תַּחֲנוּן Taḥanun~~

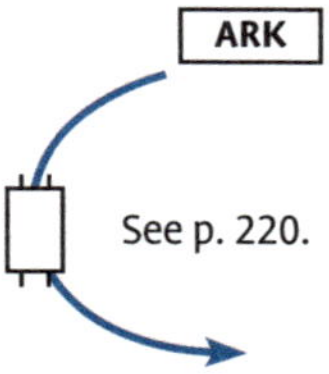

\+ חֲצִי הַלֵּל Short Hallel W50 F380
קַדִּישׁ שָׁלֵם Full Kaddish W56 F392

\+ **TORAH SERVICE** W65 F138
Remove **1** scroll from ark.

Torah 4 aliyot: פִּינְחָס Pineḥas
בְּמִדְבַּר Bemidbar (Numbers) 28:1–15
[1]28:1–3 [2]3–5 [3]6–10 [4]11–15 W320 P943

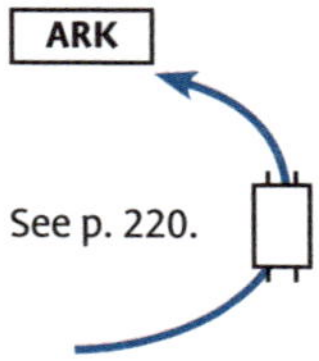

חֲצִי קַדִּישׁ Short Kaddish W71 F146
Open, raise, display, and wrap scroll.
Return scroll to ark. W76 F150

אַשְׁרֵי Ashrey W78 F152
✕ ~~לַמְנַצֵּחַ Lamenatse·aḥ (Psalm 20)~~
וּבָא לְצִיּוֹן Uva letsiyyon W80 F156

Remove and pack tefillin. (Some remove after Kaddish.)
\+ חֲצִי קַדִּישׁ Short Kaddish W103 F428
(If you remove tefillin here, do *not* pack but cover them, so as to begin Musaf together quickly after Kaddish.)

מוּסָף
\+ **Rosh Ḥodesh Amidah for weekdays:** W104 F486
Weekday קְדֻשָּׁה Kedushah W105 F488
☞ Do *not* continue to add וּלְכַפָּרַת פָּשַׁע Ulkhapparat pasha.

\+ קַדִּישׁ שָׁלֵם Full Kaddish W82 F158
עָלֵינוּ Aleynu W83 F160

If psalms for the day were not recited at Shaḥarit, add here:
קַדִּישׁ יָתוֹם Mourner's Kaddish (some omit) W84|100 F162|52
Psalm for Friday (Psalm 93) W90 F32
קַדִּישׁ יָתוֹם Mourner's Kaddish (some omit) W100 F52
\+ Psalm 104 for Rosh Ḥodesh W90 F34

קַדִּישׁ יָתוֹם Mourner's Kaddish W84|100 F162|52

מִנְחָה
Weekday Amidah:
\+ יַעֲלֶה וְיָבוֹא Ya'aleh veyavo for Rosh Ḥodesh W127 F178

✕ ~~תַּחֲנוּן Taḥanun~~ (as on all Friday afternoons)

Av 2 אָב
Sat 30 Jul

שַׁבָּת Shabbat
פָּרָשׁוֹת מַטּוֹת + מַסְעֵי Parashot Mattot + Mas'ey

Torah 7 aliyot (minimum): מַטּוֹת + מַסְעֵי Mattot + Mas'ey
בְּמִדְבַּר Bemidbar (Numbers) 30:2–36:13

Annual:	¹30:2–31:12	²31:13–54	³32:1–19	⁴32:20–33:49°
	⁵33:50–34:15	⁶34:16–35:8°	⁷35:9–36:13▮	M36:11–13
Triennial:	¹33:50–34:15	²34:16–29	³35:1–8°	⁴35:9–15
	⁵35:16–29	⁶35:30–34	⁷36:1–13▮	M36:10–13

☞°32:42 Note the rare ta'am (trope) מֵירְכָא־כְפוּלָה (֦): וַיִּקְרָא לָ֦ה נֹ֖בַח Connect לָ֦ה to the preceding and following words, without a pause; then pause after the טִפְּחָא (נֹ֖בַח), as usual.

☞°33:9–49 Chant 14 (others: 13) pairs of verses using the "desert traveling melody," based on the Shirat Hayam melody:
33:10–11 12–13 (others: 11–12 instead) 15–16 17–18 19–20 21–22 23–24 25–26 27–28 29–30 31–32 33–34 41–42 45–46

☞°35:5 Note the rare te'amim (tropes) יֶרַח־בֶּן־יוֹמוֹ (֪) and קַרְנֵי־פָרָה (֟): אַלְפַּ֪יִם בָּאַמָּ֟ה Connect אַלְפַּ֪יִם to the preceding and following words, without a pause; then pause after בָּאַמָּ֟ה.

▮ חזק When the Torah reader concludes a book of the Torah:
1. Close the Torah scroll.
2. **For Oleh:** Congregation chants חֲזַק חֲזַק וְנִתְחַזֵּק ḥazak ḥazak venitḥazzek; oleh remains silent.
   For Olah: Congregation chants חִזְקִי חִזְקִי וְנִתְחַזֵּק ḥizki ḥizki venitḥazzek; olah remains silent.
3. Torah reader repeats congregation's words (oleh/olah remains silent; if Torah reader is the oleh/olah, omit this repetition).
4. Open the Torah scroll.
5. The oleh/olah kisses the Torah scroll, closes it, and continues with the usual concluding berakhah.

☞**Haftarah**
Ashkenazic: יִרְמְיָהוּ Yirmeyahu (Jeremiah) 2:4–28; 3:4
Sephardic: יִרְמְיָהוּ Yirmeyahu (Jeremiah) 2:4–28; 4:1–2
(2nd of 3 haftarot of rebuke preceding Tish'ah Be'av)

מִנְחָה

Torah 3 aliyot from דְּבָרִים Devarim
דְּבָרִים Devarim (Deuteronomy) 1:1–10 (or 11)
¹1:1–3 ²4–7 ³8–10 (or ³8–11) W307 P927

Chanted also next Monday and Thursday.

Av 5782						
					1	2
3	4	5	6	7	8	9
10	11	12	13	14	15	16
17	18	19	20	21	22	23
24	25	26	27	28	29	30

Jul | Aug 2022						
					29	30
31 |	1	2	3	4	5	6
7	8	9	10	11	12	13
14	15	16	17	18	19	20
21	22	23	24	25	26	27

+ Add ✕ Omit ☞ Take note!

Siddurim
- **L** Lev Shalem for Shabbat and Festivals
- **S** Shabbat and Festival Sim Shalom
- **W** Weekday Sim Shalom
- **F** Full Sim Shalom (both editions)
- **P** Personal Edition of Full Sim Shalom

Av 8 אָב — Fri 5 Aug (daytime)

עֶרֶב שַׁבָּת Erev Shabbat — Day before Shabbat

Because 9 Av falls on Shabbat, the fast-day observance is delayed one day. See p. 201.

Preparing Shoes for Tish'ah Be'av

Wearing leather shoes is prohibited on Tish'ah Be'av. This year Tish'ah Be'av begins on Saturday night, immediately after the end of Shabbat. We do not diminish the joy of Shabbat by preparing during Shabbat for the mournful day that is coming. Therefore:

- Leave non-leather shoes at the synagogue *before* Shabbat begins.
- Do *not* take non-leather shoes with you to the synagogue on Shabbat.

Av 9 אָב — Fri 5 Aug (evening)

שַׁבָּת Shabbat פָּרָשַׁת דְּבָרִים Parashat Devarim
שַׁבַּת חֲזוֹן Shabbat Ḥazon

Shabbat Ḥazon, named after the 1st word of the haftarah, is the Shabbat immediately preceding Tish'ah Be'av. The mood of this mourning period intrudes upon the joyous spirit of Shabbat as some of the synagogue music foreshadows the upcoming day of destruction.

קַבָּלַת שַׁבָּת

Chant לְכָה דוֹדִי L23 S21 F262
to the melody of אֱלִי צִיּוֹן Eli tsiyyon
(Tish'ah Be'av lamentation poem).

Sat 6 Aug

Torah 7 aliyot (minimum): דְּבָרִים Devarim
דְּבָרִים Devarim (Deuteronomy) 1:1–3:22

Annual:	[1]1:1–10°	[2]1:11–21°	[3]1:22–38	[4]1:39–2:1
	[5]2:2–30	[6]2:31–3:14	[7]3:15–3:22	[M]3:20–22
Triennial:	[1]2:31–34	[2]2:35–37	[3]3:1–3	[4]3:4–7
	[5]3:8–11	[6]3:12–14	[7]3:15–22	[M]3:20–22

☞ °1:10 Although some books extend the 1st aliyah to 1:11, it is preferable to end at 1:10 so that the second aliyah does not begin with the melody of אֵיכָה (see note to 1:12).

☞ °1:12 Because the first word of this verse is אֵיכָה and this parashah is always read the Shabbat before Tish'ah Be'av, this verse is traditionally chanted using the cantillation of the book of אֵיכָה.

Haftarah יְשַׁעְיָהוּ Yesha'yahu (Isaiah) 1:1–27°
(3rd of 3 haftarot of rebuke preceding Tish'ah Be'av)

☞ °The cantillation changes twice from haftarah melody to אֵיכָה melody and back, reflecting the content of the verses:

verse	1	regular haftarah melody
verses	2–15	אֵיכָה melody
verses	16–19	regular haftarah melody
verses	20–23	אֵיכָה melody
verses	24–27	regular haftarah melody

☞ Recite אַב הָרַחֲמִים Av haraḥamim L446 S151 F420
even if congregation usually omits.

מִנְחָה

Torah 3 aliyot from וָאֶתְחַנַּן Va'et·ḥannan
דְּבָרִים Devarim (Deuteronomy) 3:23–4:8°
¹3:23–25 ²3:26–4:4 ³4:5–8 W308 P927

Chanted also next Monday and Thursday.

☞ °3:23–4:8 The reading ends with 4:8, which enables the correct configuration of the 3 aliyot.

✕ ~~צִדְקָתְךָ צֶדֶק Tsidkatekha tsedek~~

Although פִּרְקֵי אָבוֹת Pirkey Avot is commonly studied on Shabbat afternoon, do not study it on this Shabbat, the eve of Tish'ah Be'av.

Tish'ah Be'av

The 3-week period of mourning culminates in Tishah Be'av, the commemoration of the destruction of both the 1st and 2nd Temples in Jerusalem. Over the centuries, other catastrophes that befell the Jewish people also came to be associated with this day of mourning.

In contrast to the 4 minor fast days (see pp. 14, 90, 117, and 191), this fast, like Yom Kippur, lasts the full day. It begins immediately at sunset and ends after dark the next day. Some wait until 3 stars appear, or at least 25 minutes after sunset. Others wait longer. For the proper waiting time in your community, consult your rabbi.

Se'udah Shelishit before Tish'ah Be'av

- Eating meat and drinking wine are permitted.
- If three or more have eaten together, precede בִּרְכַּת הַמָּזוֹן *birkat hamazon* as usual with בִּרְכַּת זִמּוּן *birkat zimmun* (i.e., רַבּוֹתַי נְבָרֵךְ *rabbotay nevarekh*).
- The meal must be completed before sunset.

Tish'ah Be'av Prohibitions

Beginning at Arvit, wearing leather shoes is prohibited.
The other prohibitions take effect at sunset.

The following prohibitions apply throughout Tish'ah Be'av:

- Eating and drinking
- Wearing leather shoes
- Sexual relations
- Bathing (except for minimal washing to remove dirt or after using the toilet)
- Applying skin or bath oils
- Studying Jewish religious texts

  Exceptions are texts that support the mood of the day, such as מְגִלַּת אֵיכָה *megillat eykhah* (Lamentations), אִיּוֹב *iyyov* (Job), certain other biblical texts, and rabbinic or other texts dealing with catastrophes in Jewish history.
- Greeting one another, especially with the word שָׁלוֹם *shalom*

Procedures in the Synagogue

Creating the Tish'ah Be'av Mood

Most congregations remove the table cover, as well as the פָּרֹכֶת *parokhet* (decorative ark curtain) if the ark has doors or if a plain curtain is available.

- In honor of Shabbat, delay removing the table cover and the פָּרֹכֶת until after the Kaddish following the Amidah of Arvit.
- Sit like mourners—on the floor or on low seats—especially during the chanting of מְגִלַּת אֵיכָה and קִינוֹת *kinot* (liturgical lamentation poetry). See below.
- Keep lights low; candles or flashlights can provide just enough light for reading.

If it is ascertained (without causing embarrassment) that fewer than 6 are fasting, follow the procedures printed in gray and marked with ✦.

Most congregations restore the table cover and the פָּרֹכֶת just before Minḥah.

Chanting Megillat Eykhah

1. Sit on the floor or on low seats or benches.
2. Chant מְגִלַּת אֵיכָה.
3. When reader reaches the second-to-last verse:
   a. Congregation chants the verse (5:21) with reader: . . . הֲשִׁיבֵנוּ *hashivenu* . . .
   b. Reader concludes the final verse (5:22).
   c. Congregation chants the previous verse (5:21) aloud.
   d. Reader alone repeats the same verse (5:21).

Reciting Kinot

- Sit on the floor or on low seats or benches.
- Chant קִינוֹת using melodies suitable for liturgical lamentation poetry.

Av 10 אָב
Sat 6 Aug (evening)

תִּשְׁעָה בְּאָב Tish'ah Be'av

9th of Av (full-day communal fast, begins Shabbat at sunset)

מוֹצָאֵי שַׁבָּת Motsa'ey Shabbat Conclusion of Shabbat

Wait until Shabbat ends.

Before עַרְבִית

For the sheliaḥ/sheliḥat tsibbur:
End your Shabbat by reciting: בָּרוּךְ הַמַּבְדִּיל בֵּין קֹדֶשׁ לְחֹל
Barukh hamavdil beyn kodesh leḥol.

Remove leather shoes. If possible, avoid touching them until after the service. If you brought non-leather shoes to the synagogue before Shabbat, put them on.

Do not remove the table cloth or the פָּרֹכֶת parokhet (decorative ark curtain) at this time.

עַרְבִית

For the sheliaḥ/sheliḥat tsibbur:
Begin Arvit with וְהוּא רַחוּם vehu raḥum. L264 S281 W137 F200

☞ Chant Arvit in a subdued voice, using melodies appropriate for the mournful mood.

☞ Pause before בָּרְכוּ barekhu.

Before בָּרְכוּ

For the congregation:
Remove leather shoes. If possible, avoid touching them until after the service. If you brought non-leather shoes to the synagogue before Shabbat, put them on.

Continue Saturday night Arvit as usual through the Amidah.

קַדִּישׁ שָׁלֵם Full Kaddish L280 S294 W160 F688

☞ Most congregations remove the table cover and the פָּרֹכֶת parokhet.
See "Procedures in the Synagogue," p. 200.

✕ ~~הַבְדָּלָה Havdalah~~

☞ Upon seeing a flame (light a candle if necessary), recite only the בְּרָכָה berakhah over a flame. (It is preferred not to recite the בְּרָכָה over electric lights.)

+ **Megillah reading:**
Chant מְגִלַּת אֵיכָה Megillat Eykhah and קִינוֹת kinot following the procedures in the blue box on p. 200.

Aug 6 10 אָב
Aug 7

Av 5782							Jul | Aug 2022						
					1	2						29	30
3	4	5	6	7	8	9	31	1	2	3	4	5	6
10	11	12	13	14	15	16	7	8	9	10	11	12	13
17	18	19	20	21	22	23	14	15	16	17	18	19	20
24	25	26	27	28	29	30	21	22	23	24	25	26	27

+ Add ✕ Omit ☞ Take note!

Siddurim
- **L** Lev Shalem for Shabbat and Festivals
- **S** Shabbat and Festival Sim Shalom
- **W** Weekday Sim Shalom
- **F** Full Sim Shalom (both editions)
- **P** Personal Edition of Full Sim Shalom

✕ ~~וִיהִי נֹעַם Vihi no'am~~
✕ ~~יֹשֵׁב בְּסֵתֶר עֶלְיוֹן Yoshev beseter elyon~~
☞ וְאַתָּה קָדוֹשׁ Ve'attah kadosh L216 S293 W159 F684
☞ קַדִּישׁ שָׁלֵם Full Kaddish, but omit sentence: L280 S294 W160 F688
✕ ~~תִּתְקַבַּל Titkabbal . . .~~
עָלֵינוּ Aleynu L281 S297 W163 F696
קַדִּישׁ יָתוֹם Mourner's Kaddish L282 S298 W164 F698
✕ ~~הַבְדָּלָה Havdalah~~

After עַרְבִית
☞ If you wore leather shoes:
Put on the shoes to return home.
Wear non-leather shoes for the remainder of the fast.

☞ Do not recite Kiddush Levanah before Monday night after Arvit.

Sun 7 Aug שַׁחֲרִית
☞ Do not wear tallit or tefillin.

If you wear a טַלִּית קָטָן tallit katan,
put it on, but do not recite the בְּרָכָה berakhah.

Weekday Shaharit W1 F2
☞ Chant the service in a subdued voice, using melodies appropriate for the mournful mood.

✕ ~~Psalm for Sunday~~

Silent weekday Amidah:
Do not add עֲנֵנוּ Anenu.

Repetition of the weekday Amidah:
6 or more fasting + עֲנֵנוּ Anenu, before רְפָאֵנוּ Refa'enu W38 F110
Fewer than 6 fasting ✦ Add עֲנֵנוּ Anenu in שׁוֹמֵעַ תְּפִלָּה Shome·a tefillah.
Replace תַּעֲנִיתֵנוּ ta'anitenu (6th word) with הַתַּעֲנִית הַזֶּה hata'anit hazeh. W38 F110
All minyanim ✕ ~~בִּרְכַּת כֹּהֲנִים Birkat kohanim~~

✕ ~~אָבִינוּ מַלְכֵּנוּ Avinu malkenu~~
✕ ~~תַּחֲנוּן Tahanun~~
חֲצִי קַדִּישׁ Short Kaddish W64 F136

Fewer than 6 fasting ✦ Omit the entire Torah service.
Continue with קִינוֹת kinot.

Siddurim

					1	2				29	30

L Lev Shalem for Shabbat and Festivals 3 4 5 6 7 8 9 31 | 1 2 3 4 5 6

S Shabbat and Festival Sim Shalom 10 11 12 13 14 15 16 7 8 9 10 11 12 13

W Weekday Sim Shalom 17 18 19 20 21 22 23 14 15 16 17 18 19 20

F Full Sim Shalom (both editions) 24 25 26 27 28 29 30 21 22 23 24 25 26 27

P Personal Edition of Full Sim Shalom

6 or more fasting + **TORAH SERVICE** W65 F138

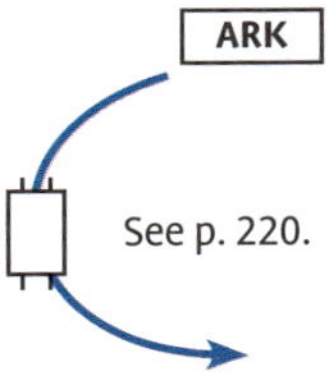

☞ Spread a טַלִּית tallit as a temporary reading table cover.

Remove **1** scroll from ark.

Torah 3 aliyot from וָאֶתְחַנַּן Va'et·ḥannan
דְּבָרִים Devarim (Deuteronomy) 4:25–40
[1]4:25–29 [2]30–35 [M]36–40 W338 P973

חֲצִי קַדִּישׁ Short Kaddish W71 F146
Open, raise, display, and wrap scroll.

Recite the בְּרָכָה berakhah before the haftarah. W74 F410 P989
This בְּרָכָה may be chanted using אֵיכָה melody.

Haftarah יִרְמְיָהוּ Yirmeyahu (Jeremiah) 8:13–9:23° W339 P975

☞ °This haftarah is chanted with אֵיכָה melody, except for the last two verses (9:22–23), which are chanted with the regular haftarah melody. (Some chant also the last verses with אֵיכָה melody.)

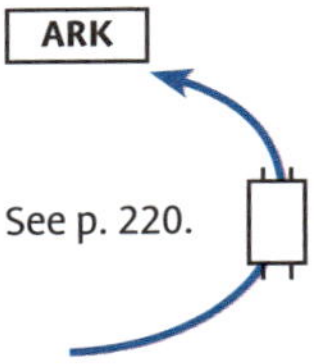

Recite the 3 concluding haftarah blessings, through מָגֵן דָּוִד Magen david. W74 F410 P989.

Return scroll to ark. W76 F150

All minyanim

Sit on the floor or on low seats or benches.
Recite קִינוֹת kinot.
Some chant מְגִלַּת אֵיכָה Megillat Eykhah, either at this point or at the end of the service.
Follow the procedures in the blue box on p. 200.

אַשְׁרֵי Ashrey W78 F152
✕ ~~לַמְנַצֵּחַ Lamenatse·aḥ (Psalm 20)~~

☞ וּבָא לְצִיּוֹן Uva letsiyyon, but omit 2nd verse: W80 F156
✕ ~~וַאֲנִי זֹאת בְּרִיתִי אוֹתָם Va'ani zot beriti otam . . .~~

☞ קַדִּישׁ שָׁלֵם Full Kaddish, but omit sentence: W82 F158
✕ ~~תִּתְקַבַּל Titkabbal . . .~~

עָלֵינוּ Aleynu W83 F160
✕ ~~Psalm for Sunday~~
קַדִּישׁ יָתוֹם Mourner's Kaddish W84 F162

מִנְחָה ☞ Immediately before Minḥah, most congregations restore the table cover and the פָּרֹכֶת parokhet.

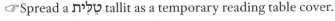

Av 5782

					1	2
3	4	5	6	7	8	9
10	11	12	13	14	15	16
17	18	19	20	21	22	23
24	25	26	27	28	29	30

Jul | Aug 2022

					29	30
31	1	2	3	4	5	6
7	8	9	10	11	12	13
14	15	16	17	18	19	20
21	22	23	24	25	26	27

+ Add ✕ Omit ☞ Take note!

Siddurim

L Lev Shalem for Shabbat and Festivals
S Shabbat and Festival Sim Shalom
W Weekday Sim Shalom
F Full Sim Shalom (both editions)
P Personal Edition of Full Sim Shalom

☞ Wear טַלִּית tallit and תְּפִלִּין tefillin, reciting the בְּרָכוֹת berakhot in the usual manner. W2–3 F4

☞ Use regular weekday melodies throughout this service.

+ Psalm for Sunday (Psalm 24) W85 F22
+ קַדִּישׁ יָתוֹם Mourner's Kaddish W100 F52

אַשְׁרֵי Ashrey W120 F164
חֲצִי קַדִּישׁ Short Kaddish W121 F166

Fewer than 6 fasting ✦ Omit the entire Torah service. Continue with the silent Amidah.

6 or more fasting + **TORAH SERVICE** W65 F138

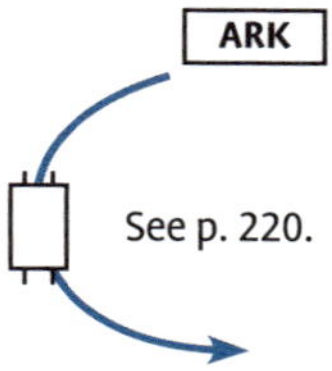

See p. 220.

If the table cover was removed and has not yet been restored, spread a טַלִּית tallit as a temporary table cover.

Remove **1** scroll from ark.

Torah 3 aliyot from כִּי תִשָּׂא Ki tissa
שְׁמוֹת Shemot (Exodus) 32:11–14, 34:1–10
[1]32:11–14° [2]34:1–3 [M]34:4–10° W341 P979

☞ °At each of the 3 passages indicated below, follow this procedure:
1. The reader pauses before the indicated text.
2. The congregation recites the indicated text.
3. Afterward, the reader chants the indicated text in the manner of the cantillation of High Holiday Torah reading.

32:12 שׁוּב מֵחֲרוֹן אַפֶּךָ וְהִנָּחֵם עַל־הָרָעָה לְעַמֶּךָ׃

34:6–7 יְיָ | יְיָ אֵ־ל רַחוּם וְחַנּוּן אֶרֶךְ אַפַּיִם וְרַב־חֶסֶד וֶאֱמֶת׃
נֹצֵר חֶסֶד לָאֲלָפִים נֹשֵׂא עָוֺן וָפֶשַׁע וְחַטָּאָה וְנַקֵּה

34:9 וְסָלַחְתָּ לַעֲוֺנֵנוּ וּלְחַטָּאתֵנוּ | וּנְחַלְתָּנוּ׃

To preserve the sense of this passage, maintain the appropriate pause after the טִפְחָא (וּלְחַטָּאתֵנוּ).

☞ Do not recite חֲצִי קַדִּישׁ Short Kaddish after maftir aliyah.

Open, raise, display, and wrap scroll.

Recite the בְּרָכָה berakhah before the haftarah. W74 F410 P989

Haftarah יְשַׁעְיָהוּ Yesha'yahu (Isaiah) 55:6–56:8 W342 P980

☞ Chant this haftarah using the regular haftarah melody.

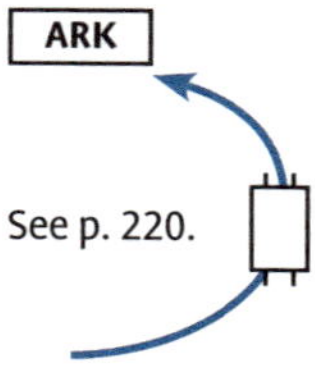

See p. 220.

Recite the 3 concluding haftarah blessings, through מָגֵן דָּוִד Magen david. W74 F410 P989.

Return scroll to ark. W76 F150
חֲצִי קַדִּישׁ Short Kaddish W121 F166

All minyanim — **Silent weekday Amidah:**
➕ נַחֵם Naḥem W126 F176
If fasting ➕ עֲנֵנוּ Anenu, in שׁוֹמֵעַ תְּפִלָּה Shome·a tefillah W127 F178
All ✕ ~~שָׁלוֹם רָב Shalom rav~~
➕ שִׂים שָׁלוֹם Sim shalom W131 F184

Repetition of the weekday Amidah:
6 or more fasting ➕ עֲנֵנוּ Anenu, before רְפָאֵנוּ Refa'enu W124 F172
All minyanim ➕ נַחֵם Naḥem W126 F176
Fewer than 6 fasting ✦ Add עֲנֵנוּ Anenu in שׁוֹמֵעַ תְּפִלָּה Shome·a tefillah. Replace תַּעֲנִיתֵנוּ ta'anitenu (6th word) with הַתַּעֲנִית הַזֶּה hata'anit hazeh. W127 F172
All minyanim ➕ בִּרְכַּת כֹּהֲנִים Birkat kohanim W131 F184
✕ ~~שָׁלוֹם רָב Shalom rav~~
➕ שִׂים שָׁלוֹם Sim shalom W131 F184

✕ ~~אָבִינוּ מַלְכֵּנוּ Avinu malkenu~~
✕ ~~תַּחֲנוּן Taḥanun~~
☞ קַדִּישׁ שָׁלֵם Full Kaddish *with* תִּתְקַבַּל Titkabbal W134 F194
עָלֵינוּ Aleynu W135 F196
קַדִּישׁ יָתוֹם Mourner's Kaddish W136 F198

Av 11 אָב
Sun 7 Aug — **עַרְבִית**

If the table cover and פָּרֹכֶת parokhet have not yet been restored, restore them before beginning Arvit.

Weekday Arvit as usual L264 S281 W137 F200

➕ **Havdalah (delayed from Saturday night)** S299 W165 F700
✕ ~~הִנֵּה אֵ־ל יְשׁוּעָתִי Hinneh el yeshu'ati~~
➕ בּוֹרֵא פְּרִי הַגָּפֶן Bo·re peri hagafen
✕ ~~בּוֹרֵא מִינֵי בְשָׂמִים Bo·re miney vesamim~~
✕ ~~בּוֹרֵא מְאוֹרֵי הָאֵשׁ Bo·re me'orey ha'esh~~
➕ הַמַּבְדִּיל בֵּין קֹדֶשׁ לְחֹל Hamavdil beyn kodesh leḥol

☞ Do not recite Kiddush Levanah until Monday night after Arvit.

At home ☞ Do not eat meat or drink wine until morning.

Av 12 אָב
Mon 8 Aug (night)

After Arvit if the moon is visible:
קִדּוּשׁ לְבָנָה Kiddush Levanah L286 W167 F704
For procedures and instructions, see p. 223.

Av 5782							Jul | Aug 2022						
					1	2						29	30
3	4	5	6	7	8	9	31	1	2	3	4	5	6
10	11	12	13	14	15	16	7	8	9	10	11	12	13
17	18	19	20	21	22	23	14	15	16	17	18	19	20
24	25	26	27	28	29	30	21	22	23	24	25	26	27

+ Add ✕ Omit ☞ Take note!

Siddurim
- **L** Lev Shalem for Shabbat and Festivals
- **S** Shabbat and Festival Sim Shalom
- **W** Weekday Sim Shalom
- **F** Full Sim Shalom (both editions)
- **P** Personal Edition of Full Sim Shalom

Av 14 אָב — Thu 11 Aug

עֶרֶב ט"ו בְּאָב Erev Tu Be'av Day before Tu Be'av

מִנְחָה ✕ ~~תַּחֲנוּן Taḥanun~~

Av 15 אָב — Fri 12 Aug (daytime)

ט"ו בְּאָב Tu Be'av

15th of Av (day of communal celebration)

Tu Be'av, according to the Talmud, is one of the most joyous days of the Jewish year. Various happy events in Jewish history are associated with this day.

During the time of the 2nd Temple in Jerusalem, the 15th of Av marked the beginning of the grape harvest. The Talmud explains that the daughters of Israel used to dress in white and go out to the vineyards to dance. Young unmarried men would follow after them in the hope of finding a bride.

שַׁחֲרִית ✕ ~~תַּחֲנוּן Taḥanun~~
☞ לַמְנַצֵּחַ Lamenatse·aḥ (Psalm 20) W79 F154

מִנְחָה ✕ ~~תַּחֲנוּן Taḥanun~~

Chanting Aseret Hadibberot

Parashat Va'et·ḥannan

Parashat Va'et·ḥannan has a second version of עֲשֶׂרֶת הַדִּבְּרוֹת *aseret hadibberot.* Although usually translated "the 10 commandments," the phrase actually means "the 10 pronouncements."

The congregants stand as they hear this section read, just as the people Israel stood at the foot of Mount Sinai and listened to the voice of God.

The proper chanting of עֲשֶׂרֶת הַדִּבְּרוֹת requires exceptional attention because this passage is marked with 2 sets of verse divisions and 2 sets of *te'amim* (tropes, cantillation marks). One set, for private study, divides the passage into verses of usual length, suitable for study. The 2nd set, for public reading, divides the passage into exactly *10* verses. Each verse corresponds to 1 of the 10 pronouncements. The congregation listens to exactly *10* pronouncements, reenacting the events experienced by the people Israel at Mount Sinai.

For further discussion of the verse divisions of עֲשֶׂרֶת הַדִּבְּרוֹת, see p. 99.

Over the centuries, the complexity of the task of separating 2 sets of verse divisions and 2 sets of *te'amim* resulted in countless errors in printed *ḥumashim.* The confusing verse divisions led to a confusion in verse *numbers,* which in fact should follow the private reading. There are 29 verses in the chapter, but many editions erroneously count 30. This leads to confusing *aliyah* divisions, which are clarified on p. 208.

The correct verse divisions and *te'amim* for the public reading appear on p. 207. Only this version presents *10* pronouncements in *10* verses.

עֲשֶׂרֶת הַדִּבְּרוֹת — פָּרָשַׁת וָאֶתְחַנַּן

For Public Reading — טַעֲמָא תְנִינָא (טַעַם עֶלְיוֹן)

דִּבְּרוֹת

1 אָנֹכִי יְהוָה אֱלֹהֶיךָ אֲשֶׁר
2 הוֹצֵאתִיךָ מֵאֶרֶץ מִצְרַיִם מִבֵּית עֲבָדִים: לֹא יִהְיֶה־
לְךָ אֱלֹהִים אֲחֵרִים עַל־פָּנַי לֹא תַעֲשֶׂה־לְךָ פֶסֶל |
כָּל־תְּמוּנָה אֲשֶׁר בַּשָּׁמַיִם | מִמַּעַל וַאֲשֶׁר בָּאָרֶץ
מִתַּחַת וַאֲשֶׁר בַּמַּיִם | מִתַּחַת לָאָרֶץ לֹא־תִשְׁתַּחֲוֶה
לָהֶם וְלֹא תָעָבְדֵם° כִּי אָנֹכִי יְהוָה אֱלֹהֶיךָ אֵל קַנָּא
פֹּקֵד עֲוֺן אָבוֹת עַל־בָּנִים וְעַל־שִׁלֵּשִׁים וְעַל־רִבֵּעִים
לְשֹׂנְאָי וְעֹשֶׂה חֶסֶד לַאֲלָפִים לְאֹהֲבַי וּלְשֹׁמְרֵי
3 מִצְוֺתָי°: לֹא תִשָּׂא אֶת־שֵׁם־יְהוָה
אֱלֹהֶיךָ לַשָּׁוְא כִּי לֹא יְנַקֶּה יְהוָה אֵת אֲשֶׁר־יִשָּׂא
4 אֶת־שְׁמוֹ לַשָּׁוְא: שָׁמוֹר אֶת־יוֹם
הַשַּׁבָּת לְקַדְּשׁוֹ כַּאֲשֶׁר צִוְּךָ | יְהוָה אֱלֹהֶיךָ שֵׁשֶׁת
יָמִים תַּעֲבֹד וְעָשִׂיתָ כָּל־מְלַאכְתֶּךָ וְיוֹם הַשְּׁבִיעִי
שַׁבָּת | לַיהוָה אֱלֹהֶיךָ לֹא תַעֲשֶׂה כָל־מְלָאכָה
אַתָּה וּבִנְךָ־וּבִתֶּךָ וְעַבְדְּךָ־וַאֲמָתֶךָ וְשׁוֹרְךָ וַחֲמֹרְךָ
וְכָל־בְּהֶמְתֶּךָ וְגֵרְךָ אֲשֶׁר בִּשְׁעָרֶיךָ לְמַעַן יָנוּחַ
עַבְדְּךָ וַאֲמָתְךָ כָּמוֹךָ וְזָכַרְתָּ כִּי־עֶבֶד הָיִיתָ | בְּאֶרֶץ
מִצְרַיִם וַיֹּצִאֲךָ יְהוָה אֱלֹהֶיךָ מִשָּׁם בְּיָד חֲזָקָה וּבִזְרֹעַ
נְטוּיָה עַל־כֵּן צִוְּךָ יְהוָה אֱלֹהֶיךָ לַעֲשׂוֹת אֶת־יוֹם
5 הַשַּׁבָּת: כַּבֵּד אֶת־אָבִיךָ וְאֶת־
אִמֶּךָ כַּאֲשֶׁר צִוְּךָ יְהוָה אֱלֹהֶיךָ לְמַעַן | יַאֲרִיכֻן יָמֶיךָ
וּלְמַעַן יִיטַב לָךְ עַל הָאֲדָמָה אֲשֶׁר־יְהוָה אֱלֹהֶיךָ נֹתֵן
7 | 6 לָךְ: לֹא תִרְצָח: וְלֹא
9 | 8 תִנְאָף: וְלֹא תִגְנֹב: וְלֹא־
10 תַעֲנֶה בְרֵעֲךָ עֵד שָׁוְא: וְלֹא תַחְמֹד
אֵשֶׁת רֵעֶךָ וְלֹא תִתְאַוֶּה בֵּית
רֵעֶךָ שָׂדֵהוּ וְעַבְדּוֹ וַאֲמָתוֹ שׁוֹרוֹ וַחֲמֹרוֹ וְכֹל אֲשֶׁר
לְרֵעֶךָ:

°Read: **to'ovdem**

°Read: **mitsvotay**
כְּתִיב: מצותו

Av 16 אָב
Sat 13 Aug

שַׁבָּת Shabbat פָּרָשַׁת וָאֶתְחַנַּן Parashat Va'et·ḥannan
שַׁבַּת נַחֲמוּ Shabbat Naḥamu

Shabbat Naḥamu, the Shabbat after Tish'ah Be'av, is the 1st of the 7 *shabbatot* of consolation leading to Rosh Hashanah. This Shabbat takes its name from the 1st word of the haftarah, "Console yourselves."

This parashah contains עֲשֶׂרֶת הַדִּבְּרוֹת *aseret hadibberot*. For the correct text and *te'amim* (tropes, cantillation marks), see p. 207. For special instructions for the chanting of this passage, see p. 206 and below.

Aseret Hadibberot and Shema in the Triennial Cycle

- **Triennial Option A:** A fuller reading. The congregation thus experiences עֲשֶׂרֶת הַדִּבְּרוֹת every year, and hears שְׁמַע *shema* in years 2 and 3 of the cycle.
- **Triennial Option B:** A more abbreviated reading. The congregation experiences עֲשֶׂרֶת הַדִּבְּרוֹת only in year 2 and hears שְׁמַע only in year 3 of the cycle.

For details, see below.

Torah 7 aliyot (minimum): וָאֶתְחַנַּן Va'et·ḥannan
דְּבָרִים Devarim (Deuteronomy) 3:23–7:11

Annual:	1 3:23–4:4	2 4:5–40	3 4:41–49	° 4 5:1–17
	° 5 5:18–6:3	6 6:4–25	7 7:1–11	M 7:9–11

Triennial:

°Option A (includes both Aseret Hadibberot and Shema)

° 1 5:1–17	° 2 5:18–23	° 3 5:24–6:3	4 6:4–9
5 6:10–19	6 6:20–25	7 7:1–11	M 7:9–11

°Option B (excludes Aseret Hadibberot, but includes Shema):

1 6:4–9	2 6:10–19	3 6:20–22	4 6:23–25
5 7:1–5	6 7:6–8	7 7:9–11	M 7:9–11

☞ °**Verse numbers in chapter 5:** In many books, the verses are misnumbered. Use these guidelines to properly divide the reading:

Annual Reading
Aliyah **4**: ends לְרֵעֶךָ (5:18 in many books).
Aliyah **5**: begins אֶת־הַדְּבָרִים (5:19 in many books)

Triennial Option A
Aliyah **1**: ends לְרֵעֶךָ (5:18 in many books).
Aliyah **2**: אֶת־הַדְּבָרִים through וְעָשִׂינוּ (5:19–24 in many books)
Aliyah **3**: וַיִּשְׁמַע through תִּירָשׁוּן (5:25–30 in many books)

☞ °5:6–17 (5:7–18 in many books) Follow the te'amim (tropes) on p. 207 for the public reading of עֲשֶׂרֶת הַדִּבְּרוֹת. For additional instructions for chanting this passage, see the blue box on p. 206.

☞ °**Triennial Option A** excludes Shema in year 1 (next year).
°**Triennial Option B** includes Aseret Hadibberot only in year 2 (last year) and Shema only in year 3 (this year).

Haftarah יְשַׁעְיָהוּ Yesha'yahu (Isaiah) 40:1–26°
(1st of 7 haftarot of consolation following Tish'ah Be'av)

☞ °40:12 For readers using Israeli pronunciation:
וְכָל Read: vekhal (**not** vekhol; this is **not** kamets katan).

מִנְחָה

Torah 3 aliyot from עֵקֶב Ekev
דְּבָרִים Devarim (Deuteronomy) 7:12–8:10
¹7:12–21 ²7:22–8:3 ³8:4–10 W309 P929

Chanted also next Monday and Thursday.

Av 23 אָב Sat 20 Aug

שַׁבָּת Shabbat פָּרָשַׁת עֵקֶב Parashat Ekev
שַׁבַּת מְבָרְכִים הַחֹדֶשׁ Shabbat Mevarekhim Haḥodesh

Torah 7 aliyot (minimum): עֵקֶב Ekev
דְּבָרִים Devarim (Deuteronomy) 7:12–11:25

Annual:	¹7:12–8:10	²8:11–9:3	³9:4–29	⁴10:1–11
	⁵10:12–11:9	⁶11:10–21	⁷11:22–25	ᴹ11:22–25
Triennial:	¹10:12–15	²10:16–22	³11:1–9	⁴11:10–12
	⁵11:13–15	⁶11:16–21	⁷11:22–25	ᴹ11:22–25

Haftarah יְשַׁעְיָהוּ Yesha'yahu (Isaiah) 49:14–51:3
(2nd of 7 haftarot of consolation following Tish'ah Be'av)

+ **Birkat Haḥodesh:** L180 S150 F418
Announce Rosh Ḥodesh Elul:
רֹאשׁ חֹדֶשׁ אֱלוּל יִהְיֶה בְּיוֹם שַׁבַּת קֹדֶשׁ
וּלְמָחֳרָתוֹ בְּיוֹם רִאשׁוֹן . . .
Rosh ḥodesh Elul yihyeh beyom shabbat kodesh
ulmoḥorato beyom rishon . . .
(Friday night, Saturday, and Sunday)

✕ ~~אַב הָרַחֲמִים Av Haraḥamim~~

מִנְחָה

Torah 3 aliyot from רְאֵה Re'eh
דְּבָרִים Devarim (Deuteronomy) 11:26–12:10
¹11:26–31 ²11:32–12:5 ³12:6–10 W311 P931

Chanted also next Monday and Thursday.

Av 5782						
					1	2
3	4	5	6	7	8	9
10	11	12	13	14	15	16
17	18	19	20	21	22	23
24	25	26	27	28	29	30

Jul | Aug 2022						
					29	30
31	1	2	3	4	5	6
7	8	9	10	11	12	13
14	15	16	17	18	19	20
21	22	23	24	25	26	27

+ Add ✕ Omit ☞ Take note!

Siddurim
- **L** Lev Shalem for Shabbat and Festivals
- **S** Shabbat and Festival Sim Shalom
- **W** Weekday Sim Shalom
- **F** Full Sim Shalom (both editions)
- **P** Personal Edition of Full Sim Shalom

Av 30 אָב — Fri 26 Aug (evening)

שַׁבָּת Shabbat פָּרָשַׁת רְאֵה Parashat Re'eh
רֹאשׁ חֹדֶשׁ אֱלוּל Rosh Ḥodesh Elul — Day 1

DURING Rosh Ḥodesh

Birkat Hamazon:

+ יַעֲלֶה וְיָבוֹא Ya'aleh veyavo for Rosh Ḥodesh L 90|95 S 340|347 W 233|239 F 762|780

+ הָרַחֲמָן Haraḥaman for Rosh Ḥodesh L 92|96 S 343|348 W 235|240 F 768

עַרְבִית

Shabbat Amidah:

+ יַעֲלֶה וְיָבוֹא Ya'aleh veyavo for Rosh Ḥodesh L 50 S 36 F 298

Sat 27 Aug שַׁחֲרִית

Before מִזְמוֹר שִׁיר Mizmor shir (Psalm 30) L 120 S 81 F 50
or after Aleynu, recite:

Psalm for Shabbat (Psalm 92) L 112 S 72 F 32
קַדִּישׁ יָתוֹם Mourner's Kaddish (some omit) L 121 S 82 F 52
+ Psalm 104 for Rosh Ḥodesh L 114 S 78 F 34
קַדִּישׁ יָתוֹם Mourner's Kaddish L 121 S 82 F 52

Shabbat Amidah:

+ יַעֲלֶה וְיָבוֹא Ya'aleh veyavo for Rosh Ḥodesh L 163 S 118 F 360

+ חֲצִי הַלֵּל Short Hallel L 316 S 133 F 380
קַדִּישׁ שָׁלֵם Full Kaddish L 167 S 138 F 392

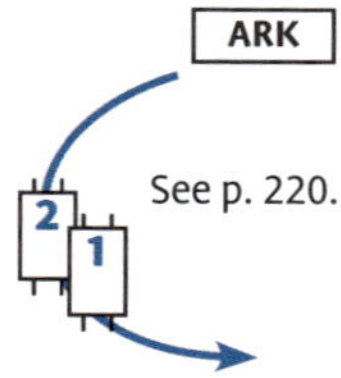

See p. 220.

TORAH SERVICE L 168 S 139 F 394

Remove **2** scrolls from ark in the order they will be read.

1st scroll 7 aliyot (minimum): רְאֵה Re'eh
דְּבָרִים Devarim (Deuteronomy) 11:26–16:17

Annual:	1 11:26–12:10	2 12:11–28	3 12:29–13:19	4 14:1–21
	5 14:22–29	6 15:1–18	7 15:19–16:17	
Triennial:	1 15:1–6	2 15:7–11	3 15:12–18	4 15:19–23
	5 16:1–8	6 16:9–12	7 16:13–17	

Place 2nd scroll on table next to 1st scroll.
חֲצִי קַדִּישׁ Short Kaddish L 174 S 146 F 408
Open, raise, display, and wrap 1st scroll.

+ **2nd scroll** Maftir aliyah from פִּינְחָס Pinehas
בְּמִדְבַּר M Bemidbar (Numbers) 28:9–15

Open, raise, display, and wrap 2nd scroll.

☞ **Haftarah** for Shabbat Rosh Ḥodesh
°יְשַׁעְיָהוּ Yesha'yahu (Isaiah) 66:1–24°

☞ °The haftarah for Shabbat Rosh Ḥodesh serves appropriately as the 3rd of 7 haftarot of consolation following Tish'ah Be'av. Then, in 2 weeks, append the usual 3rd haftarah to the 5th. See p. 215.

☞ °After 66:24, repeat 66:23 so the haftarah ends on a positive note.

☞ Most Ashkenazic congregations do **not** add verses from the Shabbat Maḥar Ḥodesh haftarah. Sephardic congregations add the first and last verses at the end.

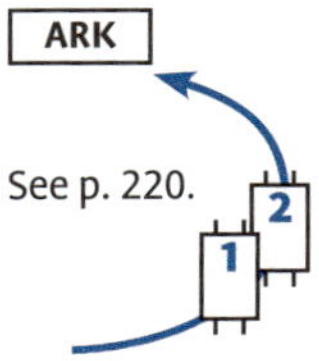

See p. 220.

✕ ~~אַב הָרַחֲמִים Av Haraḥamim~~

אַשְׁרֵי Ashrey L181 S151 F420

Return scrolls to ark in reverse order. L183 S153 F422

חֲצִי קַדִּישׁ Short Kaddish L184 S155 F428

מוּסָף

Rosh Ḥodesh Amidah for Shabbat: L193 S166 F486

Shabbat קְדֻשָּׁה Kedushah L195 S167 F490

Continuation of Amidah L196 S168 F496

☞ Do *not* continue to add וּלְכַפָּרַת פָּשַׁע Ulkhapparat pasha.

קַדִּישׁ שָׁלֵם Full Kaddish L203 S181 F506

אֵין כֵּא·לֹהֵינוּ Eyn keloheynu L204 S182 F507

עָלֵינוּ Aleynu L205 S183 F508

If psalms for the day were not recited at Shaḥarit, add here:

קַדִּישׁ יָתוֹם Mourner's Kaddish (some omit) L207 S184 F512

Psalm for Shabbat (Psalm 92) L112 S72 F32

קַדִּישׁ יָתוֹם Mourner's Kaddish (some omit) L121 S82 F52

+ Psalm 104 for Rosh Ḥodesh L114 S78 F34

קַדִּישׁ יָתוֹם Mourner's Kaddish L207|121 S184|82 F512|52

מִנְחָה

Torah 3 aliyot from שֹׁפְטִים Shofetim
דְּבָרִים Devarim (Deuteronomy) 16:18–17:13
¹16:18–20 ²16:21–17:10 ³17:11–13 W312 P932

Chanted also next Monday and Thursday.

Shabbat Amidah:

+ יַעֲלֶה וְיָבוֹא Ya'aleh veyavo for Rosh Ḥodesh L227 S237 F580

✕ ~~צִדְקָתְךָ צֶדֶק Tsidkatekha tsedek~~

Elul 5782						
1	2	3	4	5	6	7
8	9	10	11	12	13	14
15	16	17	18	19	20	21
22	23	24	25	26	27	28
29						

Aug | Sep 2022						
28	29	30	31 | 1	2	3	
4	5	6	7	8	9	10
11	12	13	14	15	16	17
18	19	20	21	22	23	24
25						

+ Add ✕ Omit ☞ Take note!

Siddurim
- **L** Lev Shalem for Shabbat and Festivals
- **S** Shabbat and Festival Sim Shalom
- **W** Weekday Sim Shalom
- **F** Full Sim Shalom (both editions)
- **P** Personal Edition of Full Sim Shalom

DURING Elul

MORNINGS

If psalm(s) for the day recited early in the service:

Every day Recite psalm(s) for the day, followed by:
קַדִּישׁ יָתוֹם Mourner's Kaddish (some omit) L121 S82 W100 F52
+ Psalm 27 for the Season of Repentance L113 S80 W92 F40
קַדִּישׁ יָתוֹם Mourner's Kaddish L121 S82 W100 F52

Weekdays + At end of service, sound the shofar* (except on 29 Elul).

If psalm(s) for the day recited at the end of the service:

Every day Recite psalm(s) for the day, followed by:
קַדִּישׁ יָתוֹם Mourner's Kaddish (some omit) L121 S82 W100 F52

Weekdays + Sound the shofar* (except on 29 Elul).
(Some sound the shofar instead after the last קַדִּישׁ יָתוֹם Mourner's Kaddish.)

Every day + Psalm 27 for the Season of Repentance L113 S80 W92 F40
קַדִּישׁ יָתוֹם Mourner's Kaddish L121 S82 W100 F52

EVENINGS

After עָלֵינוּ Aleynu:
קַדִּישׁ יָתוֹם Mourner's Kaddish (some omit) L58 S82 W100 F52
+ Psalm 27 for the Season of Repentance L59 S80 W92 F40
קַדִּישׁ יָתוֹם Mourner's Kaddish L58 S82 W100 F52

*Without anyone reciting a בְּרָכָה *berakhah* or calling out *teki'ah, shevarim*, etc., sound the shofar:
תְּקִיעָה ← שְׁבָרִים ← תְּרוּעָה ← תְּקִיעָה Teki'ah → Shevarim → Teru'ah → Teki'ah

Elul 1 אֱלוּל 1 — Sat 27 Aug (evening)

רֹאשׁ חֹדֶשׁ אֱלוּל Rosh Ḥodesh Elul — Day 2

מוֹצָאֵי שַׁבָּת Motsa'ey Shabbat Conclusion of Shabbat

DURING Rosh Ḥodesh

Birkat Hamazon:
+ יַעֲלֶה וְיָבוֹא Ya'aleh veyavo for Rosh Ḥodesh L90|95 S340|347 W233|239 F762|780
+ הָרַחֲמָן Haraḥaman for Rosh Ḥodesh L92|96 S343|348 W235|240 F768

עַרְבִית Arvit for weekdays L264 S281 W137 F200

Weekday Amidah:

+ אַתָּה חוֹנַנְתָּנוּ Attah ḥonantanu L272 S287 W143 F212
+ יַעֲלֶה וְיָבוֹא Ya'aleh veyavo for Rosh Ḥodesh L277 S289 W145 F216

Continue as on a usual Saturday night
through קַדִּישׁ שָׁלֵם Full Kaddish L280 S294 W160 F688

Some recite הַבְדָּלָה Havdalah here. L283 S299 W165 F700

עָלֵינוּ Aleynu L281 S297 W163 F696
קַדִּישׁ יָתוֹם Mourner's Kaddish (some omit) L282 S298 W164 F698
+ Psalm 27 for the Season of Repentance L59 S80 W92 F40
קַדִּישׁ יָתוֹם Mourner's Kaddish L58 S82 W100 F52

הַבְדָּלָה Havdalah L283 S299 W165 F700

Sun 28 Aug שַׁחֲרִית

Before מִזְמוֹר שִׁיר Mizmor shir (Psalm 30) W14 F50
or at end of service, recite:
Psalm for Sunday (Psalm 24) W85 F22
קַדִּישׁ יָתוֹם Mourner's Kaddish (some omit) W100 F52
+ Psalm 104 for Rosh Ḥodesh W90 F34
קַדִּישׁ יָתוֹם Mourner's Kaddish (some omit) W100 F52
+ Psalm 27 for the Season of Repentance W92 F40
קַדִּישׁ יָתוֹם Mourner's Kaddish W100 F52

Weekday Amidah:

+ יַעֲלֶה וְיָבוֹא Ya'aleh veyavo for Rosh Ḥodesh W41 F114

✕ ~~תַּחֲנוּן Taḥanun~~

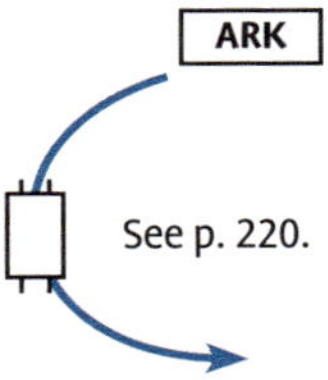

See p. 220.

+ חֲצִי הַלֵּל Short Hallel W50 F380
קַדִּישׁ שָׁלֵם Full Kaddish W56 F392

+ **TORAH SERVICE** W65 F138
Remove **1** scroll from ark.

Torah 4 aliyot: פִּינְחָס Pineḥas
בְּמִדְבַּר Bemidbar (Numbers) 28:1–15
[1]28:1–3 [2]3–5 [3]6–10 [4]11–15 W320 P943

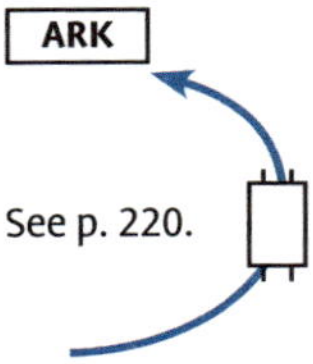

See p. 220.

חֲצִי קַדִּישׁ Short Kaddish W71 F146
Open, raise, display, and wrap scroll.
Return scroll to ark. W76 F150

אַשְׁרֵי Ashrey W78 F152
✕ ~~לַמְנַצֵּחַ Lamenatse·aḥ (Psalm 20)~~
וּבָא לְצִיּוֹן Uva letsiyyon W80 F156

Elul 5782						
1	2	3	4	5	6	7
8	9	10	11	12	13	14
15	16	17	18	19	20	21
22	23	24	25	26	27	28
29						

Aug | Sep 2022						
28	29	30	31	1	2	3
4	5	6	7	8	9	10
11	12	13	14	15	16	17
18	19	20	21	22	23	24
25						

\+ Add ✕ Omit ☞ Take note!

Siddurim
- **L** Lev Shalem for Shabbat and Festivals
- **S** Shabbat and Festival Sim Shalom
- **W** Weekday Sim Shalom
- **F** Full Sim Shalom (both editions)
- **P** Personal Edition of Full Sim Shalom

Remove and pack tefillin. (Some remove after Kaddish.)

\+ חֲצִי קַדִּישׁ Short Kaddish **W**103 **F**428

(If you remove tefillin here, do *not* pack but cover them, so as to begin Musaf together quickly after Kaddish.)

מוּסָף

\+ **Rosh Ḥodesh Amidah for weekdays:** **W**104 **F**486
Weekday קְדֻשָּׁה Kedushah **W**105 **F**488
☞ Do *not* continue to add **וּלְכַפָּרַת פָּשַׁע** Ulkhapparat pasha.

\+ קַדִּישׁ שָׁלֵם Full Kaddish **W**82 **F**158
עָלֵינוּ Aleynu **W**83 **F**160

If psalms for the day were recited at Shaḥarit:
קַדִּישׁ יָתוֹם Mourner's Kaddish **W**84 **F**162
\+ Sound the shofar (see procedure on p. 212).

If psalms for the day were not recited at Shaḥarit, add here:
קַדִּישׁ יָתוֹם Mourner's Kaddish (some omit) **W**84|100 **F**162|52
Psalm for Sunday (Psalm 24) **W**85 **F**22
קַדִּישׁ יָתוֹם Mourner's Kaddish (some omit) **W**100 **F**52
\+ Psalm 104 for Rosh Ḥodesh **W**90 **F**34
קַדִּישׁ יָתוֹם Mourner's Kaddish (some omit) **W**100 **F**52
\+ Sound the shofar (see procedure on p. 212).
\+ Psalm 27 for the Season of Repentance **W**92 **F**40
קַדִּישׁ יָתוֹם Mourner's Kaddish **W**84|100 **F**52

מִנְחָה

Weekday Amidah:
\+ יַעֲלֶה וְיָבוֹא Ya'aleh veyavo for Rosh Ḥodesh **W**127 **F**178

✕ ~~תַּחֲנוּן Taḥanun~~

Elul 7 אֱלוּל 7
Sat 3 Sep

שַׁבָּת Shabbat פָּרָשַׁת שֹׁפְטִים Parashat Shofetim

Torah 7 aliyot (minimum): שֹׁפְטִים Shofetim
דְּבָרִים Devarim (Deuteronomy) 16:18–21:9

Annual:	1 16:18–17:13	2 17:14–20	3 18:1–5	4 18:6–13
	5 18:14–19:13	6 19:14–20:9	7 20:10–21:9	M 21:7–9
Triennial:	1 19:14–21	2 20:1–4	3 20:5–9	4 20:10–14
	5 20:15–20	6 21:1–6	7 21:7–9	M 21:7–9

Haftarah יְשַׁעְיָהוּ Yesha'yahu (Isaiah) 51:12–52:12
(4th of 7 haftarot of consolation following Tish'ah Be'av)

מִנְחָה

Torah 3 aliyot from כִּי־תֵצֵא Ki tetse
דְּבָרִים Devarim (Deuteronomy) 21:10–21
^{1}21:10–14 ^{2}15–17 ^{3}18–21 ^{W}313 ^{P}934

Chanted also next Monday and Thursday.

Elul 8 אֱלוּל
Sat 3 Sep (night)

After Arvit if the moon is visible:
קִדּוּשׁ לְבָנָה Kiddush Levanah ^{L}286 ^{W}167 ^{F}704
For procedures and instructions, see p. 223.

Elul 14 אֱלוּל
Sat 10 Sep

שַׁבָּת Shabbat פָּרָשַׁת כִּי־תֵצֵא Parashat Ki tetse

Torah 7 aliyot (minimum): כִּי־תֵצֵא Ki tetse
דְּבָרִים Devarim (Deuteronomy) 21:10–25:19

Annual:	^{1}21:10–21	^{2}21:22–22:7	^{3}22:8–23:7	^{4}23:8–24
	^{5}23:25–24:4	^{6}24:5–13	^{7}24:14–25:19°	^{M}25:17–19°
Triennial:	^{1}24:14–16	^{2}24:17–19	^{3}24:20–22	^{4}25:1–4
	^{5}25:5–10	^{6}25:11–16	^{7}25:17–19°	^{M}25:17–19°

☞ °25:19 The proper reading of the 6th-to-last word is זֵכֶר, as it appears in the most reliable manuscripts and in almost all printed editions. No words should be repeated. For more information, see www.milesbcohen.com/LuahResources.

☞ **Haftarah** יְשַׁעְיָהוּ Yesha'yahu (Isaiah) 54:1–10 + °54:11–55:5
(5th + 3rd of 7 haftarot of consolation following Tish'ah Be'av)

☞ °54:1–10 + 54:11–55:5 Because Shabbat Re'eh was Rosh Ḥodesh, the usual 3rd haftarah of consolation was not read. Chant the haftarah of Ki tetse and then the haftarah of Re'eh as a single haftarah. In the book of Isaiah these two brief passages are adjacent.

מִנְחָה

Torah 3 aliyot from כִּי־תָבוֹא Ki tavo
דְּבָרִים Devarim (Deuteronomy) 26:1–15°
^{1}26:1–3 ^{2}4–11 ^{3}12–15 ^{W}314 ^{P}935

Chanted also next Monday and Thursday.

☞ °26:1–15 The reading extends through verse 15, which enables the correct configuration of the 3 aliyot.

Elul 5782						
1	2	3	4	5	6	7
8	9	10	11	12	13	14
15	16	17	18	19	20	21
22	23	24	25	26	27	28
29						

Aug | Sep 2022						
28	29	30	31 | 1	2	3	
4	5	6	7	8	9	10
11	12	13	14	15	16	17
18	19	20	21	22	23	24
25						

+ Add ✕ Omit ☞ Take note!

Siddurim
- **L** Lev Shalem for Shabbat and Festivals
- **S** Shabbat and Festival Sim Shalom
- **W** Weekday Sim Shalom
- **F** Full Sim Shalom (both editions)
- **P** Personal Edition of Full Sim Shalom

Elul 21 אֱלוּל
Sat 17 Sep

שַׁבָּת Shabbat פָּרָשַׁת כִּי־תָבוֹא Parashat Ki tavo

Torah 7 aliyot (minimum): כִּי־תָבוֹא Ki tavo
דְּבָרִים Devarim (Deuteronomy) 26:1–29:8

Annual:	1 26:1–11	2 26:12–15	3 26:16–19	4 27:1–10
	5 27:11–28:6	6 28:7–69°	7 29:1–8	M 29:6–8
Triennial:	1 27:11–28:3	2 28:4–6	3 28:7–11	4 28:12–14
	5 28:15–69°	6 29:1–5	7 29:6–8	M 29:6–8

☞°28:15–69 This is the תּוֹכֵחָה tokheḥah, verses of rebuke and warning. Because of the ominous nature of these verses, do not divide this lengthy passage into shorter aliyot. However, the chanting may be divided among multiple readers. All the readers must be present at the Torah when the oleh/olah recites the first berakhah. This serves as an implicit appointment of all the readers as sheliḥim (agents) of the oleh/olah.
Chant this section in a somewhat **subdued** voice to symbolically minimize the trepidation that the congregation experiences upon hearing the message of these verses. Be sure that all words and te'amim (tropes, cantillations) remain **clearly** audible to the congregation.
However, for verses 7–14, voicing the promise of God's protection and reward, and for the conclusion, verse 69, chant as usual.

Haftarah יְשַׁעְיָהוּ Yesha'yahu (Isaiah) 60:1–22
(6th of 7 haftarot of consolation following Tish'ah Be'av)

מִנְחָה

Torah 3 aliyot from נִצָּבִים Nitsavim
דְּבָרִים Devarim (Deuteronomy) 29:9–28°
1 29:9–11 2 12–14 3 15–28 W315 P936

Chanted also next Monday and Thursday.

☞°29:9–28 The reading extends through verse 28, which enables the correct configuration of the 3 aliyot.

Elul 22 אֱלוּל
Sat 17 Sep

מוֹצָאֵי שַׁבָּת Motsa'ey Shabbat Conclusion of Shabbat

עַרְבִית

Saturday night Arvit as usual L264 S281 W137 F200

+ Psalm 27 for the Season of Repentance L59 S80 W92 F40
קַדִּישׁ יָתוֹם Mourner's Kaddish L58 S82 W100 F52

Elul 22 אֱלוּל
Sat 17 Sep (night)

לֵיל סְלִיחוֹת Leyl Seliḥot
Seliḥot at Night

Seliḥot — Penitential Prayers

We recite סְלִיחוֹת *seliḥot* beginning the Saturday night before Rosh Hashanah to prepare ourselves for the upcoming Days of Repentance.

In a year when Rosh Hashanah begins on a Sunday night or Monday night, as in the coming year, we begin סְלִיחוֹת a week earlier so that we have enough time to prepare in advance of Rosh Hashanah.

- Recite the first סְלִיחוֹת at midnight, an expression of our eagerness to begin the process of repentance.
- On subsequent days, recite סְלִיחוֹת before Shaḥarit every morning until Yom Kippur, except Shabbat and Rosh Hashanah.

The standard סְלִיחוֹת liturgy includes:
- אַשְׁרֵי *ashrey* and חֲצִי קַדִּישׁ Short Kaddish
- Various פִּיּוּטִים *piyyutim,* distinct liturgical poems for each day
- The Thirteen Attributes of God, . . . יי יי אֵ-ל רַחוּם וְחַנּוּן *adonay adonay el raḥum veḥannun* (based on Shemot 34:6–7)
- שְׁמַע קוֹלֵנוּ *shema kolenu,* אָשַׁמְנוּ *ashamnu,* and other סְלִיחוֹת prayers that appear in the Yom Kippur liturgy
- Short תַּחֲנוּן *taḥanun*
- קַדִּישׁ שָׁלֵם Full Kaddish

Rosh Hashanah

Looking Ahead to Rosh Hashanah

Teki'at Shofar — Hearing the Sounds of the Shofar

The *mitsvah* of hearing the sounds of the shofar on Rosh Hashanah is not restricted to the synagogue. For a person unable to attend a synagogue service, arrange a shofar blowing where the person lives, so the person fulfills the *mitsvah.*

Preparing to Celebrate with a New Fruit or with New Clothes

The 2nd day of Rosh Hashanah is celebrated Monday evening with a "new" fruit (that is, a seasonal fruit that you have not yet tasted this season) or with new clothes, worn for the first time that evening. In preparation, obtain the new fruit or new clothes before Rosh Hashanah begins.

Elul 28 אֱלוּל
Sat 24 Sep

שַׁבָּת Shabbat נִצָּבִים Parashat Nitsavim

Torah 7 aliyot (minimum): נִצָּבִים Nitsavim
דְּבָרִים Devarim (Deuteronomy) 29:9–30:20

Annual: [1]29:9–11 [2]29:12–14 [3]29:15–28 [4]30:1–6 [5]30:7–10 [6]30:11–14 [7]30:15–20 [M]30:15–20 (or 18–20)

Triennial: Chant the full parashah, divided as above.

Haftarah יְשַׁעְיָהוּ Yesha'yahu (Isaiah) 61:10–63:9
(last of 7 haftarot of consolation following Tish'ah Be'av)

✕ ~~Birkat Haḥodesh~~

מִנְחָה

Torah 3 aliyot from וַיֵּלֶךְ Vayelekh
דְּבָרִים Devarim (Deuteronomy) 31:1–13°
[1]31:1–3 [2]4–6 [3]7–13 W317 P938

Chanted also next Thursday.

☞ °31:1–13 The reading extends through verse 13, which enables the correct configuration of the 3 aliyot.

Elul 29 אֱלוּל
Sat 24 Sep (evening)

מוֹצָאֵי שַׁבָּת Motsa'ey Shabbat Conclusion of Shabbat
עֶרֶב רֹאשׁ הַשָּׁנָה Erev Rosh Hashanah
Day before Rosh Hashanah

עַרְבִית

Arvit for weekdays L264 S281 W137 F200

Weekday Amidah:

+ אַתָּה חוֹנַנְתָּנוּ Attah ḥonantanu L272 S287 W143 F212

✕ ~~חֲצִי קַדִּישׁ Short Kaddish~~

✕ ~~וִיהִי נֹעַם Vihi no'am~~
✕ ~~יוֹשֵׁב בְּסֵתֶר עֶלְיוֹן Yoshev beseter elyon~~
✕ ~~וְאַתָּה קָדוֹשׁ Ve'attah kadosh~~

קַדִּישׁ שָׁלֵם Full Kaddish L280 S294 W160 F688

Some recite הַבְדָּלָה Havdalah here. L283 S299 W165 F700

עָלֵינוּ Aleynu L281 S297 W163 F696
קַדִּישׁ יָתוֹם Mourner's Kaddish (some omit) L282 S298 W164 F698
+ Psalm 27 for the Season of Repentance L59 S80 W92 F40
קַדִּישׁ יָתוֹם Mourner's Kaddish L58 S82 W100 F52

הַבְדָּלָה Havdalah L283 S299 W165 F700

Sun 25 Sep (daytime)
+ סְלִיחוֹת Seliḥot (penitential prayers)
(including תַּחֲנוּן Taḥanun)

שַׁחֲרִית
✕ ~~תַּחֲנוּן Taḥanun~~
☞ לַמְנַצֵּחַ Lamenatse·aḥ (Psalm 20) W79 F154

✕ ~~תְּקִיעַת שׁוֹפָר Sounding the shofar~~

+ Psalm 27 for the Season of Repentance W92 F40
קַדִּישׁ יָתוֹם Mourner's Kaddish W100 F52

מִנְחָה
✕ ~~תַּחֲנוּן Taḥanun~~

At home
Prepare a flame for Yom Tov. See blue box, below.
Light Yom Tov candles.
See *Luaḥ Hashanah 5783*.

Before Rosh Hashanah

Preparing a Flame for Yom Tov

On Yom Tov, kindling a *new* fire is not permitted; however, the use of an *existing* fire for cooking or other purposes is permitted.

To light candles for Day 2 of Rosh Hashanah (Monday night), ensure that you have a fire burning before candle-lighting time for Day 1 (Sunday evening) that will continue to burn until after dark on Monday. For example:

- A burning candle that lasts for more than 25 hours
- A pilot light on a gas range (*not* a gas range with an electronic starter)

The Talmud instructs: כׇּל פִּינּוֹת שֶׁאַתָּה פּוֹנֶה לֹא יְהוּ אֶלָּא דֶּרֶךְ יָמִין All the turns that you make should be only to the right (Zevaḥim 62a). The original context describes the priests circling the altar in the ancient Temple. To provide some continuity in their post-Temple world, the Rabbis here as elsewhere preserved priestly practices in everyday life. They likened the Torah reading table to the altar and prescribed that all processions should encircle the reading table and should proceed to the right, that is, counterclockwise.

This rule applies to *hosha'na* processions with *lulav* and *etrog* on Sukkot, *hakkafot* processions with the Torah scrolls on Simḥat Torah, and all weekday, Shabbat, and holiday Torah processions. When removing scrolls from the ark and returning them, encircle the reading table and proceed counterclockwise.

If the reading table is at the front of the prayer space, proceed counterclockwise from the ark. If you proceed through the congregation, you may distort the path to accommodate various aisles. But continue in a generally counterclockwise direction, completing the circuit around the reading table. When returning the scrolls to the ark, again follow a generally counterclockwise direction.

TABLE IN FRONT Sample paths for removing *and* returning Torah scrolls

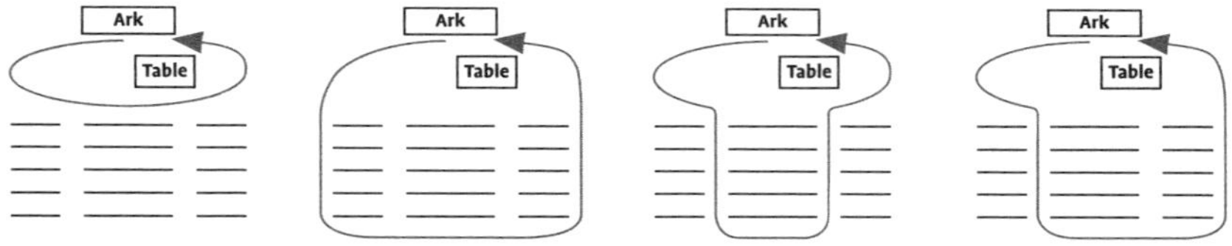

If the reading table is at the center of the prayer space, proceed counterclockwise from the ark to the reading table. You may distort the path to accommodate various aisles, but continue in a generally counterclockwise direction. When returning the scrolls, proceed counterclockwise from the reading table to the ark, completing the circuit around the reading table.

TABLE IN CENTER

Sample paths for ***removing*** Torah scrolls Sample paths for ***returning*** Torah scrolls

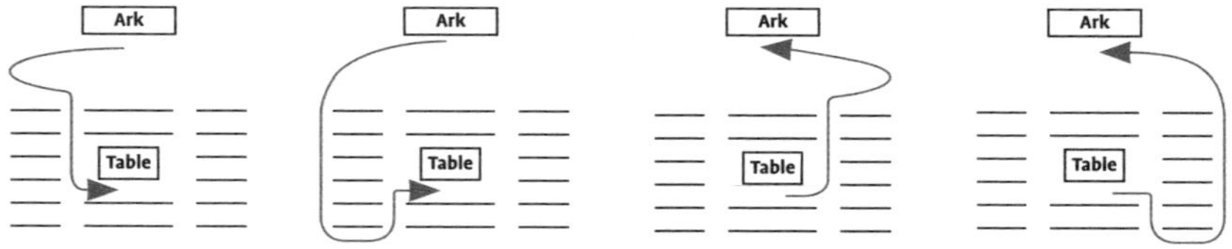

When two or more scrolls are required, remove *and* carry the scrolls in the order they will be read. To return the scrolls to the ark, carry the scrolls in *reverse* order.

Torah procession guides appear in the *Luaḥ* at Torah service procedures.

In our rituals we emulate the ancient priests, for we are to be *mamlekhet kohanim,* a kingdom of priests. These practices remind us to strive for the highest standards in our ritual behavior and encourage the same in our everyday lives.

APPENDIX B: Sefirat Ha'omer

Omer is a period of seven weeks extending from Pesaḥ to Shavu'ot. Aside from its obvious agrarian references, it serves also to tie the themes of Pesaḥ to those of Shavu'ot. As we perform סְפִירַת הָעֹמֶר *sefirat ha'omer*—counting off the days one by one every night—we realize that the freedom we gained on Pesaḥ gives us the opportunity to commit to the covenant and law that we celebrate on Shavu'ot.

Sefirat Ha'omer

Counting Omer is twofold: Each night, beginning the 2nd night of Pesaḥ, count both (1) the number of days and (2) the number of weeks and parts of weeks.

- Count Omer after dark, preferably at least 25 minutes after sunset.
- Precede the counting with the בְּרָכָה *berakhah*. L63 S55 W152 F237
- To ensure that you properly count the number of days, as well as the number of weeks and parts of weeks, use the formulas in a *siddur* or other text.
- In the synagogue, count during Arvit, before עָלֵינוּ Aleynu.
- If your congregation conducts Arvit before dark, count Omer without a בְּרָכָה. Encourage congregants to count individually with a בְּרָכָה after dark.

Although the rabbinic obligation is to count after dark, the biblical obligation can be fufilled the next day as well. Therefore, if you forgot to count in the evening:

- Count during the following day.
- Do not recite the בְּרָכָה because you are not performing the *mitsvah* in strict accordance with rabbinic law.
- Continue counting in the evening, reciting the בְּרָכָה as usual.

Most authorities consider the 7 weeks of counting to be a single *mitsvah*. Therefore, if you miss counting 1 of the days completely, fulfillment of the rabbinic *mitsvah* is disrupted. In that case, continue counting until Shavu'ot as usual, but do not recite the בְּרָכָה for the remaining days of the Omer.

Some authorities consider the counting to be 49 separate *mitsvot*. According to their reasoning, if you miss a day, you have forfeited one of the *mitsvot*, but you may continue to recite the בְּרָכָה for the remaining days.

Some people count again every morning (without a בְּרָכָה). This routine may remind them to count in case they forgot the night before.

It is advisable in the synagogue each morning to count Omer without a בְּרָכָה. This counting fulfills the obligation of those present who neglected to count the previous night.

Many congregations have continued or reinstated the traditional practice of calling כֹּהֲנִים *kohanim* forward to ask for God's blessing upon the congregation. In Bemidbar (Numbers) 6:22–27, we read that Aharon, the 1st priest, and his sons prayed for God's blessing upon the people Israel. In Temple times, Aharon's descendants continued to ask for God's blessing. Reenacting this ceremony in our synagogues today is one of innumerable ways we use elements of ritual to connect to our people's past.

Although in some communities, the ritual of בִּרְכַּת כֹּהֲנִים *birkat kohanim* (the blessing given by the priests, referred to in Yiddish as *dukhenen*) is done daily, among Ashkenazi Jews outside of Israel, the ritual is practiced only on holidays, usually at the Musaf service.

Birkat Kohanim

The ritual involves the following steps:

1. After the קְדֻשָּׁה *kedushah* at a holiday Musaf service (Shaḥarit on Simḥat Torah), the כֹּהֲנִים *kohanim* (descendants of Aharon) and the לְוִיִּם *leviyyim* (descendants of the tribe of Levi) proceed to the hand-washing area.
2. The לְוִיִּם perform a ritual washing of the hands of the כֹּהֲנִים.
3. The כֹּהֲנִים, each wearing a large טַלִּית *tallit,* return to the sanctuary and approach—but do not ascend—the בִּימָה *bimah.*
4. As the *sheliaḥ/sheliḥat tsibbur* nears the prayer רְצֵה *retseh,* the כֹּהֲנִים remove their shoes (without touching the shoes).
5. When the *sheliaḥ/sheliḥat tsibbur* begins the prayer רְצֵה, the כֹּהֲנִים ascend the בִּימָה and stand in front of the ark.
6. The כֹּהֲנִים cover their heads with their large טַלִּיּוֹת *talliyyot* and face the ark to recite the בְּרָכָה *berakhah* in advance of performing the *mitsvah:*

   בָּרוּךְ אַתָּה יי, אֱ-לֹהֵינוּ מֶלֶךְ הָעוֹלָם, אֲשֶׁר קִדְּשָׁנוּ בִּקְדֻשָּׁתוֹ שֶׁל אַהֲרֹן
   וְצִוָּנוּ לְבָרֵךְ אֶת־עַמּוֹ יִשְׂרָאֵל בְּאַהֲבָה.

   Barukh attah adonay, eloheynu melekh ha'olam,
   asher kiddeshanu bikdushato shel aharon
   vetsivvanu levarekh et ammo yisra'el be'ahavah.

7. The כֹּהֲנִים turn in a clockwise direction to face the congregation.
8. The *sheliaḥ/sheliḥat tsibbur* leads the כֹּהֲנִים in the three-part blessing, slowly chanting each word, which the כֹּהֲנִים then repeat.
9. At the end of each of the 3 verses, the congregation responds אָמֵן *amen.*

APPENDIX D: Kiddush Levanah

Our tradition teaches us not to take for granted ordinary or mundane events. Rather, we elevate even the most regular and predictable occurrences by expressing our appreciation of these events. The monthly ceremony of reciting בִּרְכַּת הַלְּבָנָה *birkat halevanah* (the blessing upon seeing the new moon), popularly referred to as קִדּוּשׁ לְבָנָה *kiddush levanah,* provides the opportunity to offer gratitude to the Creator for the miracle of regularities of creation.

Kiddush Levanah

When

Recite קִדּוּשׁ לְבָנָה each month when the moon is waxing. By common practice, the earliest we perform this ritual is after the Arvit service that begins the 4th day of the Hebrew month. The latest time is after the Arvit service that begins the 14th day of the Hebrew month. Note the following exceptions:

1. In Tishrey, the earliest time to recite קִדּוּשׁ לְבָנָה is after the Arvit service at the conclusion of Yom Kippur.
2. In Av, the earliest time to recite קִדּוּשׁ לְבָנָה is after the Arvit service at least one additional day after the conclusion of the Tish'ah Be'av fast.

(Technically, the time of קִדּוּשׁ לְבָנָה is determined by the מוֹלָד *molad,* the traditional calculation of the time the new moon is first visible in Jerusalem. In some months and and in some time zones, the permitted time period may be slightly longer.)

Within the permitted time frame: Recite קִדּוּשׁ לְבָנָה on the 1st Saturday night while still in Shabbat dress clothes. If you cannot see the moon, delay recitation until the next permitted night that the moon is visible.

Where

Recite קִדּוּשׁ לְבָנָה outdoors, viewing at least part of the moon. If the permitted time period is about to expire and the weather is inclement, you may view the moon through a window. If the moon is not visible, do not recite.

How

If possible, recite קִדּוּשׁ לְבָנָה in the presence of a *minyan*. The ceremony consists of the following: L286 W167 F704

- Recite Psalm 148:1–6.
- Recite בִּרְכַּת הַלְּבָנָה *birkat halevanah.*
- Sing or recite דָּוִד מֶלֶךְ יִשְׂרָאֵל חַי וְקַיָּם *david melekh yisra'el hay vekayyam.*
- Greet 3 people individually: שָׁלוֹם עֲלֵיכֶם *shalom aleykhem.*
  Each responds: עֲלֵיכֶם שָׁלוֹם *aleykhem shalom.*
- Sing or recite 3 times: סִימָן טוֹב וּמַזָּל טוֹב יְהֵא לָנוּ וּלְכָל־יִשְׂרָאֵל, אָמֵן
  siman tov umazzal tov yehey lanu ulkhol yisra'el, amen.
- Recite עָלֵינוּ *Aleynu.* L281 W163 F696
- If a *minyan* is present, recite קַדִּישׁ יָתוֹם Mourner's Kaddish. L282 W164 F698

Singing, dancing, and recitation of other verses and texts may be added.

APPENDIX E: Determining the Date of a Yortsayt

We memorialize our departed on various occasions during the year. One such occasion is each *yortsayt,* the anniversary of the date of death, calculated according to the Jewish calendar.

Some calendar dates do not occur every year. For a death on one of these dates, determine the *yortsayt* using the guidelines below.

Determining the Date of a Yortsayt

Death occurred on 30 Ḥeshvan (Rosh Ḥodesh Kislev — Day 1)

- If in the *next* year 30 Ḥeshvan does *not* occur, then *every* year:
  Observe 29 Ḥeshvan.
  (Thus, the *yortsayt* is observed on the same date each year.)
- If in the *next* year 30 Ḥeshvan *does* occur, then each year:
  Observe 30 Ḥeshvan in every year it occurs.
  In other years, observe 1 Kislev.
  (Thus, the *yortsayt* is always observed on Rosh Ḥodesh Kislev, either on Day 1 of Rosh Ḥodesh or on the only day of Rosh Ḥodesh.)

Death occurred on 30 Kislev (Rosh Ḥodesh Tevet — Day 1)

- If in the *next* year 30 Kislev does *not* occur, then *every* year:
  Observe 29 Kislev.
  (Thus, the *yortsayt* is observed on the same date each year.)
- If in the *next* year 30 Kislev *does* occur, then each year:
  Observe 30 Kislev in every year it occurs.
  In other years, observe 1 Tevet.
  (Thus, the *yortsayt* is always observed on Rosh Ḥodesh Tevet, either on Day 1 of Rosh Ḥodesh or on the only day of Rosh Ḥodesh.)

Death occurred during Adar (in a non-leap year)

- In a non-leap year, observe the date of death in Adar.
- In a leap year, observe the date in 1st Adar. (Some follow the custom of observing the date in both 1st Adar and 2nd Adar.)

Death occurred during 1st Adar or 2nd Adar (in a leap year)

- In a non-leap year, observe the date in Adar.
- In a leap year, observe the date in whichever Adar the death occurred.

Death occurred on 30th of 1st Adar (Rosh Ḥodesh 2nd Adar — Day 1, in a leap year)

- In a non-leap year, observe 30 Shevat (Rosh Ḥodesh Adar — Day 1).
- In a leap year, observe 30th of 1st Adar (Rosh Ḥodesh 2nd Adar — Day 1).